THE COMPLETE

Pinball Book

COLLECTING THE GAME AND ITS HISTORY

Marco Rossignoli

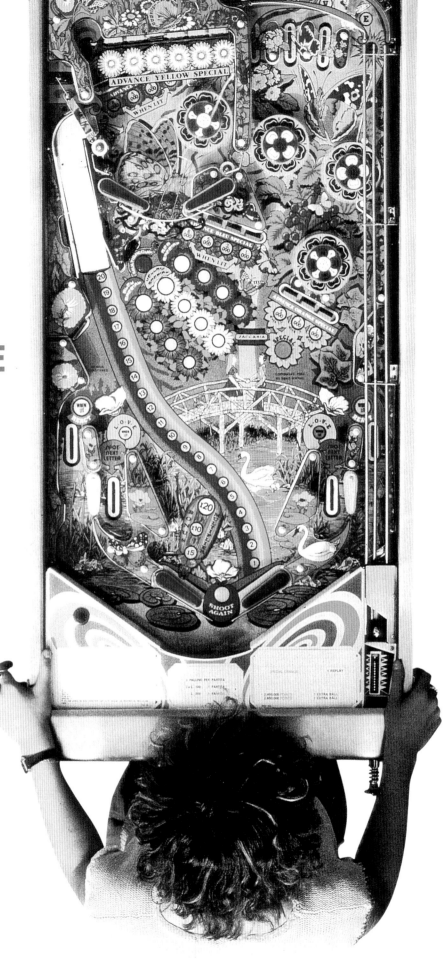

Schiffer Publishing Ltd®

4880 Lower Valley Road, Atglen, PA 19310 USA

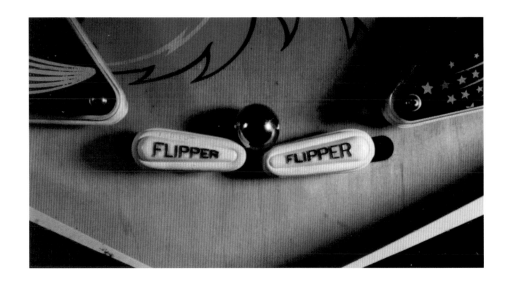

Library of Congress Cataloging-in-Publication Data

Rossignoli, Marco.
Pinball machines: everything you wanted to know / Marco Rossignoli.
p. cm.
Includes bibliographical references (p.) and index.
ISBN 0-7643-1003-8 (hardcover)
1. Pinball machines. I. Title.
GV1311.P5R68   2000
794.7'5--dc21   99-40286
CIP

Designed by Bonnie M. Hensley
Type set in Milano LET/Dutch 801 RmBT

ISBN: 0-7643-1003-8
Printed in China
1 2 3 4

Published by Schiffer Publishing Ltd.
4880 Lower Valley Road
Atglen, PA 19310
Phone: (610) 593-1777; Fax: (610) 593-2002
E-mail: Schifferbk@aol.com
Please visit our website catalog at **www.schifferbooks.com**

In Europe, Schiffer books are distributed by Bushwood Books
6 Marksbury Avenue Kew Gardens
Surrey TW9 4JF England
Phone: 44 (0)208-392-8585; Fax: 44 (0)208-392-9876
E-mail: Bushwd@aol.com

This book may be purchased from the publisher.
Include $3.95 for shipping. Please try your bookstore first.
We are interested in hearing from authors with book ideas on related subjects.
You may write for a free printed catalog.

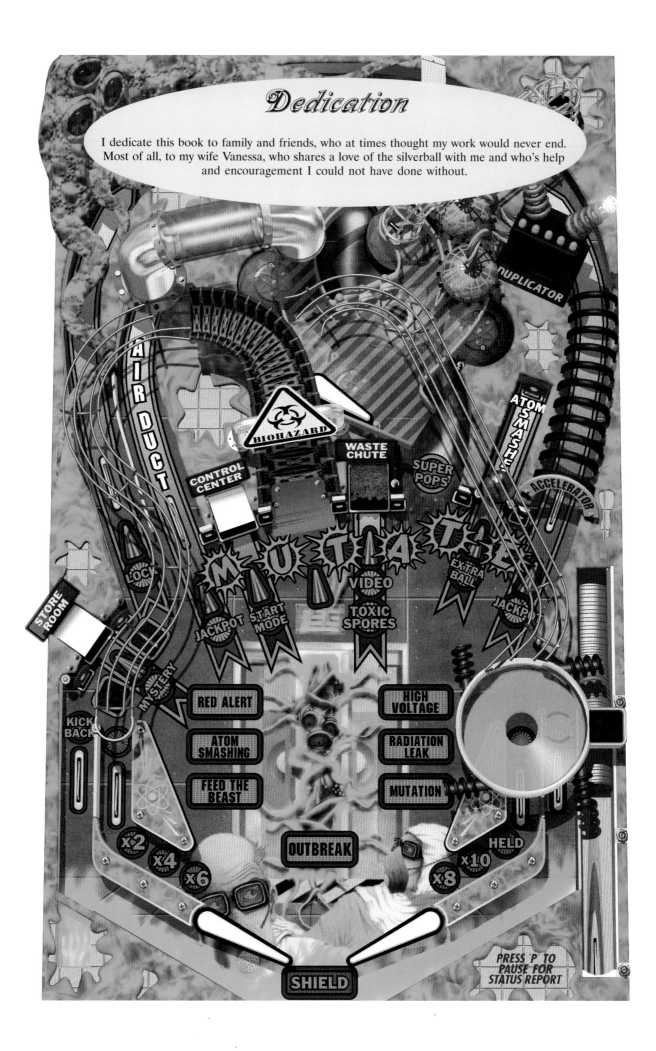

Dedication

I dedicate this book to family and friends, who at times thought my work would never end. Most of all, to my wife Vanessa, who shares a love of the silverball with me and who's help and encouragement I could not have done without.

Acknowledgements

The author would like to thank the following people for having contributed their time, knowledge and expertise in creating this book.

Australia

Andre Urfer; Anthony & Clare Moore; Blaise Myors; Craig Rutledge; Darryl Moore; David Hankin; Del Reiss/Bumper Action Amusements; Denis Bowler; Donna, Gary & Ian F. McKinnon; Garry Parr; Gary Hudson; Graham McGuiness; Graeme Beal; Gregory J. Corrigan; Herman Raspoort; Jeff Grummel; Jeffrey A. Etheridge; Joel Finch/Wildfire Studios; John A. Searles; Mac; Mark Hurry; Mark Jackson; Marta Rossignoli; Michael Tansell; Milk Marketing Pty Ltd; Phillip Brown; Phillip Paterson; Rawdon Osborne; Robert Young; Ross "Gorgar" Cockerell; Sharon Postlethwaite Buzek B.A.V.A.; Stuart Caines.

Canada

Dave Thielking; Eugene Ricci

Denmark

Peter Graabaek

Finland

Antti Hakearainen

France

Thierry Delisle; Yannick "Riffhard" Karolewski

Germany

Martin Wiest

Holland

Jan Esselman

Italy

Edoardo Frola; and a big thanks to Federico Croci for supplying me with most of the brochures.

Spain

Interflip S.A.

Switzerland

Ivo Vasella

United States of America

Alvin J. Gottlieb; Carl Heller; Carol Platt/Marvel Comics; Dan Mowczan; Dean Grover; Denny Gibbs; Duncan Brown; Eric & Gary See; Gregory A. Chance; Herb Silvers/Fabulous Fantasies; Jan J. Svach; Jay Macphee; Jim Whitemyer; John Campbell; John Hermann; John Paul Gantert; Karri E. Smith; Kevin A. Moser; Mark Gibson; Mike E. Lukacs; Mike Pacak; Orrin J. Edidin; Ray Johnson; Rick Force; Robert A. Fesjian; Russ Jensen; Tim Van Blarcom; Vernon Soehner.

Contents

IT AIN'T JUST ANY PLAIN OLD SILVER BALL...

Promotional brochure art for Stern's
QUICKSILVER (1980).

Introduction

By Vanessa Gilbert, wife of a pinball player

Whether it was wedged between the video and virtual reality games at an amusement center, or in a cramped, poorly lit corner of a local pub/hotel or laundromat; many people have had the opportunity to play a pinball machine, more colloquially termed "pinny".

Seduced by the myriad of colored flashing lights, whirls of color and design, sounds, music and the machine's own speech, the observer is enticed to "come and play". Playing pinball immerses the senses completely as one attempts to absorb it all. For the novice it can be a sensual bombardment, who simultaneously attempts to manipulate the game in order to keep the ball in play.

These tentative first games for a beginner can remain frustratingly that. However, those who have accepted the challenge of a pinball machine's unpredictability and unique charm may subsequently master the skills of play, obtaining maximal enjoyment at minimal cost. It is despairing that so many people with these game skills (and this may apply to any such amusement game) often attribute them almost apologetically as by-products of misspent youth.

Pinball machines have evolved to incorporate technological advancements, but they have also had to accommodate changes in the market, based on socioeconomic and political adjustments. As modernized societies have become more affluent, pinballs are no longer found exclusively in public haunts, but increasingly more so in private homes. Though it is true to say that due to the expense, new machines debut in the public arena, until their monetary value diminishes and they can be bought privately.

Like any commodity, a market was created to fulfill the demand for older style second-hand pinballs, as the machines became more easily procurable for the average person—whether it be the player/enthusiast wanting to own their own; those who prefer to tinker with the mechanics rather than play the game itself; or those serious collectors of pinball *objets d'art*. Like any prized object of antiquity, rare and unique pinballs can come with their own exorbitant pricetags.

As pinballs entered the home, a new service was then also created for maintenance and repairs. Older pinballs were bought mainly by enthusiasts; not a problem, as the enthusiast often knew how to fix them. However, as the scope of the buyer broadens and technology becomes more complex, owners occasionally do require the remedies offered by those professionals qualified to test, repair and replace components, who are often referred as

Playfield detail from Bally's PLAYBOY (1978). It sure does!

"Pinball Doctors". These people are often owners of small companies, which distribute machines to various public venues; as well as buy and sell second-hand machines, all of which may be approached to service, repair or adjust.

There are also businesses which produce pinball parts (such as solenoids, switch blades, bumper caps and even whole backglasses) which are no longer available from the manufacturers. This is especially so for the repair or restoration of the older machines whose components have become scarce.

Apart from the enthusiasts, few players would be aware of the historical context and technological developments that have continued to shape the game, and which differentiate their favorite pinnies of today from those 10 or 20 years before; let alone the earliest predecessors.

Two major contributing factors to this limited knowledge base, in general terms, is the lack of older pinball machines circulating through public venues; and a chronic lack of literature on the subject. Estimates place a figure of 30 books written between 1974 and 1998! This is relatively small number considering not all were printed in the English language, and smaller again if compared to more mainstream general interests, such as the history of automobiles or fighter planes. The market seems to be saturated by hundreds of titles published in the same time period for these subjects.

In compiling all the historical information and photographs for this book, this project was a "Magical Mystery Tour" through the homes and backyard sheds of those people to whom we are very grateful. They were keen to share with us the tidbits of information, personal insights, and more importantly their prized pinball collections. We found pinnies in various states, ranging from the pristine, those lovingly restored and gleamingly re-chromed; to those recently acquired and undergoing repair and restoration; to those unfortunate disjointed machines, dismantled of their legs and backboxes, all crudely stacked together amidst spiderwebs and years of dust. Of course, the machines that we were searching for were always going to be at the back of that old tin shed! On many occasions we returned home tired and hungry, drained of artistic flair, but full of stories to share about the treasures we'd found and also about the people we'd met.

It is impossible to define the type of person who would own and/or collect pinnies, except for one aspect: all of those with whom we made contact for information or to request photos were

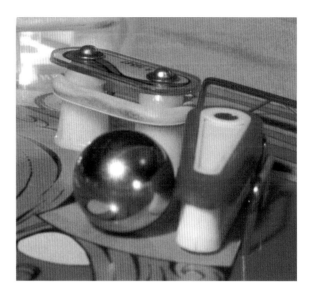

Flipper detail from Gottlieb's JUNGLE QUEEN (1977). The little bat-type device has been the backbone of pinball for over 50 years. Its history is discussed in Chapter Two. *Photograph courtesy of Ivo Vasella.*

Opposite page: Medieval mayhem on Williams' MEDIEVAL MADNESS (1997). Behold the renaissance of pinball! *Courtesy of WMS industries Inc. All rights reserved. $2700-3000.*

Greetings from the playfield of Gottlieb's SUPER SPIN (1977). More illustrations of this game can be found in Chapter Nine.

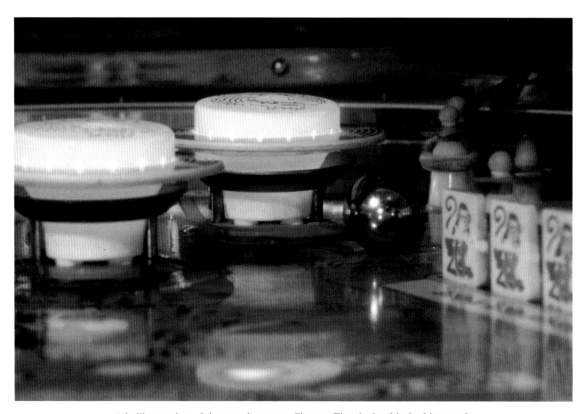

A ball's eye view of thumper bumpers. Chapter Five deals with the history of these devices. *Photograph courtesy of Ivo Vasella.*

Chicago Coin's BRONCO. How old is this pinball? It looks brand new, but is it? Someone with no pinball knowledge would have a hard time trying to answer that question. The knowledge for such a task can be found in this book. For the record, this game was built in 1963, and at the time this photo was taken it was 34 years old. *Courtesy of Rawdon Osborne.* $325-400.

Opposite page: Williams' TALES OF THE ARABIAN KNIGHTS (1996). Rescue the princess from the evil genie. *Courtesy of WMS industries Inc. All rights reserved.* $1900-2100.

TALES OF THE Arabian Nights

Your Wish Is Granted.

Williams

Williams Electronics Games, Inc.

A subsidiary of WMS Industries Inc.

Marco Rossignoli (left) and Andre Urfer (right) getting ready to take photos in the pinball workshop of Rawdon Osborne; game restorer and collector.

Playing pinball. One never knows where a pinball might turn up; they are not always found in arcades and bars. This one was at a laundromat! This photo was taken in 1991, but the pinball being played is almost 13 years old (Gottlieb's SOLAR RIDE, released in 1979), which makes it a rare find in such a public locale.

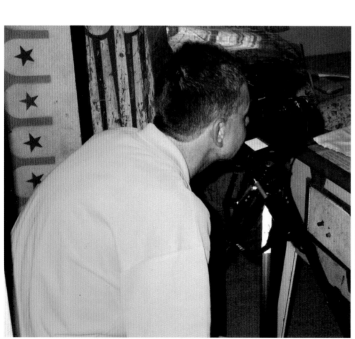

Photographing pinballs is hard work! Polishing up an old pinball kept in storage, preparing it to be photographed.

Andre Urfer hard at work taking photos. All of the photographs in this book are originals, taken by either Andre or Marco, and also by many of the contributors themselves.

Opposite page: Run for the hills! Its Bally's ATTACK FROM MARS (1995). *Courtesy of WMS Industries Inc. All rights reserved.* $2000-2400.

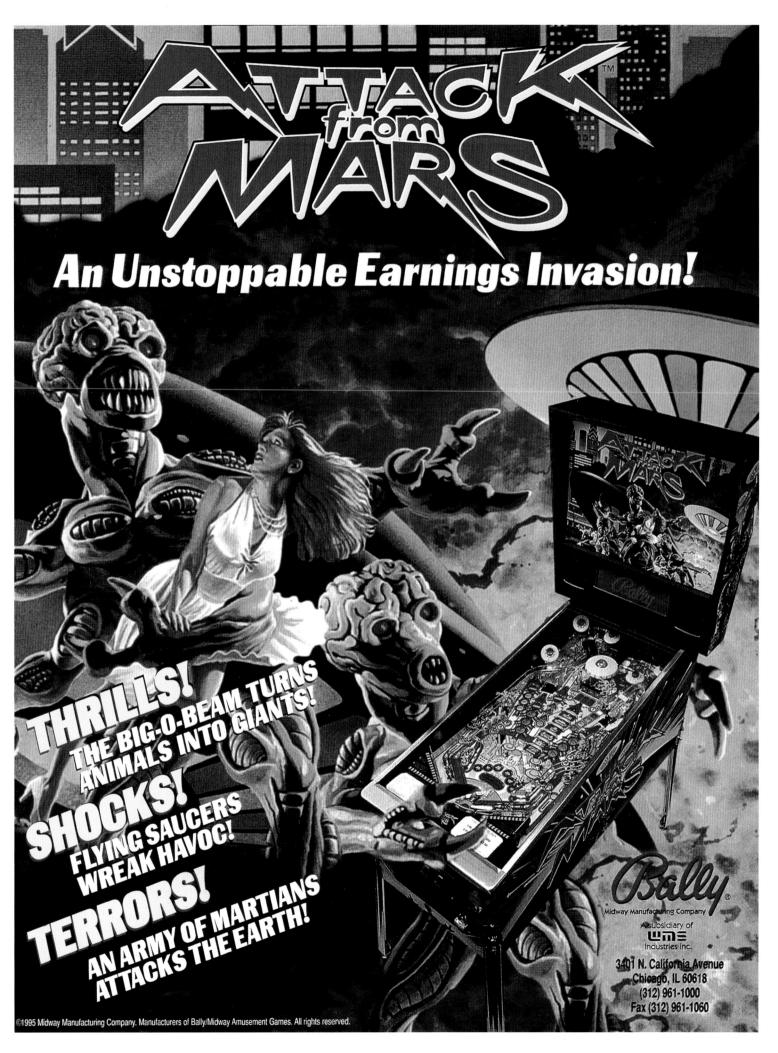

ATTACK from MARS ™

An Unstoppable Earnings Invasion!

THRILLS!
THE BIG-O-BEAM TURNS ANIMALS INTO GIANTS!

SHOCKS!
FLYING SAUCERS WREAK HAVOC!

TERRORS!
AN ARMY OF MARTIANS ATTACKS THE EARTH!

Bally ®
Midway Manufacturing Company
A subsidiary of
WMS
Industries Inc.
3401 N. California Avenue
Chicago, IL 60618
(312) 961-1000
Fax (312) 961-1060

A restorer's pinball shed—a small portion of it! One can imagine the fun we had taking photos here! Some photo shoots were easy and some were hard.

Playfield detail of Hankin's SHARK (1980). Are you familiar with this Australian-built game? If not, find out more in Chapter Eight.

Cruising down the highway on Hankin's F.J. (1978). Another game with an Australian flavor.

male. However, there was a variety of personality types among these, which caused some introspection as pinball owners ourselves (though I admit my ownership by proxy). Throughout the many triumphs and tribulations in pursuit of our quarry it was important to remind ourselves that the quest had more humble beginnings: a pinball list.

Marco began playing pinballs growing up in the late 1970s just prior to the video game revolution. Often accompanying him was his younger brother Paolo (years later, his younger sister Marta joined them on some occasions), to wherever they might play their favorite game at the time and for as long as the money would last. Subsequently, they became adept at playing the game, and would spend hours playing from their accrued credits, only paying for the initial two games. This was much to the chagrin of the owner/operator looking on.

Then came an evening sometime in 1988 when the two brothers decided to list all the names of the pinballs that they had played or seen in all those past years. Off the top of their heads they came up with about fifty titles, along with approximate age, manufacturer and even a crude rating given on playability. The list subsequently expanded to 150 machines over the following days. This original list still survives to this day, having been found by chance in an envelope tucked away in between old comic books and other "boys' stuff" in the brothers' old shared bedroom at their parents' house. It was just a few sheets of paper with crudely hand-drawn columns and scribbled names: TIMEWARP, BLACK KNIGHT, GOLD BALL, etc. The list was apparently discarded and forgotten when its contents were entered into the family computer.

In the months that followed, the brothers' interest in the game intensified, as more and more of the machines were sought out in order to play, as well as literature about the history and development of the game (particularly that information pertaining to the list, in order to fill in the blanks). It was then that Marco discovered just how little information was available on the subject. No books were to be found in bookstores (or libraries), thus requiring them to be ordered in from the U.S.A, taking months to arrive. Hence, the seed was sown that one day he might make a contribution of his own.

Attention also turned to the local newspapers where advertisements frequently appeared in the "For Sale" columns, detailing the various games on offer. Realisation of just how small the original list was became grossly apparent, as many of the games advertised did not appear on this list. Thus the list was further expanded in an attempt to repre-

sent all games manufactured, derived from the information available. Marco did not realize the task he was undertaking.

The list however, became recognized as a useful reference tool, as one could refer to a name, and it would also have the year and place of manufacture which, in combination with the background reading, could determine an electromechanical machine from a electronic one.

An interesting story as an example, while making this point, was the fact that prior to meeting my husband, I had never played a pinball in my life! I could not even remember ever seeing such a thing in the few times that I had ventured into the local amusement parlor with my friends, in my early teens. These types of [sleazy] centers were a far cry from the clean, colorful and brightly lit, family-orientated centers of today.

To cut a long story short for now, playing the pinnies is now fully integrated into my leisure time, along with much information about the game's background. So it was, that I phoned an advertisement in the paper to inquire about a machine on offer. I spoke to a man (of course!), who told me the name of the machine and the company; neither of which I had heard of. When I asked how old it was, he told me it was "quite an old one." Trying to elicit a bit more information about this, I asked him whether it was an electromechanical machine, to which I received a momentary stunned silence. "How could a woman know anything about pinball machines, let alone that particular term," he probably thought. We then had a reasonable conversation following that! The purchase of that machine made it our third pinball, and one that at the time was not on the list. Information was eventually found rummaging through pages of text. The seller later conveyed to my husband his surprise that "How could a woman know anything about...?"

As a player, the world of pinball was fully unveiled to Marco when he decided to purchase his first pinball: Bally's FATHOM (1981). It opened up another realm beyond which many players cannot venture. Owning his own pinball meant that he now had an opportunity and the time to examine and comprehend the inner workings of the machine. Experience allowed him to fix most ailments, but where all avenues drew a blank, in came the pinball doctor.

Growing experience and knowledge infused greater confidence, which imbued serious consideration of the effort and re-

Recognize this guy? Refresh your memory in Chapter Four.

quirements needed to compile a book on pinballs.

Marco's personal pinball library, containing well-known titles to some of you, supplemented a lot of information about many games and pinball development in general. However, with all progression, areas were identified where it was necessary to undertake further research. Using his personal experience he has attempted to avoid rehashing the information contained within these previous publications, other than historical milestones which cannot be ignored, though the value of these books has been undeniable.

It was difficult initially to get the ball rolling (pardon the pun!). The task seemed limited, simple and writing style-restricted. However as time passed, written expression became more fluid and did justice to the information that my husband wished to convey.

Playfield detail of one of the most successful solid state machines in pinball history. It had a production run of over 20,000 units. Do you know which game it is? The answer is revealed in Chapter Three.

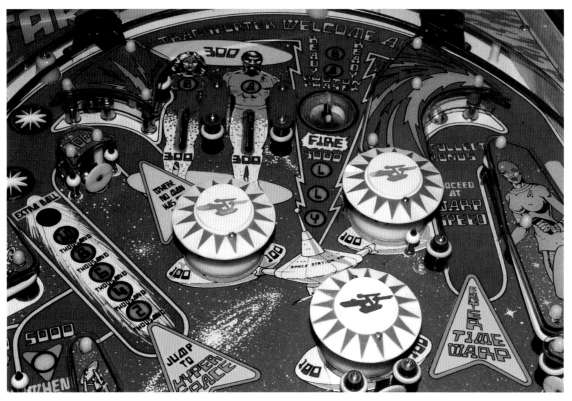

On what popular television and motion picture series was this pinball based? Find out in Chapter Eight. *Photograph courtesy of Phillip Brown.*

In the transcendence from humble list to the dream of a published book, we hope that this will be a welcome and worthy addition to the libraries of pinball enthusiasts everywhere, and for the novice an informative guide. But for those who play pinball we hope it inspires you (like us), to continue experiencing the joy and frustration of the game, to introduce others where able, and to ignore the critics. Most of all, may it inspire you to never lose sight of your reflection in a backglass or on a polished silver ball.

Vanessa Gilbert-Rossignoli

Williams' DINER (1990). The advertisement in the newspaper said, "pinballs for sale; late models, all under $1000." This particular game had already found a buyer by the time this photo was taken. Most people think that pinballs are something that only wealthy people can afford. Some even believe that it is illegal to own one privately! $625-825.

Reach for the stars on Stern's GALAXY (1980). More about this game can be found in Chapter Seven.

Pinballs can talk! Stern's FLIGHT 2000 (1980) was the first machine built by this company to feature speech and multiball. Chapter Four and Chapter Eleven, respectively, deal with the history of these concepts. *Mark Hurry collection.* $375-450.

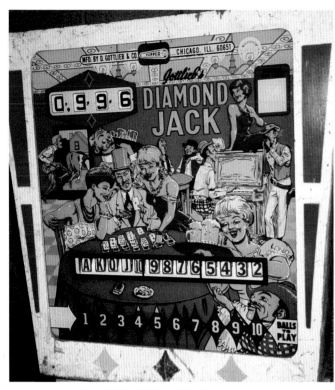

Gottlieb's DIAMOND JACK (1967). This is what is termed as an electromechanical pinball, an explanation of which can be found in Chapter Three. The distinguishing feature of such games are the score reel displays, the history of which is detailed in Chapter Six. *Courtesy of Tim Van Blarcom.* $650-800.

Photograph courtesy of Ivo Vasella.

A lost puppy on the playfield of Bally's DIXIELAND (1968). This book is filled with numerous close-ups just like this one. Enjoy!

Opposite page: Promotional brochure for Atari's TIME 2000 (1977). Atari began producing pinballs in the late 1970s. They were the first to produce what are termed as "wide body" games. This pinball was one such game. Chapter Eleven explains all. *Courtesy of Midway Games Inc. All rights reserved.*

A New Pinball

Chapter One

Pinball-ology

For those not totally familiar with the subject of pinball, its concept and the terms and devices associated with the game, then this chapter is the prerequisite for a better understanding of the chapters that are to follow. It is a helping hand for those curious enough to have picked up this book, and quite possibly have never given the subject of pinballs a serious thought. I must admit that this chapter will most definitely be overlooked by pinheads (serious pinball enthusiasts like myself), who have bought the book and have headed straight for the juicy photographs that lie beyond. However, as this book is a lot more detailed than a simple pinball photo book, and not everyone is a pinhead, this chapter seeks to inform those of you with limited knowledge of the game, or who are literally starting from scratch.

The subject itself is a tricky one. Far from being mainstream, its followers are vast and varied, and may be grouped loosely as enthusiasts, historians, collectors and general experts. There are those who enjoy playing pinball, but do not consider themselves enthusiasts. There are those who try to earn an extra dollar dealing with second-hand pinballs and other amusement machines, but do not consider themselves collectors, even though they have a garage full of old games. Then there are those who fix them, or distribute them for a living; and those who work in the factories where they build them, but they may not consider themselves experts. Then there are those towards the opposite end of the spectrum, who think they know what a pinball is—but do they really?

One will not find a single word in any dictionary that can cover the whole spectrum of the subject and the people involved. Therefore, I have decided to invent my own: PINBALL-OLOGY.

Outhole view of Gottlieb's OUTER SPACE (1972).

A collector's pride and joy. This owner has lovingly restored all these pinballs to mint condition. *Mark Jackson collection.*

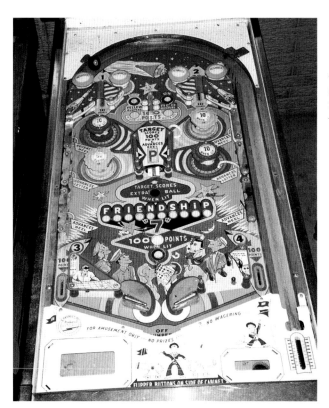

The battered and bruised playfield of a William's FRIEND-SHIP 7 (1962). There are many collectors who enjoy restoring pinballs just like this one. *Courtesy of Tim Van Blarcom.* $500-600.

Although 80% of pinball production has been based in the United States, games (and collectors) can be found all over the world. The games shown here are the proud property of a Swiss enthusiast. *Courtesy of Ivo Vasella.*

A typical pinball line up (collectively known as a bank) of a pinball arcade c.1997. Recognize any of them?

The Complete Pinball Book deals with the subject of "pinball-ology"—the study of the silverball. It is not a technical publication where one can search for knowledge on how to fix one's favorite game. It is more of a pinball history textbook (or at least it's textbookish). However, unlike other history books, this one does not take the reader on a journey through time, from the start of pinball history up until the present time, on a continuous and unrelenting stretch of road lined with milestones. Rather, it takes the modern game of pinball and divides it into its major components, looking at the history and developments of each one individually; thus allowing a more detailed explanation. A pinball history dissection in other words.

What is a pinball? To undertake the enormous task of answering that question in one short paragraph, rather than a whole chapter, I decided to cheat and seek the aid of some reputable encyclopedias and dictionaries.

1. PINBALL: A game played on a device in which the player operates a plunger to shoot a ball down along a slanted surface having obstacles and targets.[1]

2. PINBALL MACHINE: An amusement device that consists of a glass-topped cabinet in which a ball propelled by a plunger rolls down a slanting surface among an arrangement of pins and targets, with each contact between ball and target scoring a number of points indicated by a system of electric lights.[2]

3. PINBALL: Any of various games played on a sloping board, the object usually being either to shoot the ball, driven by a spring, up a side passage and cause it to roll back down against pins or bumpers and through channels which electrically record the score, or to shoot a ball into pockets at the back of the board.[3]

For a game that has been around for 60 years, it was quite disturbing to find very little (or in many cases, absolutely nothing) written about the game, in the various book encyclopedias and compact disc encyclopedias that I referenced.

My first source of reference was the old family Encyclopedia Britannica which my father had bought all they way back in 1977. To my surprise, all it had on the matter was; pinball, see bagatelle. For a book that was published in 1976, during the height of pinball

A PINBALL ORIENTATION (machine).

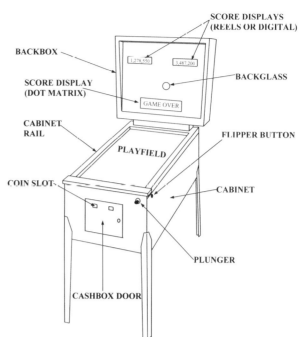

The major components of a pinball machine.

---

popularity (which had been on an upward trend that had started over ten years previously), the find was a bit disappointing.

The term "bagatelle" refers to the a table game closely related to the game of billiards, which was a popular parlor recreation for the wealthy, spanning almost two centuries from the early 18th century to the late 19th century. The game has since lapsed into obscurity. The term also refers to the equally obscure, but much closer relative of the pinball—the marble board game—despite being smaller and simpler.

In every part of everyday life, people hear and use apparently familiar terms and expressions, with partial or no comprehension of their meaning. The world of pinball is no different. The grass roots level of pinball, that of manufacturing, is a very complex world filled with many professions that each have their own technical terms. The common thread that links them all is, of course, the final outcome—a pinball machine. What can be found on a typical pinball machine, as well as other terms associated with the game, are as follows:

A PINBALL ORIENTATION (playfield).

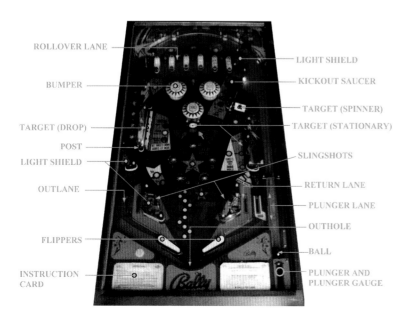

Playfield from Bally's SUPERSONIC

The most common features of a pinball playfield.

BACKBOX: Also known as the lightbox. It is the term used for the enclosure that sits on top of, and at the rear of the playfield cabinet. It contains the backglass; score unit or units; electromechanical and or electrical devices; and in some of the newer pinballs, it also contains the speakers.

BACKGLASS: The glass or plastic cover held by the backbox on which the colorful artwork, depicting the games theme and name, are displayed. On older pinballs the backglass also contained small windows from which the score display could be viewed.

Backglass detail from Gottlieb's SHIP MATES (1964). *Courtesy of Ivo Vasella.*

The backglass of William's OXO (1973). *Courtesy of Ivo Vasella.* $375-425.

BONUS: Accumulated points scored during play that are added to the total score, only after the end of each played ball or when a certain feature is completed; depending on the game rules.

BUMPERS: Also known as thumper bumpers, jets or pop bumpers. These are mushroom-shaped, cylindrical devices positioned around the playfield (generally found at the top), which score points when hit; and also propel the ball away using mechanical action.

CABINET: The term refers to the body of the pinball, not including the backbox. It holds the playfield; glass cover; internal mechanisms, and the cashbox.

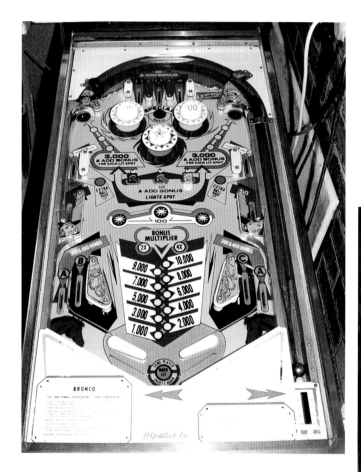

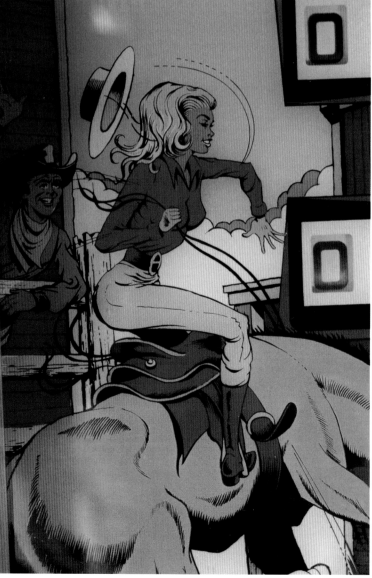

Gottlieb's BRONCO (1977). A typical game of the 70s that included the popular bonus feature. Notice the 1000 to 10,000 bonus ladder near the flippers. BRONCO backglass detail. *Gary Hudson collection.* $350-425.

CONVERSION KIT PINBALL: A pinball (in many cases, an older pinball) which has been upgraded to near new condition by the use of special kits, which change the game's theme/artwork and sometimes also the playfield layout. Converted pinballs were popular during World War II, when game production by major companies in the U.S.A was stopped for the war effort. Conversion kits again became popular during the mid-1980s, but this fad lasted only a few years. A conversion kit consisted of a new backglass, playfield (minus most working components), and new artwork panels to cover the original cabinet and backbox, which were either glued or nailed on. Some kits were suitable only for certain games specified by the manufacturer, while others were more flexible. It all depended on the amount of components re-used.

The stripped playfield of Geiger's DARK RIDER (1985), a conversion kit pinball. The playfield was originally that of Bally's STAR TREK (1978). It's one of the more exotic creations from Geiger, a company that produced several kits during the early 80s. *Ian F. McKinnon Collection.* $275-325.

CREDIT: The number of games paid for, or earned during play; the amount of which is displayed on the credit meter. Unlike gambling devices, credits obtained on pinballs are not redeemable for cash.

FLIPPERS: Appearing on the playfield, these can be any number of player controlled, bat-type devices, used to strike the ball in order to hit point-yielding targets and other playfield scoring components. Buttons positioned on the side of the cabinet activate the flippers. It is unquestionably the most well-known part of a pinball, even to nonplayers.

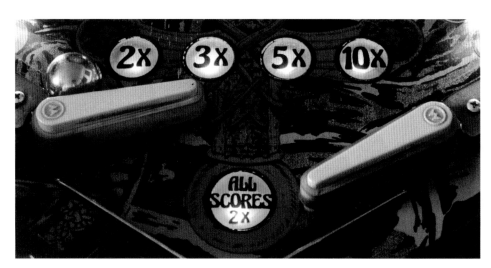

Flipper detail from Williams' JUNGLE LORD (1981). *Photograph courtesy of Ivo Vasella.*

KICKOUT SAUCER: Also known as kickout hole or eject hole. A hole in the playfield which awards points when the ball enters it; momentarily holding the ball until the points are registered and then dispelling the ball back onto the playfield. A cellar hole is also a common name for a more recent version of the kickout saucer, where the ball disappears momentarily below the playfield.

LIGHT SHIELD: A plastic covering used on playfield components that protects the playfield light source within. Its other, and most important function, is to enhance the aesthetic qualities of the playfield, and is therefore always decorated.

MULTIBALL: A term used when, during the course of a game, the player is required to play with more than one ball on the playfield at the same time. Multiball play has been a regular feature on pinballs since the early 1980s.

Lightshield detail from Bally's SUPERSONIC (1979).

OUTHOLE: The hole at the bottom of the playfield just behind the flippers through which the ball passes after its round on the playfield, and in which the ball (or balls) rests at the end of the game. It is also known in slang expression as "The guts", as in the common sentiment: "The ball went straight down the guts!" meaning that the ball was not kept in play for long.

OUTLANE: An exit lane located on each side of the playfield, usually in close proximity to the flippers. It channels the ball into the outhole, bypassing the flippers.

PLAYFIELD: The decorated topside surface of a pinball game, where the ball travels during play and which also holds various components such as flippers, bumpers and targets.

PLUNGER: The device found positioned on the right side of the cabinet; used to send the ball onto the playfield and "into play". Depending on the game, some plungers are manually operated by pulling back a spring-loaded shaft while others are electrically operated and require only the push of a button.

Lightshield detail from Bally's BAND WAGON (1965). More photos of this game can be found in Chapter Five.

Playfield of Bally's HI-LO ACE (1973). A large percentage of illustrations in this book are made up of original photos taken of pinball collections from around the world. Some games may be in mint condition, while others are pre-loved games with their fair share of wear and tear. At the other end of the spectrum are games like this one. This game no longer works and will eventually be cannibalized for spare parts, a common fate with games that have broken down completely. *Courtesy of Graham McGuiness.* $350-425.

HI-LO ACE playfield details.

PRODUCTION RUN: The total number of games produced for each particular game name/design. This is similar to a automobile manufacturer; where for instance, the production run for the latest Ford design was say, half a million cars. Pinball production runs do not reach quite so high. A production of 15 to 20 thousand these days, is considered a large run, and anything around two thousand or less is considered small.

PROTOTYPE: A prototype pinball or pinballs, as the name suggests, are the first pinballs off the production line. Ten or so of these games are built and tested, and sent out for public trials, in order to ascertain public/player response. Manufacturers then have the chance to iron out a few of the faults and inadequacies that may occur, and also obtain a better idea of how much the game will cost per unit. During this time, company executives make the hard decisions, about whether or not to scrap the game or to start full production; and if production proceeds, to determine its size.

Sega's VIPER-NIGHT DRIVING (1998). This game may look slightly different from the one that many may have seen at the local arcade—because this one is a rare prototype. *Mike Pacak collection.* $3000+

Data East's RICHIE RICH (1994). This prototype game is the only one of its kind; a very rare one-off. The game concept never made it into full production. An enthusiast with a keen eye for detail would notice that the playfield layout is almost exactly the same as Data East's TOMMY, released a few months prior. *Mike Pacak collection.* $2000+

RAMP: Any such device or feature that elevates the ball from the playfield and channels it to other parts, or to different levels.

REPLAY: A free game or credit that is obtained by achieving a specified score or objective.

RETURN LANE: A lane located near each flipper, which serves as a guide, channeling the ball down and onto the flipper.

ROLLOVER LANE: Any enclosed feature appearing on the playfield that channels the ball into one particular direction, usually either up or down the playfield. The term "rollover" refers to a switch protruding above the playfield, within the lane which scores points once the ball has rolled over it. Outlanes and return lanes are a type of rollover lane.

SLINGSHOT: Also known as slingshot kicker or kicking rubber. One of two devices generally found just above the flippers, at the bottom of the playfield. Usually triangular in shape, they form a boundary on one side, for either a return lane or an outlane. The inside face of the slingshot (that which faces towards the center of the playfield), scores points when hit, and also propels the ball away using mechanical action.

SPECIAL: A playfield scoring feature usually indicated by a bright red light. The feature light is activated after the completion of certain scoring achievements designated by the game rules. Completing a scoring feature thus lit, will in most cases award a replay.

TARGET: Any of a number of devices on the playfield that yield points (and in most cases also bonus points) when hit by the ball. Bumpers, rollover lanes, slingshots, and ramps are generally not considered as targets, despite awarding points when hit.

TILT: The term used when excessive physical force (rocking or shaking the machine) causes the game to shut down momentarily until the ball returns to the outhole and hence the player looses that ball in play.

TOMMY: "A deaf, dumb and blind kid, who sure played a mean pinball."

Ramp detail from the playfield of Williams' JUNGLE LORD (1981). The history of multi-level playfields and ramps is contained in Chapter Ten.

For a visual representation of some of the pinball components please refer to the "PINBALL ORIENTATION" illustrations in this chapter (page 22).

An introduction into the world of pinball would not be complete without mentioning some of the better-known companies (not necessarily the biggest ones) that have made up its history, and which will be noted again and again in the chapters to come. They are: BALLY (U.S.A), CHICAGO COIN (U.S.A), DATA EAST (U.S.A), GOTTLIEB (U.S.A), PLAYMATIC (SPAIN), RECEL (SPAIN), SEGA (U.S.A/JAPAN), STERN (U.S.A), WILLIAMS (U.S.A) and ZACCARIA (ITALY).

The playfield emblem of D.Gottlieb & Co, a pinball giant.

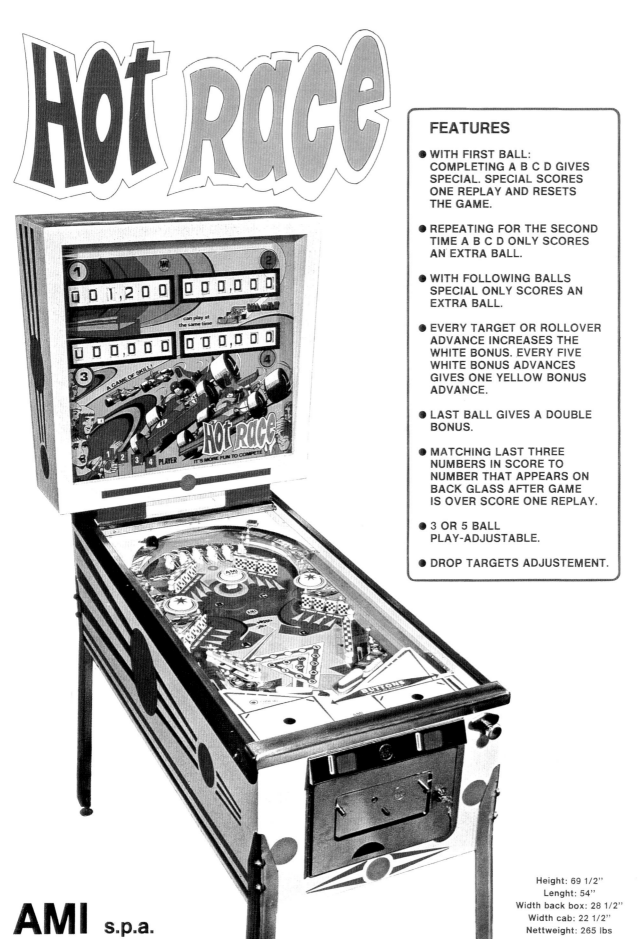

HOT RACE

FEATURES

- WITH FIRST BALL: COMPLETING A B C D GIVES SPECIAL. SPECIAL SCORES ONE REPLAY AND RESETS THE GAME.

- REPEATING FOR THE SECOND TIME A B C D ONLY SCORES AN EXTRA BALL.

- WITH FOLLOWING BALLS SPECIAL ONLY SCORES AN EXTRA BALL.

- EVERY TARGET OR ROLLOVER ADVANCE INCREASES THE WHITE BONUS. EVERY FIVE WHITE BONUS ADVANCES GIVES ONE YELLOW BONUS ADVANCE.

- LAST BALL GIVES A DOUBLE BONUS.

- MATCHING LAST THREE NUMBERS IN SCORE TO NUMBER THAT APPEARS ON BACK GLASS AFTER GAME IS OVER SCORE ONE REPLAY.

- 3 OR 5 BALL PLAY-ADJUSTABLE.

- DROP TARGETS ADJUSTEMENT.

A.M.I's HOT RACE (1976). This little-known Italian company built only a handful of pinballs during the late 70s. Most people have probably never had a chance to play this particular game, and probably never will, as there may be very few left in working condition, if any at all! One cannot compare this company to the likes of Gottlieb, Williams and Bally. Nevertheless, they are still part of pinball history, however small. $300-375.

AMI s.p.a.

Height: 69 1/2"
Lenght: 54"
Width back box: 28 1/2"
Width cab: 22 1/2"
Nettweight: 265 lbs

Logo from Italy's Zaccaria, the most successful Italian pinball manufacturer to date.

For the first-time pinball buyer, the search for a suitable pinball can be a frustrating one. The information contained within this book may be of assistance in finding the right game. If you have a particular game in mind, then all you have to do is find it; however, this can often be a never-ending search, especially when much older games are involved.

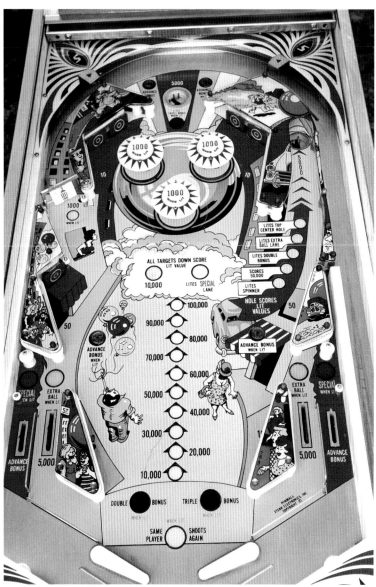

Stern's PINBALL (1977), the simplest of names for a pinball game. This well-known company began producing games in 1977 and was only in business for about 8 years. Despite its short life, it managed to create collectible games and plenty of enthusiastic supporters. *Courtesy of Mac.* $300-350.

The backglass emblem of Recel, the Spanish sister company of Petaco. Both used the same Euro-flip logo.

The reasons for purchasing a pinball can be numerous: nostalgia; something to keep the kids entertained while also providing a bit of enjoyment for the parent(s) (good trick, that one); party entertainment; as an unusual gift; or just to fulfill an urge to own your own pinball. The decisions and questions involved after you have decided to buy can also be as numerous. How much will one cost? Where or from whom can one be bought? What kind of pinball and how to get it home?! Unfortunately, this book is not a pinball buyer's guide, but anyone who has intentions of owning a pinball will benefit from the typically non-technical explanations and historical content of each chapter.

A little bit of historical knowledge can go a long way when faced with just a pinball game name or date, in the "For Sale" column of the local paper. Unlike computer games or other such electrical appliances, a new (or newer) pinball is not necessarily the best option. You may find everything that you desire all on one game, even if it is more than 20 years old. There may be certain game features or strategies and even game construction which some may find appealing, that no longer exist.

Above & opposite page: A mighty fine herd, an impressive collection. If you always liked to play the odd game in the local arcade, and then thought about buying your own game, beware! When you get a taste for pinballs you may not stop at just one. From left to right, Williams' ROAD KINGS (1986), TERMINATOR 2 (1991), F-14 TOMCAT (1987), Data East's JURASSIC PARK (1993), Williams' DRACULA (1993), DEMOLITION MAN (1994), ROLLER GAMES (1990) and finally Data East's PHANTOM OF THE OPERA (1990). *Jim Whitemyer collection.*

At the end of each chapter, a summary of the historical advancements in each case will provide an easy reference. This, along with a pinball list of over 3000 games built worldwide, and a large selection of photos (with price guide)[4] throughout the book, should provide a solid reference base for the expert and novice alike.

Gottlieb's OUTER SPACE (1972). It is not a must to buy a brand new pinball. Apart from the cost, it is not always true that "new is best". This term might apply to appliances like computers or stereos, but a pinball is different; an old pinball does not become obsolete. This may be an old game in terms of technological changes, but if you used to play this game and it was your favorite back then, chances are that its nostalgic allure will see you buying it over a relatively brand new game. One will find that most collectors' favorite pinballs are the ones they grew up with. *Graham McGuiness collection.* $300-350.

OUTER SPACE backglass detail.

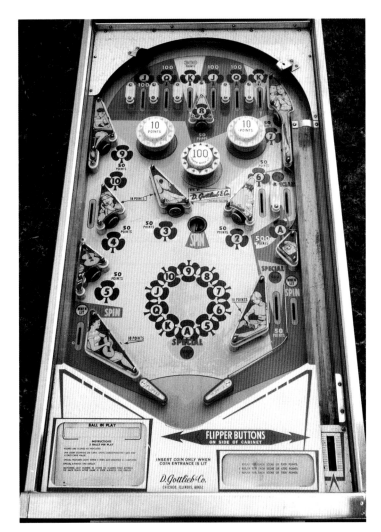

FLIP-A-CARD, a Gottlieb classic from 1970, not to be mistaken with other Gottlieb games like DROP-A-CARD, SPIN-A-CARD or POP-A-CARD. Even an expert can become confused at times. The game may sound familiar, but it may not be the game you thought. *Courtesy of Mac.* $425-525.

---

[1]The American Heritage Dictionary of the English Language, Houghton Mifflin Co.,1992.

[2]Webster's Third New International Dictionary Volume 2, G & C Merriam & Co.,1976.

[3]The Macquarie Dictionary, Macquarie University Australia, The Macquarie Library Pty Ltd., 1992.

[4]Prices shown are indicative only. They should not be regarded as firm buy-or-sell figures, but rather be used as approximate

value indicators. Values indicated refer to the price of a complete machine, even though some illustrations may show only the backglass or playfield. The price range for each game is based on an "unshopped" (meaning that it needs minor cosmetic work) complete machine in working order, with minimal/reasonable wear on the playfield surface and a good backglass. One must also note that the condition of the game's backglass and playfield may be more important to some collectors than whether or not the game is in working order or mechanically complete. Pinball prices can vary widely. A game with a price range shown as $300-$400 or $500-$600 may only be worth $100 if sold for parts, but on the other hand may be worth as much as $1000-2000 if it has been fully restored to mint condition by a professional. Relatively new games shown in this book may not vary in price as much, but will depreciate in value quite dramatically as they age, while much older games will most probably fetch the same prices year after year. Pro-

totype pinballs, very rare low production models or even "one-off" production games, do not conform to any current price trends and are usually sold for much more than one would expect to pay for a normal game. Images of such games found in this book include a minimum current price, with the possibility of a higher value, marked with a plus sign (+).

Gottlieb's PLAYMATES (1968). Sometimes a playfield may be familiar, but the name of the game may not. This is because game manufacturers have at times released pinballs with different names, but the same artwork and playfield layout. This particular game was also released as DOMINO (1968), which incidentally, was the first pinball I ever played. *Tim Van Blarcom collection.* $375-475.

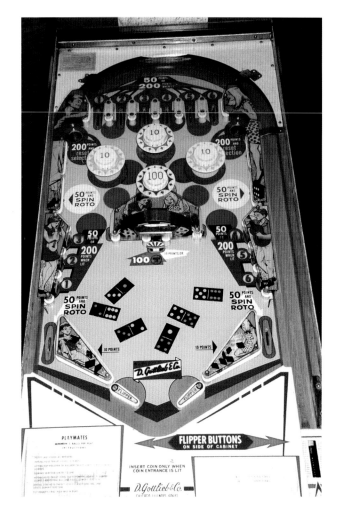

Chapter Two

The Flipper Story

A backglass close-up from a 1962 game. Gottlieb introduced the flipper to pinball. "A Gottlieb skill game"—it certainly was.

Modern pinball machines incorporate an integral component which allows us to manipulate the movement of the ball, and hence enable interaction with the playfield: the flipper. A standard pair is found at the bottom of the playfield, though additional flippers may be included further up. On contemporary machines, the flipper buttons, when pressed during play not only activate the flippers, but might provide a number of different functions. For instance, flipper buttons could change the lit rollover lanes above the bumpers in order to complete and increase the bonus multipliers and selecting various rewards or play modes, as directed by the score display panel. However, the machines of today are separated from their predecessors by technological advances which have allowed pinball designers to envisage and create new and improved components and game novelties, not least of which is the flipper.

Although flipper-type devices were not altogether new to amusement machines, with baseball games using bats to perform much the same function as a flipper since the early 1930s, the earliest pinballs were devoid of this feature.

No flippers and no thumper bumpers on Chicago Coin's KILROY, released in January 1947. By the beginning of 1948, these types of flipperless games would be out of fashion. Chicago Coin's first flipper game would be BERMUDA, released in November 1948. *Courtesy of Russ Jensen.* $275-350.

It was not until October 1947, post World War II, that the flipper made its debut on a Gottlieb pinball named HUMPTY DUMPTY. Pinball designer Harry Mabs devised the electrically operated flipper purely by mistake, while working on a new baseball machine. He was later credited with being the inventor of the modern flipper. It was an instant success, and henceforward was included on all new pinballs by every manufacturer.

Playfield of Williams' FAST BALL (1969), a baseball machine. Notice the flipper-like bat device at the bottom of the playfield. Games like this were being built as early as the 1930s, more than a decade before the flipper was introduced to pinballs. *Courtesy of Gary and Eric See.*

Backglass and machine shot of Williams' FAST BALL. It featured an extra wide playfield with underlying magnets that controlled the ball pitches. *Courtesy of Gary and Eric See.*

Prior to this revolutionary change, two other manufacturers had toyed with various player-controlled devices, but without success. In 1935 California Games introduced OLYMPIC PINS, a pinball with manually operated paddles. The handles would move these flipper-like devices, which were located on each side of the cabinet, just like today's flipper buttons. One would have thought that this idea would have caught on, but history tells otherwise. At the same time Gottlieb was marketing HUMPTY DUMPTY, Bally came up with NUDGY, a game where the playfield, with the aid of a side lever/handle, could be shifted slightly from back to front, allowing ball control. This game may have had a future had it been released before the flipper; but Gottlieb's new invention proved to be, by far, the more popular.

Gottlieb's HUMPTY DUMPTY (1947) the most famous pinball of them all! It was the first pinball to introduce the flipper, and as they say, the rest is history. *Courtesy of Russ Jensen.* $900-1100.

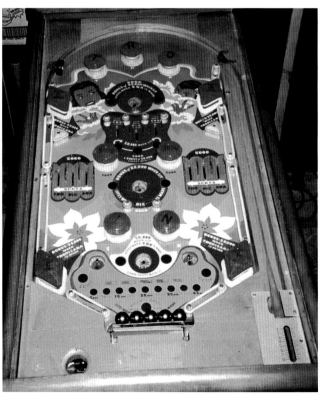

United's TROPICANA (Feb 1948), another flipperless pinball, one of the last built by this company. They introduced WISCONSIN later that same year, their first flipper game. *Tim Van Blarcom collection.* $325-400.

Treff Automaten's TREFF GLORIA
(c.1953) was the German version of
HUMPTY DUMPTY. The playfield
layout was almost identical. *Courtesy of
Jeff Grummel.* $400-500.

After the release of HUMPTY DUMPTY, the first flipper games to be manufactured by the other companies of the day were Marvel's DOLLY (Nov 1947), Williams' SUNNY (Dec 1947), Chicago Coin's BERMUDA (Dec 1947), Keeney's COVER GIRL (Dec 1947), Genco's TRIPLE ACTION (Jan 1948), Bally's MELODY (Jan 1948), Exhibit's BUILD UP (Jan 1948) and bringing up the rear, United's WISCONSIN (Apr 1948). For the record, HUMPTY DUMPTY had six flippers!

To take on a growing demand, there were even kits available to enable flippers to be added to older pre-flipper era pinballs, providing room could be found on the playfield! This concept was derived from the conversion kits used during WW II, used to update old pinballs during a time when the production of new pinballs had reached a standstill, due to the scarcity of resources.

United's MANHATTAN (March 1948), still no flippers. Compare the playfield of this game to that of TROPICANA; they are almost identical. *Courtesy of Russ Jensen.* $350-425.

Bally's MIDGET RACER (1946) had unusual flipper-like bumpers on each side of the playfield, but the were only ball guides and could not be operated by the player. Bally's first flipper pinball was MELODY (Jan 1948). *Tim Van Blarcom collection.* $350-425.

Presently, there are two significant differences between those flippers of old, and the ones used today. Firstly, the original flippers were mounted back to front (BFF-Back to Front Flippers). The tips of the flippers were pointing away from each other and facing the outside of the playfield, rather than the middle. This style of flipper play configuration soon changed, and by 1950, machines had flippers around the conventional way. Gottlieb's JUST 21 and BANK-A-BALL, both released in 1950, were some of the first machines to incorporate the new arrangement; although these two machines had the flippers quite some distance apart, on each side of the cabinet in fact!

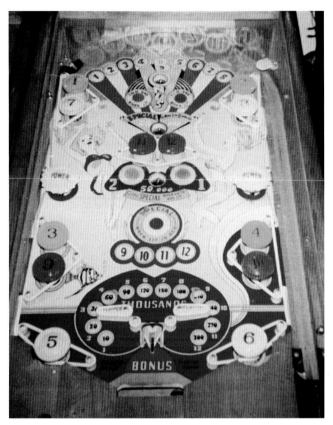

Genco's FLOATING POWER (1948). Notice how the flippers on this game are pointing the wrong way! This arrangement, introduced with HUMPTY DUMPTY, was discarded by all manufacturers by the mid 1950s. The flippers were then placed in the more conventional style we see today. *Courtesy of Russ Jensen.* $450-550.

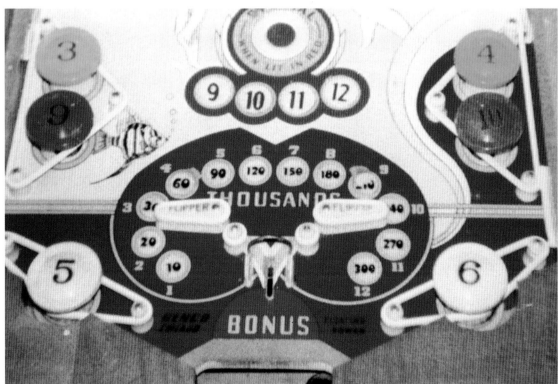

A closer look at the "back to front" flippers on FLOATING POWER.

This back to front configuration slowly disappeared within the space of ten years, and all pinballs now had this standard flipper position; but much closer at the tips. However this gap would still be considerably wider than today's machines by comparison. Gottlieb's DUETTE (1955) and REGISTER (1956), along a few German pinballs of the same year still had the BFF. Similarly with Williams' SEA-WOLF, as late as 1959. However, the latter game had two extra flippers further up the playfield, in addition to a normal set at the bottom.

The second difference was the flipper size; which was two inches long, rather than the three-inch standard of today. The "big" or 3" flipper, did not make its debut until August 1968 with HAYBURNERS II by Williams. In hindsight, the change in size seemed appropriate for this particular game, giving the player better ball control.

The mighty 2" flipper, seen here holding a ball for the proposes of size comparison, on the playfield of Gottlieb's BUCKAROO (1965).

Gottlieb's RACK-A-BALL (1962). A fairly simple game, but take a look at the gap between the flippers! This was a common sight back in those days. *Robert Young collection.* $500-600.

Approximately a year or so before the release of HAYBURNERS II, European manufacturers had also discovered that a longer flipper was beneficial to overall ball control. It was during 1967 that several two-player head-to-head games (a unique style of pinball game that will be discussed in Chapter Eleven), all built by different manufacturers, made use of a flipper size which was about 2.5" long. Such games included Germany's FUSSBALL EUROPA FLIPPER (c. 1967) by Forster and Italy's CALCIO ITALIA (1967) by Elettrogiochi.

Gottlieb's DROP-A-CARD (1971), a classic 2" flipper game of the early 70s. It was built at a time when the 3" flipper had already taken over. Those who had grown up playing with the smaller 2" flipper found it hard to adjust, and preferred to play games like this one. There are many pinball enthusiasts who still prefer pinballs this way. *Gary Hudson collection.* $350-450.

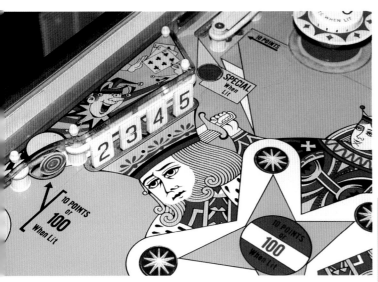

Playfield detail from Gottlieb's DROP-A-CARD.

By the end of 1971, the 3" flipper was used in preference to the small 2" flipper; of course with a few exceptions. Although Williams introduced the 3" flipper in August 1968, they did not totally commit themselves to the new style until mid 1969 with POST TIME, approximately five games later. Gottlieb adopted the longer flipper by mid-1971 on games such as PLAY BALL, and ROLLER COASTER. However Chicago Coin's BIG FLIPPER released in January 1970 went to the extremes, boasting huge 5" flippers! These "super" flippers were not to be seen again, and the now standard 3" flippers were used on their remaining games.

Backglass detail from Gottlieb's DROP-A-CARD.

STRIKE ZONE (1970), an early 3" flipper game from Williams. Williams can be said to have been the instigator of this style of flipper on games of the late 60s. This brought about the downfall of the 2" flipper, which by this stage, had already been consigned by most to a bygone era. $300-375.

Bally was the only exception in the use of the 3" flippers (whose reign was absolute by the end of 1971). Some of their games that still used 2" flippers utilized the Zipper-Flipper system.

Zipper flippers in action. When closed, they stop the ball from draining into the outhole. They are activated (and deactivated) by hitting specified playfield targets.

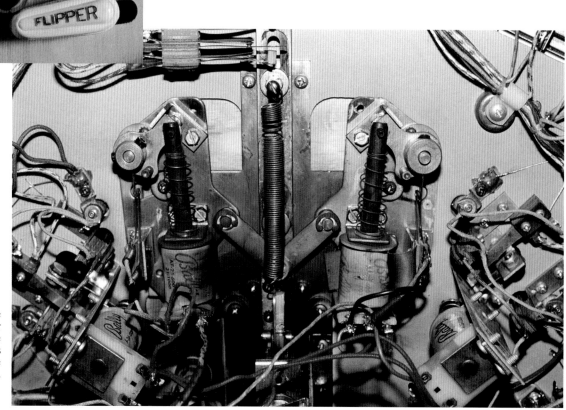

The complicated "under the playfield" workings of zipper flippers. Notice how the whole flipper assembly is mounted on a movable section.

The Zipper-Flippers, whose assemblies were mounted on tracks, allowed them to close together at the tips; effectively blocking the outhole when certain playfield features were achieved. However they would also spring back in the same manner.

Zipper-Flippers first appeared on BAZAAR in 1966, and featured on approximately seventeen out of a total of fifty pinballs built by Bally, until their demise in 1973. The three better known pinballs out of this group were FOUR MILLION BC (1971), FIRE-BALL (1972), and NIP-IT (1973). The latter game appeared regularly as a miscast in a 1950s setting on the popular 70s television show *Happy Days*, which also featured a few quick glimpses of Williams' KLONDIKE (1971) in a couple of early episodes. Williams produced a similar concept, which they named the Closing Flippers (referred to as "Closing Flipper Action" or CFA in one of their flyers). It was the same idea as the Zipper Flipper, but totally different mechanism. Only four games were released with this feature; DAFFIE, DOOZIE, STUDENT PRINCE and (surprise, surprise, with 3" flippers) HAYBURNERS II, all released in 1968. Even Spain grabbed onto the idea, appearing on T.D. Llobregat's DIG A STAR (1969), the only Spanish pinball known to incorporate it.

Zipper flippers on Bally's FIREBALL (1972). Between 1966 and 1973 Bally built approximately 17 pinballs with this feature. *Rawdon Osborne collection.*

Williams' DAFFIE (1968). It was one of only a handful of Williams games with a zipper flipper style mechanism. *Tim Van Blarcom collection.* $375-450.

Those Bally pinballs not using Zipper-Flippers did in fact utilize 3" flippers, which became standard with the company at approximately the same time as Williams in mid to late 1969. At this time, pinballs built at the turn of the decade, only two or three years prior, although practically new and still earning revenue, were unfortunately already being consigned to a previous era on the basis of their smaller flipper size.

The 2" flippers did not vanish completely, but were instead relegated by manufacturers, on some pinballs, to the upper playfield areas; which because of their size, the extra flipper or two could be more readily accommodated where the longer flipper would otherwise be an incumberance. Nearly every pinball manufacturer has included the extra 2" flippers at some time or another; EL DORADO (1975), MEDUSA (1981), GRAND SLAM (1983), JUDGE DREAD (1993), and BAY WATCH (1995), are some examples, just to name a few.

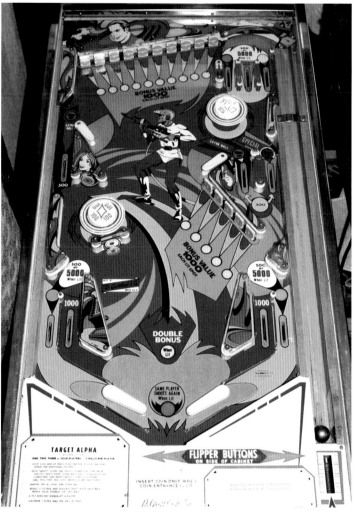

Above left & above: Gottlieb's TARGET ALPHA (1976), a game with four flippers; 3" flippers at the bottom and a pair of 2" flippers at the top. Although 2" inch flippers were replaced with the longer style in the early 1970s, they became a popular flipper for use in the upper playfield where a 3" flipper would otherwise have been an incumberance. *Graham McGuiness collection.* $400-475.

Take a closer look! Backglass details from TARGET ALPHA.

MEDUSA's two extra playfield flippers are positioned just above midfield, effectively dividing the playfield into two sections. Set out in a fashion identical to standard flippers near the outhole, the designers decided to give them the long-forgotten zipper mechanism, hence giving the game a unique feature among pinballs of the 80s.

The mechanical workings of a flipper have not changed dramatically since 1947, except that these early flippers were not as powerful as those today. For those unfamiliar with the flipper mechanism and its workings, it consists of five major components: a solenoid coil, coil plunger, lever arm, flipper shaft, and flipper.

The solenoid coil (a basic component for mechanical action on pinballs), is a coil of tightly wound insulated wire with a hollow core. It utilizes the properties of electromagnetism; and with the use of a metal plunger, produces mechanical action. This metal coil plunger sits almost completely outside the solenoid when the flipper is at rest. The lever arm attached to the flipper shaft joins the coil plunger at approximately ninety degrees, by means of a moveable joint. When the solenoid coil is energized, the plunger is drawn in by a magnetic force, causing the lever arm to "lever" and rotate the shaft attached to the flipper. Once your finger is removed from the flipper button, hence removing power from the coil, the plunger is pulled back out of the solenoid by the use of a spring mechanism and the flipper resumes its resting position.

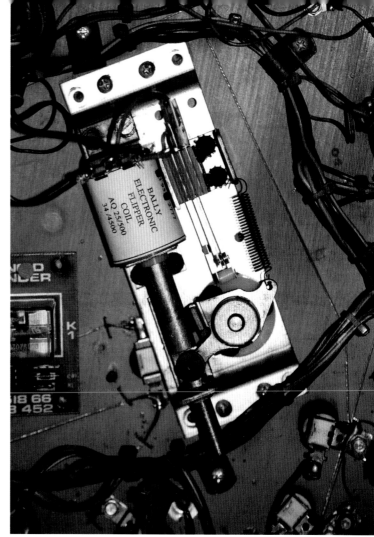

Not all flipper assemblies look the same. A flipper assembly from an electronic pinball built in the early 1980s.

A simple diagram showing the major components of a flipper mechanism.

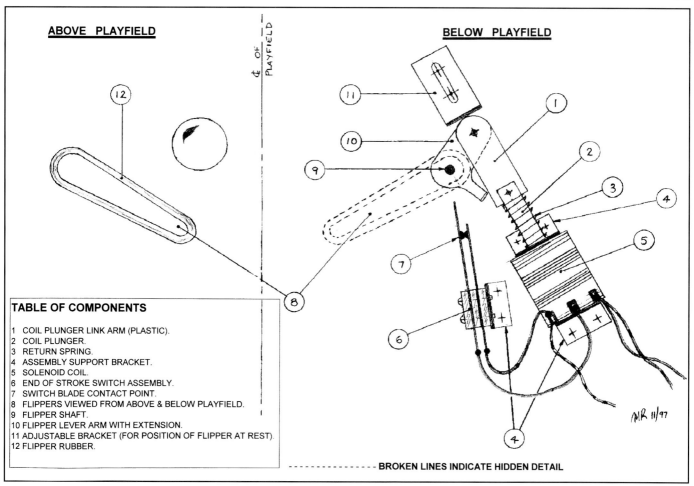

ABOVE PLAYFIELD

BELOW PLAYFIELD

TABLE OF COMPONENTS

1 COIL PLUNGER LINK ARM (PLASTIC).
2 COIL PLUNGER.
3 RETURN SPRING.
4 ASSEMBLY SUPPORT BRACKET.
5 SOLENOID COIL.
6 END OF STROKE SWITCH ASSEMBLY.
7 SWITCH BLADE CONTACT POINT.
8 FLIPPERS VIEWED FROM ABOVE & BELOW PLAYFIELD.
9 FLIPPER SHAFT.
10 FLIPPER LEVER ARM WITH EXTENSION.
11 ADJUSTABLE BRACKET (FOR POSITION OF FLIPPER AT REST).
12 FLIPPER RUBBER.

- - - - - - - - - - - - - - - BROKEN LINES INDICATE HIDDEN DETAIL

The flipper solenoid is a coil comprised of two windings; a heavier winding energized for the first strong stroke of the flipper, and a lighter winding (that uses less power) which allows the plunger to be held in for an extended period without over-heating or burning out the solenoid. The switching of power from the heavier to the lighter coil occurs with the aid of two switchblades. A switchblade is a thin flexible piece of conductive metal with a contact point attached at one end, and a hole to receive electrical wire at the other. A small extension on the lever arm is used push apart the two contacting blades mounted nearby, therefore breaking off power to the heavier winding and allowing the lighter winding to hold the plunger. These two switchblades on the flipper assembly are commonly known as a singular "end-of-stroke" switch. This type of flipper operation using an end-of-stroke switch, which is primarily an electromechanical device (see next chapter), remained relatively unchanged; even after the introduction of solid state technology, in 1976.

The next mentionable advancement in flipper technology came at the start of 1990. Data East, a newcomer in pinball manufacturing (first pinball being LAZER WARS, built in 1987), introduced their patented solid state flipper in January 1990 (Patent #4895369) on ROBOCOP. Williams/Bally devised a similar mechanism in 1992 (Williams having bought out Bally in 1988) without infringing upon Data East's patent. However, be it Williams or Data East, the working of the flipper was now tied in to the game's microprocessors. The end-of-stroke switch on the flipper assembly was now almost obsolete, replaced by its solid state counterpart within the computer circuitry.

As an example to the principle workings of a solid state flipper, we take a look at a service manual from a Data East pinball built in 1994. Doing my best to condense the technical jargon, it basically states that the "new" solid state flipper board (S.S.F.B.) contained a solenoid driver circuit, which incorporated a "one shot" timer, a 50-volt driver and a 8-volt driver. All this meant was that when the flipper coil was energized, a 50-volt current was used for the first strong "hitting" stroke, but then this was switched off by the timer and the 8-volt current now provided the holding power. The S.S.F.B. and the "one shot" timer replaced the end-of-stroke switch and the use of two separate windings on the solenoid coil. Despite this, the end-of-stroke switch was still incorporated, but strictly as an added feature and not a functional part of the circuit. Its function was now to prevent the flipper being knocked back by a fast ball. If while holding the flipper in the up position the bat was moved back by more than 0.0625", the end-of-stroke switch would make contact and hence close a circuit giving the coil another 50-volt boost, in which case the timer process was repeated again.

For the player, though, the flipper still looked and felt the same. But, for the technician, the pinball now had greater self-diagnostic abilities. Pinball self-diagnosis is something that has evolved with pinball design since the introduction of the first solid state machines. Such advancements have occurred unseen to people not associated with the game's technical aspects. The new solid state flipper system meant that the game's computer could now also activate the flipper coil independently (therefore activating the flipper), during its diagnostic cycle/sequence. This was something that has been exclusive to the other playfield solenoids—such as the bumpers; kickout saucers; and target-reset coils—since the late 1970s.

The history of the flipper basically ends here. However, this chapter would not be complete without a look at some small details, and the cameo appearances of some flipper oddities within the flipper's fifty-year history.

Gottlieb's new invention was at first named by the company "Flipper Bumpers". While Bally's flippers were named "Kicker Bumpers". However the term "flipper" was adopted (minus the extra word) eventually, in keeping with Gottlieb's device.

The word "flipper" became the German, French and Italian equivalent of the English word "pinball"; although the Italians would also occasionally use the word "biliardino", which translates as small billiard table or game.

Pinball history has always been filled with novelty ideas. Manufacturers realizing the potential of different gadgets in attracting buyers and players alike attempted many creations at least once or twice; knowing full well that the idea could be unpopular and short-lived. Having said that, let's introduce the banana flippers. No prizes for guessing their shape, they were obviously bent. Williams introduced this type of flipper on two occasions; first on DISCO FEVER (June 1978), and again a year later on TIME WARP (Sep 1979).

Williams' TIME WARP (1979). There are pinballs that are best remembered because of the unusual features which they incorporated. TIME WARP is remembered by many for its use of banana flippers. Only one other Williams pinball used this style of flipper; DISCO FEVER (1978). *Phillip Paterson collection.* $325-400.

INSTRUCTIONS

- Insert Coin And Wait For Machine To Reset Before Inserting Coin For Next Player.
- Lighting #5 On 3 Bank - Lites Top Eject For Extra Ball.
- Making A - B - C TWICE - Lites Bullseye For Special.
- Making 5 Bank - 1st Time Lites Left Outlane For 30,000.
  2nd Time Lites Right Outlane For 30,000.
  3rd Time Lites 5 Bank Special.
  4th Time Scores Special.
- Tilt Penalty - Ball In Play - Does Not Disqualify Player.
- Bullseye Special Scores _____ 1 CREDIT.
- Beating Highest Score Scores 3 CREDITS.
- Matching Last Two Numbers On Score With Numbers In Match Window On Black Glass Scores _____ 1 CREDIT.

5 BANK SPECIAL SCORES — 1 CREDIT

489-3

TIME WARP instruction card, for those interested in the game rules.

Banana Flippers had the concave, or scoop side, facing the playfield. This curvature made aiming extremely difficult and unpredictable, as the ball would sometimes slingshot off the flipper. This unpredictability appealed to some players, adding both a degree of difficulty and increasing the fun. A definite advantage with the Banana Flippers was that they made the ball easier to trap. Because of their curved tips, the ball would not roll up and off the flipper as easily. In terms of structural design, the Banana Flippers differed greatly from normal flippers, which are made from molded plastic and have a thick rubber band of sorts fitted around it, which gives

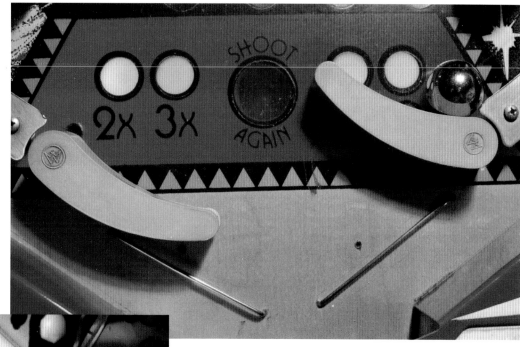

A closer look at those famous (or infamous) banana flippers.

the device more bounce and is interchangeable. Of course, this idea had inherent problems when applied to the Banana Flippers, in that the rubber would not fit to the concave side the flipper, stretching instead across the contour, between base and tip. Williams got around this problem by making an interchangeable casing out of molded rubber, which fitted over the top of the flipper like a mitten.

TIME WARP playfield detail.

At about this time, Atari came up with offset flippers. The offset, or skewed, flippers were normal flippers; the only difference was in their positioning. The left flipper was approximately 1" further up the playfield than the right. I have never played with this type of flipper configuration, and therefore I cannot comment on how it performed. However the idea did not catch on, and one can only imagine the difficulty in attempting to save a ball heading straight down the middle! MIDDLE EARTH (1978), and ROAD RUNNER (1979), both have offset flippers; the latter pinball, however, only reached prototype stage. The offset flipper was also used by Playmatic on their BLACK FEVER pinball in 1980 and by Gottlieb in 1979 on ROCK STAR.

Atari's ROAD RUNNER (1979). This rare prototype (only one of its kind produced) used the offset flipper style similar in fashion to MIDDLE EARTH (1978). *Courtesy of Herb Silvers/Fabulous Fantasies.* $4800+

It was during the early 1980s that Bally, as well as Italy's Zaccaria, came up with the outlane flipper save, or "Flipsave" as Bally named it. Zaccaria had actually named it the "React" feature, but that name never really stuck. Zaccaria took the older style 2" flipper and placed it vertically with the tip facing downwards, in between the outlane and the return lane, one on each side of the pinball. The idea was that one could activate the flipper if the ball found its way into the outlane and send it back and out into play, though it was easier said than done. Of course, in the name of fairness, one was allotted one save per flipper, per ball. Like playing any pinny, it was all in the timing; sometimes one got lucky and a perfect shot was made, but most of the time it was either a case of too soon or too late. Hitting the flipper save too soon meant that the ball would not have been struck with enough power to

A lower playfield view of Zaccaria's DEVIL RIDERS (1983), showing the "React" flipper save positioned between the outlanes and the return lanes. *Courtesy of Edoardo Frola.*

PLAY AND DANCE WITH

Black Fever

by **playmatic**

Bookkeeping Features:

Number of coins inserted in all coins rejectors.
Number of total games played (paid + free)
    "   "   "   replays by SPECIAL.
    "   "   "   EXTRA BALLS.
    "   "   "   Replays by Score.
    "   "   "   Free Games.

FEATURES:

Outside button to allow
the player to play
balls alternately or continuously.
Alarm system to protect against
robbery and Maltreatment.
DISCO MUSIC at diferents stages
of the game.

BONUS. X2. X3. X5 up to an
astounding 145.000 in combination
with Green Targets.

ADJUSTMENTS

Maximun number of CREDITS
from 0 up to 99
High Score scoring
Free game first score
Free game second score
Free game third score
Games by coins from 1/3 up to 39
in each coin rejector independently
Maximun amount of EXTRA BALLS
Match Feature or no
Free games for each player, one or severa
Several scoring on the playfield, bumpers, etc
Adjustable to all coin combination:

Playmatic's BLACK FEVER (1980). It also used the offset
flipper style. $275-325.

clear the lane and that was the end of that! Hitting the button too late, one would find oneself in the unenviable position of having the ball trapped between the flipper and the edge of the playfield; knowing full well that there was nothing else to do but take one's finger off the button and bid the ball farewell. Nevertheless, that small chance of saving the ball was better than none. One of Zaccaria's most famous pinballs, FARFALLA (1983), was one of the few pinballs with this device. Bally's device was much more user-friendly, although it still required excellent timing. It premiered on a wide-bodied game called EMBRYON (1981) and was included only on the right outlane. The main difference was that the flipper was positioned to the extreme right, and rather than trying to hit the ball back out through the lane, it just diverted the ball through a one way gate and into the return lane.

Another device, although completely without player control, was the spinning flipper. Stern's HOT HAND (1979), designed by Harry Williams; founder of Williams Electronics, had such a device. Positioned in the upper playfield, it rotated through 360 degrees continuously, every three to four seconds, throughout the duration of the game. Gathered around in a circle within reach of the flipper tip were scoring discs, where the ball could land and score continuously until the flipper came around to push it out. If the ball landed in a disc just after the flipper had been past, the player could have a whole three to four seconds of uninterrupted scoring. It it landed just before, the best hope was that the ball would get pushed through a few more discs before falling off the end of the flipper.

Stern's HOT HAND (1979), designed by Harry Williams, used a spinning flipper positioned on the upper playfield. *Courtesy of Michael Tansell.* $300-375.

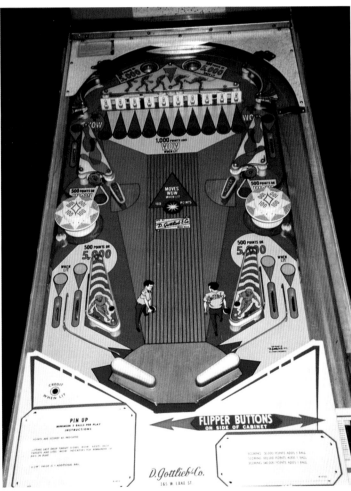

Gottlieb's PIN UP (1975) is what is termed as a deep target pinball, due to its large bank of drop targets positioned way up the playfield. Notice the position and angle of the upper flippers, positioned this way so as not to get in the way of any shots coming from the lower playfield. *Tim Van Blarcom collection.* $350-450.

A more recent pinball with this device is Gottlieb's STREET FIGHTER II (1993). The flipper is positioned above the upper part of the playfield, halfway down a long continuous ramp. The ramp starts on the right side of the playfield, turning at the very top, to deliver the ball onto the left flipper's return lane. The spinning flipper is positioned to thwart one's efforts to complete the whole journey, usually sending the ball back down to the start of the ramp.

The standard two-flipper configuration near the outhole that both players and non-pinball players have come to recognize the game by over the years, has not been without its share of experimentation. Williams' SKYWAY (1954), and NINE SISTERS (1953), had only one flipper on

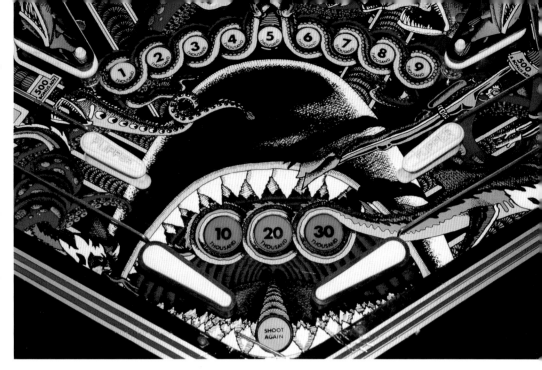

Playfield detail of Hankin's SHARK (1980). Like Bally's SPACE INVADERS (1980), it positioned both styles of flippers near the outhole, each having its own return lane.

the left side! Bally's SPACE INVADERS (1980) and Hankin's SHARK (1980), have four flippers, two standard flippers, and two 2" flippers. The smaller flippers are just over a ball width further up the playfield, and spaced further apart so as not to get in the way of the larger flippers. All four flippers have their own ball return lanes, and for those not totally familiar with pinballs, a four-flipper game does not necessarily have four flipper buttons. Even a five- or six-flipper game has only two buttons, where all flippers on the left-hand side are activated by the left button, and vice versa.

William's C.O.D (1953); cash on delivery. Notice the unusual array of flippers on this game. Other than the standard set of two, there is one positioned upside down guarding the left drain and one on the bottom right hand corner. *Eugene Ricci collection.* $600-725.

Gottlieb's JUNGLE QUEEN (1977). *Ivo Vasella collection.* $350-425.

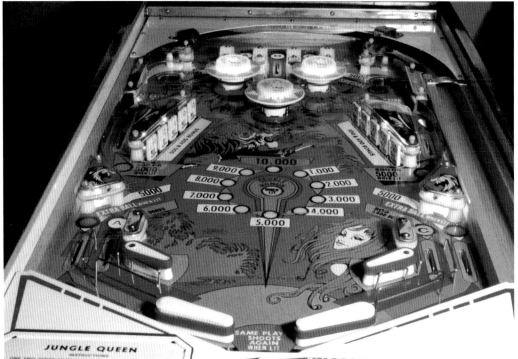

For Gottlieb's JUNGLE QUEEN, the slingshot kickers were removed and flippers put there instead, giving the player extra ball control.

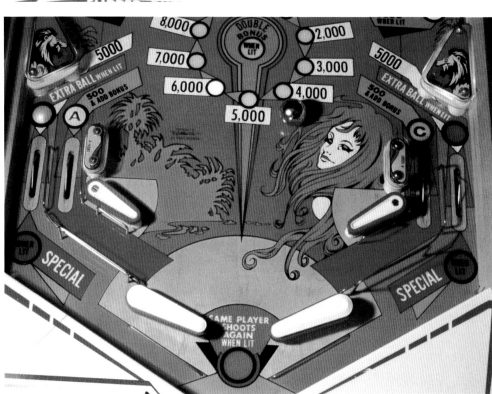

Lower playfield detail.

A flipper configuration that became popular in the 1970s, but is rarely seen in pinballs outside this decade, was the in-line flipper. The in-line flipper was an extra flipper placed directly behind the standard flipper, with its tip touching the back or shaft end of the standard one; hence the name. Because the flippers in a line (even though at an angle) took up 6" of one half of the playfield, these pinballs had no room to incorporate a ball return lane on that particular side, leaving only an outlane. The most famous part of the in-line flipper was the flipper drain.

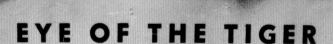

The playfield of Gottlieb's SOLAR RIDE (1979). Notice the pair of in-line flippers on the bottom left. $325-400.

The flipper drain was the gap that appeared between the flippers. Once activated, the top flipper acted like a gate, allowing the ball, usually after an unexpected bounce, to sneak through and end up in the outhole. I remember vividly the times that I lost a ball in that fashion. The flipper drain also meant that one could not hold the ball with the bottom flipper, because it would just roll off the back and therefore be lost. My brother and I, having served our pinball apprenticeships on games from the late 1970s, nicknamed the in-line flipper and drain as the dreaded "Gottlieb Trap", due to the large number of Gottlieb pinballs that used the arrangement at that time. Gottlieb's KING KOOL (1972), SINBAD (1978), and Williams' CONTACT (1978) boast two in-line flippers; one on each side. Williams' DEALERS CHOICE (1974), Bally's CAPTAIN FANTASTIC (1976), and Gottlieb's SOLAR RIDE (1979) are some of the games that have only one in-line flipper; all of which are located on the left hand side. Although this type of flipper configuration was not everybody's cup of tea, Williams'

Gottlieb's EYE OF THE TIGER (1978) was the electrome-chanical version of SINBAD (1978). Both games had almost exactly the same playfield, but different backglass art, plus of course the latter was a solid state machine with digital score displays. Notice two sets of in-line flippers, both with those dreaded flipper drains. **See next page for backglass detail.** *Courtesy of Robert Young.* $375-475.

CONTACT went some way towards giving the player an option with "Dual Action" flippers, where the bottom flipper of each set could be activated independently, de-pending on how far in one pressed the flipper buttons.

EYE OF THE TIGER instruction card, for those interested in the game rules.

EYE OF THE TIGER
INSTRUCTIONS
ONE OR TWO PLAYERS—5 BALLS PER PLAYER

INSERT COIN AND/OR PRESS CREDIT BUTTON TO RESET MACHINE. REPEAT FOR SECOND PLAYER.

RED DROP TARGETS SCORE 3000 POINTS AND INCREASES BONUS VALUE. COMPLETING RED DROP TARGETS LIGHTS RED ROLLOVER ALTERNATELY FOR "SPECIAL".

WHITE, YELLOW AND PURPLE DROP TARGETS SCORE 500 POINTS AND INCREASES BONUS VALUE. COMPLETING WHITE, YELLOW OR PURPLE DROP TARGETS LIGHTS CORRESPONDING ROLLOVERS AND BULLSEYE TARGETS. COMPLETING WHITE, YELLOW AND PURPLE DROP TARGETS LIGHTS "DOUBLE BONUS".

SWINGING TARGET AND ROLLOVER BUTTONS SCORE 10 POINTS AND ADD ADVANCE. 5 ADVANCES ADDS ONE BONUS AND 500 POINTS.

BONUS IS SCORED AND FEATURES RESET AFTER EACH BALL IN PLAY.

A TILT DOES NOT DISQUALIFY A PLAYER.

MATCHING LAST TWO NUMBERS IN SCORE TO NUMBER THAT APPEARS ON BACK GLASS AFTER GAME IS OVER SCORES ONE REPLAY.

B-18175-2

EYE OF THE TIGER backglass detail. **See previous page for more information**.

Whoops! Watch that flipper drain. One must change the style of flipper/ball action when playing a pinball with this type of flipper arrangement. Energize the flippers at the wrong time and the ball may very well disappear between them.

Bally's NBA FASTBREAK (1997). The backglass on this game is transparent, behind which a ball and flipper can be viewed. The object of this backbox playfield is to try and shoot the basket at the opposite end. With the use of a top guiding arch one can easily make the basket. It then becomes a matter of timing, not skill—trying to get as many shots in during the allotted time. $1300-1500.

The playfield has always been the flipper's domain, but there have been times when the backboard has also become a part of a pinball's playfield. Pinball enthusiasts keeping up with the latest game releases, would have come into contact with the backbox flipper used on Bally's FASTBREAK (1997). The backbox flipper is not something new to pinballs of 1997—the idea was used previously in 1981 on Stern's CATACOMB. FASTBREAK, like CATACOMB, uses only one flipper in the backbox, along with a plastic ball, rather than a heavier steel one. The backboard playfield on both games, being vertical and of course very fast-playing, is a simple affair and when activated, only takes a few seconds of game time away from the pinball's conventional playfield. The backbox flipper action does not require the same degree of skill required by the ordinary flippers, due to the absence of an outhole; allowing the ball to return and rest on the tip of the flipper, in preparation for the next shot.

In 1994, Data East introduced an entirely new mechanism that has yet to be replicated on any other pinny. The pinball TOMMY, based on the original musical score by the 1960s group *The Who*, and its subsequent success as a musical production, incorporates the various lyric themes about "That deaf, dumb, and blind kid who sure plays a mean pinball" (P. Townsend, 1969). The mechanism in question are flipper blinders. During one of the various play modes a fan unfolds to shield the flippers (themselves of standard size and location) from view of the player, who then in essence, plays "blind". These flipper blinders can also be activated at the start of the game for continuous blind play for the game's duration.

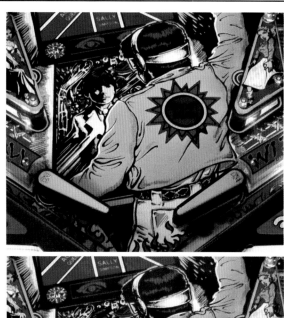

Now you see them; now you don't. Playfield details from Data East's TOMMY, showing how the game's blinders completely shield the flippers from the player's view.

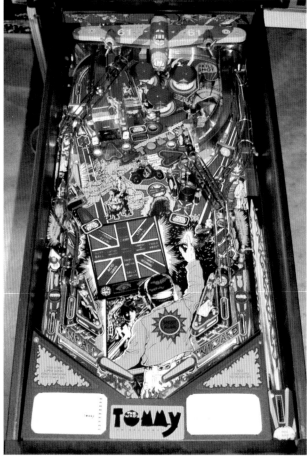

Data East's TOMMY (1994). The pinball was based on the original musical score by the 1960s group *The Who*, and its subsequent success as a musical production. The mechanism introduced on this particular game were flipper blinders. During one of the various play modes a fan would unfold, shielding the flippers from the player, in essence, playing "blind". $900-1100.

TOMMY backglass detail.

The introduction of the solid state flipper and the ability of a pinball's diagnostic program to activate the flipper coil independently lead to the logical assumption that a pinball could perhaps play by itself. Williams' MONSTER BASH (1998) introduced the novelty feature called the "Phantom Flip". Williams explained it thus; "Is the game haunted? Is it possessed? No, it's Phantom Flip! Keep those hands away and watch the spooky action!" Hitting each of the game's blue stand-up targets would light the Phantom Flip at the ball return lanes. Once the ball entered the return lane, the Phantom Flip would automatically decide which shot was the best, and try to make it for you automatically!

The final part of the flipper story looks at the flipper buttons and the pinballs of the last ten years that have offered a different approach to them.

The standard number of buttons and their position have always remained the same, since the arrival of the flipper in 1947. The standard location is two buttons, one on each side of the cabinet, near the front cash door, and at the height of the playfield. Some pinballs made in the early 1980s and mid-1990s have had four buttons, two on each side. However, these two extra buttons, in most cases, were not associated with the flippers, and had other functions, such as Williams' "Magna Save" feature (see Chapter Ten).

In the early 1990s, Italian manufacturer Mister Game decided to tackle buttons in a very different way. Mister Game replaced the traditional flipper buttons with handgrips on the end of the cabinet, with thumb operated flipper controls, much like a video game's thumb operated fire button. Williams' DEMOLITION MAN (1994) uses a similar idea; but this is in addition to a standard set of buttons. DEMOLITION MAN uses handles (as opposed to handgrips) that look rather like two silver bull's horns, and makes the game recognizable at a glance.

The conception and introduction of the flipper to pinballs could be seen as the most integral and recognizable feature, allowing us to interact purposefully with the playfield. It has become a standard inclusion along with other identifiable components that have been tried and tested throughout the decades. However, despite technological advances and vivid artistic imagery, and, of course, marketing potential, limitations have been found in terms of flipper size and location, which affect overall quality of play. Many things may affect one's play, and to be a proficient player, one must master the timing and coordination of the flippers in order to trap, aim, and strike a target or ramp, or to save a ball from being lost down the center or "down the guts!" Therein lies the secret. It might well be said that on a good playing day, the flipper can be one's closest friend; but in adversity, one's deadliest foe.

Summary

1947 Flippers introduced, two-inch size.
1947-50 Back to front flippers used on pinballs.
1950-55 Flippers slowly change position.
1955 Flippers in modern position on most pinballs.
1966 Bally introduces the Zipper Flipper (2" size).
1968 Three-inch flippers introduced on American pinballs.
1969-71 Most manufacturers convert from two- to three-inch flippers.
1973 Last pinball with Zipper Flippers, produced by Bally.
1990 Data East introduces the Solid State Flipper.

William's DEMOLITION MAN (1994). Great game to play, but personally I was never too keen on the backglass artwork. The striking feature about this game was of course its shiny flipper handles. This was quite a novel way to play pinball if one chose that option, but it never seriously challenged the traditional use of cabinet buttons. The game also featured a "captive car" in favor of a captive ball, plus loads of intertwining ramps. $825-1000.

Opposite page: Mr. Game's MAC ATTACK (1989), a pinball with pistol grip flipper control buttons. $425-525.

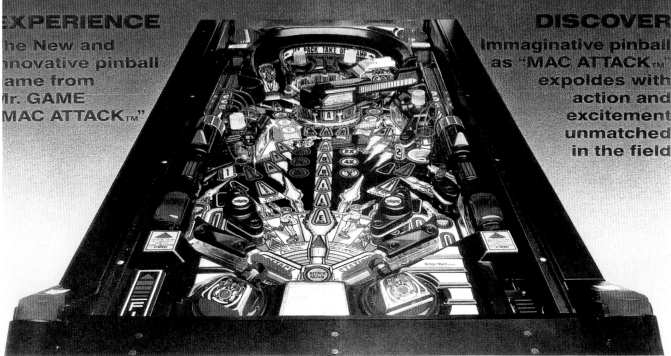

Chapter Three

Electromechanical to Solid State

The terms *electromechanical* (EM), and *solid state* (SS), are commonly used in reference to pinball type; especially if one is in the business of buying or selling second-hand pinballs. More specifically, these two terms describe the inner workings of a pinball. SS, or electronic, refers to the computer-like components used on pinballs built at present. The term electromechanical refers to the old style of pinball construction which was phased out with the introduction of SS technology in the mid-1970s. It would be the equivalent of comparing the engine of an old steam train to that of a electric train; both achieve relatively the same result, whilst utilising very different technologies.

The origins of the earliest pinball machines are shrouded in uncertainty. It seems that, like most old games and sports, the pinball slowly evolved into its recognizable form.

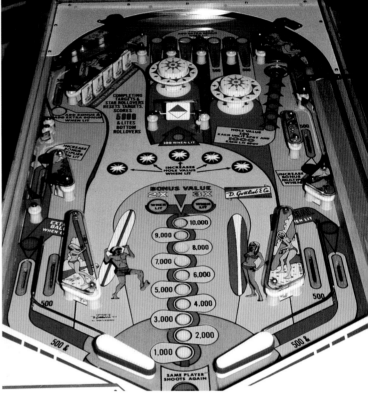

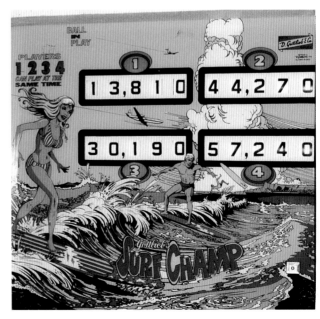

Surf's up on Gottlieb's SURF CHAMP (1976). A typical four-player electromechanical (EM) game of the '70s. It was built at a time when these types of machines were starting to be replaced with solid state (SS) technology. *Phillip Brown collection.* $400-500.

Early pinballs (bagatelles or pin tables) were very simple, comprising of a sloping, open playfield without a glass cover. The games had dozens of nails and pins (hence the derivative name of pinball) positioned to act as bumpers, obstacles, or guides, in order to direct the ball into scoring holes drilled into the playfield. Some of these games also had numbered pockets or lanes at the bottom of the playfield, maybe even a bell, surrounded by a circle of nails with a top opening, which would signal the entry of the ball into the scoring enclosure. After having played all one's marbles, one would count all scoring shots manually—not very mechanical, let alone electromechanical. Yet this type of construction is something that any average handyman today could very easily throw together in a matter of hours, using spare material. That I know for a fact, having constructed similar sorts of games as a young child during the school holidays in order to alleviate the moments of boredom. The only difference with my pin table was some added improvisation, making use of handfuls of rubber bands, stringing them across the nails to act as bumpers. I also had flippers on mine; two clothes pegs, held in place with a nail through the center of the spring. However, what may be trivial homemade games today was big business back in the late 19th century. Well-known companies like Milton Bradley sold bagatelle games, amongst other things, with prices ranging from ten cents each for small models, up to fifty cents each for the larger size, 8.25" wide by 23" long.

The first truly mechanical component used on the very early pre-pinball games was a small device still used today. A steel spiral spring used in an invention called a ball shooter, or plunger, was created by Mr. Montague Redgrave of Cincinnati Ohio, which later received the U.S. patent #115357 on the 30th of May 1871.

In the sixty years that followed Mr Redgrave's invention, bringing us now into the 1930s, bagatelle and pin tables hadn't really changed all that much. Though the games had become a little

Above & right: BIG LEAGUER, an early EM game built c. 1933/34 by American Scales (funny name for a pinball manufacturer). It was a payout pinball, awarding two nickels for every run scored. Notice the oversize balls. *Eugene Ricci collection.* $900-1000.

A simple bagatelle board game, the ancestor of the modern pinball. This particular game was manufactured c. 1900 by Glevum; a British company. *Mark Jackson collection.* $75-$100.

more refined and commercialized, the nails and scoring holes still existed, but the game had now become coin-operated. With the addition of electricity via battery, the modern pinball was born; with that also came the new word that would describe the inner workings of the game for the next 40 years—electromechanical.

In 1935 transformers were added to pinballs allowing the games to be plugged in to standard electrical outlets. These pinballs

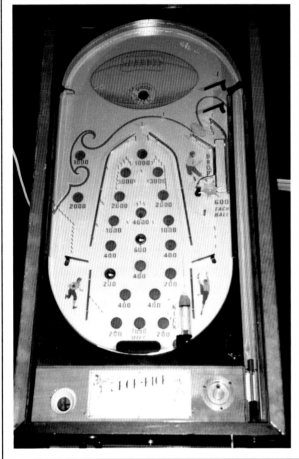

Exhibit's DROP KICK (1934), the start of the electro-mechanical era. Beautiful old games like this one are now considered more as antiques than amusement machines. *Eugene Ricci collection.* $325-$400.

were no longer the type that could be designed by a handyman on the back of a matchbox in the downstairs workshop, pinball companies now employed game designers (electrical engineers), carpenters/cabinet makers, machinists, sales representatives... The pinball business was booming.

By the late 1930s the nails had disappeared, and games required electrically activated devices like solenoids, relays and lightbulbs to power game devices like kick-out holes, bumpers, and score displays. Over those 40 years, EM pinballs became more and more complicated, requiring more and more wire to feed the ever-increasing amount of relays and switches for innovations like the flipper, multiple player capacity, and thumper-bumpers. It's difficult to estimate just how far the EM pinball would have evolved without the intervention of SS technology, for the typical four-player EM game of the 1970s was an absolute mechanical monster, almost bursting at the seams with electrical components, housed in a cabinet that had not really changed much in size since the 1940s.

See next page for caption.

Gottlieb's SING ALONG (1967). Its classic pinballs like this one that personify everything that was the EM game. Gottlieb games, especially, seemed to have an unopposed EM supremacy over their rivals during an era that lasted 40 years. **See previous page for backglass close up.** *Mark Hurry collection.* $475-575.

THE SPIRIT OF '76

computerized pinball from Mirco Games, Inc.

Finally. Something new in pinballs besides playfield cosmetics. Introducing THE SPIRIT OF '76 — MIRCO's pinball revolution. A smart, tough, 1-2 player machine. Packing a whole lot more into less with high technology, state-of-the-art microcomputer design. All the playability of conventional pinballs, plus totally *unconventional* extras. Features like:

• **Electronic semiconductor memory.** Not just a pinball to remember, but a pinball that remembers you. Players can retain bonus set-ups from one turn to the next because the computer remembers what they've done. The first playfield that doesn't quit between balls.

• **Special effects.** MIRCO's backglass adds a new dimension to exciting play. Free games, add-a-ball and high stakes bonus situations are announced by audio/visual attention grabbers. Drum rolls... whistles... light shows... a cannon that booms "the shot heard 'round the world." The only pinball with an electronic amplifier and quality speaker.

• **LED (digital display) readouts.** For all credit, scoring and ball-in-play functions. Easy to read, attractive, more reliable than electro-mechanical systems.

• **Free games/add-a-ball.** Win with high score, random match, or hit Special targets. Double bonus capabilities on last ball or optional add-a-ball.

• **Championship playfield.** Four-side kickers, 3-pop bumpers and 2-Special (free game) targets.

• **Distinctive graphics.** Crisp and clean. The look of the '70's in the game for the '70's.

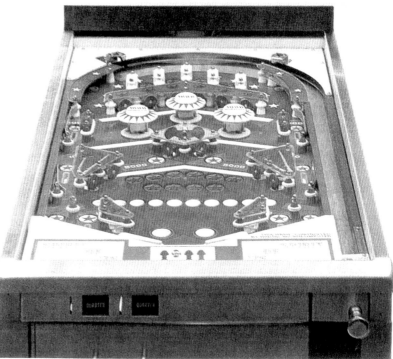

Micro Games' SPIRIT OF 76 (1975). This brochure advertised the beginning of the end for the EM game. SPIRIT OF 76 was the first non-relay based electronic pinball that used microchip technology. Only 127 of these games were built. A great advancement with SS design was the use of memory. As the brochure explains, "Electronic semiconductor memory. Not just a pinball to remember, but a pinball that remembers you." $650-800.

The beginning of the end for EM design came in mid-1975, when a small company named Micro Games released SPIRIT OF 76, the first SS pinball. The only difference that players could have detected would have been the digital scoring displays, which replaced the old score reels. This observation would be along the same lines as the "tip of the iceberg" principle, with most of the important changes occurring under the playfield and behind the backglass, away from the player's view.

For a lot of pinball enthusiasts, including myself, the first image one conjures forth whenever EM pinballs are mentioned is one of a machine with the old style of score reels that go "click click" when scoring, accompanied by a chorus of chimes; in comparison to the newer games with digital displays and electronic sounds. We would of course be aware of the significant and more elaborate technological changes, but for people with little pinball knowledge, the difference between the two game types would end there.

Backglass detail of Gottlieb's GOLDEN ARROW (1978) showing the old style EM scoring reels.

Backglass detail of Bally's EIGHT BALL (1977). The first difference that players would have detected between EM and SS games would have been the digital displays.

When SPIRIT OF 76 was released, the buzzword of the decade at that stage was microprocessors, or microchips for short. Slide rulers became obsolete overnight as pocket calculators flooded the market— watches and clocks, typewriters, scales, cash registers, and of course amusement machines all embraced the new technology.

What microchip technology did for pinballs was to completely remove every relay from under the playfield, along with the other components associated with them. A relay is a small coil of tightly wound copper wire, similar to a solenoid only smaller (in most cases the size of a walnut), which uses the properties of an electromagnet to open or close a series of switches when energized.

The other great advancement introduced with SS design was the use of memory. Microprocessors could store information, and therefore remember, for example, the bonus accumulated or the target hit by each player from ball to ball, player to player, and the highest score to date from game to game. Believe it or not, there have been EM games built with rudimentary memory capacity, involving single relays or banks of relays that enabled the machine to "remember" targets hit or sequences completed from game to game or player to player. The primary logic was simple— keep certain relays continuously energized from ball to ball, or switch from one energized bank of relays to another and back again between players or games, keeping the certain target switches open or closed as they were at the end of the previous ball or game. Simple in theory, but difficult in reality when faced with numerous relays required even for a small number of tasks, with relay and switch numbers multiplying like rabbits for every extra target included into the design. One good example of a pinball with a rudimentary memory is Williams' ALPINE CLUB (1965). This is a typical example of a one-player electromechanical machine, controlled only by relay logic, even though in fact it was one of the more complex of its kind built at the time.

A relay. In this particular case, it is a score relay positioned in the backbox, one of many found inside EM games. The paper clip (1" long) is placed there to show relative size.

See next page for caption.

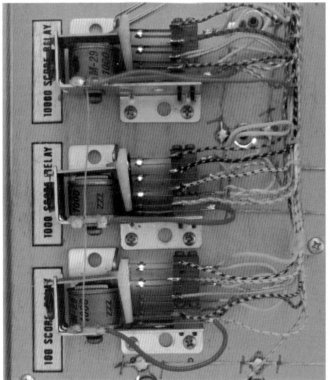

Relays at work. Notice the blue flash of electrical current between the switchblade contact points as the circuit is closed on each.

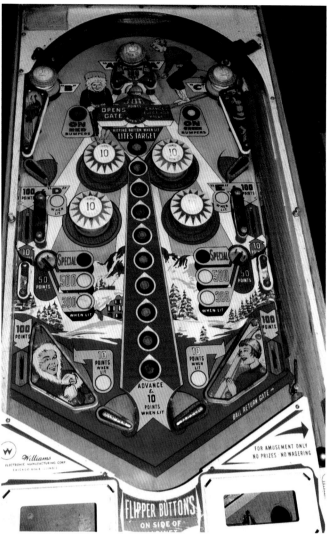

William's ALPINE CLUB (1965) uses a rudimentary relay memory which could remember from game to game the completed playfield sequence required in order to advance the figure of a lit climber on the backglass. A total of 80 sequence steps are required in order to advance the climber 16 times to the mountain summit. **See previous page for backglass close up.** *Michael E. Lukacs collection.* $375-475.

The game incorporates four sequences that the player can try to score on at any particular time during play. The rollover buttons light in sequence to enable an upper playfield target. Each of two kick-out saucers has a score-raising sequence, but the most elaborate is a deep playfield sequence that requires the player to hit each of the three top disc bumpers in order, and then the left and right side rollover channels. Completing this A, B, C, D and E sequence advances the lit image of a mountain climber on the backglass by one step. There are 16 different climber positions in total that illuminate one at a time as he climbs to the summit (the 16th position is actually a flag that illuminates at the top). The machine remembers both the climber's position and the A, B, C, D and E sequence position between games. That calculates at a total of 80 steps in order to complete the sequence from the start. This is one of the longest pinball

sequences, even by today's standards. When the climber finally reaches the top and planted his flag, the machine awarded two free games. ALPINE CLUB was also produced as an add-a-ball version called SKI CLUB.

ALPINE CLUB upper playfield detail showing the A-B-C bumpers.

ALPINE CLUB backglass detail showing one of the lit figures of the mountain climber making his way to the summit. *Photographs courtesy of Michael E. Lukacs.*

Any EM relay "memory" on such a game (not counting the use of some form of rotary switch) was of course lost if the machine was turned off. The memory on an SS game was easily kept in "storage" even after turning off the machine by the use of a small AA size battery.

If one was to examine and compare an EM pinball from 1975 to an SS game of 1978, the first thing one would notice after lifting

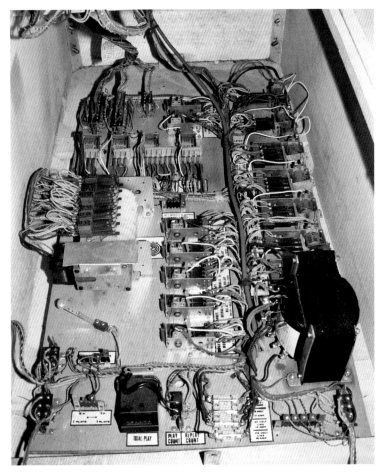

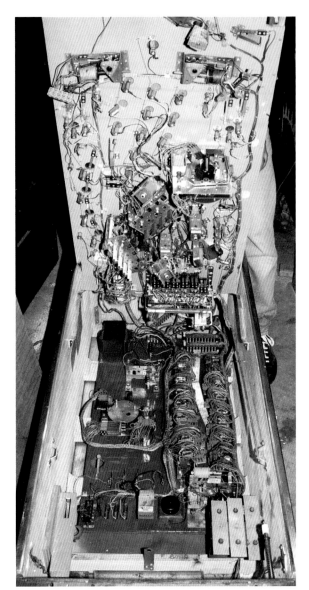

The internal working of Gottlieb's VULCAN (1977), a four-player EM game. I never understood why SS pinball cabinets were so deep, but empty. The technology had changed while cabinet construction remained the same. The bottom of this cabinet is filled with a large number of relays, a score motor, a chime unit, and several cable plugs. More relays and step up units are attached under the playfield.

both playfields is that the new SS machine is nothing more than an empty cabinet, with the exception of a cashbox, transformer and speaker which replaced the chimes. The underside of the playfield still has a lot of wire, and all the flipper and bumper solenoids are still there along with the playfield lights, however, any relays and step-up units (a solenoid-activated rotary switch) have disappeared. If an empty cabinet was all that remained in 1978, what did it contain in 1975; and where had it all gone?

A closer look, this time at the lower cabinet of Zaccaria's MOON FLIGHT (1976), a one-player game.

The cabinet of an SS pinball; Bally's SUPERSONIC (1979). Here we see that all those electrical components at the bottom of the cabinet have vanished, replaced by microchip technology. Neat disappearing trick!

Score motors. Here we see two different styles. Found on EM games, it is a motor-driven unit that controls the sequence of various circuits by the use of cam switches. One can say that it is the game's control center.

At the bottom of the cabinet back in 1975 there would have been an area approximately three-quarters the size of the playfield, extending upwards by about 6", filled with the following: numerous relays, up to 20 in some cases (depending on the game's player capacity), placed in a line or two usually, known collectively as banks. Three or four large cable plugs and sockets were used to connect the wiring from the bottom of the cabinet to either the playfield or the backbox. A transformer, step-up unit, score motor (a motor-driven unit which controls the sequence of various circuits by using a set of cam switches), and nearly one hundred (or more) switchblades. Also, we must not forget that usually just below the plunger was a set of chimes for the sound effects, which looked like a little xylophone.

All the components just mentioned, with exception of the transformer, were removed and replaced by four major circuit panels most commonly known as modules. These modules, as part of their circuits, would have the all-important microchips doing the work previously performed by the numerous relays. The set out of these modules and other components can be seen on the figure of a pinball machine provided, which depicts an electronic pinball with the front cashbox door and backbox open. The figure is typical of a Bally pinball produced in the early 1980s and although design differences have occurred in the course of time and between manufacturers, this along with the other illustrations included should help in understanding this chapter.

The working components of an SS pinball, c. 1980.

ELECTRONIC PINBALL MACHINE

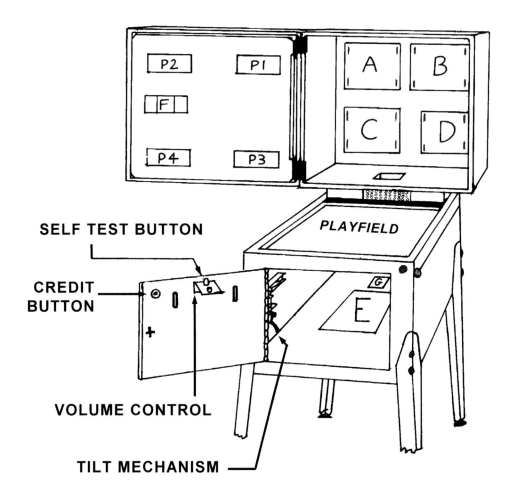

ITEM	DESCRIPTION
A	M.P.U. MODULE
B	SOLENOID DRIVER MODULE
C	LAMP DRIVER MODULE
D	SPEECH AND SOUND MODULE
E	TRANSFORMER BOARD
F	BALL AND CREDIT DISPLAY
PI - 4	PLAYER SCORE DISPLAY
G	SPEAKER

Each module was constructed from a thin circuit board; each board varying in area size, but averaging around 10" square each. Apart from the numerous electrical components sticking out of each board, these modules were relatively thin, and would not have exceeded 6" in height when each was stacked flat, one on top of the other.

A small description of each is as follows.

The MPU (module "A"), or the main processing unit is the pinball's nerve center; in charge of the scoring, game memory, diagnostic programs and signals received from the playfield and other modules.

Where did all those relays go? They were replaced by microprocessors. Inside the backbox of an SS pinball c1981, showing the four major modules.

The solenoid driver (module "B") dealt with power supply, and the regulation of voltage to playfield solenoid coils such as the flippers and bumpers.

The lamp driver (module "C"), controlled the playfield and backbox lights.

The sound board (module "D"), sometimes known as the "squawk and talk" module when speech was introduced, was usually the smallest of the four, and contained the pinball's sound effects.

The other boards included in the figure are the power transformer board ("E"), which houses the transformer and power fuses, and the display boards, each attached to the digital score displays (P1 to P4 and "F").

Back in 1975, most of the space inside the backbox of an EM game would have been taken up by the score reels, especially in a four player game. The new digital displays were but a fraction of the depth and weight of the old reels, taking up less than half of the original frontal area (even with their own circuit boards) and thus did not require a steel support housing. Other items found in the back box amongst the score reels were mechanisms such as the credit (replay) meter, the ball count unit, and the match unit. All three devices were classed as step-up units. In other words, they kept count, with the exception of the match unit, which did not count anything but acted like a random "prize wheel" at the end of each game, and is explained in more detail in Chapter Six. The credit meter kept count of the number of games available to

Gottlieb's VULCAN (1977). The backglass and backbox internals of this EM game. At the bottom left is the credit meter, appearing as a small window on the bottom right hand corner of the backglass. Bottom center is the match unit, and to the extreme right is a tall bank of score relays. The four big units taking up almost half of the available area are the score reel, four reels per score display. *Courtesy of Robert Young.* $350-425.

the player (both paid and free), with the use of a single reel, larger in diameter than a score reel and with more numbers (usually more than thirty), but narrower, with the digits appearing through a small window in the backglass. The ball count unit advised the player on how many balls were played, or left to play, with the details appearing as lit numbers on the backglass. Both of these two units plus the match unit, were all reduced to minute proportions within the microchips of the SS modules, and their read-outs shown together on a single digital display ("F").

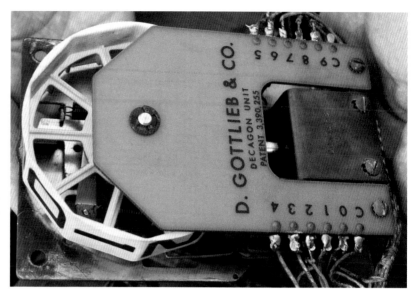

An EM score reel. Obviously, there was one reel required for each number in the score display. Compare the size of this mechanism to a complete digital display shown in the illustration on the facing page.

Several views of a EM credit meter, another mechanical device which was replaced by microchip technology.

An SS digital score display (viewed from behind). This particular display is one with a seven digit readout (score capacity of 9,999,990 points). Notice the difference in size between the two! The change to SS pinballs left a lot of space in the backbox, which was then taken up by microchip circuit boards.

The removal of all of these backbox components, plus the removal of a few score relays, would leave more than enough room for the four modules, and with some of the early SS games there was even enough room for the transformer!

Unlike SS pinballs, as the figure shows, the backbox of most EM games was only accessible via a removable metal panel positioned at the back. Therefore, to access the components in the backbox, one had to actually move the pinball out from the wall, which could be quite heavy work. The SS pinballs have the convenience of being able to open the backbox from the front, with the facade mounted on hinges to facilitate easy access.

Now that some of the differences in the two designs have been explained in a non-technical, simple way one can now comprehend the total restructuring of pinball manufacturing techniques companies had to go through.

Above right & center right: Williams' TEACHER'S PET (1965). A hinged door at the front of the backbox allows easy access to components behind the backglass, unlike the majority on EM games. Game instructions are as follows: Light all letters in name (TEACHER'S PET) and drop targets award special. Making 1-2-3 rollover lanes opens ball return gate, which remains open until used, even from game to game. Red rollover buttons raise drop targets for additional scoring. *Mark Jackson collection.* $425-500.

TEACHER'S PET playfield art detail near flippers.

allied's
2 player pin ball is
DYN·O·MITE

solid state logic

 allied leisure industries, inc.
P. O. Box 4928, Hialeah, Florida 33014

Micro Game's SPIRIT OF 76 was reputed to be not a very exciting game to play, and was not an instant success, regardless of the new technology. Nevertheless, it put the wheels in motion probably sooner than they would have been otherwise. The next SS pinball worthy of mention was Allied Leisure's DYN-O-MITE released in November 1975, which was greeted with a better player response. The pinball's popularity may have been partly due to its television tie-in, *Good Times*, a successful American sit-com featuring Jimmy Walker, whose character's catch phrase was, of course, "DYN-O-MITE!" Allied Leisure, like Micro Games, was new to the world of pinball, and enthusiasts not completely swayed by either of these two would have to wait a little longer for the idea to be introduced by the more recognizable companies, namely the "Big Three". The only setback for Bally, Williams and Gottlieb was that they had picked up so much momentum with EM machines over the decades, that for financial and technical reasons, they could not drop the EM games overnight in favor of SS machines, only slowly phase them out of production. After all, what does one do with thousands of redundant relays and score reels?

At the start of 1976 Bally was already experimenting with SS on some of their previously released EM models, namely BOW AND ARROW (Nov 1975); but the game would only reach the prototype stage. It was not until June 1976, six games later, that they released their first SS pinball, FREEDOM (also released in EM format). The few SS games released after that, like NIGHT RIDER (March 1977), EVEL KNEVEL (June 1977), MATA HARI (April 1978) and BLACK JACK (June 1978), had all been available in EM format just a few months prior, or even as much as a year. The EM versions of the last three games mentioned had all very low production runs—155, 170 and 120 units respectively, which makes these games rare as hen's teeth, in other words. Not as rare

Bally's BOW AND ARROW (1975); SS prototype. When SS technology took over the pinball industry, major game manufacturers started experimenting on games that they had previously released in EM format. This was one such game. There are claims of between 2 to 20 units of this machine being built in SS version, in comparison to approximately 7630 in EM format. *Courtesy of Herb Silvers/Fabulous Fantasies.* $2000+

as a Bally EM prototype pinball by the name of SPACE SHIP (c. 1976), of which only one was built, reputedly. Sadly, for the devoted fans of a soon-to-be bygone era, it was with these few pinballs that Bally left the electromechanical game behind forever. Here is bit of trivia regarding BOW AND ARROW. The EM version appeared regularly on television, situated in the background of a pizza bar on *Two Guys, a Girl & a Pizza Place*; a sitcom produced in 1998. The game added a nice touch to the surroundings, but in real life, vintage games like this one are rarely found in such public venues.

Bally's electromechanical NIGHT RIDER (1976). 4155 of these machines were built in this format; a further 7000 were produced as SS electronic models. *Ivo Vasella collection.* $350-425.

Opposite page: Allied Leisure's DYN O'MITE (1975) was one of the first SS pinballs built. The new "space age" digital scores set these games apart from their EM counterparts, but there was more of a difference than met the eye. $250-325.

Start a Revolution! A Profit Revolution!

Bally FREEDOM

NEW 4-PLAYER FLIPPER CONVERTIBLE TO ADD-A-BALL

NEW
WHEEL
FEATURE
BUILDS BIG
SCORES

See other side for FEATURE-GRAM ➡

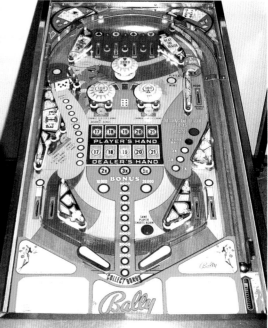

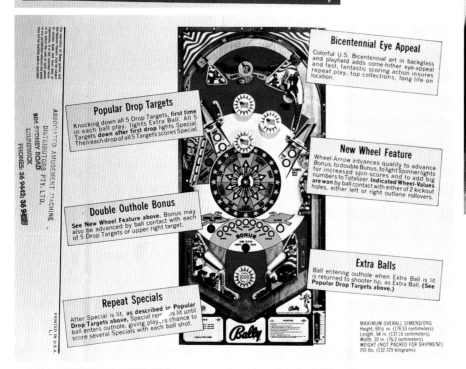

Bicentennial Eye Appeal
Colorful U.S. Bicentennial art in backglass and playfield adds come-hither eye-appeal and fast, fantastic scoring action insures repeat play, top collections, long life on location.

Popular Drop Targets
Knocking down all 5 Drop Targets, first time in each ball play, lights Extra Ball. All 5 Targets **down after first drop** lights Special. Then each drop of all 5 Targets scores Special.

New Wheel Feature
Wheel-Arrow advances qualify to advance Bonus, to double Bonus, to light Spinner lights for increased spin-scores and to add big numbers to Totalizer. **Indicated Wheel-Values are won** by ball contact with either of 2 kickout holes, either left or right outlane rollovers.

Double Outhole Bonus
See **New Wheel Feature** above. Bonus may also be advanced by ball contact with each of 5 Drop Targets or upper right target.

Extra Balls
Ball entering outhole when Extra Ball is lit is returned to shooter tip, as Extra Ball. **(See Popular Drop Targets above.)**

Repeat Specials
After Special is lit, as described in Popular Drop Targets above, Special remains lit until ball enters outhole, giving players chance to score several Specials with each ball shot.

MAXIMUM OVERALL DIMENSIONS
Height, 69½ in. (176.53 centimeters)
Length, 54 in. (137.16 centimeters)
Width, 30 in. (76.2 centimeters)
WEIGHT (NOT PACKED FOR SHIPMENT)
293 lbs. (132.729 kilograms)

Above right & center right: Bally's BLACK JACK (1978). The one seen here is the SS version, an EM version was built but in much smaller quantities and with only a two-player capacity. Total number of games produced reached 4883 units; only 120 of those were in EM format. *Craig Rutledge collection.* $375-450.

Bally's FREEDOM (1976). This game was also released in both SS and EM versions. The format shown on this game brochure is EM, that of which approximately 5000 were built. As a comparison, only 1500 SS versions were produced. One of the fascinating things about this game was that the playfield design shown here was changed. The lower playfield was completely redesigned before the game went into full production. *Courtesy of WMS industries Inc. All rights reserved.* $400-500.

Williams was still building EM pinballs up until mid-1977, without a sign of any large-scale production SS machines, when at last, on November 1977, they unveiled HOT TIP. Before this, like Bally, they had experimented with some of their previously released EM models. AZTEC (Nov 1976) was a full-scale production EM game, which had an SS prototype counterpart. The EM AZTEC reached a production run of over 10,000 units, while its SS twin only reached 10.

Major Spanish and Italian manufacturers such as Playmatic, Recel and Zaccaria were also headed in the same direction with SS games being produced in late 1977–early 1978. Italy's Zaccaria produced its last EM game, QUEEN'S CASTLE, in April 1978; the same month as Bally's MATA HARI.

Recel's POKER PLUS (1978), one of the last EM pinballs built by this Spanish company. The game was also produced in SS format with slightly different artwork. *Robert Young collection.* $300-375.

POKER PLUS backglass detail.

Gottlieb, the biggest of all the companies, was still dragging the chain, it seemed. Their first SS pinball, CLEOPATRA, released in December 1977, was followed by approximately 10 other games, most of them EM rather than electronic. Finally succumbing to the inevitable technological change, not to mention consumer pressure, they produced their last EM games—games like SOLAR RIDE (Feb 1979), TKO (March 1979) and SPACE WALK (Aug 1979). SOLAR RIDE was also released in SS format but in greater numbers. The total number of units built of this game was approximately 9,150; 365 of which were in EM format. TKO had an even lower production run of only 125 units, with no SS counterpart. SPACE WALK, like SOLAR RIDE, was also released in electronic format, but this time under a different name, COUNTDOWN. The strange thing about it all was that COUNTDOWN came out four months before SPACE WALK, and not the other way around. It had proven very popular; reaching almost 10,000 units in production, and this was probably why Gottlieb decided to give the mechanical game one last try, while at the same time getting rid of some more of those excess score reels and relays—that's my theory anyway. SPACE WALK only made it just over the 200 unit mark; it was a true sign of the times, the end of an era. Most of these late, low production Gottlieb mechanical games, including GEMINI (1978), STRANGE WORLD (1978), BLUE NOTE (1979) and ROCK STAR (1979) are now very rare, and very sought after.

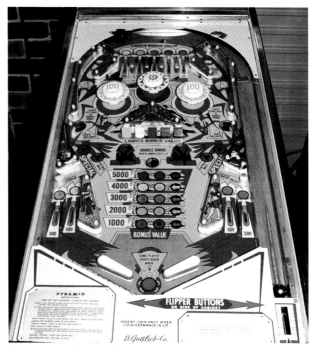

See next page for caption.

Gottlieb's PYRAMID (1977). This particular game was the two-player EM version of CLEOPATRA, Gottlieb's first SS pinball. Both were released in the same month. The player must complete the color-coded rollovers and targets in order to attain the specified bonus value. Five colors in all. The red value is the highest scoring color but the hardest to complete. Completing all rollovers and targets lights bullseye targets for extra ball, and then for special. **See previous page for playfield.** *Rawdon Osborne collection.* $325-400.

Top right: PYRAMID playfield illustration detail of Horus, the Egyptian sky god, advising players on the kickout hole value. There are two kickout holes in the game, the other, situated on the right hand side of the playfield, is attended by Anubis, the jackal-headed god of the dead.

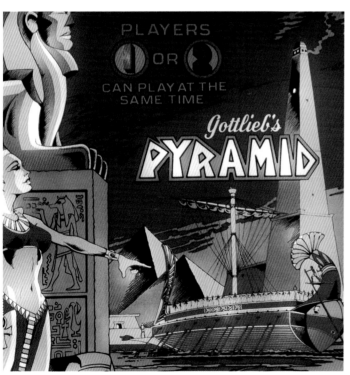

PYRAMID backglass detail.

Backglass detail from Gottlieb's EYE OF THE TIGER. This EM game reached a production run of 730 games, while its SS counterpart, SINBAD, reached 12,000.

With the exception of Gottlieb, the transition phase from the old technology to the new took three years, and luckily with few casualties. Micro Games disappeared a few years after securing a slice of history. Allied Leisure was still making pinballs in 1979, but dropped out of the pinball business by 1980. Chicago Coin, the fourth biggest manufacturer since the 1940s, was in financial difficulty; barely surviving on borrowed finance, they closed their factory doors in 1976 without ever having produced an electronic game—the SS hurdle was just too big to jump. Similarly for Nordamatic, a small Italian company from the city of Verona. They had produced only one SS pinball, ANTARES in 1979, before also dropping out of pinball construction, concentrating their efforts instead on amusement game distribution for other manufacturers.

The backglass and stripped playfield of Gottlieb's JOKER POKER (1978). Another game that was released in both EM and SS formats, the latter reaching a much higher production run. *Ian F. McKinnon collection.* $325-400.

CENTIGRADE 37 (1977). Its late EM Gottlieb games like this one that have become very collectible due to their constant low production runs. *Michael Tansell collection.* $450-550.

CARATTERISTICHE GENERALI

- Originale sistema di indicazione punteggio per i 4 giocatori;

- Convertibile esternamente nei 3 giochi: Replay - Add - Superbonus;

- Test generale di controllo su tutta la macchina;

- Ampia possibilità di programmazione sia per il gioco che per le monete;

- 4 giochi presenti sul campo per una grande soddisfazione di gioco.

Pinballs were riding on the crest of a wave between the years of 1976 and 1979, and other companies were willing to try their luck by entering the SS pinball market.

Atari, already a big name in video games, began producing SS pins late in 1976. In the far east, a Japanese company by the name of Sega (not yet famous in the west at that stage), had produced various EM games during the mid 1970s, but soon began producing electronic games of their own; games like MONTE ROSA (1977), a game name which will require a bit of explanation later.

Sam Stern bought out Chicago Coin (of which he was a former employee), and renamed it Stern Electronics; commencing production in early 1977 releasing STAMPEDE, an EM game. Stern built their first SS game later in the same year. Game Plan started building in 1978, the company also managed by another former Chicago Coin employee. Bell Games of Bologna, Italy, started producing games that same year. So did A. Hankin of Newcastle, Australia, which is a company still operating today, but unfortunately no longer building pinballs.

Stern's STAMPEDE (1977). This was Stern's first pinball after taking over Chicago Coin in December 1976. The EM era did not last long for this company, as they soon made the jump to SS technology before the start of 1978. $325-400.

Opposite page: Nordamatic's ANTARES (1979), their first and only SS pinball. Notice that there is only one display, even though it was a four-player game. $250-300.

Special
left kick-out hole after hitting the 5 left targets.

Double Bonus
hen ball goes through left ntre lane. At ic same time score on left and right bumper increases.

Advance Bonus
hen ball goes hrough left or ight top lane; ter hitting top tre target and any of the left and right drop targets.

Special
right kick-out le after hitting 5 right targets.

Especial
en picabolas izquierdo despué de abatir las cinc dianas de la izquierda.

Bonus Dobl
al pasar la bola pc el pasillo central izquierdo. Al mism tiempo aumentar el tanteo en los bumpers izquierdc y derecho.

Avance de Bonus
al pasar la bola pc los pasillos superiores derech e izquierda; despué de dar en la diana superior central y en cualquiera de la bancadas derecha e izquierda.

Especial
en picabolas derech después de abatir la cinco dianas de la derecha.

Triple Bonus
when ball goes through right centre lane. At the same time score on centre bumper increases.

Extra Ball
can be regulated from 50.000 points until 90.000 points.

Match Ball
when the last two ciphers of obtained score are the same hose appearing on the clockwork on the screen.

Bonus Triple
Al pasar la bola por el pasillo central derecho. Al mismo tiempo aumentará el tanteo en el bumper central.

Extra Ball
regulable de 50.000 a 90.000.

Match Ball
Al coincidir las dos últimas cifras del tanteo obtenido con las que aparecen iluminadas en la pantalla.

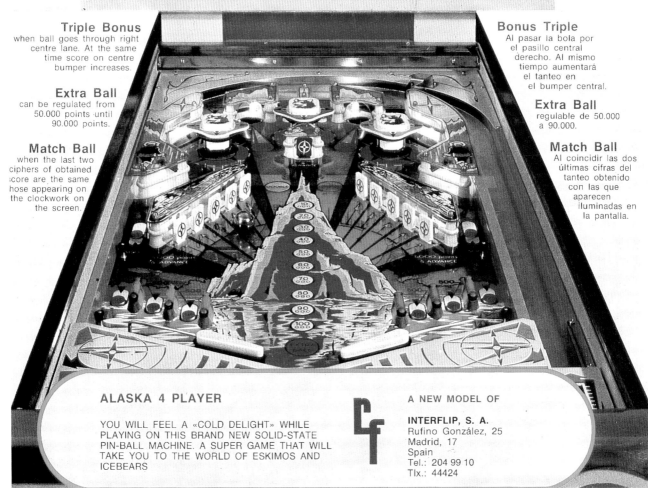

ALASKA 4 PLAYER

YOU WILL FEEL A «COLD DELIGHT» WHILE PLAYING ON THIS BRAND NEW SOLID-STATE PIN-BALL MACHINE. A SUPER GAME THAT WILL TAKE YOU TO THE WORLD OF ESKIMOS AND ICEBEARS

A NEW MODEL OF

INTERFLIP, S. A.
Rufino González, 25
Madrid, 17
Spain
Tel.: 204 99 10
Tlx.: 44424

The pinball name of Sega's MONTE ROSA is actually the Italian name of a huge, snow-covered mountain mass, comprising of ten major peaks, found in the Pennine Alps on the frontier between Italy and Switzerland. The direct translation of the name into English is actually Mount Pink, but the true meaning of the name has nothing to do with colour at all, as it is derived from the regional dialect word *roëse*, meaning *glacier*. The backglass art on the game shows a climber ascending a rock face in the foreground, with a good likeness of Monte Rosa in the background. A strange title for a Japanese pinball nevertheless, and stranger still is the fact that the game names on all of Sega's pinballs of that period were written in English instead of Japanese. The title was the only exception, it seems, as Japanese was used for the brochure slogans advertising the games.

"Solid state reliability", "solid state warranty", and "solid state superiority" were some of the power phrases used by pinball manufacturers to re-assure customers that SS pinballs were a lot better for business, and indeed it was not false advertising. Electronic games were not just visually different both inside and out, but had better built-in features to help with book-keeping, trouble shooting, servicing or maintenance, and of course they were great to play as well.

Electromechanical pinballs usually had a digit counter just inside the front behind the cashbox to help with bookkeeping. The counter could be set to show the total games played (both free and paid) or the total free games awarded. On an SS machine the bookkeeping functions would appear on the digital score display, activated by a button usually found inside the front door. This would not only show the total games played and free games awarded, but the percentage ratio between the two, to allow operators to set a reasonable replay score value relative to their customers' skill, in order to maximise their profits. It also kept a tally of the number of coins dropped in each chute (to save counting a cashbox full of coins), the number of playfield specials awarded and also, believe it or not, the total time in minutes that the game had been played for.

EM pinballs were a very hardy breed compared to the new SS games, which had more fragile electrical components making up their inner workings. However the latter, having a system of modules (as described previously), gave these pinballs an equivalent of a central nervous system which made trouble shooting and repair work a lot easier than having to contend with dozens of relays and switch blades, which were often difficult to access. A suspect module, sometimes causing total game malfunction, could be removed and set up on a test bench, which would go through a diagnostic program and inform the technician of the troublesome part within its maze of circuits.

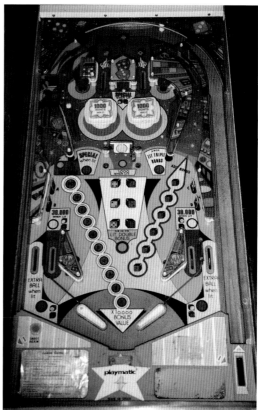

Playmatic's SPACE GAMBLER (1978), another early SS model from Spain. The playfield of most Spanish-built games (Playmatic, Recel and Petaco) were factory fitted with wear-resistant polyurethane covers. This made them almost indestructible. Almost nothing could mar the playfields, not even rusty balls! This particular game was bought by the owner from a distributor who had kept it in a barn for the better part of ten years! The playfield only needed a slight dust-off. *Dave Thielking collection.* $300-350.

Opposite page: ALASKA (1978), one of, if not the first SS pinball built by Interflip of Madrid. The game was sold with a mini-printer which supplied a print out of game statistics to help with book keeping. They had also produced a one player EM model by the same name the previous year. *Courtesy of Interflip S.A. All rights reserved.* $275-375.

THE SPIRIT OF '76

Operator Features

• **Self diagnostics.** Microcomputer design makes troubleshooting incredibly simple. An operator can exercise individual game components with the tip of a pencil. Without removing any glass. Lights, solenoids, switches—even the smallest segments of LED's can be fully checked. "Bad" components trigger corresponding digital readouts on the backglass.

• **Pre-game show.** THE SPIRIT OF '76 demands to be played. Sixty-four "working lights" flash in sequence when game is not in play, to insure it soon *will* be in play. Want more? Add MIRCO's optional show. Flippers flip, bumpers pop, kickers kick.

• **Front hinged, swing-out backglass.** MIRCO's backglass is built to get you in—and out—quickly. With a hinged panel that swings 180° to allow front-end servicing of the scoreboard. And conveniently located lights and LED's so you don't have to remove any glass.

• **PC boards.** Forget the conventional jungle of wiring and mechanical gismos. Two-printed circuit boards handle all electronic functions in THE SPIRIT OF '76. Less down time for operators—5-10 times less.

• **Low voltage/current levels.** Much lower current levels than conventional systems. Switches can't freeze. Solenoid drive currents are microcomputer controlled, preventing coil burn-out.

• **Universal (worldwide)AC power input.** Accepts 110, 115, 200, 220, 240 V.; 50 or 60 cycles.

• **Coin slots.** Easy-to-set switches provide a range of 1-4 games per coin. With a free-play mode for display or home use.

• **Operator-controlled free game levels.** Choose base level of 40,000 to 104,000. Switches (no jumpers) make changeover a snap.

• **Portable.** THE SPIRIT OF '76 requires minimum set-up time. Simply bolt on legs, tilt backglass into position and lock hinges. Light, compactable—remove legs and it fits in the back of a station wagon.

Profitable? You bet. MIRCO games have earned an international reputation for playability. And for microcomputer features that set new standards in reliability, durability, and serviceability. Take *your* best shot with THE SPIRIT OF '76.

MIRCO GAMES, INC.

Phone (602) 997-5931
1960 W. North Lane • Phoenix, Arizona 85021

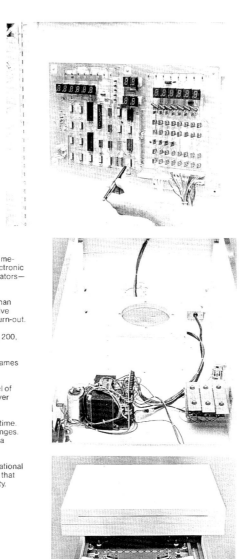

The flipside of Micro's SPIRIT OF 76 (1975) game brochure explaining the advantages of built-in self diagnostic programs.

From a player's perspective, the SS game had quite a different feel to it. Those familiar with both EM and SS pinballs soon realized that the manufacturers were not only building machines that had a memory, but also machines that could score a lot faster.

These new pinballs, with the aid of microchips, were like electronic calculators that could add up scores as fast as one could press the buttons. The game designers, knowing that players liked to hear the continuous sound of points being added, built playfield scoring features to get the same effect; something that the old EM games could not have coped with. These SS games, as fast as they were, occasionally seemed to struggle when a backlog of scoring to be added accumulated in their memory from the completion of a high scoring feature.

On EM pinballs one could only score as fast as the score reels could turn. Hit two targets, or even the same target, in quick succession and it would not register the second hit on the total score. For an electronic game it would not have been a handicap. This type of scoring problem was not a common one, but did occur from time to time (sometimes not altogether noticed by the player) and was probably the only real major playing drawback with EM games.

Bally's BLACK JACK (1978) playfield details.

To explain further, the score reels on an old EM game are rotated by a solenoid coil which uses a ratchet system. There is one coil for every score reel, and each one is activated by its respective relay. On a pinball that is capable of scoring 999,990 points there should be a 10, 100, 1000 and 10,000 point relay. For this example the ball is shot into play at the start of the game and it rolls down a rollover lane to score 5,000 points. This causes the 1,000 point relay to pulse five times which in turn pulses (amongst other things like the chimes) the score coil to turn the reel. This process from start to finish would probably take just under one second. If within this time frame the ball were to roll down, hit a bumper, and come back up the same lane, or another, the scoring signal from the lane switch to the relay would be lost because the relay is still working on the first task. It's like trying to phone someone who is already on the phone talking to someone else—you would have no way of getting through.

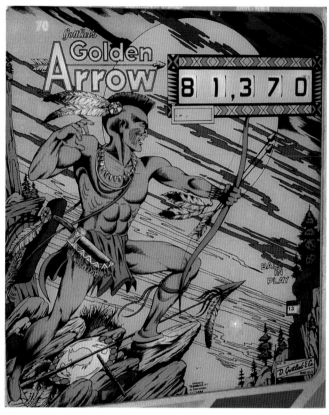

GOLDEN ARROW
playfield details.

Above & above right: Gottlieb's GOLDEN ARROW (1978), the whole picture. Completing lit rollover lanes 1 to 10 lights lane arrows for special, hence the name of the game. The arrow lights randomly from lane to lane with every point scored. *Graham McGuiness collection.* $325-400.

Solid state machines seemed to be superior in every way, and with new and better technology, quality control became a problem for smaller companies. Improving quality control for the production of SS pinballs was not a problem for the "Big Three", but for smaller American and foreign manufacturers, it became their downfall. Lack of quality control or bad design would result in games that would break down often or require constant servicing. Electromechanical pinballs from companies who have since closed their doors will often outlast their SS counterparts, as replacement microchips or other components become very rare. Although EM games can be troublesome at times, they very rarely completely break down (depending, of course, on their condition) and are not subject to corrosion as much as SS pinballs, a major cancer-like affliction that can attack the delicate circuit boards. Owners of EM pinballs consider them not only wonderful to play but also great to tinker around with on a rainy day. On these old pinballs everything that makes the machine do what it does is all there for anyone to see, not hidden away in the circuitry of a complicated set of resistors, capacitors and microchips. With a little time, what at first might seem like an elaborate but confused mass of wires, relays and switches, even for the not so mechanically or electrically minded, may turn out to be one short step away from being totally comprehensible.

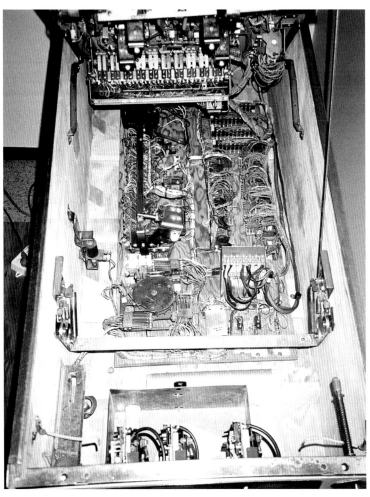

The internal workings of Gottlieb's SING ALONG (1967). Though it may look very complicated, everything that makes the machine do what it does is all there, and not hidden away in a complicated set of microchips—one advantage a lot of collectors agree on. *Courtesy of Mark Hurry.*

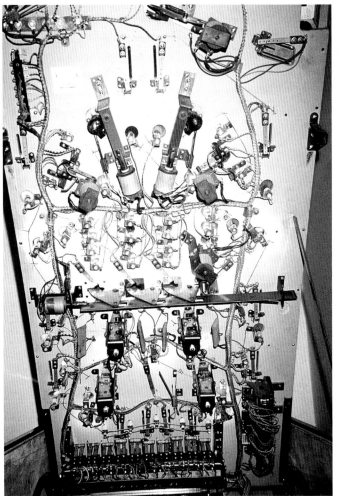

Opposite page: Nordamatic's EXPLORER (1976). EM games like this one, from small companies who have built games in both formats but have since closed down, will often outlast their SS counterparts, as replacement microchips and other components become very rare. $325-400.

Anyone who freely admits to enjoy playing an EM pinball may be giving away their age slightly; unless of course you are a true pinball enthusiast.

One final point—up until 1975 Gottlieb was considered the King of Pinball. However, due to their slow progress with SS games (as mentioned previously), they subsequently lost their top spot to Bally. With the help of a lot of promotional work on such EM pinballs as WIZARD (May 1975), which depicts characters from the motion picture *Tommy*, and CAPTAIN FANTASTIC (June 1976), which features singer Elton John on the backglass (also as the character he played in *Tommy*), helped pave the way for Bally's rise to the top at the start of the SS era. The WIZARD production run was over 10,000, while CAPTAIN FANTASTIC just made it over 16,000. Gottlieb was well and truly de-throned after the release of Bally's SS game EIGHT BALL (Sept 1977), which hit an all time high for an SS game with a production run of 20,230 units, beaten only recently by ADDAMS FAMILY, another Bally pinball released in 1992.

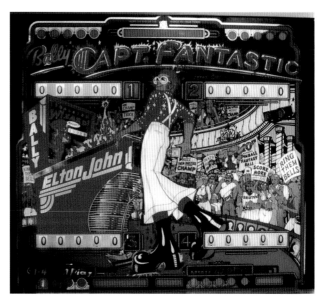

Bally's WIZARD (1975). When it came to promotional work, it can be said that Bally went all the way with this one. The pinball was linked to the film *Tommy*, a common occurrence in pinballs today, but not then. The backglass featured the stars of the show, singer/actor Roger Daltrey from the rock group *The Who*, and actress Ann Margret. The game brochure was in the same vein. In the end it all worked out for Bally; the game reached a industry production record of just over 10,000 units. The best was yet to come. *Rawdon Osborne collection.* $625-750.

Bally's CAPTAIN FANTASTIC (1976). Following the success of WIZARD, it seemed that Bally was on a roll. Hardly a year had passed when CAPTAIN FANTASTIC was released. With a production run reaching just over 16,500 units, it was the anchor that Bally needed in order to become the most successful pinball manufacturer of the late '70s and early '80s. *Rawdon Osborne collection.* $700-825.

This did not necessarily mean that Gottlieb was feeling the pinch, nor even Williams for that matter; on the contrary, the 1970s were good years for these three companies, despite the technological changes. Successful Gottlieb games included such titles as SPIRIT OF 76, released in 1976, of course (not to be confused with the first SS pinball released by Micro Games), another EM game that reached a production run of over 10,000 units. Yet another was ROYAL FLUSH (1976), which reached a run of over 12,000 units. Early SS Gottlieb games were also quite successful, averaging around the 7000 unit mark, with SINBAD (1978) reaching as high as 12,000 units. Williams' successful EM games included SPACE MISSION (1976), AZTEC (1976) mentioned previously, and GRAND PRIX (1977), all reaching above the 10,000 unit mark. While Williams' SS games were not quite successful early on, by the end of the decade FLASH (1979) and GORGAR (1979) reached production runs of 19,500 and 14,000 respectively.

Summary

Early 1930s Battery operated pinballs appear.
1935 Transformers added, pinball can now be "plugged in".
1935-1975 Electromechanical pinballs rule.
1975 First solid state pinball is built.
1975-1979 Electromechanical pinballs are slowly phased out and solid state pinballs take over.

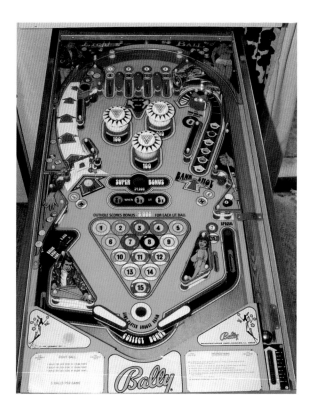

Bally's EIGHT BALL (1977). To say that this was a successful game for Bally would be an understatement. With an astronomical production run of 20,230 units, it was a statement saying that Bally was # 1 and electronic game design was the future. *Playfield and machine courtesy of Darryl Moore. Backglass courtesy of Tony and Clare Moore.* $425-525.

Bally's ADDAMS FAMILY (1992). Bally would beat its own production record almost 15 years later with this machine. With the help of the motion picture released that same year it reached a production run of over 21,000 games. *Phillip Brown collection.* $1275-1500.

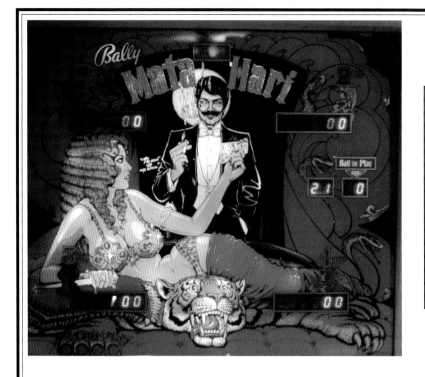

MATA HARI (1978) was a particularly successful game for Bally. Not as successful as EIGHT BALL, but it did manage to reach a production run of 16,430 units, 170 of which were produced in EM format. If you come across the EM version you know that it is a rare find. Game instructions are as follows: Making 'A' and 'B' top rollover lanes or left and right 'A' and 'B' orbits scores and advances 'A-B' lit value which is displayed in the centre of the playfield. Landing the ball in the top kickout hole first time scores 3000 points, advances bonus value 3 places, lights 2x bonus multiplier and lights left outlane for 50,000 points. Second time lights right outlane for 50,000 points and 3x bonus multiplier. Third time lights 5x bonus multiplier. Knocking down all drop targets scores 50,000 points and lights target special light. *Courtesy of Graeme Beal and Ivo Vasella.* $500-600.

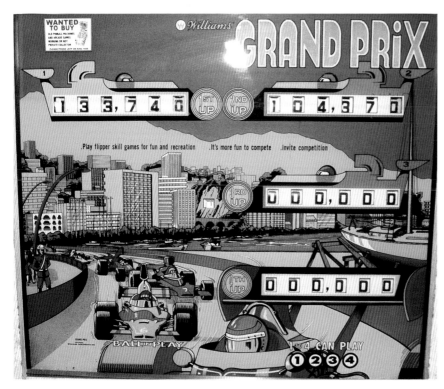

Williams' GRAND PRIX (1977). Even though the SS era had well and truly begun, EM pinballs like this one, which reached a production run of 10,550 units, were still bringing home the bacon for Williams. It seemed that for a while at least, people liked pinball regardless of the format. $350-425.

Mystery image: from which Bally playfield shown in this chapter does this belong to?

Gottlieb's SURFER (1976) was the two-player version of four-player SURF CHAMP. Compare this backglass to the image of SURF CHAMP at the beginning of this chapter. *Denis Bowler collection.* $400-500.

Chapter Four

Pinball Sounds and the Talking Machine

Sound has always been associated with pinballs, even if in the early games of bagatelle the only sound to be heard was that of the ball striking the nails on the playfield or the closing of the a little flap over the scoring holes on some of the games in the early 1930s.

The modern game of pinball requires three of the five senses; the sense of sight is obvious, the sense of touch, for the flipper buttons and the occasional nudge of the machine, and of course the sense of hearing which acknowledges the feedback from your actions. For those intending to buy their first pinball, a sense of smell will also come in handy, believe it or not—not as a game skill but as an early warning! If you smell something burning, it's probably a solenoid and you should turn off the machine.

A novice player, or more to the point, a player having his/her first game ever on a pinball may experience a form of sensory overload. Flashing lights, sounds, concentrating on keeping the ball in play so much that everything else is just too much to take in. Score? Who cares about the score when one is fighting to stay alive? Often to make things worse, they have a friend who knows how to play, and is telling them how to play, and what they are doing wrong!

Experienced players not bogged down with the learning experience will listen to a pinball for feedback while playing. What is meant by feedback is basically how well they are scoring, and with recent pinballs, listening for clues on what is best to hit or go for. For example, Bally's THEATRE OF MAGIC (1995) will tell you whether to "shoot for the magic trunk" or "go for the jets!" Williams' SWORD OF FURY (1988) will ask you to "Go for the tunnel" (a ramp on the right hand side). Even with older EM games, listening for the scoring chimes to sound after hitting, say, a stand-up bullseye target, tells the player that they have indeed scored and there was no miss-hit.

Other than the chimes, which were the loudest sounds on these pinballs, the next best thing were the score reels clicking over, but unless the chimes were for some reason disconnected or turned down (sticky taping something over them to stop the vibrating), they were usually hard to hear. Most players would agree that there is nothing worse than playing a pinball that they cannot hear, due either to a broken game at home, or one drowned out by the surrounding louder video games/pinballs in an arcade.

The sound of pinball was born in the early 1930s, and what is meant by this is not just the noise of the ball rolling around or the sound made by hitting pins or bells, but an electronically induced sound made by the ball falling into a scoring hole and closing an electric circuit. The first very distinctly audible feedback has either a buzzer or bell, telling the player that they had scored.

Outhole view of Williams' GORGAR (1979), the world's first talking machine. *Courtesy of Craig Rutldege.*

One of the first pinballs to accomplish this was CONTACT, released in 1934 by Pacific Amusements; which also has the first kick-out hole. This saw the birth of the modern pinball and the start of the EM era.

After the release of CONTACT, the pinball world was on a roll. The number of pinball games produced would reach an all-time high by the end of 1936, with an average of approximately one hundred new pinballs per year reaching the markets between 1935 and 1936.

The principle by which pinball machines produced sound in the 1930s had basically stayed the same up until the introduction of SS technology in 1975-76; although of course, pinballs of the late 60s and the reminder of the 70s had a larger repertoire of sound than those very early models.

Pacific Amusements' CONTACT (1934), a game with an incredible array of features. Pinball historian Dick Bueschel commented that it was "the game that made the game". It was with the introduction of this game that the proverbial "line in the sand" was drawn benchmarking the commencement of the EM era and the beginning of mechanically actuated pinball sounds—the use of a ringing bell. It would sound if a ball landed in the top "contact" hole; this also activated the game's two solenoid kickers. *Courtesy of Gary and Eric See.* $250-300.

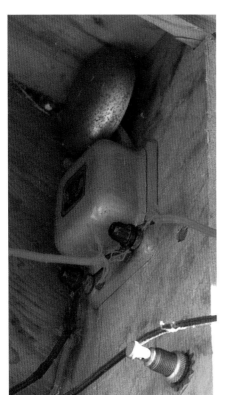

A photo of the pinball world's most famous sound producing device; the bell inside the cabinet of Pacific Amusements' CONTACT (1934) a game designed by Harry Williams. *Photos courtesy of Gary and Eric See.*

A typical EM pinball from the 70s would have had what is called a chime unit or chime box, which looks nothing like a box, but is a namesake derived from one of its components. The chime box in most EM games is comprised of three chimes of different lengths. Made from alloy, each chime was approximately 0.1" thick and 1.5" wide, the shortest being 5.5" long, with the others increasing in length by 0.4" each to provide a slightly different tone. The chimes are held horizontally by a small metal bracket. Each is loosely held to allow vibration, and each has its own solenoid underneath, with a plastic-tipped metal plunger. The namesake for this contraption comes from the plastic box that is attached to the end of all three chimes; this slightly amplifies the sound, and enhances the difference in tone of each chime. Some pinballs also utilized bell units to perform a similar function. Either the bell, or chime unit, could be found on the right hand side of the cabinet under the plunger. Sound devices, such as a single bell in some cases, could also be found in the backbox. On machines built before 1967 the chime unit was an assortment of bells situated at the back of the cabinet, usually in the left corner.

A typical electromechanical chime unit resembling a little xylophone. Also to the right lies the game knocker.

To most players the greatest sound to be heard while playing, is that of the knocker. The knocker was, and still is, what tells one that a free game has been awarded. The knocker is a solenoid with a plastic tipped plunger mounted on the inside wall of the cabinet. The plunger hits the side of the cabinet, producing a loud, hollow *thwack!* The knocker is the only mechanical sound-making device to have survived the change from EM to SS.

A small point; some people (mainly in the entertainment business it seems) still associate pinballs of today with the "chorus of chimes" of the old games. This association has come up on numerous T.V. shows where a particular scene takes place in a bar or club, where pinballs are played in the background, obviously new SS machines but the added background sound are those of chimes and bells.

Not all new SS pinballs had electronic sound, and not all EM pinballs used chimes. During the transition between SS and EM formats, pinballs had mixed technologies when it came to sound. For example, early SS pins like Bally's EIGHT BALL (1977), MATA HARI (1978) and BLACK JACK (1978), or Williams' HOT TIP (1977) and LUCKY SEVEN (1977), were fitted with EM chime units which were controlled by the game's microprocessor and thus could play extended tunes during play. Some Spanish EM pinballs from Recel, Petaco and Playmatic had analog sound modules. UNDERWATER by Recel and TORPEDO by Petaco, both built in 1976, are examples of this. The two games are identical; UNDERWATER is a four-player game while TORPEDO is the single-player version. Two of the basic sounds on these particular games are that of a torpedo hit, which sounds something like *pffffff* and *tschhhh!* More EM pinballs with electronic sounds (and no chimes) from Spanish companies included Recel's LADY LUCK (1976) and

The plastic chime box which amplifies the sound and tone of each chime. It is positioned underneath the chimes, as one can see in the previous photo.

See next page for caption.

-- 95 --

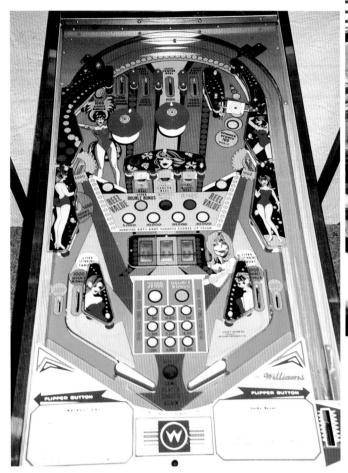

Outhole view of Bally's MATA HARI (1978), another SS game built with chimes. The game in this particular photo had its chimes removed and replaced with a sound board module. Collectors beware—if one wants such games with original components.

Williams' LUCKY SEVEN (1977). Early SS games like this one used chimes rather than electronic sound. Most used a four-piece chime unit rather than three. The units were controlled by the game's microprocessor, which gave the game the ability of extended tunes during play, something EM games could not do. *Denis Bowler collection.* $275-350.

SPACE RACE (1977), Petaco's FORTUNE (1976) and Playmatic's RIO (1977).

Electromechanical amusement machines with electronic sounds had been around for some time, not to mention the earliest video games. Rally, a French pinball manufacturer (not to be mistaken with Bally) produced pinballs with electronically synthesized sound as early as 1968, equipped with a speaker positioned in the bottom of the cabinet; much like the SS games that were to follow ten years later. Baseball games from the early 70s had small electronic sound boards that reproduced crowd noise, like whistles and cheers, while EM rifle games of the same period reproduced gun fire and ricochet bullets, not to mention background sounds to fit in with the theme of the game, be it a jungle theme or western style shootout.

Playfield detail from LUCKY SEVEN showing the game's slot machine feature on center playfield. *Photos courtesy of Denis Bowler.*

CHICAGO COIN'S

BASEBALL CHAMP

Players can hit the ball over the bleachers and out of the ball park. And the crowd roars when a home run is hit.

Chicago Coin's BASEBALL CHAMP (1973). Baseball machines like this one, not to mention EM rifle games and early video games, used electronic SS sound long before pinball games did.

HIGH SCORING ACTION, ANIMATION AND SYNCHRONIZED SOUND IN A MODERN SELF-CONTAINED CONSOLE.

- SCORES LIKE BASEBALL . . . 3 OUTS PER GAME . . . AMERICAN VS. NATIONAL LEAGUES
- BACKLIGHTED PLAYFIELD & ANIMATED RUNNERS
- PLAYERS SELECT TYPE OF PITCH . . . CURVE, STRAIGHT, SLIDER
- PLAYERS EARN EXTRA RUNS . . . OR CANCEL OUT
- EXTRA RUNS INDICATED ON PLAYFIELD WHEN HOME RUN TARGET IS HIT . . . OR WHEN BALL IS HIT INTO BLEACHERS
- EXTRA RUNS WHEN BALL IS HIT OUT OF THE BALL PARK

- EXTRA VALUE WHEN SCOREBOARD BULLSEYE TARGETS ARE HIT
- EXTRA VALUE WHEN ALL 3 BLEACHER SECTIONS ARE HIT
- EXTRA VALUE WHEN PLAYFIELD STAR IS HIT
- 25¢ PLAY • ADJUSTABLE TO 2/25¢

All these action features are packed into a new s sole with formica control panel. Caster-type rolle easy mobility. And maintenance is made easy wi out service panel.

BASEBALL CHAMP cabinet art detail. *Rick Force collection.*

BASEBALL CHAMP MEANS MAJOR LEAGUE PROFITS FOR YOU.

HERE IS BASEBALL ACTION AT ITS BEST.

LOADED WITH ACTION TARGETS

All the excitement of real baseball play is packed into BASEBALL CHAMP. Players control type of pitch and batting. There are 7 playfield targets, 3 bleacher targets, 2 scoreboard targets . . . and a unique extra value target, the bleacher roof top. When a ball is hit over the bleachers, it's out of the ball park for extra value.

BUILT-IN SOUND

The atmosphere of the major league ball park is part of Baseball Champ, too. When a home run is hit, the actual roar of the crowd is heard through a built-in sound system. This is an extra play-reward designed by Chicago Coin to keep player interest high.

SELF-CONTAINED CONSOLE WITH PANORAMIC VIEW

Players feel that they are right in the ball park because the new console styling gives them a close up, panoramic view of the complete play-field. They can watch all the action . . . the hits, the outs, the animated base runners. Console has formica control panel for durability. Caster-type rollers at back permit easy movement. A slide-out front panel provides maintenance access.

PACKED DIMENSIONS AND WEIGHT

Height	Length	Width	Shipping Weight	Power Source
75 in.	48 in.	34¾ in.	380 lbs.	115-220V/AC 50-60 HZ

CHICAGO COIN MACHINE DIV.
CHICAGO DYNAMIC INDUSTRIES, INC.
1725 W. DIVERSEY BLVD., CHICAGO, ILLINOIS 60614

By the start of 1979, with the new electronic pinballs ousting the old electromechanicals from the games arena, the sounds emanating from amusement centers were purely electronic. I remember that "old" EM games were still lurking around in some of the less amusement-orientated venues like bars and such, or pool halls, but they too would soon be replaced. Pinball sounds were no longer mechanically actuated, but electronically created from within the sound module in the backbox, and transmitted audibly via speaker.

The new SS pinballs could now also play tunes, and not just sound at the drop of a target. Tunes were usually played at the start or the end of a game, and also upon the insertion of a coin into the money slot. These were very simple tunes though, and with Bally pinballs, they sounded very much like a an electronic version of the old chimes, although an EM game would have needed

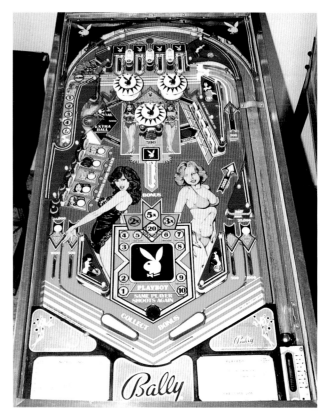

The early electronic chime unit (sound module) of a pinball from 1978. Approximately 6" by 6" in size, and although seemingly complicated in the eyes of a layman, it can be considered primitive by today's standards.

A rather risqué detail from the backglass of PLAYBOY.

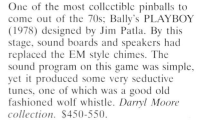

One of the most collectible pinballs to come out of the 70s; Bally's PLAYBOY (1978) designed by Jim Patla. By this stage, sound boards and speakers had replaced the EM style chimes. The sound program on this game was simple, yet it produced some very seductive tunes, one of which was a good old fashioned wolf whistle. *Darryl Moore collection.* $450-550.

a chime box with ten or more chimes instead of three to compete. Bally's PLAYBOY (Dec 1978) has a seductive little eleven-note tune. KISS (June 1979), another Bally pinball which depicts the famous rock band, plays the tune from one of their songs "Wanna rock and roll all night" lasting seventeen notes, if my memory serves me correctly. Gottlieb was also playing simple music on pinballs like GENIE (Aug 1979), which has an Arabian-style tune, however, the notes sound more electronic than Bally's, with more of a "hum" rather than a "ding" chime-like sound.

An extreme close up on the backglass of Bally's KISS reveals the game designer's signature (Jim Patla) on a guitar headstock.

Bally's KISS (1979). Drop a coin in the slot, press the start button and listen to a simple Kiss tune before the start of play. Pinball tunes were very simple back in 1979, no match for the complex stereo sound/music of today's games, but far more superior than the old chime box. KISS was a very popular game, and many were played to death in the arcades; a fate reserved for only the most favored of pinballs. It is still a game on demand even today, not only by collectors of pinballs, but also by collectors of Kiss memorabilia, the purchase of which would no doubt be regarded as their *piece de resistance. Backglass courtesy of John A. Searles. Playfield courtesy of Darryl Moore.* $775-950.

A. Hankin produced pinballs that incorporated Australian icons, one of these is HOWZAT (1980). Its theme is that of the game of cricket (a popular Australian sport), which features game legend Dennis Lillie on the backglass. The pinball's end-of-game tune is something that initially was only recognizable to Austra-lians and New Zealanders, but is now identifiable internationally: the repetitive chant of Aussie supporters "Come on Aussie, Come on, come on; Come on Aussie, come on!" As for the actual title of the pinball, "howzat" is the shortened version of "how is that?!" Commonly shouted by players when appealing to the umpire.

Players found the new electronic sounds a great accompaniment. However most, including myself, could not see beyond the obvious. What did pinballs have now that they did not previously? Up until the introduction of SS technology, every new EM pinball arriving on the market had something different—new name, artwork and playfield layout, basically the same as the pinballs today, except that they all sounded the same! Pinballs were now not only visibly different, but audibly so. If one knew their pinball machines (which a lot of us pinball-crazy kids did), the games were now identifiable purely by their particular sound content, before even seeing the machine. This was a by-product of the new technology that game designers sank their inventive teeth into.

The mustached grin of cricket legend Dennis Lillee on Hankin's HOWZAT! (1980). The end-of-game tune was that of a popular sporting chant sung by Australian supporters during cricket matches. *Graeme Beal collection.* $550-600.

Backglass detail depicting Dennis in action, doing what he did best; bowl (pitch) very fast.

See next page for caption.

Two EM games from the 70s; Gottlieb JET SPIN (1977) and ATLANTIS (**see previous page**) (1975). Although both were quite different in artwork and game design, both were almost identical soundwise; most EM games were. One would find it hard to distinguish one game from another. Solid state sound changed all that. *Courtesy of Gottlieb Development LLC. All rights reserved.* $350-475.

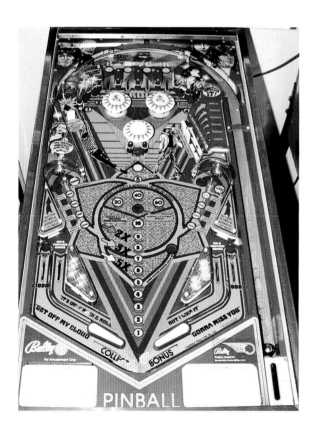

Bally's ROLLING STONES (1980). Like Bally's KISS, it too incorporated simple tunes from some of the group's songs, although I must admit it did take me a while to figure them out. *Darryl Moore collection.* $700-850.

As mentioned previously, Bally had become the "Pinball King", having stolen the crown from Gottlieb, but Williams was ever-present, waiting to strike for the top spot. Williams' pinballs were heading in a different direction with sound. They did not adopt the tunes of Gottlieb and Bally, but instead experimented with continuous background sound; a concept that the other companies would eventually pick up on and remain with.

Some of the SS pinballs mentioned earlier, such as PLAY-BOY, have static sound, just like EM pinballs once had. That is, in

order to have sounds produced, targets had to be struck. However with the introduction of continuous background sound, as first seen on Williams' FLASH (Mar 1979), this target stimulation was no longer required. The sound was now always there; stopping only momentarily when interrupted by the different scoring sounds of a target or rollover, which had priority.

The background sound also increased in pitch and intensity when more and more points are accumulated; which makes TIME WARP (Sep 1979) seem as though it is about to explode if the ball stays in play long enough. The sound pitch and intensity returns to normal at the commencement of a new ball. This particular sound concept was first pioneered on video games like Midway's *SPACE INVADERS* (1978) where a "hi-lo-hi-lo" monotonous sound increases in speed during play as the player reaches the end of each stage. Bally put this idea to good use on some of their now-"classic" pinballs. CENTAUR (Nov 1981) has an idling motorbike as background sound, while FATHOM (Sep 1981) has the sound of lapping waves.

A few months after FLASH, Williams had another first with GORGAR (Dec 1979), the first talking pinball.[1] Though the phrasing is very simplistic, with phrases like "Me Gorgar, beat me" spoken at the end of the game or "You hurt Gorgar" during play, it was at least a beginning. GORGAR's voice at this stage seemed only a novelty to players, who were far more interested in how the new game played—and played well it did! Had GORGAR been built around the speech concept much like Micro's SPIRIT OF '76 was built around the SS concept, it would have been a flop. But, it has a great background sound, that of a beating heart, which gets faster and faster, and a great playfield which includes "the pit", an electromagnet located in the upper left hand side of the field which grabs the ball for increased scoring. Apparently, Bally had also been playing with speech concepts for their earlier release of KISS, but dropped the idea at the prototype stage.

Backglass of Williams' FLASH (1979), the first pinball to include continuous background sound. *Courtesy of Robert Young.* $350-425.

The stripped playfield of William's FLASH. Popular games like this one, that had a long arcade life, usually end up so worn that large areas of bare wood appear, especially near the flippers. Original unrestored games with a good playfield are hard to find. *Ian F. McKinnon collection.*

See next page for caption.

-- *102* --

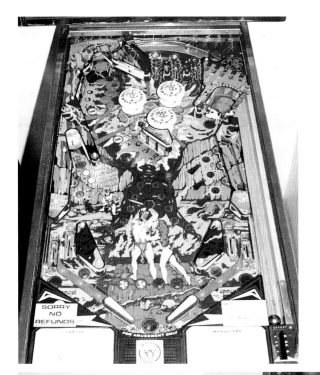

INSTRUCTIONS

- Insert Coin And Wait For Machine To Reset Before Inserting Coin For Next Player.
- Making G - O - R Targets Advances "PIT" Value.
- Making G - A - R Targets Lites Jet Bumpers For 1000, Lites G - A - R Targets For 5000 Each & Lites Outlane Specials.
- Lighting GOR & GAR Advances Eject Value.
- Making 1 - 2 - 3 - 4 Lites PIT For 50,000 & Lites Next Star. When Both Stars Are Lit Making 1 - 2 - 3 - 4 Lites Red Arrows Alternately For Special.
- Making "D" & "E" Spots 1 - 2 - 3 - 4.
- Making A - B - C Advances "X" Value.
- Tilt Penalty - Ball In Play - Does Not Disqualify Player.
- Special Scores _____ 1 CREDIT.
- Beating Highest Score Scores _____ 3 CREDITS.
- Matching Last Two Numbers On Score With Numbers On Match Window On Back Glass Scores _____ 1 CREDIT.

496-3

An old-looking original GORGAR instruction card; find out how to play!

A close-up of Gorgar himself on another dirty and worn out playfield found in storage.

Williams' GORGAR (1979), the first talking pinball machine. With a vocabulary of seven words, combined to make a total of seven phrases (two words or longer), the talking pinball had finally taken form. In many cases one could be excused for not taking any notice of this new development as it was sometimes hard to hear it speak in the middle of a noisy arcade full of other (much louder) games. **See previous page for backglass.** *Craig Rutledge collection.* $425-525.

GORGAR playfield detail showing "the pit"; the game's most popular feature.

Upper playfield detail from Bally's KISS (1979). The game could well have been the world's first talking pinball, but the idea was dropped during the prototype stage; or so the story goes.

has a range of approximately 30 words, not to mention that it could laugh! It also had a reverberation program that gave its half-man, half-motorbike character a more menacing voice.

XENON was the first game to speak with a female's voice. It includes some very sexy sounds and spoken phrases like "Aaaaaah" and "Try me again", when depositing coins in the machine and at the end of a game respectively. Other phrases included are; "Welcome to Xenon" and "Try tube shot" (the game's ramp shot). This of course was very appealing to male players, and it attracted them like bees to honey. It also includes a very limited male repertoire like "Enter Xenon" at the start of the first ball, and "Ooww" when hitting selected bumpers/slingshots. These male "Ooww" and certain female "Aaah" are ambiguous sounds that could be interpreted as either pleasure or pain. Hit a male bumper; "Ooww" then a female bumper or slingshot; "Aaah" and back to a male bumper again; "Ooww!" It was during this kind of play between slingshots or bumpers that the game sounds like a couple having sex right in front of you! A very erotic pinball indeed, back in my teenage days.

Williams' next talking game was FIREPOWER (March 1980). It proved a little bit more sophisticated, if only just, with phrases like "Enemy destroyed" spoken when all of the six stationary targets are completed, or "Mission accomplished" when scoring a special.

For almost a year after the release of GORGAR, Williams stood apart from the other companies, who did not follow the lead taken in producing talking pinballs. Stern's FLIGHT 2000 (Oct 1980) was one of the first to cross the line, followed closely by Bally's XENON (Dec 1980) and Gottlieb's MARS (March 1981). Italy's Zaccaria also started experimenting with speech in 1982 with PINBALL CHAMP 82 (April 82). Due to the close proximity of foreign markets available to Zaccaria, PINBALL CHAMP 82 and several other games to follow (like SOCCER KINGS in September 1982) were built in different language versions—Italian for the home market, English for the U.K, U.S.A and Australia, and even in French and German.

The increased vocabulary of these pinballs were evidence of the growing development taken in speech production from the primitive concept first introduced in GORGAR. Bally's CENTAUR

Stern unveiled its first talking pinball with this game, FLIGHT 2000 (1980). *Mark Hurry collection.*

XENON (1980), Bally's first talking pinball. It is still considered by most as one of the sexiest pinballs ever built. *Peter Graabaek collection.* $500-600.

XENON playfield detail. *Photographs courtesy of Peter Graabaek.*

An interesting spin-off on the talking machines was the "Game attract" feature. The feature activates when a pinball is left idle. The machine says something every two to three minutes, in order to turn the heads of unsuspecting potential players roaming about. Williams' BLACK KNIGHT (Dec 1980) taunts players with "The Black Knight will slay you" followed by a belly laugh, while Bally's FATHOM, having an underwater theme, yells, "Help, surface, surface... Fathom" or warns you that "Danger, sea nymphs await...Fathom." This was a usual feature on pinballs by this time. But, there were always exceptions, and I have to mention CENTAUR once again.

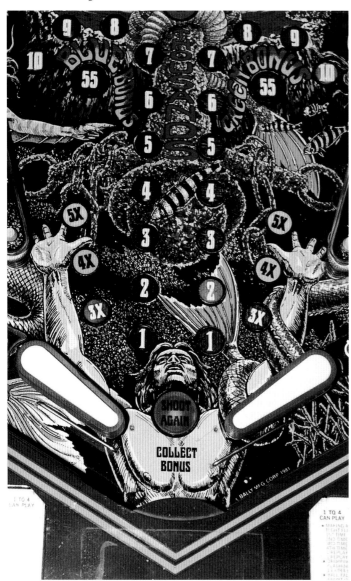

Playfield detail from Bally's FATHOM (1981). "Help surface surface...Fathom."

CENTAUR does not have a "Game attract" feature as such, but more of a "Game browsing" feature; if a potential customer/player happens to touch one of the flipper buttons while looking over the machine it introduces itself by saying "Challenge me" and then goes on to outline the game's five major playfield features. Not only does it tell you what to shoot for, but also shows you by flashing the playfield lights pertaining to that particular feature as it was speaking. For example, it lights its captive ball and in-line targets (see Chapter Nine for explanation of a captive ball target) and says "Chamber feature" and then goes on to say "Guardian feature" while lighting both out lanes and return lanes. The same methods have been used on more recent pinballs, but with less flair. Data East's STAR WARS (1992) has the voice of Darth

Vader saying, "The force is strong in this one" if the credit button is pressed without depositing money. While Bally's JUDGE DREAD (1993), has a female's voice telling you "You wanna play, you gotta pay" if one tried the same thing.

Above & opposite page: Bally's CENTAUR (1981), a talking machine with a vocabulary of around 20 short phrases. My personal favorite was "bad move human" exclaimed at times when one was too slow on the game's lane change, or when the game was tilted. Only 3700 games were built, but the pinball became so popular that it went back on the production line in 1983. CENTAUR II, the remake, had the same playfield but the backbox design was uniquely different. *Courtesy of WMS industries Inc. All rights reserved.* $625-775.

Despite these new innovations—including multiple levels (see Chapter Ten)—pinballs were in trouble. Game popularity started to decline in 1979 due to the increasing popularity of video games such as the blockbuster games from Midway like the previously mentioned *SPACE INVADERS, GALAXIAN* (1979), Atari's *ASTEROIDS* (1979) and, of course, another one of Midway's classics, *PAC-MAN* (1980). The video games' allure was too strong. I for one spent much time enjoying video games like Atari's *BATTLE ZONE* (1981) and Midway's *GALAGA* (1982). The situation then worsened with the introduction of home video game units like the Atari 2600, and the Intellivision by Mattel, which kept players at home and away from amusement arcades altogether.

Amongst all this change, adult venues like bars, taverns, and pool halls were still pinball strongholds, with the older generation frequenting them. Having been brought up on nothing but pinball, they did not care as much for the new video games.

To stay alive, pinball manufacturers started cutting back on production costs by keeping production runs low, reducing the number of company staff, and keeping pinballs simple. Multiball was used sparingly, multiple levels even more so, and speech was dropped altogether. Some of the pinballs that had their vocal chords removed were Bally's SPEAK EASY (1982), GOLD BALL (1983), GRAND SLAM (1983), KINGS OF STEEL (1984),

CYBERNAUT (1985), Williams' COSMIC GUNFIGHT (1982) and LASER CUE (1984). Others included those by Gottlieb and Stern, who also produced non-speaking machines during this period.

It wasn't all bad news, especially for Bally. At the end of 1982 player response from two of their games released nearly a year before was so great that it was financially beneficial to re-release them; because these games had already been designed, the design cost was practically nothing. The two pinballs in question were EIGHT BALL DELUXE (1981) and of course CENTAUR; which subsequently became EIGHT BALL DELUXE LIMITED EDITION (1982) and CENTAUR 2 (1983).

EIGHT BALL DELUXE was one of the first games that talked to the player instead of at the player during play. It gives the player hints on what to shoot for next, such as "Shoot the eightball corner pocket" (a target near the plunger exit lane), but it also taunts you at the start of each game with "Quit talking and start chalking."

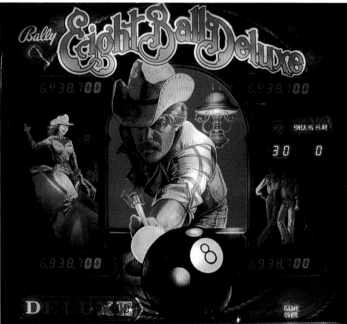

Bally's EIGHT BALL DELUXE (1981). "Quit talking and start chalking" was the phrase used at the start of the match, one of many throughout the course of a game. This pinball used its voice abilities to guide the player on what to do or where to shoot next, even though at times it was blatantly obvious. *Rawdon Osborne collection.* $625-750.

Williams' ALIEN POKER (1980). During the early 80s manufacturers were facing hard times, so a lot of previously released pinballs made their way back to the production line. ALIEN POKER was re-released with minor modifications and became LASER CUE (1984). *Kevin A. Moser collection.* $350-425.

Meanwhile, across the Atlantic, Zaccaria seemed to be defying the odds. While American companies were cutting back, Zaccaria was increasing production, producing some of Italy's best-known pinballs. Zaccaria was not a big manufacturer in comparison to the "Big Three", but between 1982 and 1985 four of their ten pinballs were multi-leveled and most had speech. FARFALLA (Sep 1983) would remind the player with, "One more coin, please" on the amount of coins needed when depositing money in the coin slot and would also say, "For this score... No comment" if one's final score was below average. FARFALLA (Italian for butterfly), like Bally's XENON, also has both male and female voices, while ROBOT (Jan 1985) has a robotic voice asking one to "Challenge the robot from Zaccaria."

What I found particularly striking about Zaccaria's pinballs of this era, were their plastic molded backglasses, which gives a slight, but very effective, 3-D effect much like Gottlieb's CLASS OF 1812 released in 1991.

The next stop in the pinball sounds tour is the beginning of 1985. Stern became a victim of the pinball recession and closed down by the end of 1984, while Gottlieb had just barely remained viable. However, unknown to all, the situation was going to improve.

The downward trend in pinball popularity, which started in 1979, had come to an end. With the aid of a few good Williams pinballs like SPACE SHUTTLE (Oct 1984) and HIGH SPEED (Feb 1986), the pinball game had been saved and was talking once again. It was SPACE SHUTTLE in particular that marked the return of the talking machine, and in the words of this same game, the pinball world was, "Ready for lift off."

Pinball sounds had come a long way from the days of EM chimes just ten years before, and the next ten years would provide a few more innovations.

Backglass details from Gottlieb's HAUNTED HOUSE (1982). Talking pinballs were popular but still relatively new at this stage. Players did not seem to notice at first, that this particular game had no speech. This was because most were taken in by the continuous background music, that of Bach's Toccata and Fugue.

Williams' SPACE SHUTTLE (1984) marked the return of the talking machine. *Kevin A. Moser collection.* $400-500.

Continuous background sound became background music, a concept far from new, but SS sound/music had improved substantially since Gottlieb had used it on HAUNTED HOUSE early in 1982. The machine plays Bach's Toccata and Fugue throughout the duration of the game, accompanied by great spooky sound effects. The game would have been perfect had Gottlieb decided to give the machine the ability to speak, and to speak with a ghoulish voice.

Music and speech sounded much better than it did a few years prior, in part due to the addition of two extra speakers placed in the backbox. Both occupied each side of the bottom part of the backbox facing the player. On some machines the extra speakers ended up on the very top of the backbox. Either way, this helped the introduction of stereo sound which first appeared on Data East's LAZER WARS in 1987. This style was used earlier (or should we say experimented) by Atari on 4X4, a pinball built in 1983 which unfortunately only reached the prototype stage.

Atari's 4X4 (1983). Although having only reached the prototype stage, it was one of the first pinballs to use dual speakers mounted in the backbox. Courtesy of Herb Silvers/Fabulous Fantasies. $4800+

Bally's POOL SHARKS (1990). Welcome to Sharkey's Billiard Emporium and Seafood Bar where you will meet Great Whitey (Trickshoticus Magnificus), Hammer Head (Probosisicus Ridiculus) and Tiger Shark (Bankshoticus Tremendicus). Here we have a typical example of how the speakers where placed right on top of the backbox. $550-675.

By the start of the 1990s music had become a feature that was very hard to ignore. Tunes were so catchy that I found myself humming them long after having left the arcade much like someone finds themselves singing the last song they heard on the radio before getting to work.

Data East's CHECKPOINT (Feb 1991) gives the player a choice in background music styles between rock, rap, country, jazz, classical, or even soul! One has to choose the style before the start of each game. It did not take long before the novelty wore off with a lot of players, who wanted to just get on with the game without having to go through the process every time. The only other occasion that a pinball has been built with this "multiple choice music" feature, to my knowledge, was Sega's FRANKENSTEIN (1994). The player can choose between the two theme versions from the movie of the same name, directed by Kenneth Branagh in 1994, upon which the pinball was based. One of the themes was actually written way back in the 1970s!

Pinball music of the 1990s has been a mixed bag of original and adopted compositions. Pinballs based on motion pictures and popular T.V. shows picked up again where they left off in the late 70s and early 80s, and of course the music and themes followed.

Sega pinballs (Sega took over Data East in 1994) seem to have chosen this path, and the company has been building pinballs exclusively linked (with the exeption of CHECKPOINT) to either films or T.V. shows since 1990. Original playfield themes along with original sound and music still play a big part today; even though it seemed that at one time all manufacturers were following Sega's direction. Some of the more memorable original compositions in the past years have been; Williams' FISH TALES (1992) with banjo accompaniment, an old sea shanty tune on Bally's BLACK ROSE (1992), a kooky rap tune on Gottlieb's CLASS OF 1812 (1991), which also included the 1812 overture during multiball (accompanied by a singing chicken), and a truly grand theatrical organ piece on Bally's THEATRE OF MAGIC (1995).

See opposite page for caption.

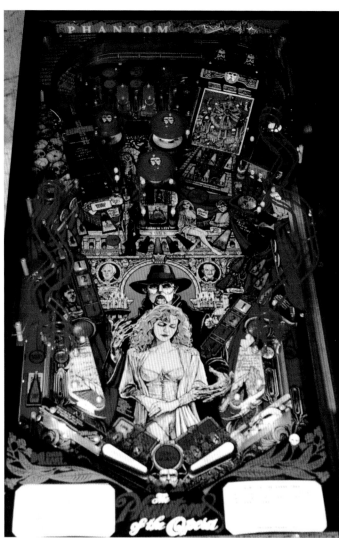

Data East's PHANTOM OF THE OPERA (1990), one of my favorite games from this company. It had very good sound indeed! The background organ music was very impressive; Johann Sebastian Bach in stereo! The match feature was also very nicely done, a long organ tune played, with musical notes shown flying over on the alphanumeric displays. The match number then appeared on the display accompanied by a deep loud sound followed by a rock-tune that faded away slowly. The game had various other music sounds, screams, and speech. One of the most noticeable was the long scream of a woman; "Nooo!....Nooo!" when the ball exited the playfield via the outlanes. *Ivo Vasella collection.* $575-700.

Left & opposite page bottom right: Backglass and backglass detail of Data East's PHANTOM OF THE OPERA (1990). Notice the transparent mask on the Phantom's face, this gives this part of the backglass a 3-D effect. On the top left hand corner there is also a mirror, where the figure of the Phantom is standing. Small stripes making up the picture of the Phantom alternate with small stripes of the mirror, this allows one to see oneself in the mirror with the picture of the Phantom at the same time. *Photos courtesy of Ivo Vasella.*

Since the resurrection of speech in the mid 1980s the talking machine has also advanced. From its humble beginnings with GORGAR, way back in 1979, to a pinball like that of THEATRE OF MAGIC, for example, the game's speaking ability has increased almost ten fold. GORGAR was only programmed to say a handful of phrases using a very limited vocabulary. Its program contains 7 words in total combining to form 7 phrases of two words or longer; "Gorgar speaks", "Me hurt", "Me got you", "You beat me", "You beat Gorgar", plus the two phrases mentioned previously. A few years later, CENTAUR's vocabulary of 30 words gave the machine the ability to speak with a capacity of approximately 20 phrases. CENTAUR's speech program was one of the biggest around for pinballs at that time, other games averaging around 10 phrases. On Bally's SPECTRUM (1982) this capacity was increased even further with a vocabulary of 44 words combining into approximately 30 phrases! Thirteen years later THEATRE OF MAGIC had a speech program that held a vocabulary of over 100 words; in the course of a game one would have been able to hear somewhere between 55 and 60 different

Backglass detail from Bally's CENTAUR (1981). Say cheese! *Photo courtesy of Peter Graabaek.*

Williams' STAR TREK T.N.G (1993). With its large vocabulary and eleven or more different voices, this game sure proved that a lot of things had changed since the release of GORGAR in 1979. *Courtesy of Ivo Vasella.* $1275-1550.

(but much more elaborate) phrases. Williams' STAR TREK: THE NEXT GENERATION (1993), like THEATRE OF MAGIC, has a large vocabulary; the only difference is that the whole crew of the Enterprise gets a chance to say something, along with the ship's computer and a few aliens. The last time I played this particular game I counted 11 different voices!

With music and speech all mixed in together, what ever happened to the good old fashioned electronic sounds of yesteryear? Electronic sounds like background sound have become sound effects themselves. You name it, and there is probably a pinball out there with it. From machine gun fire on Williams TERMINATOR 2 (1991), to a crying baby on Gottlieb's RESCUE 911 (1994); cats purring and meowing on Williams' BAD CATS (1989), a Saint Bernard dog barking on Gottlieb's WIPE OUT (1993); wolves howling along with thunder claps on Williams' DRACULA (1993); fire works going off on Bally's WORLD CUP SOCCER (1994); the cracking of whip on Williams' INDIANA JONES (1993), and of all things, the sound of EM chimes on Data East's TOMMY (1994)!

What will happen to pinball sound next? Who knows? In the near future even though the basic sound systems may not have changed, one could find oneself talking to a pinball; asking it simple questions and getting spoken answers in return! One thing is for certain, if the volume is turned right down during a game one should still be able to hear a sound that has not changed in over a century; that of a ball rolling along the playfield.

Summary

1934-1976 Electromechanical sound produced using chimes, bells and buzzers.

1976-1978 Solid state sound introduced but no continuous background sound available.

1979 Continuous background sound and first talking pinball introduced by Williams.

1982-1985 Due to pinball recession and cost cutting, few talking machines produced.

1985 Talking machines back in production.

1987 First pinball with stereo sound introduced by Data East.

[1] NOTE: The two main abbreviations in regards to this chapter shown in the pinball list remarks column will be; "V" for talking machines and "NV" for non-talking machines.

These will be used mostly between the years 1979 and 1986, as it was the only period in time where talking and non-talking machines have been produced together.

Outhole view of Data East's TOMMY (1994). As seen previously in Chapter Two, this game was based on the rock opera come stage play composed by *The Who*. The game's background music incorporated many of the 24 themes from the opera, as well as the lyrics in some cases, all of which could be heard during the different stages of game play, a unique feature among pinballs. Some of the songs included were *Cousin Kevin*, *Tommy's Holiday Camp* and *Pinball Wizard*.

Gottlieb's CLASS OF 1812 (1991), a pinball with a spooky game theme and unique rap music speech. Other game features included an animated mechanical beating heart, chattering teeth synchronized to the music and speech and a 3-D vacuum formed backglass. *Courtesy of Gottlieb Development LLC. All rights reserved.* $725-825.

Chapter Five

The Bumper Story

The unmistakable bumper arrangement on Gottlieb's SLICK CHICK (1963). *Photograph courtesy of Jan J. Svach.*

Bumpers have been a pinball feature for a very long time now. They preceded the introduction of the flipper in 1947, and have always been present on playfields; with the exception of a small percentage of games like Gottlieb's BANK-A-BALL (1950), Williams' DERBY DAY (Oct 1967) or Bally's SPECTRUM (1982), all of which purely by coincidence had no plunger and shot the ball into play from the outhole! While pinballs like Stern's LIGHTNING (1981) had no bumpers due to sheer lack of space. Apart from these, the number of bumpers has varied from only a solitary bumper, on games such as Allied Leisures DYN-O-MITE (1975); Bally's FLICKER (1975); and Gottlieb's PRO POOL (1973), to as many as twenty-eight on Bally's CAROM (1937), which was a payout pinball.

Up until 1937, the word "bumper" was not readily used in association with pinballs. Bumpers referred to those metal bars attached to either end of one's motor vehicle. Although the term could (and may well have) been used to describe

There is only one bumper on the playfield of Gottlieb's PRO POOL (1973), and one can see that one is enough in this case. *Courtesy of Tim Van Blarcom.* $475-600.

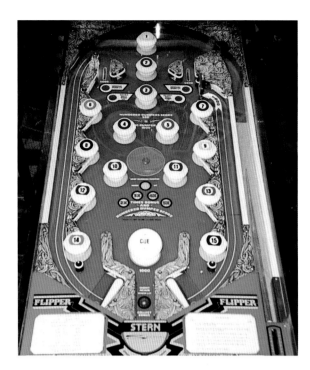

Stern's CUE (1982). This bumper-studded playfield is almost like that from a game built in the 1940s. Look closely at the playfield layout; definitely not your conventional type of game. This game never made it to full production, and only five prototype games were built. *Courtesy of Herb Silvers/Fabulous Fantasies. Photographs courtesy of Ray Johnson.* $2000+

The game that made pinball what it is today; Bally's BUMPER (1937). It was not the flipper that changed the way that pinball was played, its introduction merely refined the concept. It was the coil bumper that revolutionized the game and set it apart from its bagatelle-style predecessors. *Courtesy of Russ Jensen.* $350-400.

a number of different springy devices used on pinballs, it seems the stage was about to be set by Bally.

In January 1937, the first bumpers appeared on Bally's BUMPER. It poses the question; was this pinball named after the playfield device, or was the device named after the pinball? Anyway, the new bumpers were a sensation to say the least, and all of the other game manufacturers from that time onwards, had no other choice, but to include them on new pinballs in order to remain competitive.

Bally's new pinball, made the old bagatelle type games, with the pins and scoring holes, look obsolete—as FM pinballs did when SS was introduced, though more so. What Bally introduced was a whole new way of playing and scoring. No longer was the game one of dodging, but one of hitting. On the old style pinballs, prior to the introduction of the bumpers, one had to dodge pins in order to land the ball into a scoring hole. That was the end of that ball, unless the hole had a solenoid kicker, in which case the whole process repeated itself. It was still quite a static and staid sort of action, but BUMPER offered a totally different concept; to hit as many things as possible, much like the pinballs of today.

What made BUMPER so popular was not only the bumpers, but the backboard totaliser, a projection device which projected the score on the back of a semi-opaque area on the backglass, which would advance in value every time a bumper was hit. Bumpers would not have been practical without this device (or some other form of automatic scoring), and of course the use of electricity, which had only been successfully introduced a few years prior.

The construction of the new bumpers was a simple affair. They consisted of a metal post approximately 2" high, much the same height as today's bumpers. On top of this sat a metal disc or

cap, with a diameter just slightly bigger than that of the ball. The metal disc was held on by a cap nut on Bally pinballs, while other manufacturers had slightly different forms of fasteners, all fulfilling the same purpose while attempting to look different.

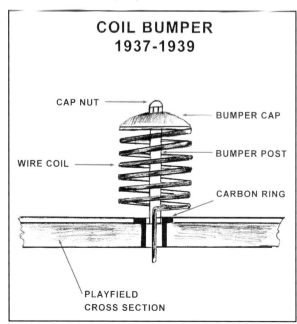

The components of a coil bumper.

COIL BUMPER
1937-1939

CAP NUT

BUMPER CAP

WIRE COIL

BUMPER POST

CARBON RING

PLAYFIELD CROSS SECTION

Spiraling down towards the playfield from the underside of the disc/cap, was the bumper coil, which, having the same diameter as the cap, made it look like a fat spring. This spring or coil spiraled approximately seven to eight times before straightening vertically, going through the playfield; with the wire surrounded at the entry point by a carbon ring.

The force of the ball in play hitting the bumper coil would push the protruding wire against the live carbon ring and therefore close a circuit, which would then register on the scoreboard as points.

These new bumpers did not pass on any mechanical push to the ball, but the coil had enough rigidity to allow the ball to bounce off slightly (with the assistance of a well-timed nudge from the player), in readiness for the next bumper on the way down. It now became more important to keep the ball alive and bouncing all the way down to the outhole, than to just try and land it in a scoring hole somewhere on the playfield, as had been the case before.

It was not long before bumpers began appearing internationally, turning up on games in 1937-38, made by companies such as Jentsch and Meerz, and Bergmann & Co of Germany.

With the release of bumper machines after Bally's BUMPER came a substantial change in playfield design. The pins that once dominated "pin" balls, which were placed with artistic flair and mathematical precision, disappeared. The kickout holes that were once hailed as a great invention, as well as any wire-form rollovers, were also removed; but not forgotten. The playfield between the bumpers was left free of any obstacles that might otherwise impede the ball, except for ball guides or posts placed on both edges of the playfield to help a stray ball back into the middle.

The next technical advancement for the bumper would come two years later in 1939, where by then, wire-form rollover lanes were reintroduced to playfields along with kickout holes. Wire-form rollovers have not changed a great deal in design terms since they were first introduced in the mid-1930s; a good example can be spotted on the playfield photo of FLYING HIGH (1936) included in Chapter Six. A curved wire protruding through the playfield, positioned within a laneway, when pushed down by the weight of the ball, would force two switchblades together and close a circuit, thus registering points. The same basic principle is still used today.

The introduction of molded plastics saw a drastic change in bumper design, and by the end of 1940, the now old style coil bumper was superseded by something that appeared very similar to the bumpers on today's pinballs.

The new bumpers had a plastic body and a plastic cap. The metal coil used to repel the ball that also acted as a circuit switch was replaced by a thick rubber ring around the middle of the bumper body, for pushing the ball away, and a bumper disc, slightly elevated from the playfield to act as the circuit switch.

There were two types of bumper discs, hence the name "disc bumpers". The first, the double disc, used metallic wafer contact discs—one for the disc/skirt and one on the playfield. The disc/skirt, as mentioned previously, was slightly raised off the playfield and pivoted from the center of the bumper body; the same as the bumper skirts on pinballs today. When the ball rolled onto the skirt, the skirt would push down, contact between the two metal discs would be made, and the circuit completed. More importantly for the player, points were added onto the backboard score.

The second type used the same principle, except that instead of wafer contact discs, a rigid wire or metallic post would hang down from the center of the skirt (at ninety degrees to the plane of the skirt), and underneath the playfield. The ball, having run on top of the skirt, would then also tilt the wire from its vertical position, making it touch a metal ring of small diameter encircling the wire, and therefore closing the circuit.

Disc bumpers with no solenoid action. Notice the thick rubber ring around the mid-section and the bumper disc/skirt at the bottom. This type of bumper replaced the coil bumper in 1940 and remained on the playfield up until the late 1960s, even after the introduction of the thumper bumper in 1948.

Playfield detail of a simple rollover lane. Notice the scoring information "lites pop bumpers" at the bottom.

The new disc bumpers, though, having a plastic bumper body that was hollow (since the coil was removed) gave designers an added artistic dimension; the opportunity to include lighting within the device, utilising what would otherwise be an empty space. Perhaps that was the whole reason why the bumper took this particular shape, as game designers were possibly trying to include lighting on the device, in some form or another. Many of the old spring bumpers did in fact have lights sticking up through the playfield just under them, while others had lighted center posts.

A lit playfield, with different colored bumpers, along with a full size lit backglass (introduced in early 1938), really pulled in the players. The new lit bumpers were not just for aesthetics, but played an active part in the new type of playfield scoring strategy, marking the beginning of that immortal pinball term "when lit". For example, hit a bumper for the first time, and score 100 points; but now the bumper has been "lit", so now it's worth 1000 points. Other pinballs would give out free games if one managed to light all the bumpers with five balls per game. While with others, certain bumpers on the playfield had numbers or letters on the cap. Light those bumpers in order, and get a free game or increased scoring. The combinations that manufacturers applied to bumper pinballs were numerous.

Bumper detail from Gottlieb's MISS ANNABELLE (1959). *Photo courtesy of Jan J. Svach.*

The reign of the disc bumper lasted nearly ten years from mid-1939 to late 1948, being replaced by the new "thumper bumpers" or "jet bumpers" or "power bumpers"—take one's pick of names.

The disc bumper, as good as it was for those days, had its obvious limitations when compared to the newer thumpers. Despite this, they continued to appear with regularity on playfields for the next 19 years, up until 1967, when they became almost extinct.

Bumpers by night. Ocean blue bumper caps fit the theme on Bally's FATHOM (1981). An unlit bumper is worth 100 points. Lighting each bumper by making the respective rollover lane increases their value to 1000 points.

Playfield detail from Gottlieb's EGG HEAD (1962), a mix of thumper bumpers (Gottlieb preferred to call them "pop" bumpers) and disc bumpers. The old style disc bumper had obvious limitations when compared to the newer thumper bumpers, despite this, its popularity lasted up until the late 60s.

The deep orange bumpers on Bally's EIGHT BALL DELUXE (1981).

Stern's METEOR (1979), notice the old style bumpers positioned on the upper playfield. Disc bumpers vanished from playfields by the start of the 1970s, but as always, a game like this one was an exception. *Courtesy of Mac.* $375-450.

they are occasionally placed in close proximity to the flipper's territory, on such games as Williams' MAGIC CITY (1967), SPANISH EYES (1972) and PAT HAND (1975), Bally's OLD CHICAGO (1976), and Gottlieb's ABRACADABRA (1975).

Upper and lower playfield of Bally's OLD CHICAGO (1976). Notice the unlikely position of two bumpers in the lower playfield. *Denis Bowler collection.* $450-550.

Bumpers are usually found in the upper playfield, but not in this case. William's SPANISH EYES (1972) had a total of four bumpers, one of them could be found below the flippers!

In October 1948, Williams released SARATOGA, the first pinball with the all new thumper bumper. By then the bumper had already conceded defeat to the flipper as the number one playfield component, introduced exactly one year previously.

Due to the dual action of the flipper and the new power bumpers, the number of bumpers included on the average pinball of the 1940s was reduced by more than half, in the 1950s. It was no longer possible to pack a playfield with 15 to 20 bumpers, as they would now interfere with a good flipper shot. So, from then on, bumpers have occupied the upper half of the playfield, although

The construction of the 1948 thumper bumper was basically the same as a bumper from the 1990s, plus all the EM components of course, like the end-of-stroke switches and bumper relays, which were not required for the latter.

For people who do not own a pinball, and have only been playing pinballs for a short time, the action of the thumper bumper can be quite intriguing. I recall as a young player, trying to take a look at a bumper in action, thinking "how does it do that" while at the same time trying to keep the ball in play.

The traditional and most recognized bumper cap design of the '60s and '70s.

The thumper bumper uses a skirt mechanism similar to the old disc bumpers, to provide a ball activated switch for it to operate on. However, instead of one function, it has two. The first being a score signal just like the old bumper and the second to provide power for a solenoid.

A metal striker (see bumper illustration) sitting below the bumper cap is connected by two rods to the solenoid plunger, which in turn is being held up out of the solenoid by a spring. When the solenoid is activated by the ball rolling onto the skirt, the plunger, along with the metal striker, are drawn downwards, causing the striker to hit the ball before it has had time to roll off the skirt. The conical section of the striker against the round surface of the ball is what makes the ball really fly off.

Bumper cap design from Hankin's SHARK (1980).

Although bumpers have been around for quite some time now, their scoring importance on the playfield has gradually diminished. No longer are they regarded as the ultimate scoring feature on the pinball. Despite this, their ability to keep the ball alive, especially with the standard set of three bumpers in triangular formation, is still as good now as it was then. Fortunately, it is because of this quick scoring action that many modern pinballs now include certain play modes during a game that require the player to hit as many scoring devices as possible within a specified time, regardless of their actual scoring value. Making the ball bounce around the bumpers during this stage of a game is usually the best strategy.

See next page for caption.

THUMPER BUMPER ASSEMBLY

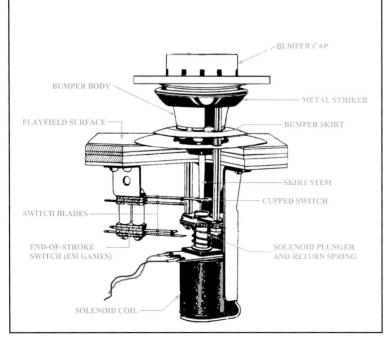

BUMPER CAP

BUMPER BODY

PLAYFIELD SURFACE

METAL STRIKER

BUMPER SKIRT

SKIRT STEM

CUPPED SWITCH

SWITCH BLADES

END-OF-STROKE SWITCH (EM GAMES)

SOLENOID PLUNGER AND RETURN SPRING

SOLENOID COIL

The inner workings of a thumper bumper.

Gottlieb's SKY JUMP (1974), one for the thrill seekers. Bumpers "bump" the ball away and most importantly they score points, but in this case the red middle bumper does more than that. Hitting this bumper (when lit) moves the 10x drop target value light, and thus in some cases one may not want to hit the bumper at all, only until the lit targets have been hit. **See previous page for backglass.** *Mark Gibson collection.* $300-400.

The bumper story would not be complete without mentioning a few of the odd bumper styles that have arisen over the years.

In October 1940, Genco Manufacturing released METRO, a pinball game with bell-shaped bumpers, which would pivot from the top and close a circuit when struck by the ball, then would move back to push the ball away. Incidentally, METRO was one, if not the first pinball to include the end of ball bonus points.

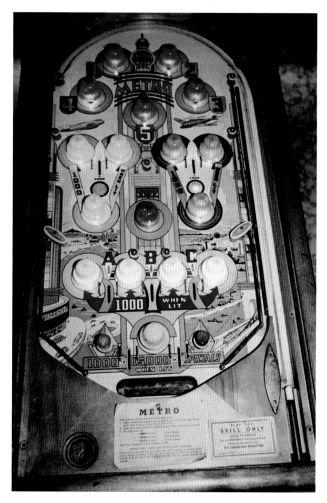

Left, above right & bottom right: Genco's METRO (1940), with those beautiful and unmistakable bell-shaped bumpers. *Russ Jensen collection.* $375-450.

In the same month as the thumper bumper was introduced (Oct 1948), Exhibit Supply Co. released their own powered bumpers. These looked similar to the old coil bumpers that had appeared 11 years previously, except that the whole bumper body would be drawn down by the solenoid and therefore the wire coil would flare out and push the ball away.

The caricature of Elton John on Bally's CAPTAIN FANTAS-TIC (1976), one of the most instantly recognizable bumper caps in the history of pinball.

Williams introduced the disappearing bumper on GUSHER (Sep 1958), after receiving a patent for it in April that same year. This bumper had a flat top that could sit flush with the top of the playfield, once it dropped down after completing a certain game feature. The bumper acted like a normal thumper bumper when above the playfield. Williams re-released this expensive device on SEA WOLF in 1959 and again on METRO (not to be confused with Genco's version) in 1961. For interest's sake, as some pinballs often have hidden meanings that are usually forgotten as time passes, Williams' SEA WOLF was named after one of the first American nuclear submarines, the USS *Seawolf*. It set an endurance record for underwater operation of 60 days between August 7 and October 6, 1958. The game suddenly makes a whole lot more sense now, doesn't it?

Disappearing bumpers were used on Zaccaria's TIME MACHINE, released in 1983; instead of one bumper there are three. All three bumpers are situated on a circular platform, which drops down (bumpers and all) below the playfield, exposing valuable targets that were otherwise unobtainable. A clear perspex roof over the bumpers would then become the playfield, once the whole platform had dropped. TIME MACHINE was the official game for the 1983 Italian pinball championships. The single disappearing bumper has not been left forgotten. Almost 40 years after its debut, Bally picked up the design and used it on CIRQUS VOLITARE in 1997.

Bumper and playfield detail from Genco's METRO. *Photographs courtesy of Russ Jensen.*

Qualitá al piú alto livello

Flipper ufficiale
del campionato
italiano '83

Flipper equipaggiato con il
sensazionale dispositivo
GAME TIME BONUS ® *

Zaccaria's TIME MACHINE (1983) had three disappearing bumpers
set on a large movable platform. $325-400.

During the mid-1960s, Bally introduced mushroom bumpers—
a bumper that was purely a scoring device with no solenoid action—first appearing on MONTE CARLO in 1964. It actually
looked like a mushroom, and a ball, sliding underneath the mushroom lid, lifted it just slightly, closed a circuit, and activated the
scoring motion. The Bally "mushroom" can be found on other
pinballs like GOLD RUSH (1966), SIX SHOOTER (1966), NIP-
IT (1973), SKY KINGS (1973), LOOP THE LOOP (1965), and
many more.

The spinning bumper can also be found on SIX SHOOTER
and LOOP THE LOOP. This device again had no solenoid action,
but utilized a motor to keep the bumpers' three posts (forming a
triangle) rotating, sending the ball flying in all directions. The
spinning bumper was also used on Stern's ORBITOR 1 (1982),
which has rubber discs instead of triangles.

Bally's BAND WAGON (1965), a game with pictures
of pretty girls, lots of candy colours (like pink and light
green) and a good example of a mushroom bumper
pinball. *Ivo Vasella collection.* $350 425.

The mushroom bumper. Both photos were taken from the playfield of Bally's
FIREBALL (1972).

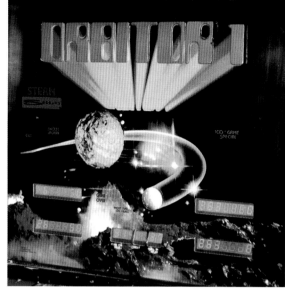

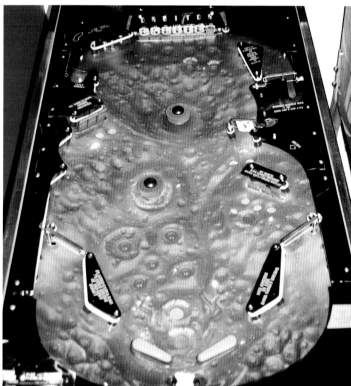

BAND WAGON backglass details. *Photos courtesy of Ivo Vasella.*

Stern's ORBITOR 1 (1982). To say that this pinball is unusual is an understatement, and obviously the format did not catch on. As one can see, the playfield was a moulded contoured surface with craters, high areas and depressions. Not a flat spot to be seen! The conventional bumper was replaced here by spinning disks, as mentioned in this chapter. Other features included a minimum game time (maximum of 180 seconds) where free balls were awarded if all balls were played and lost before the time ran out, and a "100th game special" which awarded a free game for every 100th game played. *Mark Gibson collection.* $425-525.

ORBITOR 1 lower playfield detail. From this angle one can pick up the various contours of the game, and even the crater like formations around the indicating lights. *Photos courtesy of Mark Gibson.*

Bumpers have always been connected to either a sound chime or a particular sound-producing circuit. One of my favorite bumper sounds was featured on a Stern pinball named QUICKSILVER released in 1980. The bumper makes a sound when hit, which I can only describe as an electronic version of a hooting owl.

Stern's QUICKSILVER (1980), a pinball with unusual electronic bumper sounds; one of my favourite games from this company. $325-425.

Finally, the last bumpers to mention are those on Data East's THE SIMPSONS (1990). These are normal thumper bumpers (or "jets", as they are more commonly known today), but they have caps in the form of cooling towers found on nuclear power stations. These caps are quite tall and stick up, but the feature is that they are attached directly to the metal striker and bob up and down when the bumper is hit. However, this is not the first time that bumpers have been disguised to blend in with the overall theme of the game. Bumpers on Bally's SPECIAL FORCE, released in 1986, have square brown thatched roofs to accompany the game's jungle/guerrilla warfare theme.

Summary

1937 Coil bumpers introduced.
1937-39 Coil bumpers used exclusively on most pinballs.
1939 Disc bumpers introduced
1939-48 Disc bumpers used on most pinballs, replacing coil bumpers.
1948 Thumper bumpers invented.
1948-67/68 Thumper bumpers and disc bumpers used together on most games.
1964 Bally introduces the mushroom bumper.
1968 to present Thumper bumpers used exclusively.

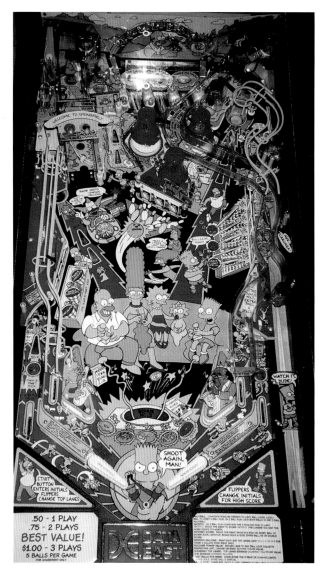

Data East's THE SIMPSONS (1990), with those cooling tower bumpers. *Ian I Svach collection.* $625-775.

The vibrant and hypnotic red bumpers from Data East's TOMMY (1994).

Chapter Six

What's the Score?
The Amusement Adding Machine

What's the score? 1,437 on Bally's ROCKET 3 (1967). Visit all the planets in the solar system; all except Pluto, that is. $450-525.

Playing pinball can be a truly engrossing task. Even for the experienced, a moment's loss of concentration can result in the loss of the ball in play. As a consequence of the concentration required at times, players often manage only a quick glance at the backglass scoreboard during play, to see how their score is progressing. This next section will address the differences in score displays over the past 60 years of pinball.

Take a pinball from any era, be it an EM machine from the 1960s or the latest release this year, and remove all its cosmetic components, such as art work, sound, and all the parts that make it look like a game, and what remains? An adding machine! Does one want to know what two thousand, plus five hundred, plus ten, equals? Press the corresponding value switches that would otherwise have been on the playfield and one has the answer.

This machine is best suited for continuous addition; it operates at a level of speed that is virtually impossible for most people to achieve an answer mentally, without falling behind. By reinstalling the playfield and adding a ball, one once again has a game, an amusement adding machine. However, having already read the previous chapters, one is aware that in the history of pinball, the game appeared before the adding machine.

The journey commences once again in the 1930s, at the apparent roots of modern pinball. Scoring on games built early in this decade was carried out manually, which was not a problem, as a ball could only score once. Quite simply, the ball was plunged into the playfield, bouncing off a few pins, and with some luck, landed in a scoring hole. Depending on the pinball manufacturer, the number of balls played per game varied, from five balls for one

cent, seven balls for one cent, ten balls for three cents, or ten balls for five cents. However, in playing all these, regardless the number, one would note which scoring holes they had landed in, and add up the values shown.

The first mechanical scoring devices appeared on Gottlieb's BIG BROADCAST (Jan 1933) and Bally's AIRWAY (Feb 1933). Gottlieb introduced the idea, but Bally got the credit. The new features were a ball trap, and a score display.

Both games had an array of scoring holes, all of which had the new ball trap with a hinged lid (nicknamed the "toilet seat"), this would close over the scoring hole once the ball dropped in, therefore eliminating the possibility of the hole scoring again with the following ball. Once the ball fell beneath the playfield, it would roll down to the front of the machine and land on a small lever, which would flick up a little card displaying the score. For example, ten holes, therefore ten score counters, all displayed on a protruding bar at the front of the machine. The player still had to add up the points at the end to get a total score, but at least he (I apologize to the female readers, but in those times, it was a pastime dominated by the male sex) no longer had to locate the balls on the playfield. Erich Buttner, a German game manufacturer, later copied BIG BROADCAST almost identically and released it as ERBU BALL late in 1933. AIRWAY also became a very popular game in Europe at the time.

By 1934 the pinball scene was beginning to boom, with the introduction of battery operated machines. However the scoring remained a manual operation.

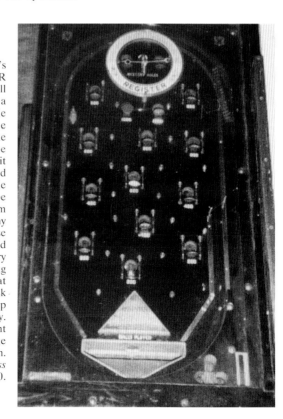

Gottlieb's REGISTER (1934). A ball landing in a scoring hole would activate the hand dial on the round clock-type face, advancing it by the specified amount. The hole then would be eliminated from scoring any further by the use of a lid that would snap shut. A very simple scoring mechanism that removed the task of adding up scores manually. The amusement adding machine was born. *Courtesy of Russ Jensen.* $325-400.

In this same year, some manufacturers did experiment with ideas concerning automatic scoring, and the results turned up in the form of mechanical clock counters. The best-known pinball with this device is Gottlieb's REGISTER (1934). A ball landing in a scoring hole would activate the hand or dial on a round clock-type face, advancing it by the specified amount. REGISTER had the clock counter on the playfield (along with those famous "toilet seats"), rather than on a backglass. A full size backglass and backbox similar to today's games was, at this stage, still a few years away.

The first hint of a backglass came in mid 1935, with Stoner's BALL FAN, and Bally's ROCKELITE. BALL FAN's backglass (if one could call it that), although stretching across the width of the game, was only about 4" high! However both of these games incorporated a scoring feature which would dominate for the next 20 years: light-up scoring.

Sequential light-up scoring appeared soon after, on Rock-Ola's TOTALITE (1936). Sequential light-up scoring used a series of numbers in increasing increments displayed on the backglass, each with the ability of being individually lit from a light source behind the glass.

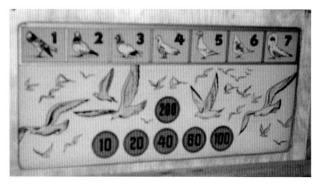

Bally's BALLY DERBY (1935) payout pinball, the modern pinball begins to take shape. Early lighted backglasses (also known as a marquee) like this one did not count up scores, they only registered where the ball had landed. *Eugene Ricci collection.* $375-450.

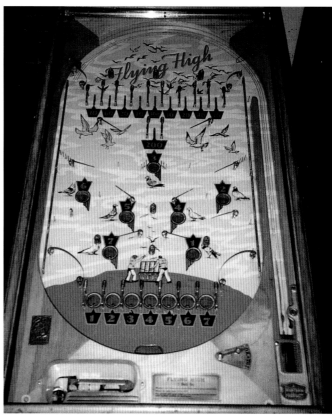

Western Equipment's FLYING HIGH (1936), a huge one-ball payout pin. Another early example of a lighted marquee, but in this case the glass advised the player which scoring holes (1 to 7 birds) paid out money. One of these would light up at random at the start of the game. A score number (10 to 200) would also light up once the corresponding rollover was made, this indicated the payout amount won if the scoring "bird" hole was made. *Eugene Ricci collection.* $575-650.

TOTALITE's scoring displayed the total score as either a single lit number, or a series of lit numbers forming a total score. For example, if after having played all five balls of one's game the total score was 900, then only that number would be lit on the backglass. But if the score were say, 2,300, then two numbers would be lit—the 2,000 and the 300. Light-up scoring pinballs of the mid-1950s by this stage had scores reaching into the millions. For example, a score of 3,560,000 was made up of a 3 million, a 500,000 and a 60,000 lit score values.

The year 1937 was a big one for pinball. It was the year that the coil bumper was unveiled on Bally's BUMPER, a device which went hand-in-hand with automatic scoring. As mentioned previously in Chapter Five, the bumper changed the way pinball was played, but it required some form of automatic scoring in order to succeed, hence the introduction of these two complementary components. With the bumper requiring the efficiency of automatic scoring, it subsequently turned the backglass into a necessity for pinballs, rather than the eye-catching novelty that it had begun as.

Automatic scoring was now an essential part of pinball. Remove the "adding machine" from a pinball in 1937, and just like a pinball from 1997, the game would have little point. "What's the point of playing, if I don't know what the score is?!" A phrase that has been uttered countless times in the last 60+ years, at the sight of a broken scoreboard. But, if the backglass scoring were to fail on the older style of pinballs prior to BUMPER, the game would still be playable; as the game's strategy was as it had been for years without automatic scoring, filling holes to make scores. The evidence of one's skill (or lack of it) was there for all to see, until the balls were returned to the outhole at the drop of a coin to start a new game.

BUMPER's backboard and backglass were approximately 8" high; not quite full size yet, but included a score window, where the progressive score was displayed by means of a rotating disc being projected onto that window. This type of score display was almost a hybrid of light-up scoring and reel scoring, but it appears not to have lasted beyond 1937.

1938 was the year of the full size backglass, and it soon became evident that it provided a greater area to spread eye-catching graphics and gimmicks in order to attract players. The possibilities were endless! The backglass was not just a score display, it had now become the on-site advertisement for the pinball. There was a lot of room on the new backglasses to be filled apart from displaying the ever-increasing score values, which went from an average game score in the thousands in 1938, to the hundreds of thousands in the 1940s, and millions in the 1950s. The manufacturers overflowed in artistic flair and included animation.

The ladies are spending up big on Williams' C.O.D (1953). The scores are up into the millions. As one can see, a department store setting was used for this backglass. Notice how the artist has incorporated score numbers on the side of the escalator, increasing in value from 40,000 at the bottom, "rising" to 90,000 at the very top. *Eugene Ricci collection.*

An animated backglass came not in the form of cartoons, but simple figures made to simulate movement, with the aid of rotating discs or cardboard like puppets with moveable legs, and so on. Animated backglasses have appeared intermittently through the decades, becoming less popular by the 1970s, and rare in the decades to follow. TAPS by Harry Hoppe (1939) had a black and white Minstrel figurine (named Sambo), whose moveable legs would tap dance when scoring features were made. The theme, though highly relevant to the 1930s and 40s, would not be considered appropriate in this politically correct age. Williams' SPARK PLUGS (1951) and HANDICAP (1952) each had six horse & jockey figurines which would advance separately on a racetrack, by hitting the bumpers and rollover lanes that carried their numbers. Gottlieb's BUCKAROO (1965) had an animated bucking bronco and a doubled over cowboy who would spin as though kicked from behind by the bucking horse. CROSS TOWN (1966) featured subway doors which would open and close when a replay was awarded,

Gottlieb's A-B-C BOWLER (1941), an example of an early 40s backglass (a "modern" full size, I might add) where the scores were still pretty low in value. *Ivo Vasella collection.* $300-400.

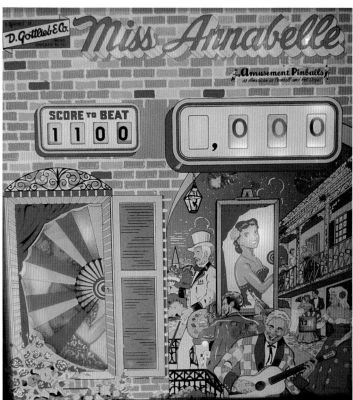

See next page for caption.

revealing a tuba-tooting passenger. Italy's Zaccaria also dabbled in animation with DEVIL RIDERS (1984), where a motorbike riding daredevil performs a loop-the-loop.

Backglass (see previous page) and backglass detail of Gottlieb's MISS ANNABELLE (1959). The detail is that of the game's animation unit, a fan which during the course of a game unfolds to reveal the beautiful Annabelle. *Courtesy of Jan J. Svach.* $575-725.

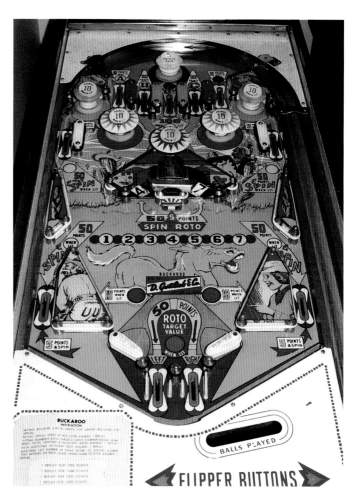

Above right & right: Gottlieb's BUCKAROO (1965), a pinball legend! There is no doubt in my mind that when the words "animated backglass" are uttered amongst pinball enthusiasts, that for many of them this game would be one of the first to pop in their heads. Its claim to fame is its appearance in the 1975 cult movie *Tommy*. The game rules are as follows: Completing top A-B-C-D rollovers, lights center rollover for special. Hitting numbered roto targets lights corresponding light on playfield. Completing four in a row awards one replay. Additional adjacent spot awards another replay. Easier said than done! *Mark Jackson/Robert Young collections.* $750-900.

Details of BUCKAROO's animation unit. *Jeff Grummel collection. Photograph courtesy of Phillip Brown.*

BUCKAROO playfield detail.

Some of the more recent animated backglasses have been CYCLONE (1988) and RIVERBOAT GAMBLER (1990). Both were built by Williams, and both have spinning wheels—a score prize wheel and a roulette wheel, respectively. Data East's THE ADVENTURES OF ROCKY AND BULLWINKLE (1993) feature the famous cartoon characters, and has Bullwinkle the Moose pull something out of a magician's hat. On SCARED STIFF (1996),

Bally claimed "Industry First, a 3D Interactive backbox, featuring a player-controlled spinning spider used to collect special features and start unique modes." The mode is heralded by the audio cue: "Look up! Stop the spider!" The player then has the opportunity to select the desired prize, depending on accuracy. "The large hairy spider is sure to send shivers down the spines of experts and novices alike" the brochure states.

Bally's SCARED STIFF (1996) a pinball that will send shivers down your spine! The rim of the backglass is shaped in the form of a T.V screen, and within is a player-controlled spinning spider. Hitting the ball into a playfield trap starts the spider spinning. Pressing a flipper button stops the spider. It's a prize wheel basically, used to collect special features and start unique modes. Other pinball features include a "stiff-o-metre" and plastic moulded bony flippers. Turn out the lights...It's time to get SCARED STIFF! *Courtesy of Jan J. Svach.* $1800-2200.

In 1938, the ever-changing face of automatic scoring, which had started only four years before, had begun to settle down, and backglass light-up scoring settled in for a comfortable 15-year stretch.

The first sign of change appeared in late 1953, with the drum score reel. The score reels, probably the feature most associated with EM pinballs, was used on everything else but pinballs before 1953, on such things as amusement bowling machines and baseball games. Williams unveiled ARMY-NAVY in October 1953, the first pinball with scoring reels. ARMY-NAVY was followed by GUN CLUB (Oct 1953), STRUGGLE BUGGIES (Nov 1953) and NINE SISTERS (Dec 1953), all of which had scoring reels. In order to keep abreast with light-up scoring's high game scores (which reached into the millions), Williams built these machines with seven reels, capable of scoring up to 9,990,000 points. The last four reels however, were dummy reels, all fixed at zero, and non-operational.

Despite this innovation, mechanical problems ensued, and so Williams went back to light-up scoring almost straight away, cutting their losses to a minimum.

Up until this time, pinball had been strictly a one-player game; unless of course one wanted to play "doubles" (also called "flippers" or "halvies", where two people control a flipper each, and alternate with each ball). It remained this way because the light-up scoring was too intricate to allow a score to be kept for more than one player. The only way around this problem would have been to incorporate separate scoring panels, one for each player. This idea was not fully realized until 1956, with Bally's release of BALLS-A-POPPIN', a two-player game. It was one of only a few pinballs produced by Bally in the 1950s. The company diverted most of its manufacturing ability into the production of bingo machines—a flipperless pinball look-alike purposely built to side-step the gambling law active at the time, while still allowing operators to award payouts.

Williams' ARMY NAVY (1953). This was the first pinball to incorporate a set of score reels for points tabulation, as opposed to the common form of light up scoring. Williams' released three more pinballs in this format, but because of design problems, they returned to the more conventional light-up scoring by the end of the year. Only the first three reels were operational, the rest were "dummy" reels fixed at zero. This gave the illusion of high scores, which were in style at the time. *Courtesy of Russ Jensen.* $600-700.

Williams' SMOKE SIGNAL (1955). Williams' went back to producing light up games like this one after the failure of drum reel scoring. One problem with games such as these was that only one player could have a game at any one time. *Eugene Ricci collection.* $500-600.

Pinballs with multiple player capacity were not a Bally first; that prize had gone to Gottlieb, not in 1956, but in 1954. Gottlieb had decided to take the drum reel idea which Williams had used without success in October 1953, and almost one year later, the idea reached its full potential on a four-player game called SUPER JUMBO. It was played exactly as one would today, with each player alternating turns until each of the balls had been played (five each), and each player having their own score. A wise choice for Gottlieb was also the reduction of the score display, with only a set of three reels per player instead of the extended bank of dummy reels which Williams had used to simulate larger scores. This effectively reduced the maximum score to 999 points per player.

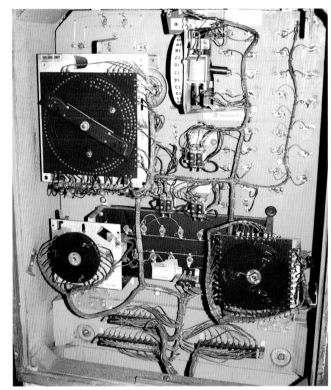

Inside the backbox of ROTO POOL. The only reel in this backbox is that of the credit meter. The score is controlled by a set of rotary switches.

Genco's JUMPIN' JACKS (1952), a vertical "pachinko" style marble game. Notice the score reels, and in 1952! Electro-mechanical reels, whether for score tabulation or credit count had been around for a while, it was only a matter of time before designers used them on pinballs. *Tim Van Blarcom collection.*

Top left & left: Gottlieb's ROTO POOL (1958). Although Gottlieb perfected drum reel scoring in 1954, single player games still utilised light-up scoring up until 1960. The score is 1,580,000 points. The lit pool balls inside the backglass indicate the number of pool balls scored on the playfield. Notice the old style wood rail and the cigarette holders. *Robert Young collection.* $800-975.

A closer look at the vertical playfield of JUMPIN' JACKS without the front cover. *Photos courtesy of Tim Van Blarcom.*

The multiple-player layouts took some getting used to, especially for those accustomed to the single-player games. It was a little confusing at first, not knowing if it was possible to have a game by oneself, or whether one required three other players, despite advertising slogans and instructions such as "1,2,3 or 4 players can play at the same time!"

However, no advance comes without a price, and the addition of score reels made pinballs slightly more expensive. Manufacturers preferred to use them on multiple-player games only, leaving single player pinballs unchanged with the now older style light-up scoring. By 1960, even single-player games had adopted the score reels. There were a few reluctant Spanish companies like Faer and T.D. Llobregat, who maintained single player light-up scoring well into the mid 60s, but in America, the last such game became Williams' SPACESHIP (Dec 1961). The way was then clear for the score reel to also sit back for its own 15-year stretch.

There was an exception to this general trend (as there inevitably is!), provided by French company Rally-Play (Rally for short) mentioned previously in Chapter Four. Rally was better known at first for the manufacture of electronic marine equipment, then for some reason expanded into pinballs, incorporating their electronic knowledge into the game. The company's pinball produc-

Rally's RALLY GIRL (1966), the first game to include digital scoring displays. Notice the clear coloured plastic playfield parts (the bumper caps especially), not the kind of components associated with American pinballs of the late 1960s. They were to become standard components there almost fourteen years later. *Courtesy of Russ Jensen.* $325-400.

Not many single-player pinballs using light-up scoring made it past the end of 1960, but this one did; Williams' SPACESHIP (1961), one of the last pinballs to include this type of score display. The backglass art is somewhat reminiscent of a cover one would expect to see on an old science fiction/fantasy comic book. *Courtesy of Russ Jensen.* $600-700.

tion life spanned six years, from 1962-68. Within that time they managed to fabricate some quite remarkable pinballs, displaying ideas that were far beyond their time, almost a premonition of what was to come. For Rally, the age of digital scoring came in 1966, ten years before the "Big Three" and the rest of the world! Being a small manufacturer, Rally's market was limited to a few European countries. Their games remained virtually unknown in the U.S.A, unlike the manufacturing giants Gottlieb and Bally, which became major exporters into Europe (especially to Italy and Germany) in the mid 1960s. Despite their digital score, these pinballs were EM in design, incorporating miniature self-contained "plug-in" relay units, a technology not used by American manufacturers until the start of the SS era. The digital displays were achieved by the use of decade counters; display components used in early large-scale general purpose electronic computers of the era. It was a clever adaptation of a technology that had been around for some time, which had its uses in a large number of appliances (like weight scales, for example) well into the 1970s. RALLY GIRL (Nov 1966) was their first pinball to incorporate digital scoring. Only five more games were produced after this before pinball production was stopped.

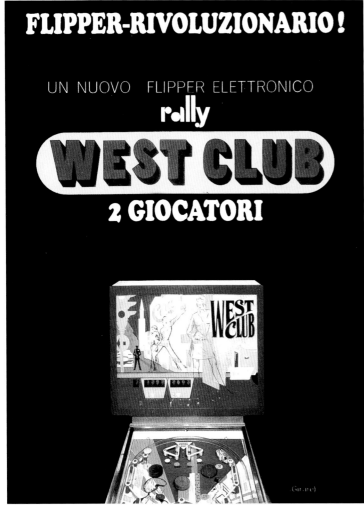

Italian brochure for Rally's WEST CLUB (1967), another game with digital scoring. The sight of digital decade counters, rather than score reels, must have been an awesome sight. The reasons why this type of display never caught on with American manufacturers will always remain a mystery. $325-400.

Score reel numbers may appear similar when hidden by a backglass. Some may look smaller in size or have different shaped numbers, but all in all they look pretty much the same. The mechanisms that turn these reels however, change in design from one manufacturer to another. Some companies have relied on the successful designs of others. Both score reel assemblies shown here are from Italian pinballs, but both have copied designs from those of Williams and Gottlieb.

Since the start of multiple player pinballs in 1954, until the end of the EM era in 1976/77, the choice of player capacity has never been the same. Players and distributors could choose between single-player, two-player and four-player models (not of the same game), something that disappeared after the introduction of SS technology; with almost all pinballs built as four-player models. The reason being the price differential. With EM games of the 1970s, the price tag between a single-player game and a four-player game may have been as high as 15-20%, the four-player obviously being the more expensive. Solid State technology reduced that differential to a minimal amount, thus the majority of manufacturers only built four-player machines, which were more versatile. Here are some interesting figures. Between the years 1955-1976, 56% of all pinballs built were in single-player format, 24% two-player and 20% four-player (not counting two EM pinballs built with six-player capacity). As a comparison, between the years of 1979-1998 (skipping two years due to the EM and SS transition period) only 4.5% of pinballs built were in single-player format, many of them coming from Spain and Italy, 2.1% two-player (not counting head-to-head games), 92.7% four-player and 0.7% six-player format.

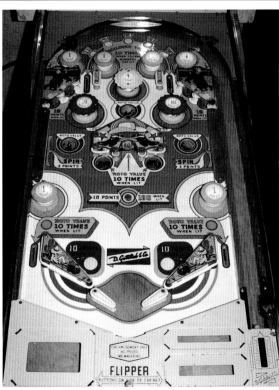

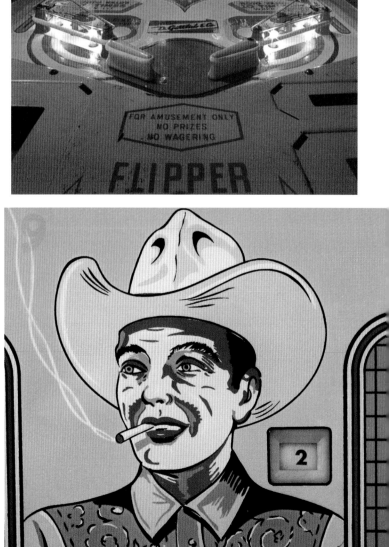

Top left, bottom left, & top right: Gottlieb's TEXAN (1960). Yee Haa! Four-player games were not all that common back in 1960. Since the introduction of multiple player pinballs only six years before, the ratio of four-player pins built by Gottlieb, relative to their other single or double player pins, was one out of every six. Notice the "one thousand" indicator light at the front of each score and the advertising slogans. Note: Game shown during restoration. Cabinet not original. *Robert Young collection.* $500-600.

Bottom right: TEXAN backglass detail. This guy looks a little sunburnt!

Another multiple player game, this time Gottlieb's two-player PICNIC (1958). *Courtesy of Tim Van Blarcom.* $525-625.

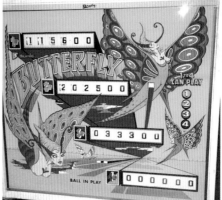

Sonic's BUTTERFLY (1977) featuring one of my favorite backglasses to come out of Spain. Notice the scores reaching up to 999,900 points. It was during 1977 that the numbers of EM pinballs built with score capacities this high reached a peak. The exponential rise in their numbers since 1975 was soon to be taken up by electronic pinballs. *Jeff Grummel collection.* $300-350.

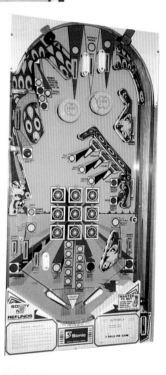

A phenomenon that started with the introduction of automatic scoring and is well-known among long time players is the ever-increasing game scores and replay values which have reached an equilibrium only recently. I have already mentioned how light-up scoring values increased from thousands to millions in the space of approximately 15 years; the same trend continued after 1954, starting from an average score in the hundreds, to one in the billions (one thousand million) in the mid-1990s. The average game scores have remained lower since then, with some of the latest games offering replays below 100 million points. A simple chart has been compiled, titled "Reels of time" which depicts this trend for the EM drum reel era, between 1954 and 1978.

REELS OF TIME

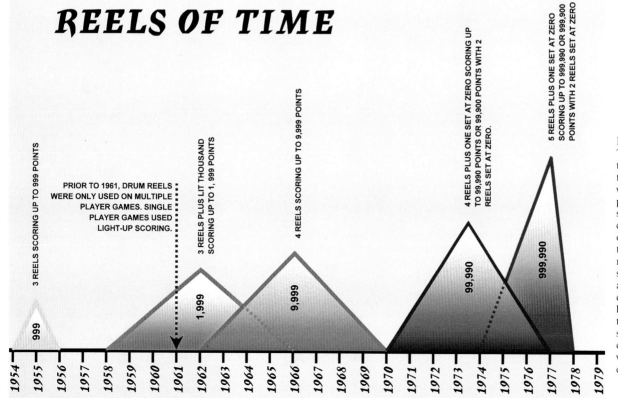

3 REELS SCORING UP TO 999 POINTS

PRIOR TO 1961, DRUM REELS WERE ONLY USED ON MULTIPLE PLAYER GAMES. SINGLE PLAYER GAMES USED LIGHT-UP SCORING.

3 REELS PLUS LIT THOUSAND SCORING UP TO 1, 999 POINTS

4 REELS SCORING UP TO 9,999 POINTS

4 REELS PLUS ONE SET AT ZERO SCORING UP TO 99,990 POINTS OR 99,900 POINTS WITH 2 REELS SET AT ZERO.

5 REELS PLUS ONE SET AT ZERO SCORING UP TO 999,990 OR 999,900 POINTS WITH 2 REELS SET AT ZERO

999   1,999   9,999   99,990   999,990

1954 1955 1956 1957 1958 1959 1960 1961 1962 1963 1964 1965 1966 1967 1968 1969 1970 1971 1972 1973 1974 1975 1976 1977 1978 1979

Reels of time graph. The base of each triangle represents the time period where 90% of EM pinballs with the specified score capacity have occurred. The triangle shapes represent an over-simplified version of a mean curve for each case, where the height is relative to the base width. The size of each triangle does not indicate the volume of pinballs in each.

The chart is comprised of five triangles, with the base of each representing the time period where 90% of the pinballs with the specified score capacity have occurred. The reason for choosing the 90% margin was because it was found that 100% gave the chart too many overlaps. For example, as early as 1970-71, Williams built a handful of pinballs such as 3 JOKERS, JIVE TIME and STRAIGHT FLUSH, which already had scores reaching into the hundreds of thousands. Incorporating these pinballs into triangle 5, meant that triangle 4 would have been almost completely eclipsed. The same

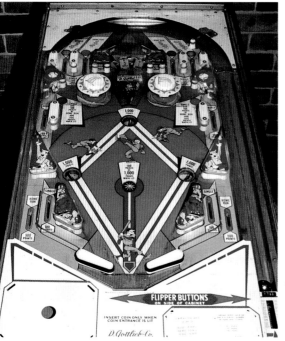

Gottlieb's GRAND SLAM (1972). Take a close look at the backglass. This is not a two-player game, but a single-player game with two separate score displays. One display (on the left) is for the standard point score while the other smaller score is the home run counter. Replays are awarded for reaching a certain score as per usual, but also for reaching a certain number of runs. *Phil Paterson/Mark Gibson collections. $325-400.*

Gottlieb's GRAND SLAM (1972). Playfield art detail showing the pitcher, batter and fielders, all portrayed in the typical Gottlieb cartoonish style.

problem occurred with triangle 3, where the 100% spread would have covered from 1960 to 1972; again almost covering triangle 2. The triangular shapes also represent an over-simplified version of a mean curve depicting frequency for each case where the height of the triangle is relative to the base width. Triangle 5 shows a slight lean, as EM pinball numbers dropped dramatically after 1977.

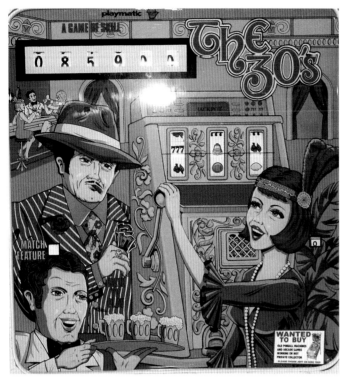

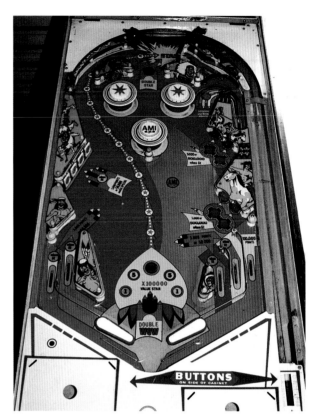

Playmatic's THE 30S (1977). There's reels, and then there's reels. The slot machine feature on the backglass was activated by shooting the ball into any one of the game's five kickout saucers. *Jeff Grummel collection*. $275-325.

A.M.I's BIG HUNT (1976). One of several EM games built by Italian manufacturers around this period that had score reels reaching into the millions of points. It really was, however, two dummy reels fixed at zero placed on the end of a set of five operational reels. A closer look at the backglass reveals another interesting feature. The artwork on it is a copy of Bally's BOW AND ARROW (1975). It is almost exactly the same in content, but it has been simplified and compressed to fit into a smaller area. *Graeme Beal collection*. $300-375.

There are always exceptions to every case, like Williams' first attempt with drum reels in 1953. Scores did again reach into the millions for a short time around 1976-78, but very few pinballs with this score display were built, and most of them came from European manufacturers. For example, A.M.I.'s BIG HUNT (1976) and Zaccaria's QUEEN'S CASTLE (1978), both Italian pinballs, can score up to 9,999,900 points; but in reality, their score displays actually consist of two dummy zero reels in addition to the standard set of five scoring reels. An interesting fact about BIG HUNT is that some of the machines were fitted with digital credit displays rather than with the standard EM step unit reel in use at the time. Perhaps these were experimental games.

Backglass detail of BIG HUNT showing the chief of the tribe supervising the hunt. It is a slightly different detail than that of Bally's BOW AND ARROW.

MOON FLIGHT backglass detail.

By the year 1979, the absolute end of the EM score reel had eventuated, and players were now looking at their score displays as a more compact unit and giving off their own light; not enhanced by any other light source. In fact, the darker the surroundings the better one could see the score.

Zaccaria's MOON FLIGHT (1976). Like A.M.I's BIG HUNT and many other Italian and Spanish pinballs, this game used an over-inflated score display which incorporated two dummy zeros, pushing the score into the millions of points. This did not fool anyone, but the games were fun to play nevertheless. $300-375.

Backglass detail from Bally's FATHOM (1981). Digital delight. Digital scores were perfectly suited for the dark; in fact, the darker the surroundings, the better.

The now-compact digital score set within the space of the unchanged standard size backglass gave the artist a slightly greater area for expression. Whereas a standard bank of six reels would have once taken up an area approximately 10" long by 1.5" high, a digital score with the same capacity took up only approximately 6" by 1.25", less than half the area!

HIT THE DECK playfield detail.

Gottlieb's HIT THE DECK (1978), a pinball that has become famous for all the wrong reasons. The reels on this EM game were painted to look like a digital display. This may have been done to purposely fool players into thinking they were playing an SS game; the fact is it did not work. On the other hand, because of that, the game has now become sought-after. The game was also released as NEPTUNE (1978) and POSEIDON (1978), and all three were produced in very low quantities. *Jeff Grummel collection*. $350-425.

The unmistakable blue digital display of a Gottlieb pinball. A. Hankin & Co., and Juetel, a French company, also used the same type of display. One particular difference with this display was the use of an extra digital component for the number "1". As one can see, this number appears in the center of the digit counter and not on the left side, as was common with other displays. Digits measure approximately 1" high by 0.55" wide.

Not every digital display was the same, however. They appeared in various sizes and colors, depending on the manufacturer. Gottlieb always had to be different; their larger digital display had digits almost equal in size to the old drum numbers, approximately 1" high by 0.55" wide, emitting a pale blue light. Hankin and France's Juetel also used this type (called a Futuba display). A tinting on the backglass display window enhanced the colour on Gottlieb games.

Williams, Bally, Zaccaria and Stern all had similar displays, with digit size 0.75" x 0.4" emitting a dark yellow light. The internal design of the displays varied from game to game, but the outcome was basically the same. However, the blue display on a Gottlieb pinball made it readily identifiable amongst its rivals, especially in a darkened, smoke-filled pool hall or pinball parlor, typical of the early 1980s. What made Gottlieb displays different was their construction, running on 55 volts DC with a fluorescent type illuminant, rather than the 200 volts DC and neon illuminant used by the others. Green was also another colour chosen for use by Gottlieb on games such as DEVILS DARE and HAUNTED HOUSE, both released in 1982. On the other hand, what made early Atari pinballs identifiable at a distance was lack of backbox score displays altogether! The backglass artwork on these games was stunning, to say the least, unobstructed by the lack of digital displays, as they were located on the left side of the scorecard plate were the instruction card would normally reside.

Playfield of Atari's AIRBORNE AVENGER (1977). Early Atari pinballs like this one did not have the score displays positioned in the backbox, behind the backglass. Instead, they were located on the left-hand side of the scorecard plate, as seen here. This made the backglass an uninterrupted work of art. *Courtesy of Midway Games Inc. All rights reserved.* $375-450.

Gottlieb's DEVIL'S DARE (1982), a wide bodied game which used green displays. It definitely suited the overall look of the game. *Courtesy of Gottlieb Development LLC. All rights reserved.* $400-475.

My favorite colour, but one seldom seen, is the deep red display used predominantly by Spanish manufacturers like Recel, Playmatic and Interflip. It was given limited use by Bally and Atari on games like CENTAUR II (1983), and SUPERMAN (1979) respectively; where it seems that the change in colour for Bally was used only for aesthetic purposes. For the record, Atari's SUPERMAN used the more conventional backbox score displays.

Pinballs were, if only for a limited time, being manufactured in Japan. As previously stated in Chapter Three, today's amusement giant, Sega, were building EM and SS pinballs during their humble beginnings, back in 1976; but were only in production for

a few years, cutting back on pinballs to concentrate on their video games. Universal was another Japanese company that gave pinball a try, producing HAREM CAT late in 1979. It was the first pinball game to use a TV/video monitor for the score display.

HAREM CAT is a six-player game with the video monitor mounted in a corner of a standard backbox, behind the backglass. One can imagine how versatile this type of display seemed at the time. Not only does it show scores, but also video game style animation of that era; appearing if only briefly, when an important scoring feature is made, or replay awarded. Despite using different materials, this type of display could be said to have had almost exactly the same visual effect as the dot-matrix display first used on pinball machines almost 12 years later, in early 1991. Universal built only one more pinball after HAREM CAT, that being ASTEROID KILLER in early 1980, before disappearing into the unknown like so many other companies involved in the amusement machine industry.

By the end of 1980, mainstream pinballs had already added an extra digit to the front of the display, putting scores up into the millions once again. But unlike the light-up scores of the 1950s, where the lowest denomination was 10,000 points, these displays had only one fixed digital zero, with the lowest possible score obtainable being ten points (the score value usually reserved for bouncing off a slingshot). Have you ever missed out on being awarded a replay by just ten points? I have, and remember it well!

The year was 1980. The pinball, Bally's SPACE INVADERS (1980). I had only been playing pinballs for one or two years at that stage, but seemed like an eternity, possibly because the chances to play the silverball came too few and far between. Barely a teenager, it was straight home after school, and that sort of thing.

Not having cracked a replay on points before, I felt that my luck was finally about to change, when on the third and final ball of this particular game, my score was tantalizingly close to that of 350,000, the score needed for a free game. Unfortunately due to my lack of skill in those days, I lost the ball too soon. Looking up at the score with fingers crossed for good luck, as the bonus score added up. Final score, 349,990! Unbelievable! Knowing that I could not afford another game, all that was left was to step back, take a deep breath, and give the machine a good "kick in the guts" (the act of kicking the front cashbox door in disgust); but I held myself in check, for fear of getting kicked out and/or banned. I had just declared war on that particular game, and I would be back!

Incidentally, SPACE INVADERS the pinball met with a violent death at the hands of Richard Kiel (the bad guy that played Jaws in the James Bond movies) in the 1981 screen comedy *So Fine*, which also starred Ryan O'Neill. Kiel's character smashes the pinball into pieces following a bad game (I know how he felt!). As for the rest of the movie, a regrettable forgettable, it had something to do with jeans with a plastic see-through backside...Anyone remember?

It might seem puzzling that with such high scores required for a free game, then and even more so now, there are still features of the playfield, like the slingshot kickers, that award such an insignificant value as 10 points. The reason for this has to do with the match feature.

The match feature is the pinball's way of offering a second chance to the player at the completion of the game, irrespective of how well the person may or may not have played. A free game is awarded to the player if the last digit or digits of the final score matches a random number appearing on the backglass at the end of the game. The player's odds being a 1:10 chance of receiving a free game.

Since the 1970s, the match number has consisted of two digits; a total of 10 numbers from "00" to "90". During the 1950s and 1960s, when drum reel scores were not as high, the match number consisted of only the one digit; the lowest obtainable score being one point. The feature first appeared on pinballs in 1957; it was not restricted to pinballs with drum reel scoring but was also included on single player light-up games. The match indicator on these games came in the form of an extra set of lights adjacent to the scoring lights. On Gottlieb games, for example, it was usually a lit star appearing on the backglass next one of the lower score panels (the lower score indicators in this case being from 00 thousand to 90 thousand). If at the end of a game the star appeared next to the lit value, a free game was yours. On EM score reel pinballs, the match number would appear in the form of lit numbers somewhere on the backglass; with the exception of a few games, like Zaccaria's MOON FLIGHT (1976), where the match number is on a separate drum reel which reveals itself at the end of the game. On SS pinballs built between 1976 and 1986, the

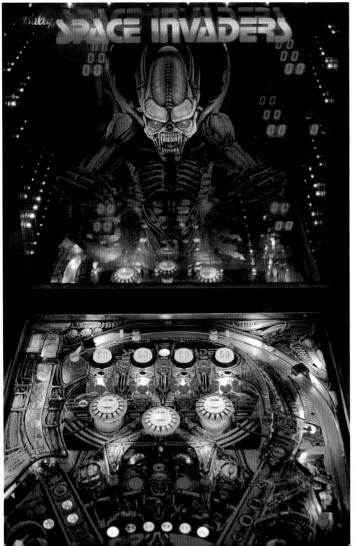

The backglass of Gottlieb's HIGH HAND (1973). Compare this to the flip-side image of the glass. *Rawdon Osborne collection.*

Playview of Bally's SPACE INVADERS (1980). The game featured in the 1981 movie *So Fine* which starred Ryan O'Neill and Richard Kiel.

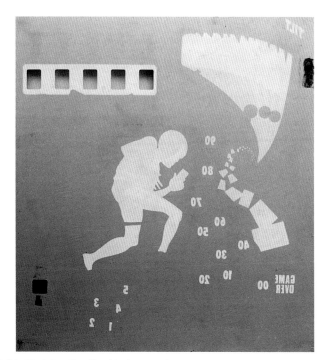

HIGH HAND. The flip-side image of the glass showing all the light-up indicators. The grey area of the glass is where light cannot penetrate from behind. The lighter areas, like the game name for example, allow light from bulbs placed directly behind to shine through. Other areas, such as the 1 to 5 "ball in play" numbers on the bottom left and the 00 to 90 "match" numbers, are not visible to the player until such time as they are lit from behind. The same applies for the "game over" sign and the "tilt" sign on the top right hand corner.

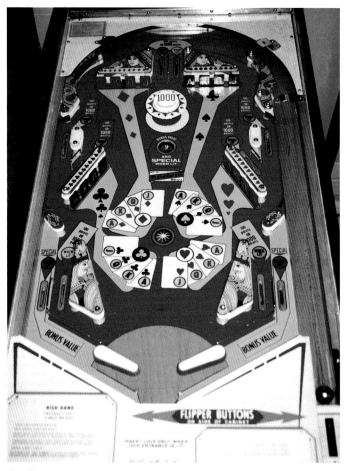

Gottlieb's HIGH HAND (1973). If you were wondering what the playfield of this game looked like, here it is. It might look simple, but games like these require great flipper skill-shot accuracy in order to pick off the remaining targets in each bank. Knocking down a target in each bank lights the corresponding light in each bonus hand. *Mark Gibson collection.* $425-500.

match number would appear on a separate two-digit display next to the credit meter. This display was also used as the ball count during the game. The exceptions come from Spain this time, with Playmatic having a completely separate display and Recel again having a separate display in the form of a digital roulette wheel. On pinballs from 1986 onwards, the match feature would appear somewhere on the score display, usually after some eye-catching routine.

An interesting sight, that found behind the backglass of Zaccaria's MOON FLIGHT (1976). Rather than using light-up numbers for the match feature, this game used an extra reel, seen here as the first on the left. The reel was obscured by a metal arm, which would drop down at the end of the game revealing the number. Notice how there are two "dummy" zeros, and hence the match numbers shown on the reel ranged from 000 to 900.

MOON FLIGHT outhole view.

The match feature is the great equalizer among pinball players. The "Hot-Shot" pinball wizard might miss out on a replay by a few thousand points, while the novice may win a free game by pure luck. The main idea for this latter group is that one must wait around to watch the match feature come up. Many first-timers win games in this fashion, but because they are unaware of the feature, and a possible second chance, they wander off when they have lost the game on points. If awarded, a free game is often referred to simply as a "match" but it will obviously vary depending on the country one resides in. In the Australian schoolboy slang, it is known as a "scab". Derived from the derogatory term, it infers that the game was easily obtained, without having to work for it. It is often ruefully joked about between my wife and I, in terms of "Confucius say." Two worthy mentions relevant to this topic are: "Confucius say, pinball will always match when player walks away" and "Confucius say, pinball will always match when player in hurry to leave."

The next big change in how players viewed their score came in 1985. Alphanumeric score displays hit the spotlight in May 1985, on Gottlieb's CHICAGO CUBS TRIPLE PLAY. The displays not only show the score, but spell out messages, directing players to important scoring features and allowing the top scorers to enter their initials into the pinball's memory. Pinballs were now also capable of storing lesser scores in order of magnitude, displaying them during times of non play, along with the top score—something that had been only available on video games in past years.

Gottlieb's EL DORADO (1984), one of the last Gottlieb games to use standard digital displays before they converted to alphanumerics. *Ivo Vasella collection.* $550-625.

The most common score display configuration on the backglasses of pinballs prior to alphanumerics was one display per corner. With the introduction of alphanumerics, this setup was no longer favorable. For example, a simple phrase like "Great score – Enter initials" would not have been presented effectively, broken up across four display units and not totally within the player's field of view. The answer was to bring the displays closer together.

A typical alphanumeric display, able to show comments as well as score values. Their introduction to pinballs in 1985 saw a rise in pinball popularity, if only for a brief period of two years.

Some displays formed a line at the bottom of the backglass, while others were grouped into a block. Gottlieb decided to reduce its oversized digits to facilitate the grouping, but rather than conform with Bally and Williams (who kept theirs the same size as before), they went one size smaller, still maintaining the blue coloration.

The first Bally and Williams pinballs to include alphanumeric displays were MOTORDOME (May 86) and HIGH SPEED (Feb 86) respectively. The last games from each of the "Big Three" to feature standard digital scoring were Bally's LADY LUCK (Feb 86), Williams' COMET (Sep 85) and Gottlieb's ICE FEVER (Feb 85).

During this time, Williams, with the help of a string of pinball hits, became the leader of the Industry. It all started back in late 1980 with FIREPOWER and BLACK KNIGHT, topping it all off with the release of HIGH SPEED.

HIGH SPEED was the first pinball to feature a progressive jackpot (see Multiball, in Chapter Eleven). It also introduced the backbox ornament, a flashing red light in this case, which over the years has taken many different forms; from a fan on WHIRLWIND (1990) to a fish on FISH TALES (1992). HIGH SPEED was so popular that it was released as a pinball home video game in 1991 for Nintendo. It was also re-released by Williams in 1992 as THE GETAWAY; with some differences, such as an electro-magnetic ball accelerator called the Supercharger. Lastly, HIGH SPEED also had something new to offer the operator; Average Replay Percentaging; ARP for short.

See next page for caption.

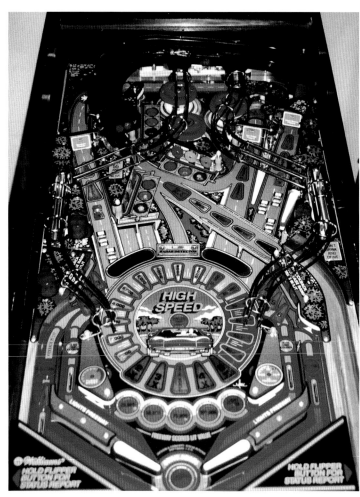

There was always that fine line between keeping the replay value low enough to allow players a reasonable chance of a free game, and hence keep the players paying and playing; but not too low as to award too many free plays. ARP now took care of that.

Upper playfield detail of THE GETAWAY showing that famous ball accelerator loop.

Williams' HIGH SPEED (1986), a tremendously successful game. The first pinball by Williams to use alphanumeric displays (Gottlieb was first in 1985), but more importantly the first pinball in the industry to feature a progressive jackpot feature during multiball, average replay percentaging and a backbox ornament, clearly visible in the photo. **See previous page for backglass.** *Mark Gibson collection.* $475-600.

Pinballs have never come with a factory-set replay score; it has always been adjustable. Manuals accompanying each pinball stated a recommended replay value for either a three- or five-ball setting; but it has ultimately been the operator who has chosen a setting that he/she felt was most suitable for his/her business and clients.

Williams' THE GETAWAY (1992), the remake of the highly successful HIGH SPEED. The playfield has almost exactly the same layout, except for the "supercharger", a magnetic ball accelerator loop. Other extras not in the original include a video mode and a plunger gear shift lever where the player had to change gears during play. $725-875.

After the operator set the initial replay score, the pinball's computer would do the rest. It would automatically adjust the replay value, higher or lower, depending on how many free games had been awarded to players in comparison to paid games.

ARP also made the score card redundant. The card, advising players of the replay score, was usually situated on the bottom panel below the flippers. With ARP it could no longer be used, due to the constant changing of the replay score. The replay value was now displayed on the score board with the use of alphanumerics. "Replay at 1,500,000" for instance. I remember the first time I played HIGH SPEED, the first thing I did was to look at what I thought was the score card. Having read the instructions which said, "Refer to backglass for replay value," I ended up looking for another score card on the backglass, not knowing a great deal about alphanumerics at that stage.

ARP, or some other form of automatic replay score adjustment, became very much the standard for all pinballs very quickly. Unfortunately, from a player's perspective, it was not all such a good idea, especially when the new innovation started being abused by the operators. Most operators skipped the average and percentage bits, so that the machine increased the replay values immediately after it had been beaten, but they never decreased. The worst cases involved beating a pinball's replay value to receive a free game, but the new replay value then became your own highest score! In other words, in order to receive a free game, you had to beat the highest score that was set by you or someone else. It is always a good idea to check the replay value before inserting your hard-earned money!

Bally's DR. DUDE (1991). If one wasn't to busy playing pinball, there was plenty to read on the backglass. Bally usually lined up their alphanumeric displays in a line at the bottom of the backbox. *Jan J. Svach collection.* $700-850.

These new alphanumeric pinballs also had what is known as a Status Report. The status mode, which has now become a standard feature on all pinballs since, could be activated during play by trapping the ball on either flipper, and holding the two flipper buttons down. The status mode, advised the player of his/her current standing by way of the alphanumeric display: "Replay at 1,500,000", "Jackpot value at 400,000", "Bonus value at 50,000", "Current Ramp value at 25,000", etc etc.

Flipper instructions on the score-card plate of an alphanumeric game from 1988, showing the status report feature first introduced with this style of display.

The alphanumeric display, unlike its predecessors, only lasted just under six years. The new face of scoring appeared on Data East's CHECKPOINT in February 1991; the dot matrix display.

Williams was the next to use the new display on TERMINATOR 2 in July 1991, followed by Bally with PARTY ZONE in August 1991, and bringing up the rear more than a year later was Gottlieb with SUPER MARIO BROTHERS, released in April 1992.

The last alphanumeric games from the major companies are as follows: Data East's THE SIMPSONS (Oct 1990), Bally's HARLEY DAVIDSON (Feb 1991), Williams' THE MACHINE (Feb 1991) and Gottlieb's OPERATION THUNDER (March 1992).

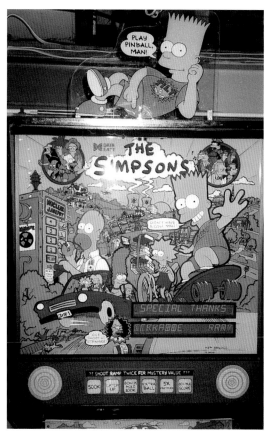

Data East's THE SIMPSONS (1990), the last alphanumeric pinball from this company. *Jan J. Svach collection.*

An extreme close up of a dot matrix display. Now you know were the name comes from. One inch covers approximately 11 dots both vertically and horizontally.

Dot matrix is immeasurably superior to alphanumerics. The new display was the equivalent of having a TV screen in the backbox, like Universal had 12 years earlier! The standard dot matrix display, as the name suggests, is made up of thousands of dots, each about 0.05" in diameter. The overall size of the standard display, is approximately 3" high by 13" wide, whereas the original Data East displays were only about half the height, although the same width. The dots within are evenly spaced and for a total of around 4,000 for each unit!

William's THE MACHINE: BRIDE OF PINBOT (1991). The last pinball built by Williams with an alphanumeric display. *Jan J. Svach collection.* $600-725.

OPERATION: THUNDER™

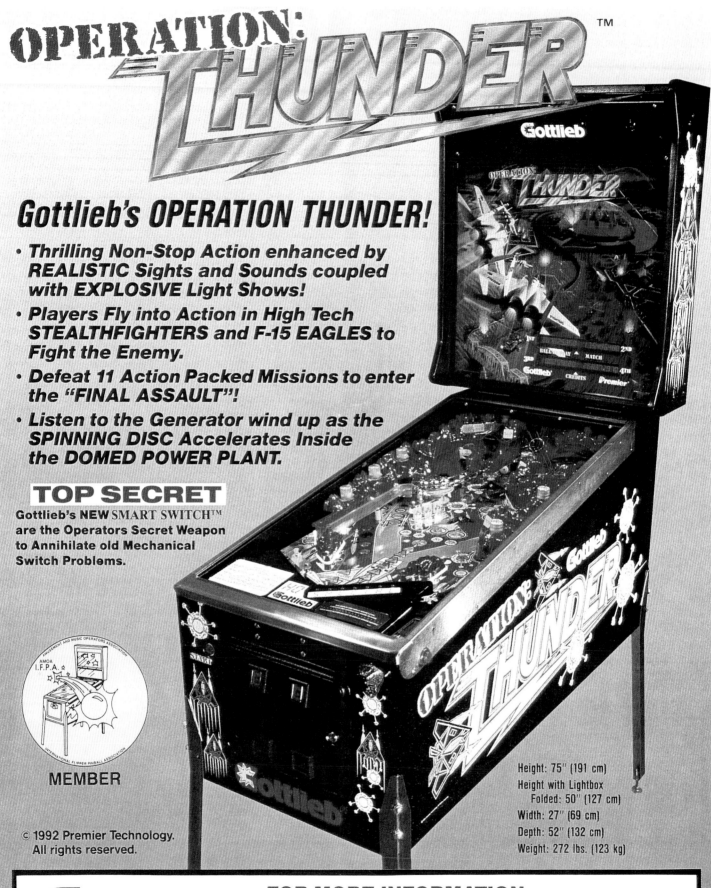

Gottlieb's OPERATION THUNDER!

- **Thrilling Non-Stop Action enhanced by REALISTIC Sights and Sounds coupled with EXPLOSIVE Light Shows!**
- **Players Fly into Action in High Tech STEALTHFIGHTERS and F-15 EAGLES to Fight the Enemy.**
- **Defeat 11 Action Packed Missions to enter the "FINAL ASSAULT"!**
- **Listen to the Generator wind up as the SPINNING DISC Accelerates Inside the DOMED POWER PLANT.**

TOP SECRET

Gottlieb's **NEW** SMART SWITCH™ are the Operators Secret Weapon to Annihilate old Mechanical Switch Problems.

MEMBER

© 1992 Premier Technology.
All rights reserved.

Height: 75" (191 cm)
Height with Lightbox
Folded: 50" (127 cm)
Width: 27" (69 cm)
Depth: 52" (132 cm)
Weight: 272 lbs. (123 kg)

There have been very few pinballs that have had a different colored display in the dot matrix. The standard display emits an amber colored light; much the same as the old digital scores and is changed simply by inserting a tinted plastic cover over its front. Even Gottlieb surrendered its trademark blue display, but most of their pinballs still used a tinted cover. So did one particular pinball offered by Williams with a variant in colour, DRACULA released in 1993. It had a red display.

The dot matrix display has added a little more fun and enjoyment to the game, with lively and truly original animation. The best spin-off to emerge from dot matrix has been the video mode. The video mode is usually obtained by completing certain scoring features and then is activated by "locking" the ball, normally in a kickout saucer or cellar hole. The video mode is exactly what it means; one plays a short video game shown on the dot matrix display while the ball is held captive. After the game is finished, usually not lasting longer than 30 seconds, the ball is released, and the pinball game resumes. During this time, the flipper button and the electronic plunger button become the joystick equivalent. There is always a short description on the score display describing what to do and what to use for the game just prior to the mode commencing.

Not every video mode starts while the ball is safely tucked away. On quite a few Data East pinballs (now Sega) one must attempt to co-ordinate pinball play with video mode play, which in most cases involves shooting someone or something with the plunger trigger or button, while still trying to play the ball.

Williams was the first to incorporate a video mode on TERMINATOR 2 (1991), Data East, probably not realizing to what extent they could have used the new technology, missed out. Not every pinball manufactured with dot matrix has incorporated a video mode. However, at the completion of this book (Appendix One) a list has been compiled, with the numerous different video modes and a brief description for each.

Thus ends the journey of discovery through the amusement adding machine. The dot matrix system and its duration of use has already lasted longer than the previous alphanumeric display, but its longevity may be less than assured. With the release of Williams' new "Pinball 2000" game designs early in 1999, a new generation of score displays may soon take over. Nevertheless, so long as the game of pinball remains alive, I may very well be writing another pinball book describing the dot matrix display to a new generation of players with the same historical twist that I have used for the old drum reels of yesteryear.

Summary

1934 Automatic scoring first appears in the form clock counters.
1935-36 The small backglass appears and light-up scoring is introduced.
1937 Automatic scoring becomes an essential part of pinball.
1938 The full size backglass appears along with backglass animation.
1953 Drum score reels first appear on pinballs.
1954 First multiple player game is produced by Gottlieb using score reels.
1957 Pinballs begin using a match feature at end of game.
1961 Last American pinball built with light-up scoring.
1966 French company Rally produces the first pinball with digital scoring.
1976-77 With SS technology introduced, drum score reels are replaced by digital score displays and 99% of all pinballs produced now have a four-player capacity.
1981 Most pinballs now have a score capacity up to 9,999,990 points.
1985 Alphanumeric displays introduced.
1986 Automatic replay percentaging (ARP) introduced.
1991 Dot matrix displays introduced along with a video mode feature.

Dot matrix display panel from Williams' INDIANA JONES (1993), giving the player tips on how to tackle the video mode.

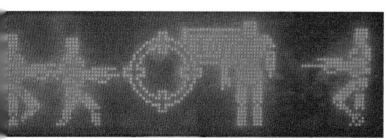

A scene of the first pinball video mode from Williams' TERMINATOR 2 (1991). The object of the game was to shoot all the advancing cyborgs before they shot you. *Photo courtesy of Ivo Vasella.*

Opposite page: Gottlieb became the first manufacturer to use alphanumeric displays in 1985. They also became the last to drop this type of display in favor of dot matrix displays. OPERATION THUNDER (1992) was the last alphanumeric pinball from them. *Courtesy of Gottlieb Development LLC. All rights reserved. $475-575.*

Bally's CIRQUS VOLTAIRE (1997). Notice anything missing on the backglass? What is missing is the score display. It was removed and placed at the back of the playfield, as one can see in this photo. A sign of things to come? Perhaps not. $2200-2500.

Chapter Seven

Plungers, Skill Shots and Lane Change

Outhole view of Gottlieb's ICE REVUE (1965), a classic "push up" pinball.

Three headings for the price of one. Plungers, skill shots and lane change are all in some way connected to each other, the last of which however has absolutely nothing to do with changing traffic lanes on the freeway on the way home from work.

The plunger is the mechanism used for sending the ball into play. It was first introduced on bagatelle games back in 1871, and has evolved with the game ever since. This spring-loaded device, known then as a "ball shooter", gave the player a form of mechanical ball control. Pull the lever back to exactly the same spot every time, and one knew how the ball was going to react; these were the first skill shots. Mastering the plunger shot was very important to pinball players of the 1930s. It was the first and last chance that they had of affecting the ball's future course, not taking into account the unpredictable action of nudging.

To facilitate a more accurate plunger skill shot, graduated gauges were incorporated on some pinballs at first, then on all. The gauge was fitted on the left-hand side of the plunger lane or sometimes placed over the whole lane with a slotted window in the middle to allow the plunger tip to be seen. If the first shot was too hard, having pulled back the plunger to the fourth graduation say, then the next shot could be tried from the third, and so on. Some German manufacturers went as far as putting gauges graduated in millimeters on their pinballs! This was extremely accurate, providing one let go of the plunger with exactly the same grip or in the same manner every time.

The plunger skill shot lost some of its importance with the removal of the scoring hole and the introduction of the coil bumper. When disc bumpers replaced the coil, the plunger shot was once again back in vogue. Now that the new plastic-capped bumpers could be hit, and lit, the importance of avoiding certain bumpers in favor of others reinstated the calculated plunger shot.

Top rollover lanes have become almost as standard an inclusion on pinballs as flippers and bumpers. Even on some of the more recent games, one can find the now typical set of three lanes just above the bumpers at the extreme top of the playfield. By the middle of the 1960s the pinball playfield had assumed the modern look that most people today can associate with. Flippers were located near the outhole, with slingshots side by side, and two outlanes either side of those. Bulls eye targets, or maybe even drop targets, and kickout saucers lay in mid-field; thumper bumpers in the upper mid-field, and at the very top, a line of rollover lanes; and the occasional kickout saucer right in the center.

Color-coded top rollover lanes on Williams' CABARET (1969). *Photo courtesy of Ivo Vasella.*

A close up from an old Gottlieb woodrail pinball c. 1958, showing the plunger (or shooter) gauge. Notice also the entry point into the plunger lane from the manual ball lift.

Upper playfield view of Gottlieb's GOLDEN ARROW (1978). An unusual set out of spinners and top rollover lanes. Spinners are seldom found up this far, but notice the left #1 rollover lane tucked in behind the rebound rubber—a very challenging plunger skill shot.

Upper playfield view of Gottlieb's TEXAN (1960). The 1 to 5 value of the two top rollover lanes corresponded to the current value of the game's roto-target.

A good plunger shot was like an entree before the flipper's main course. Land in that hard-to-get kickout saucer or roll down that hard-to-get top rollover lane before anything else, and one had a good start, otherwise it would have been hard work for the flippers.

The most common strategy behind top rollover lanes, and rollover lanes in general, has basically remained the same over the years: to complete the set during the course of the game, or each ball, depending on the rules. On some pinballs, for example, having completed all the lanes, the player would be awarded an extra ball. On others, the target values may have been increased; the permutations of these rules have been numerous.

Upper playfield of Gottlieb's SHIP MATES (1964) showing the top rollover lanes. The lanes increased the value of the game's roto target from 1x to 10X, and even to a staggering 100X! Plunging the ball just right, plus a few good nudges, and the player is on the way to a good start.

Gottlieb's SHIP MATES, the complete view. *Ivo Vasella collection.*
$400-500.

How does a player keep a count of which lanes have been completed? Located at the top entry of each lane, there is almost always a light bulb under the playfield which when lit, indicates that the lane has been "rolled over". However, on a number of pinballs the reverse is the case. All lanes are lit at the start of each ball and will go out as the player completes them.

There is always an exception to every rule. While a large percentage of pinballs use and have used a set of rollover lanes at the very top of the playfield, Bally's HI-DEAL (1975) had none! It used a spread of tiny rollover buttons. The game was released at approximately the same time as the film release of *King Kong*, which explains the backglass somewhat. *Denis Bowler collection.* $350-425.

On Gottlieb's SOLAR RIDE (1979) the player had to complete the playfield's four top rollover lanes in sequence at the start of each ball in order to increase the bonus multiplier. The first lane that had to be scored was always the first on the left. The easiest way to get it, was from a calculated plunger shot, otherwise it was hard work trying with the flippers. Fortunately the game had a wire gate which allowed the player to hit the ball back into the plunger lane for another attempt.

Gottlieb's ICE REVUE (1965). The top rollovers on this game were a main feature. Completing each lane lit the corresponding bumper for increased scoring. When all the lanes were completed, one lane would light for special. *Graham McGuiness collection.* $550-675.

ICE REVUE

HITTING TOP ROLLOVERS LIGHTS CORESPONDING BUMPER.
LIGHTING ALL BUMPERS LIGHTS TOP ROLLOVER FOR SPECIAL.
TARGETS 1-2-5-6 LIGHT BOTTOM ROLLOVERS
WHEN ALL 6 TARGETS ARE MADE, HOLES SCORE INCREASED
VALUE AS INDICATED.
SPECIAL AWARDS ONE REPLAY.

1100..	1 REPLAY
1500..	2 REPLAYS
1600..	3 REPLAYS
1700..	4 REPLAYS

221   A-9401-2

The instruction card for ICE REVUE explains further.

Playfield detail from Gottlieb's ICE REVUE.

Backglass and playfield details from Gottlieb's ICE REVUE.

When playing Bally's SUPERSONIC (1979) one had to complete all five lanes (not necessarily in order) to increase playfield scoring. The game could remember from ball to ball which lanes had been lit, so players did not have to start from the beginning at the commencement of each ball. The top middle lane (marked as # 2) was by far the hardest to get by flipper shot—it was again a job for the plunger. My friends and I knew exactly how far to pull back the plunger tip in order to eliminate that obstacle, all made easier with the use of the gauge.

Countless numbers of pinballs, like SUPERSONIC, have used a playfield ball entry design which first appeared with the very earliest of bagatelle games; the "top arch". The top arch lies at the very top of the playfield, and as the name suggests, it spans this upper area in an arch. Once the ball is plunged, it enters the upper

Backglass and backglass detail from Bally's SUPERSONIC (1979). The playfield illustration of this game can be found in Chapter One. The object of the game was to complete the numbered targets and rollovers in order to increase playfield scoring. The #2 top rollover lane (top center) was best scored with an accurately measured plunger shot using the shooter gauge mounted in the plunger lane. $325-425.

playfield through a one-way gate, the start of the arch. The ball makes it way across the top of the playfield hugging this curve, due to its centrifugal force. Hitting a rebound device on the other side, the ball then heads back from where it came; backwards and forwards until the momentum is lost, in which case it then drops and bounces around the entry point of any number of top rollover lanes. Plunge the ball with force, or softly, and one can control the number of rebounds the ball makes (if any) along the top arch before it drops onto the playfield in the desired location ready for a gentle nudge into the proper rollover lane. Not all games have been built this way however, and one will learn more of this in the paragraphs to come. Some of the more flamboyant game designers did away with both top arches and rollover lanes! Other game designers were not so drastic in their attempts to create something out of the ordinary, keeping both features intact, but changing their posi-

GALAXY instruction card explains all.

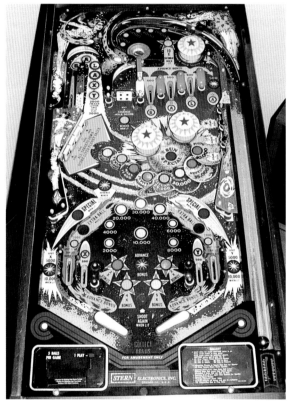

tion and construction just enough to surprise the unsuspecting player. One such designer was non other than Harry Williams, and the game in this case was Stern's GALAXY (1980). Harry removed the all-important rebound rubber, and curved the left side of the top arch so that it provided a slingshot effect to the ball. The player could no longer plunge the ball with a full stroke unintentionally, for it would send the ball flying over the entire row of top rollover lanes, enter a small scoop positioned on the far right of the playfield that then re-directed the ball, sending it hurtling towards the flippers. Ouch! What a surprise for the first time player!

GALAXY backglass detail.

Center left & bottom left: Stern's GALAXY (1980). When a game is designed by none other than Harry Williams, it's sure to be interesting. This game incorporated an unusual top arch design, which made players think twice about how they would plunge the ball into play. *Tony and Clare Moore collection.* $325-400.

A closer look at the unusual top arch design on Stern's GALAXY.

Digressing slightly from the main subject now, is to discuss a quite significant, but often over-looked part of pinball history; the mechanical ball lift.

Since the early days of pinball, where one received ten balls to play for five cents, up until 1966, where one played five balls for a slightly higher price, the ball lift was the mechanical device operated manually by the player to move the ball up onto the playfield from underneath, and into position in front of the plunger. After 1966 the device was replaced by the ball return kicker; a solenoid placed in the outhole used to eject the ball back into the plunger lane. The ball lift was always found just under the plunger and was similar in appearance. The routine that players had to go through at the start of each ball was to first push in the ball lift, and then pull the plunger. With the introduction of the ball return kicker, one played the same ball over and over again (not counting multiball games) with the machine keeping count until the end of the game. Not so with the older ball lift "push-up" games. A five-ball game meant that there were five separate balls to be played. The balls would be held on a metal track called the ball trough, used to guide them to the front of the ball lift. Lift the ball; plunge it; play it; and on many games, when it drained into the outhole, it would remain in full view to the player in a smaller trough, a reminder of how many balls had been played.

The internal workings of a mechanical (or manual) ball lift. Notice the spring-loaded, rubber tipped plunger shaft directly above.

Photograph showing the mechanical ball lift push handle situated under the plunger. A common sight on pinballs that were built before the introduction of the ball return kicker in the mid-1960s.

An upper ball trough displaying the "balls played" sign. Before the introduction of the ball return kicker, a five-ball game meant that there were actually five balls in total. The balls were held in this upper compartment until a new game was started, in which case they would then all drop into a lower trough that led to the manual ball lift. The particular design on this Gottlieb pinball always reminds me of an undertaker carting the dead balls away.

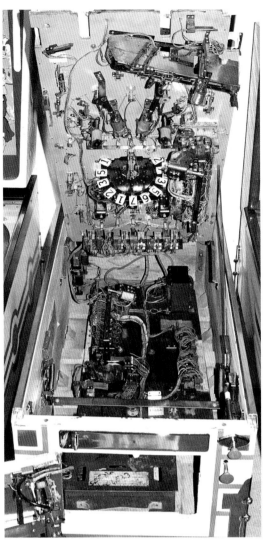

The guts of Gottlieb's BUCKAROO (1965). Notice the ball trough on the top right corner and how much room it occupied. All this was removed with the introduction of the ball return kicker. *Courtesy of Mark Jackson.*

The number of machines with mechanical ball lifts began declining in 1963, and by 1967 they had become a thing of the past. The removal of the ball lift and trough made room for the three-piece chime unit, which then became the standard "sound" device on all EM pinballs.

See next page for caption.

Several views of a ball return kicker and how it works. The weight of the ball landing on the outhole switch energizes the solenoid. The energized coil draws in the plunger and with the aid of a lever arm, the ball is kicked out and is retuned to the plunger lane.

The plunger skill shot also became a thing of the past when Williams released FIREPOWER in March 1980, introducing "Lane Change" to the world of pinball. It is a feature that allows the player to rearrange the lit lanes by using the flipper buttons. It does not matter how hard or how soft one shoots the ball into play; one can skillfully manipulate the lights allowing the ball to

Williams' FIREPOWER (1980), the first to introduce the "lane change" feature on the top rollover lanes and the first SS pinball with multiball (see Chapter Eleven). It was also the second machine produced with speech after the success of GORGAR. *Rick Force/Jim Whitemyer collections.* $385-400.

Bally's HARVEST (1964). While Gottlieb games like BUCKAROO and ICE REVUE still had "push up" mechanical ball lifts, Bally had already converted to the newer ball return mechanisms on most of their machines, like this one for example. **See previous page for backglass.** *Courtesy of Mark Gibson.* $475-575.

enter through an unlit lane, thus rendering the plunger skill shot obsolete. More recently, on pinballs like Bally's HARLEY DAVIDSON (1990), the lane change was even incorporated on the out and return lanes. Top rollover lanes and lane change still form part of the modern pinball play strategy, but have diminished somewhat in their importance.

Williams' BLACKOUT (1980), the next game produced after FIREPOWER and the second to include lane change. Much to the disgust of the of the purists, who declared it took away the skill of a well-placed plunger shot or nudge, it looked like lane change was here to stay. $475-575.

Following a five-year absence, the plunger skill shot was reinstated—this time officially! The skill shot had become a little game all in itself. Not forming part of the playfield, it tested the player's skill as always. Plunging the ball haphazardly, as one had become accustomed to doing with lane change, could lose valuable points. Shoot too hard or too soft and receive little, shoot just right and one was well rewarded. Williams' PINBOT (1986) uses a spiraling ramp. Bally's FIREBALL CLASSIC (1985) uses the same tricky ascending ramp shot as on its previous FIREBALL released in 1972; while Williams' POLICE FORCE (1989) uses a spinner attached inside the plunger lane. This spinner, being a little bottom-heavy, can only spin a certain number of times before coming to rest. It is used as an equivalent of a prize wheel. As the spinner spins, playfield values marked inside the plunger lane also light on and off in sequence. When the spinner stops, the lit value is the prize awarded.

Scorecard plate on Williams' DRACULA (1993) advising players of the trademarked "Lane Change" feature.

Incidentally, the tricky ramp shot used in FIREBALL is similar to that first used on Bally's FOUR MILLION BC (1971), which was known then as the "cliff-hanger" shot. FOUR MILLION BC is perhaps best known for its peculiar runway, one that has been rarely used in pinball design history. Instead of the usual plunger runway (which sent the ball up to the top arch from the right-hand

The colorful playfield of Bally's SKATEBALL (1980), utilizing the breakaway plunger lane. This design gave the game extra playfield area. *Courtesy of Tim Van Blarcom* $475-550.

side), it was shortened, and at about one third of the way up, bent approximately 30 degrees towards the playfield at the tip. This diagonal plunger shot (occasionally termed the "breakaway") meant that after pulling back the plunger all the way and letting go as normal, the ball would enter the playfield one-third of the way up, but then, almost defying gravity, it would shoot diagonally across a bare playfield with no form of guide, reaching the end of its run at the arched opening on the left. This variation was also successfully used on Bally's LOOP THE LOOP (1965), Williams' FLASH (Mar 1979) and again on Bally's SKATEBALL (1980).

At the beginning of 1991, 120 years after the plunger was invented, the familiar springed shaft and knob was replaced by a button. The ball could now be shot into play electronically, with the slight touch of a finger, or by the pull of a trigger; as the most popular electronic plunger has taken the form of a gun grip and trigger rather than just a large button. This gun grip plunger first appeared on Williams' TERMINATOR 2.

The old style plunger has not been discarded entirely, however. It has appeared on recent games, such as Bally's THEATRE OF MAGIC (1995) and CIRQUS VOLITARE (1997), Williams' TALES OF THE ARABIAN NIGHTS (1996), and Sega's MAVERICK (1994), based on the so titled movie.

Having just stated that the electronic plunger (EP) was introduced in 1991, I will now contradict myself by saying that the idea was far from being a new one. Before the likes of TERMINATOR 2, one could launch the ball from the plunger lane by using the right flipper button, that is if one was playing Gottlieb's SPRING BREAK (1987), four years before the EP became a standard item.

MAVERICK backglass detail.

Sega's MAVERICK (1994). This game was built during the Data East/ Sega changeover. The plunger knob still carries the Data East logo but the pinball was marketed as a Sega. The plunger is manual and not the prevalent electronic type. The plunger lane is an elevated ramp with three skill holes. At the start of each ball the player has to skillfully plunge the ball into the lit hole to collect the "skill shot" prize. $1000-1200.

Similarly, Bell Games' F1 GRAND PRIX (1987) introduced some industry firsts; some of them are still unique today. With no plunger, the ball is launched into play again by pressing the right flipper button, while a set of three horizontally revolving targets and a disappearing spinner target makes this Bell Games' most complete and complicated game. It was a big step forward for an Italian company who was better known for manufacturing conversion kits, but unfortunately the game had very little playability. Even so, one can still look further back than this.

A type of electronic plunger had been invented way back in 1950 by none other than Harry Mabs, the inventor of the flipper. What Mr. Mabs designed was not exactly the same as the modern EP; it was perhaps a bit more complicated. The device was termed

Gottlieb's SELECT-A-CARD (1950), one of a few games built by Gottlieb that featured a turret shooter. The ball was shot from the outhole by pressing either of the flipper buttons. *Courtesy of Russ Jensen.* $450-550.

the "turret shooter". The few pinballs built by Gottlieb with this device—first JUST 21, SELECT-A-CARD, then BANK-A-BALL—shot the ball not from a plunger lane (the conventional plunger and plunger lane did not exist on these games) but from the outhole, in between the flippers.

The turret shooter was engaged by using the flipper buttons. What made the shooter so different was that one could also aim and shoot the ball in the direction desired. A pointer at the outhole, which continually oscillated back and forth within a 40-degree range, indicated ball direction at any given time if the flipper buttons were pressed. All one had to do was to decide when to fire. This would explain why the term "turret" had been used, as the word itself describes a self-contained structure, capable of rotation, in which weapons are mounted, especially in tanks and warships.

JUST 21 and the rest of the Gottlieb gang were radically different in regards to playfield design, having wide-open playfields with targets lined up along the rear and sides of the cabinet, with absolutely nothing to obstruct the way of the shooter. A good example is BANK-A-BALL, which is in a sense a miniature pool table with flippers. Having a green playfield and kickout saucers placed where the pockets would be, it cannot be mistaken for anything else other than a "pinball pool table".

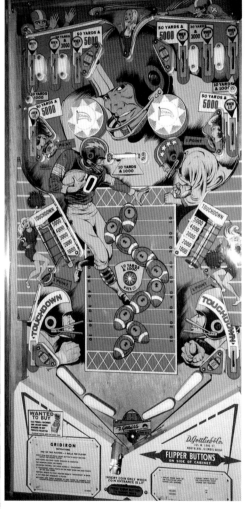

Gottlieb's GRIDIRON (1978), a copy of PRO FOOTBALL. With a production run of just over 1000 units, it was the last EM pinball from Gottlieb to use this game design. *Jeff Grummel collection.* $350-425.

Gottlieb's PRO FOOTBALL (1973). Not a typical pinball, as one can see upon closer inspection. With no plunger, the ball was shot from between the flippers. It was somewhat similar to games like SELECT-A-CARD and JUST 21, with one major difference being the absence of a turret shooter; the ball was shot out in the same direction without any player control. Gottlieb used this game design several times during the 1970s on games like PLAYBALL (1971) and BIG HIT (1977). *Michael Tansell collection.* $375-450.

After 1950, the turret shooter reappeared on Midway's RO-DEO and FLYING TURNS, both released in 1964, both with the same open playfield, but the latter equipped with a separate button for the "new ball aiming shooter" as it was called. Other turret shooter games a la Gottlieb mode included Williams' DERBY DAY (1967) and HAYBURNERS II (1968), and Chicago Coin's HIGH SCORE POOL (1971).

With the arrival of electronic plungers, the turret shooter again became a novelty item. This time, it is not a means of delivering the ball onto the playfield (a standard electronic plunger takes care of that), but as an added playfield feature not restricted to the outhole.

First used on Williams' TERMINATOR 2, the turret shooter (or ball gun as most players call it) really lives up to its name this time. Located just above the game's breakaway plunger exit and two inches above the playfield surface, the gun can be loaded by shooting the ball into the top kickout saucer, which then loads the gun via a ramp. In order to start multiball, one has to shoot the loaded gun (using the plunger trigger) as it oscillates back and fourth, aiming at a bank of five bullseye targets across the other side of the playfield. Hit the designated flashing target and multiball starts. The voice of Arnold Schwarzenegger speaks out just before reaching this stage saying, "Take your best shot...Fire at will." Because this turret shooter is an added extra placed above the playfield, the overall design of the game was not compromised in order to accommodate it. Other games with this feature include Bally's BLACK ROSE (1992), with the ball being shot from beneath the playfield like a surface to air missile; Williams' DIRTY HARRY (1995) and STAR TREK T.N.G (1993)—the latter boasting a set of two; and Sega's STAR WARS TRILOGY (1997), where the ball is shot from an X-wing fighter model. All of these, of course, have the same oscillating movement.

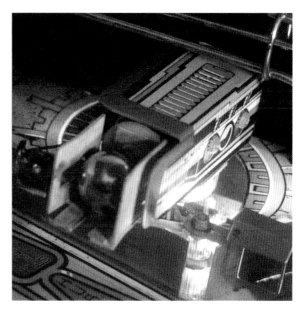

A close up view of that famous ball gun on Williams' TERMINATOR 2.

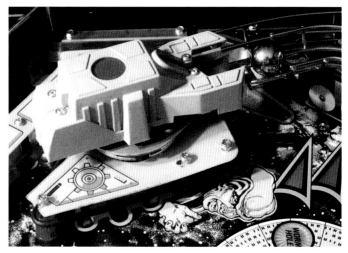

Another ball gun, this time from the playfield of Williams' STAR TREK T.N.G (1993), seen here being loaded. This particular game had two!

Williams' TERMINATOR 2 (1991), a truly awesome pinball. This game was famous for its ball gun, located on the right hand side of the playfield and the electronic plunger's pistol grip. It was an arcade essential. Designed by Steve Ritchie, it was the first Williams pinball to include a dot matrix display, but more importantly the first in the industry to incorporate a video mode. $775-950.

With introduction of the electronic plunger, like the turret shooter, skill shots requiring the right touch were no longer viable because the player could not change the velocity with which the ball ejected. It was now all a matter of timing. Like a miniature video mode, some skill shots were tied in to scenes taking place on the dot matrix display. Others did away with the plunger skill shot altogether by sending the ball immediately to the flipper for a "flipper skill shot" requiring the player to hit a specific target before any other. One of my favorite video skill shots was that of Sega's FRANKENSTEIN (1994). This pinball's plunger button is that of an old-style electrical switch, like in those old horror movies. On the dot matrix display, a Jacob's ladder-type animation shows a bolt of electricity jumping unpredictably up and down between award values. Wait for the lightning to jump onto a high value, then throw the switch!

The gear stick plunger on Williams' THE GETAWAY (1992). Not only was this lever used to launch the ball into play, it was also used to shift gears while the ball was in play, not to mention its use during the game's video mode.

We know for a fact that not every pinball ever built has had a plunger. This was revealed earlier, but nevertheless such a game is always bound to extract comments from a first time player like "where is the plunger on this thing!?" Those were the exact words uttered by many a player when confronted by one pinball released in 1982, Bally's SPECTRUM.

SPECTRUM was a pinball experiment that failed. It failed because the game strategies were too complex to be understood by the average player; it was a "mind game" pinball, and after all, that is not what amusement machines were all about. Unfortunately it will be remembered by most as the game that had no plunger.

The game design was based on a popular two-player board game called "Mastermind", which I remember reaching its height in popularity in the late 1970s. One player set a colour code using a set of colored pegs (yellow, red, blue and green), while the other player tried to break this code in the least number of attempts, with the help of some standard cryptic clues given by the opponent as the game progressed. SPECTRUM was a simplified version of this, where the pinball set the color code and the player had to guess which colour was in what position, and just like the board game, the pinball handed out clues along the way to expedite the process.

At the start of each game, the pinball would choose a colour combination; for argument's sake lets say it was red-green-blue-red (the same colour could be used more than once). The ball was shot into play from between the flippers by a kickout saucer. This was triggered by the right flipper button, or shot automatically by the machine after a brief period. The player then made an attempt to guess the first colour in the code by knocking down sets of colored drop targets. Each of the four colours were represented by a bank of three drop targets; knocking down two out of three targets is the way one made a guess. The bank would then reset and your guess was registered on a massive bank of lights located centrally in the lower half of the playfield. This was known as the "computer code array", listing each guess (correct and incorrect) for each of the code's components and colour (four colours in four positions) for three complete sets of guesses (three columns). That's a total of 48 separate indicator lights! Does all this sound a bit confusing? It took a while to understand the rules, which was the biggest problem. On top of this, SPECTRUM had a playfield layout that took some getting used to. Apart from no plunger and plunger lane, the playfield had no outlanes, a large gap between the flippers, and two very long "hidden" return lanes which commenced at the top of the playfield. On top of this it was also an add-a-ball game!

SPECTRUM was designed by Claude Fernandez, who also designed games like FLASH GORDON, ELEKTRA, and BABY PAC-MAN. It had a production run of approximately 990 machines, with rumors of a significant number of machines never being sold. After poor sales, about half of the machines were disassembled and the parts returned to inventory. I sometimes wonder, that maybe all of this could have been avoided if only the game had been built with a standard plunger!

See next page for caption.

Backglass detail from Bally's SPECTRUM (1982), one of the most misunderstood games in the history of pinball. Based on the then popular *Mastermind* game, it was too complicated for players to understand and thus fared poorly in the arcades. Because of this, it has become a sought-after pinball over the years. *Courtesy of Carl Heller.* $500-625.

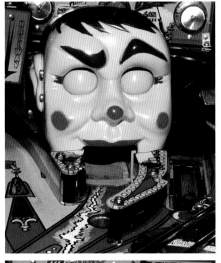

Williams' FUN HOUSE (1990); this game is watching you! The game's most striking feature was the use of a dummy's head (Rudy) on the playfield. Second to this, and probably more unusual than striking, was the use of two plungers. If one thought pinball was fun to play, than this game made it even more so. One of my all-time favorites. **See previous page for backglass.** *Phillip Brown collection.* $800-900.

The many facial expressions of the amazing Rudy. *Photos courtesy of Phillip Brown.*

The next chapter departs from all the gadgets, gizmoes and inventions to take a look at what has made pinballs look appealing over the years: the art of pinball.

Summary

1871 The plunger is introduced on bagatelle games.
1950 Turret shooter first used.
1963-1966 Mechanical ball lifts replaced by ball return kickers.
1980 Lane Change introduced.
1985 Plunger skill shots used on pinballs.
1991 Electronic plungers become a standard feature on pinballs.

Chapter Eight

Pinball Art

Backglass detail from Bally's MATA HARI (1978), a great piece of pinball art.

Sometimes the smallest detail on a backglass can prove to be the most interesting. This little fish, found on the backglass of Bally's FATHOM (1981) is just over 1" long.

Pinballs have long since been more than just a game, they are works of art! After all, can you imagine the appeal of playing a blank machine, devoid of all colour and design? The use of colour and a particular design style to best reflect the theme is like any form of advertising. Best represented in all its glory, the backglass is like the game's billboard, a hanging masterpiece to which people approach gazing upon it, digesting the details, before looking at the playfield below. It's the combination of design and colour that can be an irresistible attraction to such sensitive and appreciative beings as ourselves, inviting us to come forward and take a closer look. However, like all artwork, what appeals to one may not necessarily appeal to another.

The positive effect on both mood and behaviour in the presence of the aesthetically pleasing can never be underestimated. The reverse is also true; the types of subjects represented and how they are presented are a great determinant of the game's attractiveness and general appeal, and it's a bonus when the game plays well. Having played a new machine, it's not unusual to either make or hear the comment, "Good game, 'shame the artwork isn't better" or "Great artwork, shame about the game." Meanwhile, those games that apparently have all the right ingredients are a pleasure to play.

The earliest machines; the 1920s bagatelles were indeed devoid of all artwork, consisting essentially of the materials required to construct the game, wood and metal pins, without any elaboration other than the values shown for each scoring hole. However, by the 1930s, manufacturers were becoming more innovative and a greater emphasis was placed on artwork. Though extremely simplistic initially, consisting of bright colours arranged in eye-catch-

ing shapes and patterns, the artwork was becoming increasingly more detailed. Manufacturers began seeing it as a way of distinguishing their games from those of another. Images and themes were being introduced and explored, such as Rock-ola's WORLD'S FAIR JIG-SAW (1933). Commemorating the World's Fair in Chicago, an image of the fairgrounds appeared on pieces of a jigsaw that flipped up as balls landed in the corresponding score holes; the obvious aim was to complete the puzzle.

The artwork until the mid 1930s had been confined to the perimeters of the playfield, but with the introduction of electricity and the backbox, the scope broadened. Used to incorporate automatic scoring, scores were illuminated by small light bulbs placed strategically behind the backglass. It provided a greater area for artistic application, but it also had to include the scores, which were usually assimilated in some very creative ways. Scores had a fanned appearance on Chicago Coin's TOPPER (1939), or shined more unobtrusively as the lit clams on Genco's FLOATING POWER (1948), and were integrated into the colored stripes of the circus tent on BIG TOP (1949), again by Genco.

Backglass detail from Genco's METRO (1940). The letters on the wall represent the A-B-C rollover lanes situated on the lower playfield. METRO is an early example of artwork by Roy Parker. He would later join up with Gottlieb for a great art romp through the 60s. Unfortunately he died later than same decade. METRO, a city of the future, with art-deco cars and planes. The game name and artwork has always reminded me of Fritz Lang's 1927 film *Metropolis*. Maybe there is some connection? *Courtesy of Russ Jensen.*

Genco's BIG TOP (1949), with the backglass showing how the score numbers are integrated into the artwork. *Courtesy of Russ Jensen.* $350-450.

By this time, the backglass and backbox had increased to a size comparable to those of today, and popular themes were really making the most of this space. This available space to devote purely to art was to increase even further with the introduction of drum reel scoring. The trade-off was that the artist did not have to include numbers in the backglass art, but had to allow space for the reels. Digital scoring increased the available free space area even further and with the subsequent introduction of alphanumeric and dot-matrix displays, the backglass became an uninterrupted artwork.

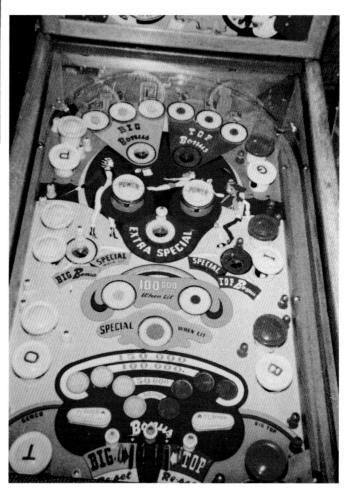

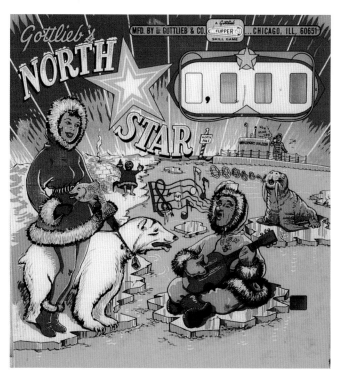

The art of Roy Parker. The backglass of Gottlieb's NORTH STAR (1964). Roy's artwork was always full of hidden messages connected to the events of the period—this time expressing the ability of U.S. nuclear submarines to navigate under the North Pole, a feat first accomplished by USS *Nautilus* in August 1958. *Robert Young collection.* $675-800.

Sega's X-FILES (1997), the finished product. $1800-2100.

Uninterrupted artwork on the playfield, however, has always been very scarce. The old saying that one has to "play with the cards one is dealt" is a close description of the artist's dilemma of having to cover the playfield with art the best way he/she can after the designer has "dealt" the final design of the playfield layout. Spare a thought for the artist when you next gaze upon a playfield. Not only does the artwork have to fit around playfield devices like bumpers and targets, but playfield lights that indi-

cate rollover lanes, bonus points and scoring modes. On older pinballs, artists would also have to incorporate target values, as well as bonus values, within the art, similar to the backglasses with light up scoring.

Artwork has not always been restricted to the playfield and backglass. The surfaces in question are those found on the light shield and the cabinet.

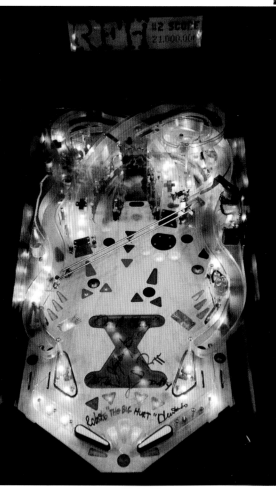

A pinball with no art. The development "whitewood" prototype of Sega's X-FILES (1997), signed by the design team. Pinballs would be pretty boring to look at if they were all like this. *Courtesy of Herb Silvers/ Fabulous Fantasies. Photograph courtesy of Ray Johnson.* $2000+

Areas of playfield that have become unusable due to the arrangement of components have always been put to good use by the placing of general illumination. With the introduction of plastics, proving popular on components such as bumpers, these areas became covered by decorated plastic light shields, which gave the playfield artistic and aesthetic continuity. Like miniature backglasses, light shields have always carried artwork associated with the game theme, each different from one game to the next (not to mention different sizes and shapes), and have therefore become sought after by restorers and collectors as spare parts.

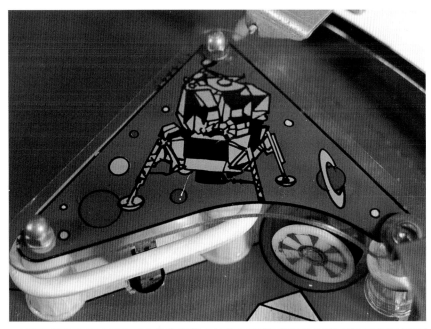

Light shield details from games shown in the previous chapters; Gottlieb's OUTER SPACE and GRAND SLAM, and A.M.I.'s BIG HUNT. Can you guess which belongs to what?

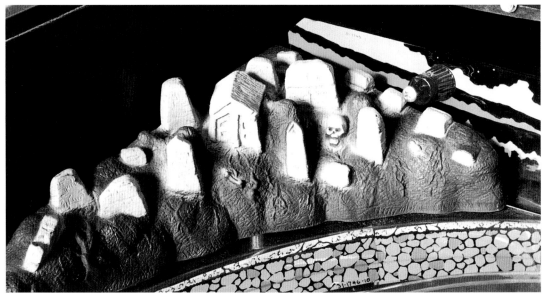

The haunted graveyard on William's' DRACULA (1993). Molded plastics have also been used as light shields, giving games a more attractive 3-D effect.

Coin operated countertop pinball games, unlike their thin bagatelle ancestors, required a cabinet to house their inner workings. Most were just decorated with carved trims and no art of which to speak of. A sign of things to come appeared on games like Bingo Novelty's IMPROVED BINGO (1931), which included a five-pointed star comet design, carrying the game name on its tail. By the end of the decade cabinet designs were in full swing, soon followed by more designs appearing on the sides of the backbox cabinet. From the 1940s to the 1980s, cabinet designs remained very simple, containing a small combination of contrasting colors, forming stenciled designs from geometric shapes to theme graphics and of course, the name of the game. Since the late 1980s cabinet designs have taken on full-colour graphics and much more elaborate designs, almost as elaborate as the backglass.

Backbox panel art from Bally's FATHOM (1981).

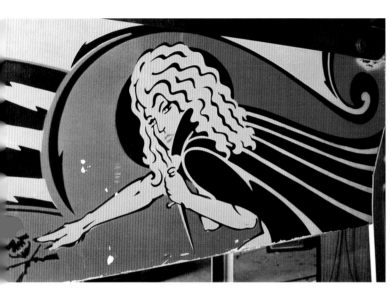

Cabinet art from Bally's MATA HARI (1978).

Cabinet art from Williams' DINER (1990).

Backbox panel art from Bally's PARAGON (1979).

Themes over the years have continued to center around the popular pastimes. Games and sports, particularly card games (poker) and ball & cue (pool), have been by far the most popular. Gottlieb was the self-confessed card theme king, with advertising slogans like "from the master of playing card games" on the brochure of JACKS OPEN (1977). While Bally was making a name for itself with pool themes like EIGHT BALL (1977), featuring an unauthorized portrait of Arthur Fonzarelli (Fonzie), from the T.V. hit show *Happy Days*, on air at the time. Other sports to have made their mark on pinballs include motor racing, soccer, American football, surfing, boxing and even polo, used in Gottlieb's POLO (1970) which was featured, if only briefly, in the motion picture *Marathon Man* (1976). As always, pinballs seem to get portrayed in a bad way, one way or another, and in this particular movie, a hitman plays POLO while waiting for his victim.

Game themes can be many and varied, and here are two pinballs from Gottlieb which feature themes from opposite ends of the spectrum. The theme of tennis on a pinball has been very rare indeed, used here on VOLLEY (1976). On the other hand, how many times has a playing card theme been used on a pinball? Hundreds of times, and on this particular game brochure from JACKS OPEN (1977), Gottlieb even admits to be the "master maker" of playing card games. $425-550.

Playfield and playfield detail (**see next page**) of Gottlieb's VOLLEY (1976). The overwhelming majority of pinball art has always portrayed white males and females. On the playfield of VOLLEY however, one can find two little figures of a black male and a black female tennis player. The male looks remotely like Arthur Ashe, who in 1975 became the first black tennis player to win Wimbledon. Was the connection intentional? *Jeff Grummel collection.*

Playfield detail, **see previous page for caption.**

Backglass detail from Bally's EIGHT BALL (1977). The unauthorized likeness of the pool playing character to that of "Fonzie", from the popular television show *Happy Days* on air at the time, landed Bally in hot water. *Courtesy of Tony and Clare Moore.*

The artwork on Bally's EIGHT BALL can almost be mistaken as being a Dave Christensen creation, but Paul Faris took care of that by placing his signature on the bottom part of the pool table.

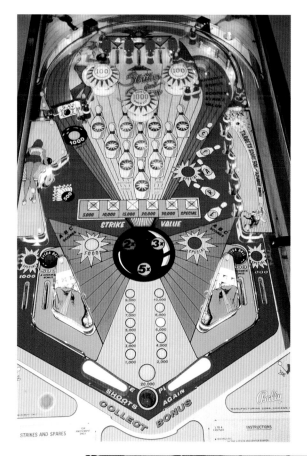

Think of a popular sport and there has probably been a pinball built with that theme. Many other leisure activities have been represented including science & technology, fantasy and space travel. No matter what the theme, the style in which it is represented contains the essence of that particular era; a time-portal to the past, or even the perceived future. The most striking aspect is perhaps the fashions in vogue at that particular time, especially since females are more often portrayed. The themes show strong influence that the male orientation of pinball has had, and still has on the game; but it is not just in terms of themes, but more how the figures in these themes are portrayed.

Right & bottom right: TOP CARD (1974), another card theme game from Gottlieb. Want to know how to play? Here are the game rules: Hitting targets from 2-7 or 8-K or ace (the "top card") lights bumpers for 1000 points. Hitting all targets lights special on the top card, center rollover button and return lanes for duration of game! Not bad if one can manage to hit all the targets on the first ball! Notice the diagonal return lanes. *Mark Jackson collection.* $325-425.

Playfield and playfield detail of Bally's STRIKES AND SPARES (1978). A very simple playfield layout using a very popular theme of the times, ten pin bowling. Pinballs have always portrayed the most popular of pastimes, sports, and images from the era in which they where manufactured, and in fact many ten pin bowling theme games were produced during the 1960s and 1970s but very few during the 1980s and 1990s. Maybe this sport has lost some of its appeal, as far as pinball manufacturers are concerned. *Courtesy of Ray Johnson.* $400-475.

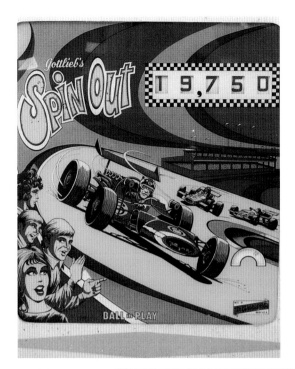

Backglass and backglass detail of Gottlieb's SPIN OUT (1975). It was built at a time when formula one racing was a popular theme amongst manufacturers of both pinball and video or mechanical driving games. Others included A.M.I's HOT RACE (1975), Bally's TWIN WIN (1974), Recel's TOP SPEED (1975) and Williams' GRAND PRIX (1976). *Robert Young collection.* $400-475.

Since the earliest pinballs, women have appeared in a converse relationship, shown to be performing or participating in activities considered almost exclusively masculine. One for the hedonists! It is therefore no great surprise that the female form presented is nothing short of voluptuous, and almost always scantily or revealingly clad. It is interesting to note that male figures are either very masculine and heroic, as on Paul Faris' art on LOST WORLD (1978) by Bally, or appear in caricature. Williams' KINGS (1957) or Gottlieb's ROYAL FLUSH (1957) shows an interesting mix of exactly this point; comical male figures (playing card king caricatures), versus the undisputed glamour and voluptuousness of the accompanying Queens.

See previous page for caption.

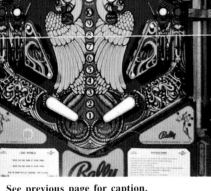

Williams' STARDUST (1972). The unmistakable artwork of Christian Marche, represented by long, angular paper-cut figures. *Ivo Vasella collection.* $300-375.)

Returning to the female form, they too have on occasions been caricatured, but only to accentuate already well-proportioned attributes; such as those by game artist Gordon Morrison, featured on Gottlieb's JUMPING JACK (1973), KING ROCK (1972), and many others. This is a stark contrast to the angular, almost psychedelic paper cut figures of Christian Marche found on Williams' STARDUST (1972) and GULFSTREAM (1973). Jerry K. Kelly also used a similar style on Williams' A-GO-GO (1966) and Bally's CAPERSVILLE (1966).

Gottlieb's JUMPING JACK (1973). A typical example of Gordon Morrison's exaggerated cartoonish style, depicted here in the female form, showing women with ample breasts, long legs and tiny, ultra-thin waistlines. If you like wide open playfields, you can't get any wider or more open than this. This pinball was an exact copy of the four-player game JACK-IN-THE-BOX, released by Gottlieb only three months earlier. *Courtesy of Robert Young.* $375-450.

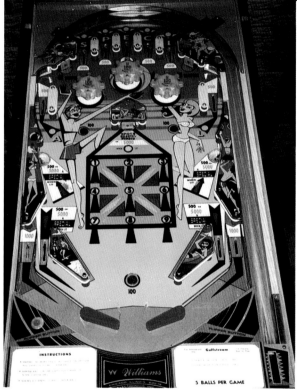

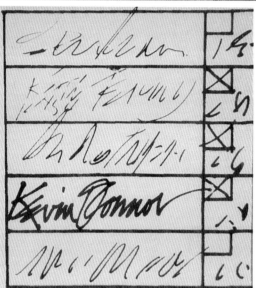

Find the artist's signature. Backglass and backglass detail of Bally's STRIKES AND SPARES (1978), where the artist, Kevin O'Connor, has inserted his signature in the scoreboard on the upper right hand corner. The pinball was featured in French magazine advertisements during the early 90s, promoting a popular brand of beer. *Robert Young collection.*

Having fun in the sun on Williams' GULFSTREAM (1973). Another very distinct Christian Marche creation. His type of angular artwork does not favor everyone. As discussed with a number people that I have met through the years, it is definitely an art style that seems to have died out in the 1970s. *Tim Van Blarcom collection.* $300-375.

Certain styles have definitely served to identify particular artists, and raise them out of anonymity, with the added help of signatures and initials craftily worked into the intimate details of their artwork. Take a close look at a pinball's playfield in today's arcade and one will most certainly find a small list of credits covering the efforts of the main production staff. Names included are those of the artists, game designers, sound and music designers, software designers, etc. On the other hand, in the EM era of the early 1970s, a close look would reveal absolutely nothing.

The first to take credit for their work were, of course, the game artists with those hidden backglass signatures which began

to appear on Bally games like MONTE CARLO (1973) by Dave Christensen (signature on champagne bottle) and OLD CHICAGO (1976), by the same artist, (name on car number plate). By the end of the 1970s, almost every pinball produced by Bally featured the artist's signature, usually on the bottom left or right of the backglass, no longer camouflaged or concealed. The artists in question were Kevin O'Connor and Paul Faris, followed by Greg Freres and Tony Ramunni. The father of the hidden signature, Dave Christensen, still preferred to do just that. His name can be found hidden amongst the tiger's fur on Bally's MATA HARI (1978-see photo) and at the bottom of Oscar Goldman's coat on SIX MILLION DOLLAR MAN (1978). The hidden signature of Constantino Mitchell, a Williams artist, can also be found on the backglass of FLASH (1979), TIME WARP (1979) and GORGAR (1979); on the wall of the citadel, on the glove of the "time wizard", and on the right corner of the sacrificial altar, respectively.

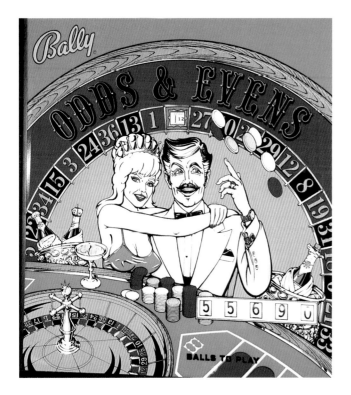

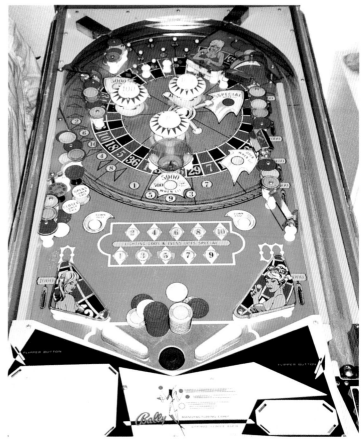

Top left, bottom left & top right: Bally's ODDS & EVENS (1973) was the single-player version of the four-player MONTE CARLO (1973). The playfield on both games were almost identical, but the backglass art, although being quite similar, included some major changes. The most significant change was the use of only one girl, as compared to two on MONTE CARLO. While a less noticeable one was the removal of the artist's signature (Dave Christensen) from the champagne bottle on the right. *Jay MacPhee collection.* $375-450.

Dave Christensen's minute signature on the bottom of the fourth player score display on Bally's MATA HARI lies almost camouflaged amongst the tiger's fur.

Backglass detail of Williams' FLASH (1979) showing the signature of game artist Constantino Mitchell.

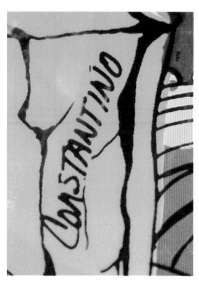

Constantino Mitchell leaves his mark once again, this time on the backglass of Williams' GORGAR (1979).

The almost microscopic signature of Jim Patla on the backglass of Bally's PLAYBOY (1978).

Not to be outdone by the artists, game designers also managed to incorporate their names amongst the artwork. Greg Kmiec, designer of countless Bally games, placed his on the flight captain's nametag on Bally's SUPERSONIC (1979). It can be found on a lightshield on the top left hand corner of the playfield, while the almost microscopic signature of Jim Patla can be found on the backglasses of both PLAYBOY (1978) and KISS (1978) pinballs. One can also find the name "Pemberton" on the oxygen tank of the diver found on the playfield of Bally's FATHOM (1981), placed there by game designer Ward Pemberton.

Ward Pemberton, game designer on Bally's FATHOM (1981), places his name on the diver's oxygen tank.

Spot the designer's name; with a bit of help. Greg Kmiec puts his name on the airline pilot's nametag on Bally's SUPERSONIC (1979). You can find this detail on the lightshield situated on the top left-hand corner of the playfield. The pilot himself looks a bit like Mr. Kmiec as well.

For an artist, drawing from life can be easier than drawing from an imaginary source, especially when it concerns the faces of characters. Although backglass and playfield scenes may be purely fictitious, the faces within may include the artist's family, relatives and even work colleagues in crowd scenes!

Dave Christensen is perhaps one of the better known and most mentioned artists to capture the imagination with his detailed crowd scenes on such pinballs as Bally's NITRO GROUNDSHAKER (1980) and CAPTAIN FANTASTIC (1976). These were typical examples of the brash, suggestive but amusing style that became his hallmark. Typified by busty women whose attire left little to the imagination, and a fascination with interesting belt buckles, Christensen has produced some astonishing work not only in terms of quality, but more often in the content, and his career has been nothing short of controversial because of it.

Backglass detail from Bally's WIZARD (1975) featuring typical Christensen artwork, the 3 Bs: broads, boobs, and belt buckles. Notice the inscription on the buckle—"Take me".

Bally's NITRO GROUNDSHAKER (1980), another Dave Christensen mayhem masterpiece of backglass artwork. $475-575.

Backglass detail from Bally's CAPTAIN FANTASTIC (1976). Another one of Christensen's favorite tricks; hidden detail. Spot Adolf Hitler's face in the crowd.

Take a close look at the crowd scene on Bally's CAPTAIN FANTASTIC (Chapter Three), and one can see some rather risqué behaviour depicted. However, the original glass was worse, containing a couple involved in sexually explicit activity that somehow went unnoticed by management at the time of its release. Promptly rectified, the few originals produced are much sought after by collectors. These were far different images than the one that had capitulated Christensen into the spotlight earlier that decade with Bally's FIREBALL (1972).

Undisputedly the most explicit pinball designed by Christensen was the custom-built machine by the name BIG DICK, produced by Fabulous Fantasies of North Hollywood California. A flyer was found for this machine during one of our photographic forays. The X-rated art content caused quite a bit of debate among us.

The power of art can never be underestimated. Gottlieb used this knowledge as a tool when faced with a highly successful playfield design, that of EL DORADO (1975). Further taking advantage of it, Gottlieb produced TARGET ALPHA (1976), CANADA DRY (1977) and SOLAR CITY (1977), all with the same playfield layout but each equally as popular on the basis of their individual artwork.

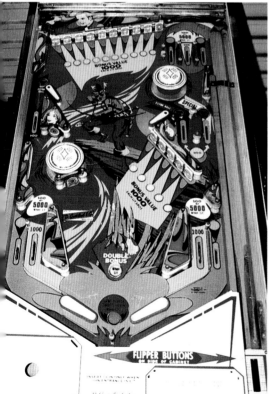

Gottlieb's SOLAR CITY (1977). When Gottlieb released EL DORADO in 1975, the playfield layout was so successful that they built several other differently named games with exactly the same playfield, but different artwork. These games were TARGET ALPHA (1976), CANADA DRY (1977) and this game. *Graeme Beal collection.* $375-450.

SOLAR CITY backglass and playfield details.

Gottlieb went one step further with this idea, using the artwork to change the gender of a particular pinball from male to female! This was the case of VULCAN and FIRE QUEEN, both released in October 1977. Both games were identical in playfield layout and art but had different player capacity—4 player and 2 player respectively. The backglass of VULCAN depicted a muscle bound, god-like male figure grasping thunderbolts in a powerful stance. For FIRE QUEEN, the god was replaced by a goddess who still commanded the force of thunderbolts, but with a lighter feminine touch.

It was during the 1970s that celebrities began to make their appearance on pinballs, including rock groups and musicians, popular T.V serials, comic book and sporting heroes. Already mentioned in Chapter Three were the Bally pinballs based on the stage rock-opera and subsequent movie of *Tommy*; WIZARD featuring Roger Daltrey and Anne Margaret, while Elton John appeared CAPTAIN FANTASTIC. Others to be immortalized in pinball art have been Bally's ROLLING STONES (1980), DOLLY PARTON (1979), EVEL KNIEVEL (1977), HARLEM GLOBETROTTERS (1979) and STAR TREK (1979). Gottlieb captured JAMES BOND (1980), BUCK ROGERS (1979), SPIDERMAN (1980), INCREDIBLE HULK (1979), CHARLIE'S ANGELS (1979), PINK PANTHER (1981), Mohamed Ali as "the greatest" in Stern's ALI (1980) and even Elvis Presley in Bell Games' THE KING (1978). In the 1990s THE SIMPSONS (1990), ROBOCOP (1990), BATMAN (1991) and STAR WARS (1992), were all produced by Data East, plus a string of movie releases all undertaken by Sega.

Bally's STAR TREK (1979). Many pinballs of the 70s used popular characters from contemporary television programs/series. This pinball was somewhat different. Although it coincided with the release of the first *Star Trek* motion picture, it was (and still is) more closely associated with the television series, which was taken off the air ten years prior. *Phillip Brown collection.* $625-700.

Playfield light shield detail from Bally's ROLLING STONES (1980), featuring Mick Jagger.

William's TAXI (1988). Williams used a few well-known faces in the artwork of this pinball; Santa Claus, Dracula, Pinbot, Mikhail Gorbachev and Marilyn Monroe (**close up on next page**). The estate of Marilyn Monroe objected to the unauthorized use of the star's likeness, so the character was given brown hair and renamed Lola during the production stage. Quite a number of "Marilyn" games made it off the production line unchanged (an example seen here); a lot of them were shipped overseas. *Gregory J. Corrigan collection.* $675-750.

Marilyn Monroe, **see previous page for caption.**

Backglass detail from Bally's DOCTOR WHO, with the evil Davros, creator of the Daleks, seen here commanding his troops against the seven Doctors.

Bally's DOCTOR WHO (1992). A large percentage of "celebrity" pinball machines have been based on popular U.S. motion pictures and T.V shows, this game was one exception. This British television series grew from its humble black-and-white beginnings into a worldwide cult following, and I guess it was only a matter of time before it was immortalized as a pinball. It goes without saying that it is sure to become a sought-after item amongst devoted fans and collectors of Doctor Who memorabilia. $725-875.

However, possibly one of the earliest connections between the big screen and pinballs, although perhaps purely by coincidence, was the backglass art featured on Bally's FOUR MILLION B.C., released in 1971. Five years prior was the movie release of *One Million B.C.*, produced by Hammer productions, a British company better known for their horror films. It was a film with a story set in prehistoric times, which starred the scantily clad Rachel Welch in the role that shot her to fame. The backglass depicts a scene suspiciously and uncannily similar to one from the movie in which a tyrannosaur attacks a triceratops, but comes out of the fight second best — dead, in fact. The film's animation during this scene was superb, even by today's standard of computerized images, and it is not impossible to imagine that the game's artist (Dick White) may have been influenced when deciding on a backglass layout.

in the late 1960s. The comic book in question is *"Nick Fury—Agent of S.H.I.E.L.D."* issue # 6, published by Marvel Comics in 1968. It appears that this particular comic book series (or comic book cover) may have been one of the artist's favorites.

Playfield detail of the intricate and exquisite art on Data East's PHANTOM OF THE OPERA (1990). Artwork by Paul Faris. *Photo courtesy of Ivo Vasella.*

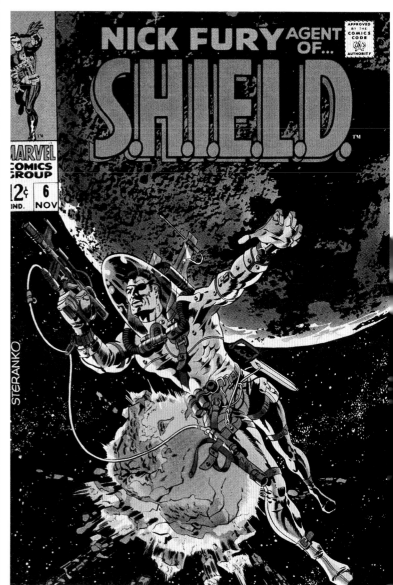

Inspiration for a pinball's theme or its art may come from many sources. When Constantino Mitchell designed the artwork for Williams' BLACKOUT (1980), he may have been thinking about one of his favorite pieces of comic art, or perhaps his favorite comic book, Marvel Comics' *NICK FURY–AGENT OF S.H.I.E.L.D.* (issue 6–1968), shown here. The figure of one of the astronauts featured in the backglass has an uncanny but definite resemblance. *Courtesy of Marvel Comics. Nick Fury: TM & ©1999 Marvel Characters, Inc. Used with permission.*

A similar situation can easily be interpreted when it comes to the backglass artwork on Williams' BLACKOUT (1980), and Constantino Mitchell, the game's artist. The glass depicts two astronauts in dire straits. There is absolutely no doubt in this case that the figure of the astronaut in the foreground is almost an exact replica of the figure found in a comic book cover published

Influential material does not necessarily have to come from sources recognised the world over, they can be localized to the country of origin. For the Australian population, for instance, nothing could surpass the depiction of some of the "Aussie" icons produced by A.Hankin of Newcastle. Having lived in Australia most of my life and in Newcastle especially, the influential factors are easily explained. Games such as HOWZAT (1980), featuring one of Australia's mainstream sport, cricket, and the mustached grin of cricket legend Dennis Lillee. The game has become a sought after item for lovers of cricket paraphernalia. Only 350 HOWZATs were built.

The pinball FJ (1978) depicted one of the country's historical motoring favorites; the F.J Holden, a car idolized by millions of Australians. First produced in 1953, it is one of the true Aussie legends, the car that has become synonymous with everything that is "fair dinkum" and "true blue". The playfield graphics illustrate a long stretch of flat road disappearing into the distance, typical of some of the outback roads, and the slight hint of the illegal sport of street drag racing. Maybe the artist frequented the local Saturday night drag races on Kooragang Island (part of Newcastle), underneath Stockton Bridge? In reality what may have influenced the game theme could have been yet another film! The motion picture in question was one produced and filmed in Australia, named funnily enough *The F.J. Holden*. Released in 1977, it centered on a group of youths living in the western suburbs of Sydney, with the central character the proud owner of an F.J. It attained a cult movie status for a short period of time, especially amongst young adults, due to its documentary type atmosphere that included plenty of swearing, sex, plenty of beer drinking and (surprise, surprise) illegal drag racing.

F.J instruction card. Learn how to play!

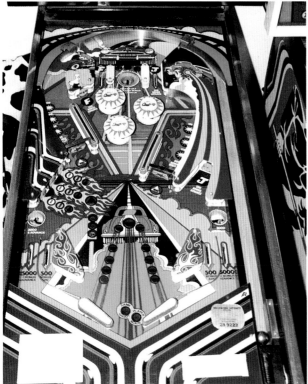

Hankin's FJ (1978). It commemorated an Australian motoring icon, the F.J. Holden. The idea for the theme of the pinball may have come from an Australian movie released in 1977 titled *The F.J. Holden*, or maybe it was just coincidence. *Robert Young/Darryl Moore collections.* $375-450.

Upper playfield detail of Hankin's FJ.

FJ backglass detail.

fish, and the intertwined bodies of eels with humanoid heads. This is not to mention scuba divers "diving" down every rollover lane with sharks in apparent hot pursuit, all escaping the giant octopus' tentacles. It has been estimated that only 200 SHARK pinballs were built.

Newcastle is a city by the ocean, with sand, surfing and sharks. SHARK (1980) was produced at a time when local boy come hero, Mark Richards, had just won his third World Professional Surfing Championship. SHARK featured a backglass with some rather futuristic looking surfies riding a wave with highly reflective boards, on top of a school of wide mouthed sharks. The playfield was just jam-packed with colour and detail. The open jaws of a shark near the "guts" is almost overshadowed by schools of brightly colored

Top right & right: Backglass details from Hankin's SHARK. Groovy helmets!

Surf's up on Hankin's SHARK (1980). The style of artwork between the backglass and the playfield does not seem to have much in common except that they have both something to do with sharks and the sea. The wide-body playfield of this game is absolutely jam-packed with art detail. Scuba divers, sharks, anglerfish, eels and other strange fish, all superimposed on what appears to be a giant octopus. Lovers of pinball art will absolutely adore this playfield; unfortunately this game was produced in low quantities and you would have to travel to Australia to find one. $550-600.

Backglass detail from Hankin's SHARK. Groovy helmets!

Minute SHARK playfield detail showing a small school of angler fish heading for safety.

Bally produced one photographic backglass pinball during this time, HARDBODY (1987), a body building theme with the backglass photo of a female bodybuilder. Data East used the same concept on LAZER WARS (1987), their first pinball. This time the backglass featured a male and a female shooting it out in a futuristic battle of the sexes. The graphics of the mid-'90s pinball has greatly improved in terms of colour mixing and overall precision. Sega introduced the curved (convex) backglass, first seen on SPACE JAM (1996) and then on STAR WARS TRILOGY (1997), which included another industry first—a 3-D optical backglass.

Machine shot of SHARK.

Another SHARK playfield detail, this time showing a group of sharks chasing scuba divers through the top rollover lanes.

The start of 1986 saw Gottlieb exploring a new avenue in pinball art with RAVEN, the first pinball with a photographic backglass. Rather than hand-drawn art, an artistic photo was used with the game's name superimposed. RAVEN was followed by several more games with this style of backglass, but still featuring traditional artwork on the playfield. They included games like HOLLYWOOD HEAT (1986), GENESIS (1986) and ARENA (1987), just a sample of a small number of games produced. The Gottlieb experiment only lasted a few years before backglass art returned to the more conventional style, much to the purists' delight.

Pinball machines come and go, and not all of them end up in loving relationships with their owners. When all attempts to restore a game fail, the artwork may be the only "non-mechanical" salvageable aspect. Backglasses are popular collector items from pinball graveyards, and are often framed and hung. Playfields in good condition whose components no longer work, can find themselves set into glass-topped coffee tables. In contrast, on working games the value can be vastly decreased if the backglass has been damaged or destroyed—try to find a replacement, especially for a rare game!

One can now see how important the visual medium has been (and continues to be) in determining or favorite games. The collective works of the masters of pinball art may never be found hanging in famous art galleries. The galleries for these works have always been the thousands of arcades scattered throughout the world.

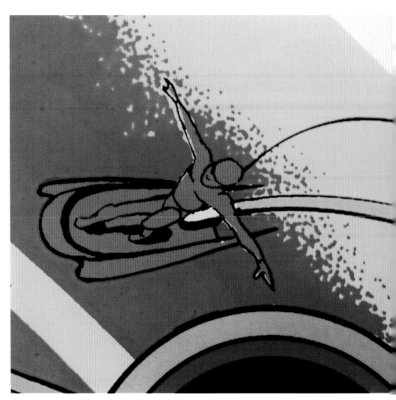

Mystery backglass detail. The next chapter features a full view of this well-known Gottlieb game. Do you know which one it is?

This backglass from Gottlieb's SKY LINE (1965) was saved from the scrap heap and framed to make an excellent wall hanging. The elevator doors are missing, as they were part of the game's animation unit. *Mark Jackson collection.* $650-800.

Backglass detail of SKY LINE, with a view of the city below.

Chapter Nine

The Chronicles of Scoring Devices

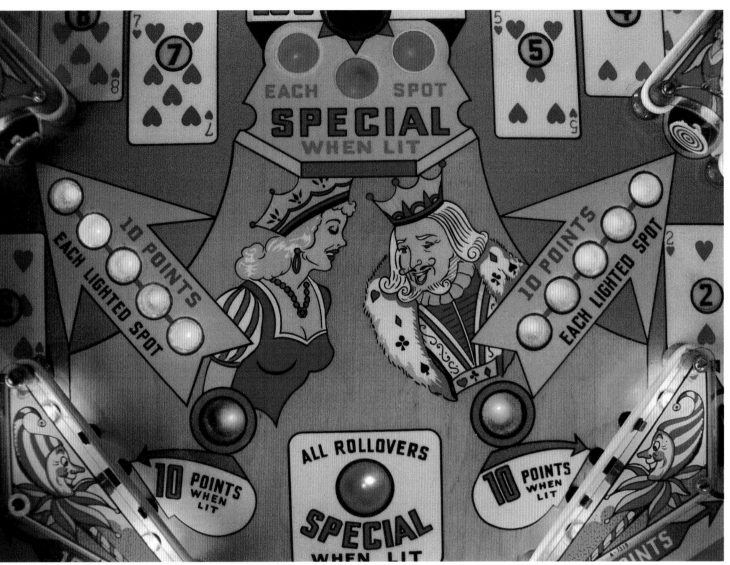

Playfield detail from Gottlieb's
SWEET HEARTS (1963).

Thus far, this book has only covered the history of three major playfield components—the flipper, bumper and to a lesser content, the top rollover lane. Here now, grouped together, is the history of over ten different playfield scoring devices, with a few other miscellaneous historical details thrown in for good measure.

Wire form rollover lanes (not necessarily positioned at the top), strategically positioned around a flipperless playfield came out as early as 1936-37 and have been in use ever since. Their simple construction (explained in Chapter Five) could only allow a ball to pass over them in a direction parallel to the switch wire, hence their exclusive use within laneways. The introduction of rollover buttons by 1950 allowed designers to place a device similar in function to the wire form, anywhere on the playfield without the use of a lane. Rollover buttons were, in a visual sense, the same as flipper buttons on the playfield. The ball rolling over them from any direction would push down a little plunger and force two switchblades together. With the button sitting almost flush with the playfield, the ball was not greatly deflected upon contact. This

An old style rollover button an Williams' TEACHER'S PET (1965). Compare this "piston" type button style to the "star" button used predominantly in the 1970s and early 1980s.

Star buttons. These types of rollover buttons became popular with game designers in the early 1970s. Detail of a row of rollover buttons on Gottlieb's CHARLIE'S ANGELS (1979).

was a great advantage, as they could be placed anywhere, even in front of the flipper, and not get in the way of a shot or obstruct any other scoring device. Since the early 1970s the rollover button took on the now well known and familiar appearance of the "star" button, which remained popular until the mid-1980s. The button now only appears occasionally having since gone out of vogue.

A closer look at some star buttons on Bally's SUPER-SONIC (1979).

Solenoids have always been the pinball world's quiet achievers, hidden under the playfield away from sight, but powering most of the well-known devices. The solenoid's success has come from its simplicity: a coil of wire, a metal plunger and electromagnetism combined to produce mechanical action. What got the ball rolling (pardon the pun once again) was the kickout hole (better known today as a kickout saucer). The premier electromechanical device made its first debut in the early 1930s. For the reader, the typical ball-activated action used should not hold any surprises; ball lands in saucer, pushes two contacts together and engages the solenoid. However the ball is not shot out vertically, but is instead pushed out by a claw-shaped metal tip forming part of a lever arm attached at one end to the solenoid. Games with kickout saucers are numerous, well beyond the thousand mark, to reach at a guess. Not so for the bi-directional kickout saucer which could launch the ball out in more than one direction. Three of the very few pinballs with this device are Bally's FLASH GORDON (1981), VIKING (1980) and Williams' CONGO (1995).

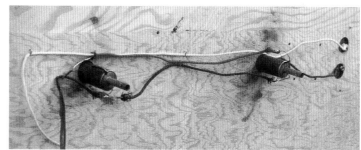

Undoubtedly two of the most famous solenoids in pinball history; those from the kickout holes on Pacific Amusements' CONTACT (1934).

Gottlieb's DODGE CITY (1965) used a row of rollunder gates, rather than rollover buttons. Courtesy of *Tim Van Blarcom*. $600-725.

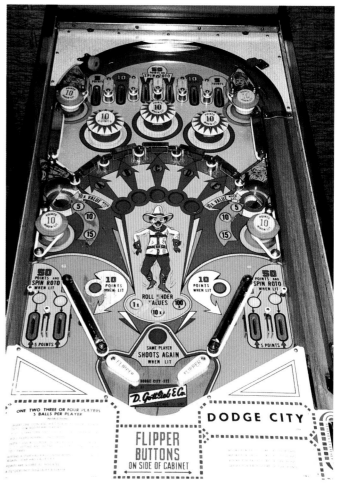

A close-up view of one of the solenoids from CONTACT.

Playfield detail of CONTACT showing one of the kickout holes. *Photos Courtesy of Gary and Eric See.*

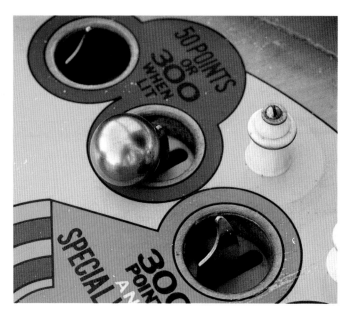

A row of kickout holes activated at the same time from Gottlieb's 2001 (1971), showing the claw tip as the ball is kicked out.

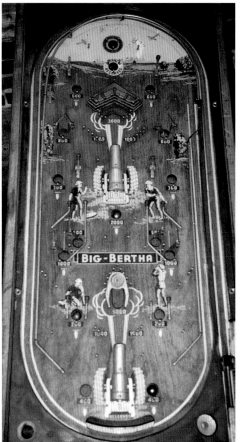

Daval's BIG BERTHA (1934). Rather than using kickout holes, this game took the concept one step further and used kickout cannons! In order to make the cannons fire, one had to land the ball into the "advance reserves" hole positioned at the top of the playfield. *Eugene Ricci collection.* $375-450.

Other solenoid-activated devices appearing after the kickout saucer were, of course, the flipper and thumper bumper; but hot on their heels came the slingshot kicker. Those familiar triangles near the flippers first appeared in the early 1950s. Some were not in the form of triangles, only having two sides, but their purpose was still the same. The flipper domain of the lower playfield had been devoid of ball-activated solenoid action up until this time. The job of keeping the ball alive before the arrival of the slingshot (and even before the flipper), was left to rebound rubbers. These thick, round rubber bands, each stretched across two or three posts and placed around the playfield, (with the biggest and most bouncy residing at the bottom) acted like a trampoline. The idea behind the slingshot was to incorporate a solenoid kicker within that existing feature, making it more powerful. Positioned halfway along the slingshot's stretched rubber was a level arm that extended down through the playfield. It would push against the rubber, bouncing the ball away once activated; the solenoid was energized by the ball pushing together a set of switchblades placed on the same side of the rubber band as the lever arm. The slingshot soon became a standard playfield feature (just like the flipper), and still is to this day. There have been pinballs built without slingshots, of course; one such game was Gottlieb's JUNGLE QUEEN (1977), where a pair of two-inch flippers replaced the devices.

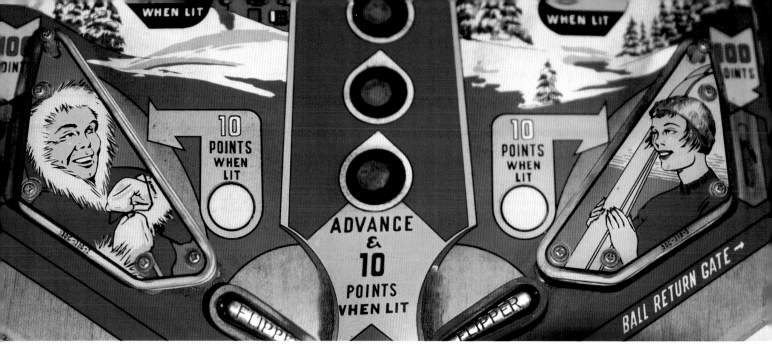

When Bally introduced the coil bumper in 1937, the old baga-telle-style scoring holes were removed and not seen again...until they re-emerged at the start of the 1950s. The two new terms describing these old features were the ball trap and the gobble hole. Both were aptly named, as having landed the ball in one of them, it was "trapped" or "gobbled up" and never returned into play. I always used to think of the two as being one and the same. The fact that both features occupied the same time frame in pinball history does not help.

The name near the scoring hole says it all, its a close-up of Pacific Amusement's CONTACT (1934). The hole was not a scoring hole as such, it was the "contact" hole; much like a gobble hole. Once the ball fell in, it would drop though the playfield and activate a switch which would energize the game's two kickout holes positioned further down the playfield.

An interesting sight. Once again we are looking at a close-up of a component inside CONTACT. This funny-looking scoop device is the switch situated beneath the "contact" hole. Once the ball falls through the playfield, it lands on the cantilevered scoop. The weight of the ball causes the scoop to drop at one end. This then completes an electrical circuit, ringing the game's bell and activating the solenoids and the two kickout holes. The ball then rolls off under gravity and the switch then returns to its normal position, ready for another ball. *Photos courtesy of Gary and Eric See.*

A perfect couple. A pair of slingshot kickers as seen on the playfield of William's ALPINE CLUB (1965). These devices were first introduced onto the pinball playfield in the early 1950s and have been there ever since. They are the pinball world's quiet achievers, providing ball movement without too much scoring reward. At times they can prove to be frustrating when they seem to juggle the ball between themselves; as if playing piggy in the middle with the player. *Photo courtesy of Michael E. Lukacs.*

The ball trap was something that found its way into the game from the amusement/gambling world's exposure to bingo machines that first appeared in 1951. The trapped balls, like on the older pinnies, remained on the playfield until the start of a new game. The ball trap, unlike its earlier counterpart, was very deep. This allowed the top of the ball to sit almost flush with the top of the playfield so as not to get too much in the way of a flipper shot with the remaining balls. Some of the best known pinballs with the ball trap have been Gottlieb's QUARTETTE (1952) with four ball traps, DRAGONETTE (1954) with five and FLYING HIGH (1953) with eight.

The gobble hole, as the name suggests, did not just trap the ball, it swallowed it! This sinister Gottlieb invention first appeared on HAPPY DAYS in 1952 and last appeared on SWEET HEARTS in 1963. This little playfield outhole or outholes (as games sometimes had more than one), like the ball trap, seemed to contradict the basic flipper game strategy of keeping the ball in play as long as possible. It was a danger shot, that is granted, but game designers

did not expect players to give the ball away without proper compensation. The gobble hole was a trade-off feature, often awarding high scores or multiple specials (free games). Unlike all playfield devices, and this goes without saying, there was always a good time and a bad time to loose the ball down a gobble hole, an example of this is to be found on SWEET HEARTS.

Kickout hole on the left, gobble hole on the right—notice the difference? The court jester does. The gobble hole in this case is worth 200 points, not bad considering the replay value on this game is 1200 points with five balls to play.

Unfortunately for SWEET HEARTS, the game has always been known as the last gobble hole pinball, and its place in history has been pigeon-holed to express that fact and nothing else. Even for the average pinball player, not to mention the pinball wizard, the rewards for having a good game on SWEET HEARTS were enormous. What lay in wait for these silverball prospectors was a free game mother lode. It is my personal opinion that pinballs today (referring to the late 90s) are not as liberal in awarding free games from playfield specials as they once were prior to (at least) the mid-1980s. Generally one can pick up an average of only one to two free games while having a great game at the local arcade today, compared to four or five free games on a pinball built back in the late '70s early '80s. Back then, there was more than one replay value (usually two but sometimes three) and one had a chance to earn a special on every ball—something almost non-existent now. SWEET HEARTS, even as far back as 1963, was a champion for this cause.

When referring to the playfield photo of SWEET HEARTS, one can see five top rollover lanes. Completing those lights the middle special light at the gobble hole. Completing lanes 6 through to 9 on the left (6 is the outlane) lights the left special light at the gobble hole and completing lanes 2 through 5 lights right special light. Once all the lanes are complete this lights the "all rollovers special" light near the flippers for a free game each time a rollover is completed from then on. That's a possible total of thirteen free games, not counting three more if you make the gobble hole! The gobble hole at any other time was only worth 100 points, a relatively small compensation for losing the ball.

Targets were the by-products of flippers. The very first flipper pinballs used flippers as a means of keeping the ball in play for extended periods, though considerably shorter periods when compared to today's, but far longer than the flipperless games. Once players became proficient with the popular devices, designers gave them something to aim for: enter the target.

Gottlieb's SWEET HEARTS (1963). A pinball better known for being the last game produced featuring the infamous gobble hole. Once all the rollover lanes were completed, landing the ball in the gobble hole (located in the center of the playfield) awards three free games. *Mark Jackson collection.* $575-700.

The backglass of SWEET HEARTS.

Those early targets are now known by various names; stationary targets, stand-up targets or bullseye targets. These targets were by far the simplest and cheapest of components and are still used today. Their construction has always consisted of a plastic target face (usually round) attached to a switch or switchblade, which is pushed closed by ball contact. The first two of many variations on this simple device came in 1957 and 1960, with the introduction of the roto-target and the moving target, respectively.

dom, displaying a new target/value after a front stationary target, or the wheel itself in most cases, was hit. Activated by the ball, the random spin of the selection wheel was created by a solenoid and gear arrangement. The electromechanical workings of a roto target meant that the feature did not pass through into the SS era, keeping its appeal with game designers intact. Some of the few roto-target assemblies on SS machines can be found on Gottlieb's CLOSE ENCOUNTERS (1978) and TORCH (1980); the former of which was released in both EM and SS formats. There have been a few pinballs throughout the years that have incorporated electronic versions similar a roto-target, without the moving parts. Examples can be found on Bally's GOLD BALL (1983) and on Gottlieb's VEGAS (1990).

Stationary targets. These types of targets have been the most common of scoring devices, they have also been very versatile. Here we see one placed in front of a bumper, and one positioned inside a small lane.

The roto-target was invented by Gottlieb designer Wayne Neyvens, and was first used on MAJESTIC (March 1957). The idea behind the roto-target was an existing stand-up target coupled with a new random value selection wheel. A wheel assembly of rotating targets (hence the name "roto") would change at ran-

The roto-target. Roto-targets have been produced in different styles and have in most part been an exclusive Gottlieb device. Here we see the two most popular versions. Another style, unfortunately not shown here, was the horizontal type first used on KING OF DIAMONDS (1967). It was sometimes known as the "carousel" because of its merry-go-round appearance.

Due to its patent, the roto-target was a Gottlieb exclusive, but despite this, another similar device did appear around the same time. Rather than a familiar spinning target wheel, it used a score reel-type device which protruded vertically through the playfield and displayed the current score value. Hitting a stationary target placed in front of the wheel scored the points shown and made it spin to the next value. It was used on several French and American games like Alben's SAMBA (1961) and Williams' FIESTA (1959), MARDI GRAS (1962) and EL TORO (1963).

Williams' KLONDIKE (1971). Gottlieb's roto-target was a patented device, but despite this, Williams devised a similar mechanism in the late 50s. It used a score reel which protruded vertically through the playfield. On this machine, three such targets were placed at the top of the playfield. *Jeff Grummel collection.* $350-425.

Gottlieb's TORCH (1980). Many Gottlieb EM games included the roto-target, but when it came to SS machines, very few had this scoring feature. Notice the unusual playfield design near the flippers. The pinball was to have commemorated the Olympic games in Moscow, but it was the year that the games were boycotted by the U.S. *Michael Tansell collection.* $275-375.

KLONDIKE playfield detail showing the slot machine style roto targets.

The moving target was first used on Williams' MAGIC CLOCK, released in December 1960. The moving target is a standard bullseye target mounted on a metal arm attached to a motorized assembly. The target oscillates continuously from left to right during play, in much the same manner as a metronome. A well-aimed flipper shot was no longer enough to guarantee a hit; one had to achieve the correct timing as well. One of the best-known moving target pinballs of the EM era was Williams' SPACE MISSION (May 1976), a 4-player game which was also released as the 2-player SPACE ODYSSEY two months later. The backglass artwork featured an American Apollo and Soviet Soyuz space capsules during a rendevous and docking procedure. The tricky space maneuver was simulated in a way by the game's moving target. Data East's STAR TREK (1991) and Bally's WORLD CUP SOCCER (1994) are two of the more recent pinballs with this component. The latter, depicting the World Cup soccer tournament held in the U.S.A in 1994, uses the moving target as a goalkeeper, thwarting the player's attempts at scoring a goal.

The 1960s seemed to be the decade of invention and expansion for pinballs, including the introduction of add-a-ball pinballs (see Chapter Eleven); the exporting and importing of games between countries; the debut of the 3" flipper, and a swag of other innovations, including drop targets. Williams' VAGABOND, an add-a-ball game, released in 1962 was the first drop target game. As always, the name of the feature describes its action. This target, after being hit, would drop below the playfield out of view and effectively be removed from playfield scoring until such time that it was reset by the game play. The reason why the term has been

Backglass of VAGABOND. **See next page for caption.**

Playfield of Williams' SPACE ODYSSEY (1976). Probably one of the best-known moving target games of the '70s. *Eugene Ricci collection.* $375-475.

Gottlieb's PALACE GUARD (1968) used an equivalent of a moving target; it was named the "Snap" target. *Courtesy of Tim Van Blarcom.* $475-575.

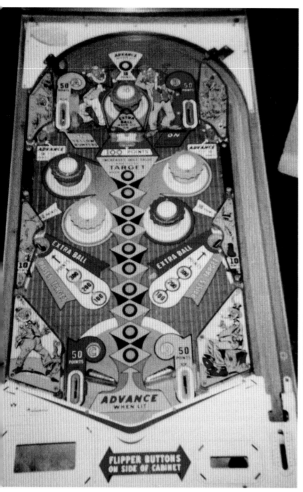

Williams' VAGABOND (1962) introduced the drop target to the world of pinball, one of the game's most popular scoring features. **See previous page for backglass.** *Courtesy of Russ Jensen.* $575-700.

SEVEN UP backglass detail.

iams' SEVEN UP (Dec 1969), a pinball with a skiing theme. SEVEN UP had six stationary targets, three on each side of a drop target, positioned in the upper playfield. Hitting all six stationary targets would reset the drop target, hence the name of the game. It also utilized a similar feature to that of ALPINE CLUB mentioned in Chapter Three. Completing the game's A-B-C-D rollover sequence advances one of a series of lit-up skiers (on the backglass) further down the mountain slope towards a finish line.

The first multiple drop target bank was unveiled on Gottlieb's GALAXIE, released in January 1971. This add-a-ball game built for the Italian market was re-released one month later in the U.S. as 2001, the replay version, and DIMENSION, yet another add-a-ball. Players could not believe their eyes! Twenty drop targets set up in two ten-target banks, facing each other on either side of the playfield. It was a drop target feast, to say the least! Since then, drop target banks have been built in various capacities. Some had as few as two targets, such as Gottlieb's SINBAD (1978), while others trying various quantities and combinations, all of which, to my knowledge, have not equaled to the amount as first appeared on GALAXIE, 2001, and of course, DIMENSION.

used in a singular fashion is because VAGABOND only had one drop target, set in the middle of the playfield, at high mid-field. The features popularity ensured its inclusion in other Williams games; and it remained for the next nine years in the single-target bank format.

One of the last single target games released before the introduction of the multiple target bank in the early 1970s was Will-

Williams' SEVEN UP (1969). After the initial success of VAGABOND, Williams produced several games with the single drop-target bank format. SEVEN UP, released in December, was one of the last, as Gottlieb was to introduce the multiple target bank in early 1971. The seemingly artless area in the middle of the backglass revealed lit figures of skiers descending when a playfield scoring sequence was completed. *Graham McGuiness collection.* $325-400.

Backglass of 2001.

-- 195 --

2001 playfield details.

Gottlieb's 2001 (1971). The replay version of GALAXIE (released a month earlier), it was the second game to feature a multiple target bank. The game rules are simple. Each target is worth 50 points. Completing a bank of coloured drop targets lights corresponding kickout hole and rollover lane for increased scoring. Completing any three sets of colored drop targets lights special. Notice that the game still has the older style 2" flippers. *Graham McGuiness collection.* $275-350.

2001 backglass detail.

Playfield detail from Gottlieb's BRONCO (1977). This single drop target row style first appeared on Gottlieb's CRESCENDO (1970). Almost a target bank, but not quite.

The idea of a target bank almost came to fruition for Gottlieb a few games earlier on CRESCENDO (May 1970), a two-player game re-marketed a few months later as a four-player GROOVY (July 1970). The center playfield area was equipped with a row of five separate "Flower-Power" targets spanning the entire playfield from left to right, each separated from the other by just over a ball's width. Only a small post guarded the back of each target; not quite what one would call a target bank.

In-line drop targets, or sometimes known collectively as a "target tunnel", was a variant to the standard target bank, and first appeared on Bally's PARAGON (1979). Rather than placing targets side by side, in-line targets were placed one behind the other, usually increasing in value. The obvious objective was to knock down the front target of lesser value in order to make the second and more valuable target accessible, and so on. Bally received a patent for this target design (pat #4257604) in 1979.

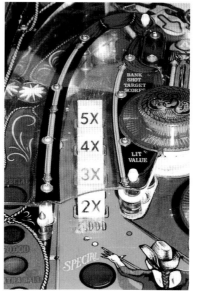

A bank of in-line targets on Bally's EIGHT BALL DELUXE (1981). Knocking each target down increases the bonus multiplier to the amount shown, 2x, 3x, etc. When all the targets are knocked down, hitting the bullseye target at the end of the tunnel awards 50,000 points on the first hit, then special on the second. The targets reset at the beginning of each ball.

Targets within a bank are wired in series. Each closes its own switch when hit down, and when the last one is dropped, the whole circuit is complete, the reset coil is energized, and all the targets are pushed back up above the playfield. With the aid of an electronic pinball's memory, target banks could be reset in exactly the same way as they were left at the end of the previous player's ball. This could be done from player to player, ball to ball for the duration of the game. This was known as a target "recall" feature in most pinball manuals. In order for the machine to achieve this, the target bank assembly was equipped with a small solenoid for each individual target, along with the standard reset coil. At the start of a new ball, all the targets in the bank would first be reset as normal, then with the aid of each target's separate coil acting in a similar fashion to a ball, the targets remembered as being "down" would then be knocked down from underneath the playfield automatically. The considerable amount of extra coils required for this target assembly made it an expensive choice and was therefore not used often.

Playfield detail from Bally's ROLLING STONES (1980). A strategically placed "satisfaction" single drop target blocks the access to a kickout hole.

Top left & bottom left: Bally's HARLEM GLOBETROTTERS (1979), one of the first pinballs to introduce in-line targets, located in the upper right corner of the playfield. The game also included a return gate within the right outlane and a pair of those dreaded in-line flippers. *Courtesy of Ivo Vasella.* $400-475.

If simplicity is an assured way to a successful playfield component both in player appeal and cost effectiveness, then the spinner and the captive ball represent a pinball designer's ability to please both game fanatic and the equally unforgiving bean-counting company executive. Both features have appeared together or on their own in countless games throughout the years, and are still favored by designers today. The captive ball can be found on games as early as 1961, such as Gottlieb's FLYING CIRCUS, while the spinner was first introduced in 1963 on SWING ALONG, another Gottlieb game.

Gottlieb's SWING ALONG (1963) introduced the spinner to the world of pinball. *Jeff Grummel collection.* $450-525.

A captive ball is a standard size game ball trapped inside an open-ended chamber, much like an enclosed rollover lane. The open-ended section, always facing downfield, has a large enough opening to allow the trapped ball to peek out. At the other end of the closed lane there is usually a stationary target or a rollover wire switch. Hitting the captive ball hard enough will send it up the lane and onto the target. The other name commonly used for this feature is the "messenger ball". Once the shot is made, the captive ball then returns back to the open end of the chamber under gravity. The feature's popularity comes from the skill required not only just to hit the captive ball, but to hit it with enough force in order to score. It is the pinball's equivalent to the old "test your strength" attractions at the fairground—swing the sledgehammer hard enough to make the bell ring!

The captive ball. A simple but popular scoring device found on hundreds of pinballs, its appeal has not faded since its appearance in the early 1960s. Playfield detail from Gottlieb's PINBALL POOL (1979).

Another captive ball (or sometimes known as a messenger ball), this time from Bally's FIREBALL (1972). Notice that the chamber is slightly more elaborate. It has a pair of rollover switches and also a stationary target placed at the end.

Captive balls have come in various quantities and in different styles. Recel's CRITERIUM 75 (1975) uses three captive balls set up in a row, much like a target bank. The word criterium describes a specific type of bicycle race held around a short circuit or track; Recel used the cycling theme in two other similarly named games. The same concept was used again on Atari's 4X4 (prototype-1983), but with two substantial differences. One, each captive ball was guarded by a drop target placed directly in front (a common Atari captive ball design) and two, it had a total of eight captive balls split into two banks! Gottlieb's FLYING CIRCUS and SUNSET (1962), and Williams' WHOOPEE (1965) had several captive balls held within two interconnecting chambers. A ball or balls from one chamber could be hit and then transferred over to the other chamber and vice versa. Bally's CENTAUR (1981) has a captive ball chamber with four in-line targets in front of a stationary target. The "queen's chamber", as it is named, is unusually long, but once all the targets are completed the player has the opportunity to score a replay. Captive ball chambers have also been enlarged sideways in order to accommodate thumper bumpers or even a bank of drop targets! A good example of the latter can be found on Petaco's ICARUS (1977), a Spanish pinball. RIO (1977) by Playmatic, another Spanish game, includes several chambers in a line, but only one captive ball! A small arch connected all the chambers. Hitting the captive ball hard enough sends it into the next chamber on its left. Another hit, and another jump to the next chamber on the left, and so on until the ball comes to rest inside the last chamber. From this point however, one final hit sends the captive ball on a long loop to the right, jumping over all the previous lanes, and back to the starting chamber in readiness for the whole sequence to begin again.

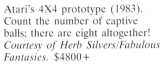

PINBALL POOL instruction card.

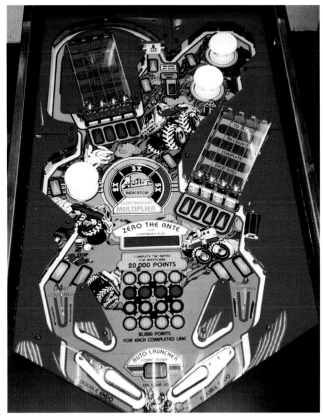

Gottlieb's PINBALL POOL (1979) one of the earliest SS pinballs from this company. The most outstanding playfield feature is the captive ball, clearly visible in the centre of the playfield. What is not so apparent is the "remotrip" drop target feature. The game's instruction card explains "hitting an even-numbered drop target drops opposite corresponding target" hence the name; hitting targets by remote control! *Courtesy of Robert Young.* $300-375.

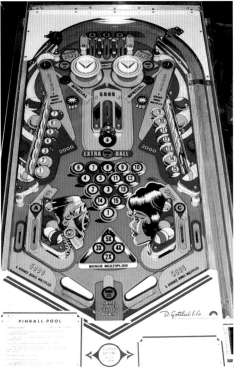

Atari's 4X4 prototype (1983). Count the number of captive balls; there are eight altogether! *Courtesy of Herb Silvers/Fabulous Fantasies.* $4800+

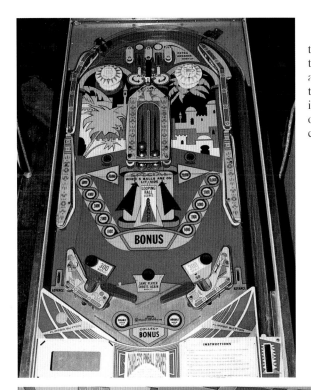

A spinner is a balanced, free spinning horizontal target, held up between two posts, or other playfield components. The ball rolling under and through the target causes it to spin, its action similar to that of a water wheel. Points are awarded at the completion of each full rotation and thus the harder one hits the target the more points awarded. Its compact construction has guaranteed its inclusion on most games, and like the rollover button, is non-obstructive to overall play. Unlike the captive ball, the spinner has not varied a great deal in its construction or style through the years.

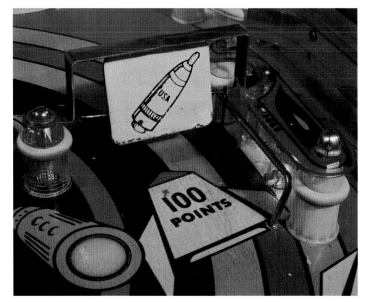

Williams' DARLING (1973) boasted five captive balls held within two interconnecting chambers. Looping balls from one side advanced the bonus. Special was awarded if all five balls were looped on the lit side. *Courtesy of Robert Young.* $250-300.

Top right: The spinner. A scoring device that is simple but effective, and has been used on hundreds of pinballs since its introduction.

Center right: Playfield detail from Gottlieb's SWING ALONG. Note: art detail on outside spinners not original.

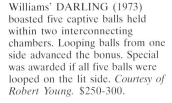

DARLING backglass detail.

The year 1965 saw a change in lower playfield layout that would dominate pinball by the start of the 1970s, the placement of return lanes. First used on Gottlieb's BANK-A-BALL (Sep 1965), the return lanes gave play-

BANK-A-BALL playfield detail.

---

ers better ball control, made even better in time by the use of 3" flippers. The lanes made it easier to trap the ball by channeling it directly onto the flipper, and acting as a damper, slowing the ball's speed in the process.

The traditional return lane positioned on the inside, and outlane on the outside, was not always so when it came to Bally pinballs. The crossover return lane can be found on FATHOM (1981), SPEAK EASY (1982), MR & MRS PACMAN (1982), GOLD BALL (1983), CITY SLICKERS (1987), HARLEY DAVIDSON (1991) and others. With the return and outlane now

---

There are return lanes, and then there are return lanes. A typical return lane layout. Return lane on the inside, outlane on the outside—but things haven't always looked like this.

Gottlieb's BANK-A-BALL (1965), the game that introduced return lanes. It was also released in add-a-ball format as FLIPPER POOL. Tiny pool balls in the backbox drop into view as the corresponding targets on the playfield are hit, and furthermore, the corresponding lit balls appearing on the pool table in the backglass are switched off. The rules of the game are simple. Hitting numbers 1 to 7 or 9 to 15 lights center eight ball target. Hitting eight ball target lights either left or right rollover lane for special depending on which set of numbers were completed. *Mark Jackson collection.* $600-725.

positioned in reverse, the ball was channeled across the outlane width to land safely across the other side, through a one-way gate and back onto the flipper. This arrangement also allowed one to save the ball if it entered the outlane by nudging the machine to one side at the right moment.

while still visible to the player. Captive ball spinners have been included on only a handful of pinballs throughout the last three decades since their invention. The last pinball to have included this device thus far was Gottlieb's TEE'D OFF (1993), a golfing theme game with a talking gopher.

Compare this return layout to the traditional; notice the switch? These type of cross-over lanes were primarily used on Bally machines, but I know of at least one Williams game which incorporated it, COMET (1985). These type of lanes gave the player a second chance of getting the ball back into play after it had entered the outlane. All one needed was a well-timed nudge on the side of the cabinet.

The name of the game is golf, with the help of a mischievous gopher, on TEE'D OFF (1993). This was the last Gottlieb game to include a roulette wheel. **See next page for close up of backglass and playfield.** $875-1100.

The year was 1966. The machine: Williams' A-GO-GO. The device: the captive ball spinner. Was this a captive ball and spinner hybrid? Not quite. The new scoring device was actually a mini-roulette wheel, totally self-contained with its own marble-sized steel ball. During the course of a game, the wheel would spin, sending the tiny ball flying, and the player was then awarded the points corresponding to the hole where the ball landed. The first wheels used were housed above the playfield, taking up a considerable amount of room usually in the lower playfield near the flippers. Since then they have been placed beneath the playfield

Williams' FAN-TAS-TIC (1972). The game incorporated a captive ball spinner (a.k.a. roulette wheel) that could be activated by landing the ball in any one of three kickout holes. *Jeff Grummel collection.* $300-400.

Backglass of TEE'D OFF. **See previous page for caption.**

This chapter is not exclusively devoted to scoring devices. Through the years there have been some simple but effective innovations in the field of "ball saving". Ball saving devices gave the player a chance to block or save the ball from going out of play via the gap between the flippers or the outlanes. This field can be further divided into two categories: player-activated and game-activated.

A player-activated ball saver is where one is given a choice whether to save or not to save, even if the latter does seem illogical; (in the event of saving) it is a process which requires quick reflexes. A good example of this is the flipper save, as mentioned in Chapter Two. Bally produced a similar, but much more user-friendly ball saver on BMX (1982). This game featured an extra pair of flipper buttons that activated the device and allowed the player a limited number of attempts to close the outlanes. The apparatus consisted of a moving/retractable metal ball guide which closed the outlane and redirected the ball onto the return lane and its corresponding flipper. One of my favorite ball saver devices from this category is Williams' "Magna-save". I will not be explaining this gadget here as I have devoted a much larger section of the next chapter to it.

The game-activated ball saver is one where the game saves the ball automatically, or the device is activated continuously while the ball is in play. This removes the skill in its activation but requires the player to hit certain specified targets in order to enable the feature.

The "grand-daddy" of ball saving devices appears to be a contraption used by Gottlieb in the early 1950. It involved a V-shaped device located between the flippers, which was raised at the start of each ball, effectively blocking the entire outhole. The V-shape pointing up field acted as a ridge, diverting the ball onto either flipper tip. Once the player reached a certain score, the device would then drop down flush with the playfield and out of the way. Some of the Gottlieb pinballs with this device were FOUR HORSEMEN (1950), KNOCK OUT (1950) and MINSTREL MAN (1951).

The "king" of all ball saving devices, due to its popularity, is the up-post. This game-activated feature also resides between the flipper tips and can be found on pinballs as early as 1967/68, such as Rally's PLAYBOY (Nov 1967) and Chicago Coin's STAGE COACH (June 1968) for example. It is a large cylindrical lighted post which sits flush with the playfield and "pops" up when activated, again effectively blocking the outhole. This does not guarantee complete protection, as it can only stop the ball while the flippers are at rest. The post does not remain up for any great period of time of course, and some games even had targets marked "down post" (which were usually hard to avoid, despite trying very hard to) which disabled the feature, while others gave the up-post a time limit of approximately 10 to 15 seconds in some cases before the feature automatically turned off.

Playfield of TEE'D OFF. **See previous page for caption.**

Captive ball spinner detail from Gottlieb's TEE'D OFF.

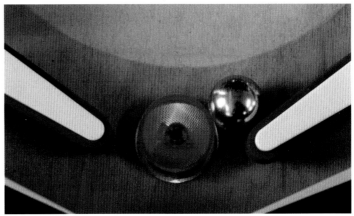

The mighty up-post, the king of ball saving devices. The up-post at work between a set of 3" flippers in Bally's SPACE TIME (1972).

The same device, only this time between a pair of 2" flippers; Williams' CABARET (1969). *Photos courtesy of Ivo Vasella.*

There has also been a few player-activated up-post type devices included in games over the years. Unlike normal up-posts, these were much smaller in diameter and did not completely block the exit; such as the aptly named "little demon post" found on Bally's MEDUSA (1981) or FIREBALL 2 (1981). However, even if they did (like the "claw-save" on Gottlieb's A NIGHTMARE ON ELM STREET (1994)), the action time is less than a second and thus timing is imperative if you are even able activate the feature at all! These devices require great skill in timing and decision making, as the player first has to decide whether or not the ball was salvageable with conventional flipper action. The feature is activated using an extra flipper button, which means that unless one has a friend providing a hand (or finger, literally), it is almost impossible to attempt to save the ball by flipper play while trying to reach the other button simultaneously.

Having covered the "guts" area, the only exits left are the two outlanes. These have been the domain of the kickback (formerly known as the "recovery kicker"), usually residing in the left outlane; and the return gate (sometimes known as an outlane gate) predominantly on the right. Both devices are game-activated.

The idea behind this odd couple came from Bally during the late 1960s and early 1970s, and driving the idea was game designer Thadius Zale. The kickback is a solenoid-driven, plunger-like device that sends the ball back into play from the bottom of the outlane before being lost. The ball rolling onto the lane's wireform switch activates it. It is impossible to always have an explanation as to how and why some things occur, they just do—this is particularly applicable to playfield devices, as they fall into and out of favor with designers. As an avid pinball player in the early 1980s, the kickback was unknown to me. It was not until later that decade that the kickback returned to pinballs on games like Bally's FIRE-BALL CLASSIC (1985), and then on Williams' HIGH SPEED (1986). Unaware of its history at that stage I thought it was something new, but it had in fact just come back into fashion, with at least one or two pinballs every year appearing with the device. Its popularity reached into the mid-90s.

The same cannot be said about the return gate. A prominent feature on a lot of Williams pinballs of the 1960s and popular on most games in general up until the late 1970s, it has now become virtually non-existent. In the days when outlanes and return lanes were separated by simple guide wires, and plunger lanes were separated from the playfield only by a thin piece of timber, the return gate was a simple gate that when activated, would channel

the ball from the outlane back into the return lane. Bally's KISS (1979) and HARLEM GLOBETROTTERS (1979) makes use of such an apparatus. Most common by far, however, the ball was returned back to the plunger via a small exit cut into the plunger lane rail. Examples of this latter type can be found on games from both Bally and Williams, as mentioned previously. Gottlieb also began using them in the 70s on games like KING KOOL (1972), SOCCER (1975), ROYAL FLUSH (1976) and WILD LIFE (1972).

A ball return gate. This device is positioned within the outlane and saves the ball from going into the outhole by channelling it back into the plunger lane for a second shot, or diverts it into the return lane and back onto the flipper, as in the case shown here on Bally's KISS (1979).

A more conventional gate diverting the ball into the plunger lane. This photo is from Bally's SUPERSONIC (1979).

WILD LIFE, like so many other Gottlieb pinballs of the 60s and 70s, was released under a different name for the Italian market, though the artwork and presentation remained the same. The same was applied for certain pinballs sold within the U.S. or other foreign markets. SHERIFF (1971) became LAWMAN, and games like FAR OUT (1974) became OUT OF SIGHT (1975). Two-player WILD LIFE became a single-player JUNGLE LIFE released early in 1973. JUNGLE LIFE has a film credit, believe it or not. It appeared, if only briefly, in the 1975 Italian horror movie *Profondo Rosso*, better known to English speaking moviegoers as *Deep Red* (or a.k.a. *The Hatchet Murders*) and starred British actor David Hemmings. It was a gory film for the 1970s, but tame by today's standards. The scene in question takes place in a coffee bar where our hero tries to make a phone call from a wall mounted pay-phone (no mobile phones in those days) but is unable to hear because of a noisy cappuccino machine next to him and someone playing JUNGLE LIFE nearby.

Another device rarely seen nowadays, coming back amongst scoring components, is the vari-target. Vari, short for variable, was a Gottlieb-patented target first used on AIRPORT in April 1969. Similar in appearance to a captive ball layout, the ball was replaced by a metal target which could be pushed back in a similar fashion. The harder a ball hit it, the further it was pushed back, thus the higher the score. The most recent pinballs with a vari-target have been Gottlieb's SILVER SLUGGER (1990) and SHAQ ATTAQ (1994). After AIRPORT, the vari-target became a moderately successful device, appearing on numerous Gottlieb games. This included pinballs like POLO (1970), ORBIT (1972), BIG BRAVE (1974) and DRAGON (1978). The original layout of two vari-targets used on AIRPORT also proved popular, and was re-

Views of a vari-target. Notice the different scoring zones as the target is pushed back. The further back, the higher the scores.

A quick peek under the playfield, and the vari-target looks relatively simple in design.

Gottlieb's AIRPORT (1969). This game introduced the vari-target (vari, short for variable), which was a Gottlieb patented design. As one can see on the playfield photo, two targets were used, one each side of the middle bumper. *Courtesy of Russ Jensen.* $400-500.

peated several times soon after among games like COLLEGE QUEENS (1969), SKIPPER (1969), WILD WILD WEST (1969), PLAY BALL (1971), PRO FOOTBALL (1973), and again but much later on BIG HIT (1977). BIG HIT and PRO FOOTBALL were close re-makes of PLAY BALL, both used a popular sporting theme (baseball and football respectively), and both were built with a center ball shooter and no plunger.

Gottlieb's SUPER SPIN (1977), a game with a fabulous combination of Gottlieb's exclusive roto-target and vari-targets, a seldom-encountered combination. Roto-targets were usually found in the center of the playfield, but in this case, the device was suitably placed at the top left corner of the playfield. *Gary Hudson collection.* $400-500.

Backglass details from Gottlieb's SUPER SPIN.

Finally, out of the 1960s, things had begun to slow down considerably. The biggest thing to happen in the 70s was of course the change from EM to SS technology, which grabbed most of the pinball headlines. Before then designers were still inventing bits and pieces to catch the player's attention, including spinning posts. Here is another fine example of a feature that has come and gone, then come back again. Almost completely forgotten but then resurrected. Phew!

Take two posts which would otherwise be normal components that have been everpresent since the game began, mount them on opposite sides of a free-spinning circular platform flush with the playfield, and hey presto! A new scoring device is born. It scores when rotated by the impact of the ball striking either of the two posts. Similar to the spinner invented years earlier, the harder one hits it, the higher the score. First appearing on French pinballs of the late 1960s on such games as Rally's PLAYBOY (1967), it made its debut on the U.S. game scene on Williams' ACES & KINGS in 1970. It was then used on various other pinballs like STAR ACTION (1974) and STAR POOL (1974), both by Williams, and GOLD RECORD (1975) by Chicago Coin, but then became virtually extinct during the 80s and early 90s. The spinning posts have now been re-introduced only recently on Williams' TALES OF THE ARABIAN KNIGHTS (1996), a pinball dedicated to the spirit of Harry Williams, and on Bally's SAFE CRACKER (1996).

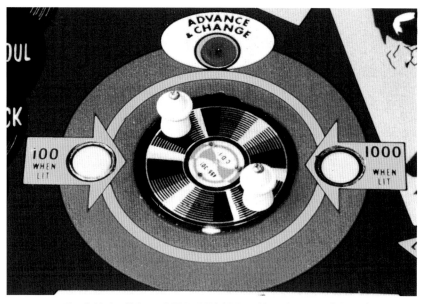

Playfield detail from GOLD RECORD, with a close-up of the spinning posts, depicted in the form of an old style vinyl record.

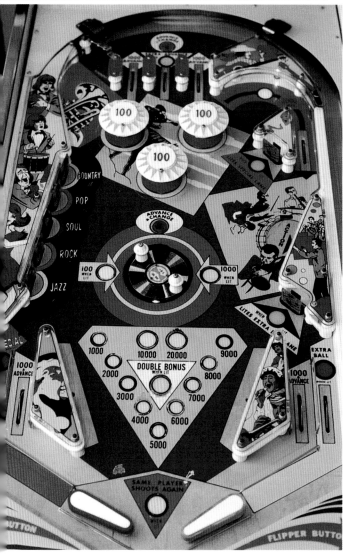

Chicago Coin's GOLD RECORD (1975), a game which included the spinning posts feature. *Rick Force collection.* $350-400.

A clever invention will always provide a springboard for other ideas to come forth. There will always be someone who takes an existing product, re-arranges it, adds to, or subtracts from it to create something new. Whose idea was it to combine a digital alarm clock with a radio? Having steered your thoughts in the right direction you will see the similarities between spinning posts and our next device, the whirlwind spinner.

The whirlwind spinner was not a scoring device, it manipulated the ball to send it flying off in unexpected directions. In the words of the advertising flyer for Bally's FIREBALL (1972), the first game with the device, "Whirlwind spinner twirls ball into a frenzy of scoring action." What could cause such ball movement? A motorized playfield turntable, that's what. Taking the existing spinning post feature, the posts were removed and a motor added to the platform. Am I right in thinking that is what happened, or was it pure coincidence? Only Ted Zale can answer that question.

I have read nothing but praise for FIREBALL, the game mentioned in almost every book on this subject as being the best in its time, and now the most collectible machine of the EM era. Some people have also told me that the game is slightly overrated, and that the whirlwind spinner made the game unpredictable (a dog of a game, in fact). A game of skill became at times a game of chance. Speaking from experience, having played FIREBALL and other games incorporating the device, once the ball hits that rotating disc, all the laws of silverball physics go down the gurgler. Slow balls are accelerated and shot off unpredictably. Fast balls catching the disc rotating in the opposite direction are slowed down, then briefly held motionless before being shot back from whence they came. One can just imagine the mayhem.

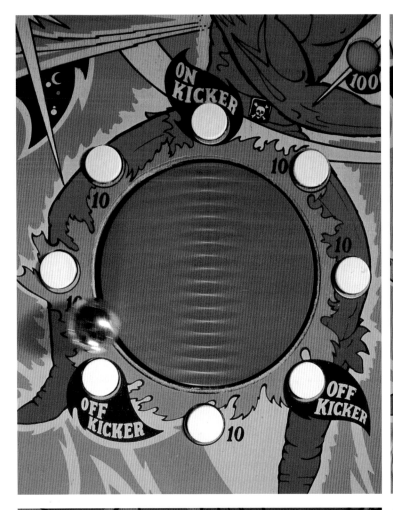

Top left, bottom left & top right: A whirlwind spinner as seen on the playfield of Bally's FIREBALL (1972). Ball enters spinner. Ball is stopped momentarily by the spinning rubberized disk, before being shot off unpredictably in both speed and direction.

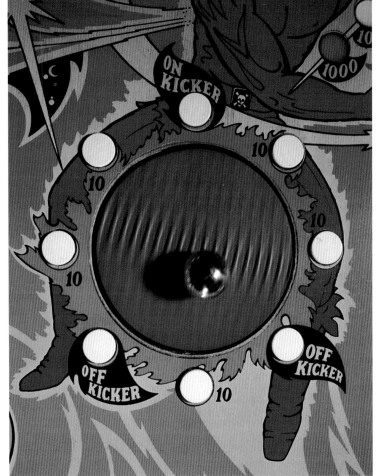

Four months after the release of FIREBALL, Chicago Coin produced a game with twin spinners, CASINO, released in July 1972. Chicago Coin also produced games with features that resembled whirlwind spinners, games like SOUND STAGE (1976) and JUKE BOX (1976). The rotating disc on these pinballs was set under the playfield and covered by clear plastic. Its main function is to give a visual (and somewhat hypnotic) effect, other than just scoring points each time it spins. The disc is engaged by hitting two large targets clearly marked "spin". SOUND STAGE had an amusing movie credit. Not another movie tie-in, I hear you say! More on that later. Someone wanting to experience the whirlwind will not have to resort to seeking out these older games as more recent ones are at hand. Williams' WHIRLWIND (1990), Data East's TEENAGE MUTANT NINJA TURTLES (1991) with spinning pizzas, Sega's TWISTER (1996) and finally Williams' NO GOOD GOLFERS (1997).

If this type of ball manipulation does not suit one's pinball tastes, and something subtler is required, then magnets are in order. Rather than whirlwind spinners, Bally's ADDAMS FAMILY (1992) uses a set of magnets. Three magnets set out under the playfield in triangular formation just above the slingshots energize intermittently, causing ball deflections. The same concept was then used again on Data East's GUNS N'ROSES (1994). The way the ball gets pulled around by the magnets can be quite comical if one does not take the game too seriously, though anyone having played these games under the influence of certain drugs or alcohol may not have noticed anything special.

You should not be surprised if I said that playfield magnets were used on pinballs before; it seems to be a fact of pinball history that what may appear to be a new device could have links to the past going back decades! Back in 1938 two such pinballs were produced and both by Exhibit; LIGHTNING and BUTTONS. Both designed by Lyn Durrant and Harry Williams, they incorporated field coils from radio loudspeakers to do the trick. When the ball passed over the hidden magnets, it would swerve in odd ways.

Now, back to that SOUND STAGE movie appearance. This is something that my brother and I always joke about when we get together and play pinball like we did in the "good old days", something that now happens very rarely. The movie in question was *Odds and Evens,* an Italian production released in 1978 that starred Terrence Hill and Bud Spencer; the "Trinity" duo better known for their spaghetti westerns. The pinball scene once again takes place in a bar where Terrence Hill is playing a mean pinball and scoring big. His unusual playing style is what we joke about (in fact the whole movie was a bit of a joke). He kicks the side of the cabinet, turns around and plays with his back to the machine, and then for the grand finale, he turns back around and jumps on top of the game while still holding on to the flipper buttons! Don't try this at the local arcade! A Mafia gang later smashes up the pinball. I believe it was actually a prop that they destroyed, the film producers probably could not afford to do it to the real thing.

Imagine the task involved in cataloguing every single scoring device produced? From the likes of drop targets and spinners used hundreds of times, to playfield novelties only used once or

Chicago Coin's SOUND STAGE (1976). What looked like a whirlwind spinner was actually a rotating disc set under the playfield and covered by clear plastic. Points were scored by making the disc spin, this was achieved by hitting the designated "spin" targets. *Jeff Grummel collection* $300-350.

SOUND STAGE playfield detail.

twice. While we are at it, what about a list to mention all those "celebrity" pinballs that have appeared in movies or T.V shows? I have vague recollection of pinballs played long ago, usually lesser-known ones, with strange targets or features. Lesser-known pinballs, meaning foreign pinballs (meaning pinballs not built in the U.S.A to be exact), are a treasure trove of weird and wonderful contraptions. For example, I remember playing CLOWN (1985) by Zaccaria, a pinball with a circus theme which includes a moving target suspended by a rail spanning the playfield! Another Zaccaria creation, ROBOT (1985), has peculiar barrel drop targets. The pinballs are real and do exist, that's for sure, but as for the features...well, I guess I will have to wait until someone refreshes my memory or the chance to play the two games once again arises.

SPACE TIME playfield detail with a close-up of the tunnel. This same device was used on a Bally slot machine named *CIRCUS*; the only difference was that the segments were marked with the amount of coin payout one would receive if and when the tunnel was stopped during one of the machine's special feature modes. A similar device was also used on Playmatic's SPACE GAMBLER (1978), but was housed in the backbox. *Photos courtesy of Ivo Vasella.*

Playfield detail from Williams' DINER (1990), showing an ingenious but simple scoring device called the whirlpool. Found on only a handful of games, like Williams' TAXI (1988) or Gottlieb's SURF AND SAFARI (1991), it makes use of the ball's centrifugal force—the more loops, the more points one scores, until the ball looses speed and falls through a hole and onto the playfield.

Bally's SPACE TIME (1972), a game with a very unique scoring feature; the Tunnel, a segmented cone which extends below the lower playfield. There are five segments, each ranging in point value from 1000 at the top to 5000 at the bottom. Lights inside each segment indicate the scoring value at any particular point in time. The values constantly change at a quick rate, but one can "stop" the tunnel and collect its value. Other targets also restart the tunnel. The tunnel is active at the start of each ball, and can be stopped with a well-timed plunger shot, as there is a "stop tunnel" rollover wire inside the plunger lane. The obvious strategy is to stop the tunnel at the 5000 mark. *Courtesy of Ivo Vasella.* $325-425.

Zaccaria's CLOWN (1985) had a moving target (similar to a flyaway target) which travelled back and forth suspended above the playfield by a rail; a kind of "high wire" act which fitted in well with the game's circus theme. $325-400.

Unlike American pinballs, foreign pinballs have not been very well documented through the years, and thus a lot information regarding some of their features have yet to become part of the better known history of the game. One such feature was that used by Europlay (Italy) during the 1970s and was named the "biri-biri" feature. The biri-biri was not actually a scoring feature but proved interesting nevertheless. Based upon the gambling laws during this time in Italy, like in some states in the U.S.A, a free game was considered illegal. As a small reward, Europlay introduced the biri-biri; a small set of bells inside the machine that would sound a little tune once a certain score was reached. More importantly though, the biri-biri would signal the location owner that one of the patrons was entitled to an "under the counter" prize.

CASINO ROYAL playfield detail showing the roulette wheel and the collect saucer.

Segasa's CASINO ROYALE (1976). Little-known foreign pinballs, like this Spanish game for instance, can be full of surprises. The game has a roulette wheel in the center of the playfield which uses a lit arrow to indicate the prize amount. At the start of each ball the indicating light slowly rotates around the wheel until the player hits the "stop" target. One can now collect the shown amount or prize by shooting the ball into the kickout saucer. One can also advance the light one step by hitting the "advance" target. *Courtesy of Ivo Vasella.* $325-400.

Returning to American pinballs now, the hub of the industry, the draught horse pulling the weight of the future of pinball. A timely reference to the horse at this point brings the subject along to the next mentionable device—the horseshoe.

Although the origins of the horseshoe feature are uncertain, it can be found as early as 1968 on Williams' DING-DONG and SMARTY. It has also appeared on various other games, including Williams' SPANISH EYES (1972), SPACE ODYSSEY (1976) and BIG DEAL (1977), Hankin's SHARK (1980), Bally's SPACE IN-VADERS (1980) and even on Gottlieb's MAGNOTRON (1974) and CUE BALL WIZARD (1992). Picture a horseshoe-shaped laneway with two openings (rather like a U-turn lane), the ball enters one side, turns through 180 degrees, and comes out the other; it is that simple. Inside the horseshoe lane, rollover buttons or switch wires reward the player with points. A well-placed horseshoe, such as that found on Bally's SPACE INVADERS, gave the player an opportunity for repetitive shots. The sequence first trapped the ball on either bottom flipper (the game had four flippers, two further up the playfield). If the ball was on the left flipper, then the best shot was for the right horseshoe entrance. The ball would then swing around, come out the left entrance/exit and head for the tip of the left flipper once again. With a well-timed shot (a volley shot to be precise) the sequence could be repeated again and again, until a mistake was made. If one completed seven loops during the same ball (not neces-sarily in succession), then the horseshoe special would light up. If this was obtained with one more loop, then another loop would light it again. One can imagine the obvious benefits of repetitive shots dur-ing this time!

There are two more features that require explaining before concluding this chapter. Niether one are quite historical essentials to compare with the likes of drop targets or kickout saucers, but there is not much remaining on a pinball to point out. The list of designed features is not exactly endless, but slight variations al-ways tend to arise, like mutations of spinners or captive balls. One has to draw the line at some stage, and this is it: flyaway targets and the buy-in option.

The flyaway target is a cousin of the drop target. Both are eliminated from the playfield and taken out of scoring action once

Horseshoe detail from SPANISH EYES. This device is much like a curved rollover lane, which in most cases is positioned in such a way as to sling-shot the ball back to the player.

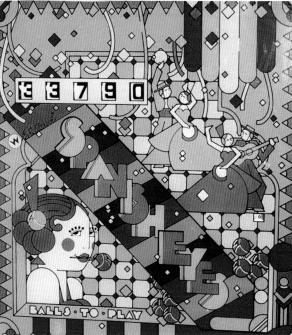

William's SPANISH EYES (1972), with a horseshoe lane as the prominent feature. The striking artwork (like it or not) and the unusual playfield made this game stand out from the crowd. Completing all of the top rollover lanes scores an extra ball. Hitting targets one to six increases kickout hole value and completing all of them lights the center loop for extra ball or 5000 points, and outlanes for 5000 points. *Rawdon Osborne collection.* $375-475.

SPANISH EYES backglass detail.

hit by the ball. First appearing on Bally's SPEAK EASY (1982), and later on Bally's GRAND SLAM (1983), the feature consists of a bank of five targets suspended just above the playfield, hinged at the top and hanging vertically like a row of laundry items out to dry. These square, thin pieces of plastic can be eliminated from play by rolling the ball under them, causing the bottom part of the target to flip up and clip to the underside of the bridge-like structure from which all are hanging. In the case of the two pinball machines mentioned, the structure is situated across the middle of the playfield. The targets can only be hit from one direction, that is, if the ball is heading up field. A ball heading through the targets on the way downfield would have no effect, as the targets would just swing freely back and forth.

Finally, the buy-in option, well-positioned at the end of the chapter as it is a game option/feature that is only available to the player at the very end of the game.

Imagine losing the ball just points away from achieving a free game, or maybe reaching that second, more difficult video mode round that has always been so elusive. It may also be that you were so close to beating the highest score, that all you needed was another ball, even just a few extra seconds of play. You think, "It might be ages before I get that close again!" All hope is not lost; you can buy an extra ball for the cost of a game or credit. The idea

Sonic's MARS TREK (1977), another classic Spanish EM game from the late 1970s. The standout feature in this case was a horseshoe lane with a seemingly unobtainable kickout hole for its hub, and a set of entry/exit spinners. *Jeff Grummel collection.* $325-400.

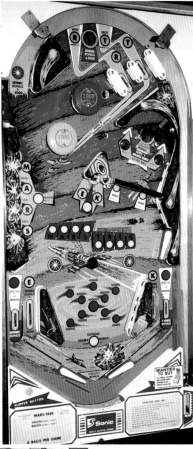

MARS TREK horseshoe and spinners playfield detail.

goes back as far as the 1940s on games like Bally's TRIUMPH (1940) for instance, when the fifth and last ball drained one could insert another nickel and get a sixth ball.

As expensive at it might sound (a rip-off, in other words) no one can appreciate the option unless they have been in that position. Exchanging one credit (earned, not paid) for an extra ball in order to get a credit back may sound absurd, but there is more to a pinball these days than just scoring free games. For example, completing all the magic illusion modes on Bally's THEATRE OF MAGIC (1995) grants the "Grand finale" mode. Similarly, on Williams' STAR TREK THE NEXT GENERATION (1993), completing all the missions grants the "Final Frontier" mode. These final modes consist of regular game play or multiball with the advantage of incredibly high scoring. One may have already won a free game on points long before reaching these stages, and this is where the buy-in option enables the player to reach a certain stage in the game that he/she was not able to reach before. In some ways, it is the same concept used on video games, where the player has the option of continuing on at the end of the game, providing more credits are available.

The first SS pinballs equipped with a buy-in option appeared in 1993, but by 1996, like on Bally's SCARED STIFF, the feature was no longer included. At the end of game, before the match feature commenced, the player usually had 10 seconds to decide whether or not to buy a ball. If one chose to buy-in, an extra start button on the front of the cabinet activated the option. If one chose not to, the countdown could be aborted by hitting both flipper buttons simultaneously or pressing the plunger button/trigger and hence starting the match feature.

Targets, eye-catching gadgets, playfield devices usually referred to as "toys" and other similar scoring features, have been an integral part of the game for almost a century. It would be pointless (pardon the expression) to flip a ball around the playfield with nothing around to shoot for. Needless to say, it is because of this that such devices will always be incorporated, but in what form? Virtual targets, perhaps? Something that Williams and Bally have already perfected. Stay tuned, the next great step in the evolution of pinball may be just around the corner.

The next chapter covers the field of multi-level pinballs, the game design that shaped the early 1980s and created some of the best-known and most collectible pinballs of that era.

Summary

1934 Kickout holes already appearing on pinballs.
1936 Wire form rollover lanes already appearing on pinballs.
1948-50 Flipper pinballs use bullseye targets.
1951 Slingshot kickers first used.
1952 Bingo style ball traps become popular with designers.
1952 Gottlieb introduces the gobble hole.
1957 Roto-target introduced on Gottlieb's MAJESTIC.
1960 Williams first uses a moving target on MAGIC CLOCK.
1961 Captive ball targets already appearing on pinballs.
1962 The drop target is first used on Williams' VAGABOND.
1963 Last gobble hole pinball built.
1963 Spinners introduced.
1965 Return lanes first used on Gottlieb's BANK-A-BALL.
1966 First appearance of the captive ball spinner.
1967 Spinning posts and up-post features appearing on French pinballs.
1969 First appearance of the vari-target.
1970 First appearance of the spinning posts feature on American pinballs; Williams' ACES & KINGS.
1971 Multiple drop target banks first used by Gottlieb.
1972 FIREBALL, by Bally, uses the whirlwind spinner.
1979 First appearance of in-line targets on Bally's PARAGON.
1982 Flyaway targets first appear on Bally's SPEAK EASY.
1993 Buy-in option available on Williams/Bally pinballs.
1996 Buy-in option no longer available on pinballs.

A multi-level pinball is a pinball with more than one playfield. The extra playfield or playfields may be smaller in size and situated either above or below the standard playfield connected to it by ball ramps or ball lifting devices.

What is the fascination that people have with all things and possessions that are multi-leveled? A house with an upstairs and downstairs seems to appeal more than one with just a ground floor. The same applies to boats, buses, and for kids, the good old bunk beds. The same fascination is what took the pinball world by a storm at the end of 1980 with the release of Williams' BLACK KNIGHT.

As one may well know by now, the pinball world had begun to feel the effects of the introduction of video games (PAC-MAN fever had broken out in 1980). The "Roman Empire" of amusement that was pinball was heading for a fall, and something had to be done.

Game brochure from Bally's ELEKTRA (1981). *Courtesy of WMS industries Inc. All rights reserved.*

The success of BLACK KNIGHT was what the whole of the pinball industry (not just Williams) needed. One can indulge in endless speculation on how the game of pinball would have eventually survived without BLACK KNIGHT (BK). It may not have halted the slide in game popularity, but it did appear to have slowed the downward spiral at that time, and possibly prevented the game of pinball (like some of its predecessors), from falling into oblivion. Who knows? As Australians would say "You had to bloody be there matc!" And indeed one had.

A completely restored playfield, with correct bumper and target decoration. *Courtesy of Mac.*

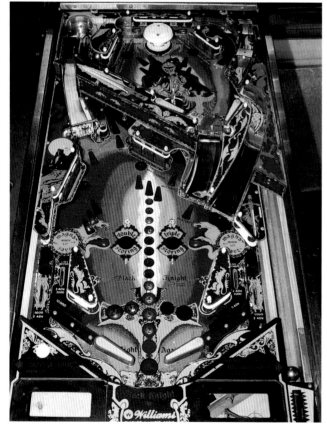

Williams' BLACK KNIGHT (1980), a game that requires little introduction. It has been said that it was the game that got people off video machines, and made them play pinball again, which is just about the highest compliment that a pinball can get. This particular game was photographed while under restoration. The white bumper was not the original (red), the targets lacked the original decorative stickers and the backglass was starting to flake (a common problem with Williams glasses of this era) but the playfield was in near mint condition, which is more important, as most of these games endured a very long and hard arcade life. *Courtesy of Robert Young.* $625-725.

The first time that I played BK was some time in 1982, almost two years after its release, and the game was still highly popular and sought after; hot, in other words. What initially attracted players to BK was, unquestionably, its multi-level layout; but this alone cannot account for its arcade longevity. After all, soon after its release, multiple level pinballs were turning up left, right, and center. I cannot answer the question for everyone who played the game, but I can at least give my point of view.

As an early teenage pinball player (and looking back now, still quite green at the game), I found BK an intimidating machine. The fact that there always seemed to be older boys wanting to have a game on the thing and scrutinizing my every flipper shot definitely did not help things. However, that, in some weird way, was for me part of its charm. From memory, I don't think that I ever managed to reach a replay score back then, because it was such a demanding game relative to my skills. The denial of this achievement, (and this did not occur to me until much later), was another appealing aspect. In a nutshell, it was the ultimate pinball challenge for me, and one that cost a fair share of my pocket money!

BLACK KNIGHT's layout consists of two playfield levels. The bottom level is the conventional playfield on the lower half of the game, while on the upper part, occupying almost half of the total game area, is the top level. Each level has two flippers and two banks of three drop targets. The two levels are connected by three ramps; two short steep ones on the right side, and a much longer one, which includes a switchback, on the left.

The first lesson to be learned on BK is how to master the plunger shot. The game has no top rollover lanes and the ball enters the upper level straight in front of its flippers, catching almost everyone with no prior knowledge of the game off guard. And that's just the start. The plunger exit, the face of the top right flipper; the whole length of middle ramp and the outhole are almost in a straight line. Plunge the ball without thinking, and it will zip across the entire playfield, heading straight for the outhole, or at least one of the flipper tips. Not a very good start. The remedy for this is to energize the top left flipper immediately after you plunge the ball. Once that playfield design trap is overcome, you can then proceed in the discovery of the game's other traps, pitfalls and devices.

BLACK KNIGHT has an array of features that really make the game quite challenging. The first challenge is the drop targets. Normal drop targets reset once all are knocked down, but not so with this pinnie—it has a timed reset feature. Once any one or two targets in each bank of three are hit, those remaining have to be dropped within a certain time (approx 10 seconds depending on game setting), otherwise the bank will reset automatically and one has to start all over again in order to collect the reward.

First appearing on BK was the ball saving feature (briefly mentioned in Chapter Nine), called Magna Save. Magna Save consists of an electro-magnet hidden under the playfield, one at the top of each return lane. With the aid of an extra flipper button on each side of the cabinet, the player can save the ball from exiting play down the outlane by energizing the magnet which grabs the ball and holds it momentarily before delivering it safely down the return lane. Knocking down a complete target bank can restore each Magna Save, once used. As with all player-activated saving devices, one has to be quick. One advantage with Magna Save is that if one is tad slow to react, the magnet is still strong enough to literally suck the ball out of the outlane. Activating the magnet prematurely however, is not an advantage in most cases. First, once the magnet is activated, it remains live for only a few seconds, just enough time to catch the ball, slow it down, and finally hold it still. If the ball is out of range from its magnetic pull (a good player knows just how far that is), then the Magna Save is wasted. Sec-

BLACK KNIGHT had an array of features that made the game quite challenging, the most famous of all was the Magna Save feature. The device consisted of a player-activated magnet positioned under the playfield, used to save a ball from exiting play via the outlanes.

ond, if on the other hand the magnet does manage to grab the ball during its final seconds before switching off, it creates a problem for the player. Not having had enough time to stop the ball completely, the magnet will switch off and send the ball flying off unpredictably—as luck would have it in my case, usually straight down the outlane.

Other features include a mystery score shot (awarding from 20,000 up to 99,000 points) on one of the three ramps, and bonus timed play. Bonus timed play (I think it is actually called Bonus ball) is only available when more than one player is playing. The player with the highest score usually receives (depending on the game setting) an extra thirty seconds of continuous multiball play with unlimited Magna Save. The round commences at the end of

Artist Tony Ramunni's signature on the backglass of BLACK KNIGHT.

the last player's final ball, with the score display showing who has won the honor. This encouraged people, even if playing by themselves, to play more than one game at the same time. When reaching this stage of the game, it was always good to have a friend to help plunge lost balls back into play (no electronic plungers back then), as you concentrated on scoring as many points as possible during this short time. If you did manage to get a game, all hell broke loose! Rather than having a conventional solenoid knocker, BK has a loud ringing bell, almost like a fire alarm. A bit embarrassing for some players, I would think.

It is time now to move on, but before that happens I would like to add one final comment regarding this game, which is one of the best known amongst collectors. In terms of artwork, for myself, the game was not as grand as some of its contemporary counterparts, like Bally's CENTAUR. It does, however, have a singular striking feature, that of a diamond-encrusted sword; the diamonds are the bonus ladder and bonus multiplier lights. It is a fabulous sight.

What came after BLACK KNIGHT? Soon after, Williams produced more multiple level games to take advantage of BK's success. They were JUNGLE LORD (March 1981), PHARAOH (July 1981) and SOLAR FIRE (Oct 1981), all of which include Magna Save. The sequel to BK came in 1989 with BLACK KNIGHT 2000. The game is not a carbon copy of the original; it was built with alphanumeric displays, has only three flippers, and the left outlane is now equipped with a kickback rather than a Magna Save. Fortunately the right outlane was left unchanged in that respect, still packing that magnetic wonder.

Backglass of Williams' JUNGLE LORD (1981), one of a series of multi-level games produced following the huge success of BLACK KNIGHT. *Courtesy of Ivo Vasella.* $450-550.

Top right & bottom right: The playfield of JUNGLE LORD; by day and by night. One could not help but compare this game (and the other two multi-level games that followed) to BLACK KNIGHT. There were some obvious similarities, but also many differences. One such difference was the self-contained mini bagatelle style "chamber" playfield, found on the top left-hand corner.

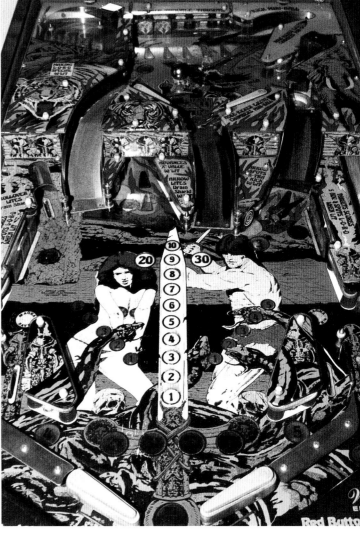

A closer view of a slightly worn JUNGLE LORD upper playfield, along with the enclosed "chamber" bagatelle. Landing the ball in the upper level kickout saucer released a tiny steel ball into the chamber, which consisted of four rollover lanes spelling L-O-R-D.

This popular ball saving device has also appeared on Williams' GRAND LIZARD in 1986, and can now also be found on more recent pinnies by Bally; THEATRE OF MAGIC (1995) and WORLD CUP SOCCER (1994). Both are not quite in the original concept; THEATRE OF MAGIC's are automatically energized by the game, while WORLD CUP SOCCER has a player-activated Magna Goal Save placed near the left flipper to rescue the ball from an unsalvageable situation.

JUNGLE LORD backglass detail.

Williams' SOLAR FIRE (1981), the last of the "awesome foursome" of multi-level games. The next Williams game, BARRACORA, returned to the single-level layout. *Courtesy of WMS industries Inc. All rights reserved.* $500-600.

Hot on the heels of the "Big W" came the rest of the pinball world, all jumping on the multi-level bandwagon.

Bally's first multiple level game, FLASH GORDON, may have been released too close for comfort as far as Williams was concerned, just one month after BK in January 1981. This proves that both companies had been working on the same concept during the same period of time, and that Bally may have been tipped off as to Williams' impending release, or vice versa perhaps. The creative process of building a pinball is a long one and takes several months, hence the release of FLASH GORDON (FG) was merely a second placing for Bally in a race that had been in progress for some time. A far better title than that of a "copy cat" pinball, as some may see it.

Flash Gordon, the motion picture, had just been released in the USA sometime in 1980. The pinball was based on the movie which, in turn, was based on the comic strip character created by Alex Raymond in the 1930s.

FG is a talking machine, as is every game from that time, and the lines come from the bad guy, "Ming the Merciless". The villain was played in the movie by Swedish actor Max von Sydow. Ming says "Miserable Earthling" or "Lucky shot, Earthling" in apparent disgust during play and then rounds it off by saying, "Try again, Earthling" at the end of the game. The attract feature is also quite memorable with "Emperor of Doom awaits."

Bally's FLASH GORDON (1981), was released hot on the heels of BLACK KNIGHT which hit the arcades a month previously. It may not have been as popular as its rival, but it did offer the player some interesting challenges, like 15 seconds of double or triple playfield scoring and a separate bonus system for each level. *Courtesy of Carl Heller.* $475-575.

Just like BLACK KNIGHT, this game is fast, furious and hard to beat. The ramps are especially fast on both machines, accelerating a ball traveling down them like a shot, which then heads for the flippers. The playfield layout and game rules for FG are unique in their own right, but the obvious omission is a multiball feature. There are three ramps connecting the two playfields. The middle one, which is flanked at the bottom by two bumpers, is also guarded at the entrance by a bi-directional kickout saucer which can kick the ball either up the ramp onto the top level or return it into play on the bottom. Both of the other ramps include spinners at their base. The upper level is manned by a solitary two-inch flipper (three flippers on entire game) which make the job of keeping the ball up there quite hard at times. Other standard features include a good selection of drop targets; a bank of three targets, plus a solitary target in front of the plunger lane exit on the upper level; a bank of four targets plus three in-line targets on the lower level.

The more unusual features include two bonus systems, one for the upper playfield scoring and one for the lower, and a 15-second game clock for double or triple playfield scoring. The game clock can be activated in two ways. Knocking down the upper playfield's 1-2-3 bank of drop targets in sequence awards the player a 50,000-point mini bonus and lights the kickout hole for the award of double playfield scoring for 15 seconds. Similarly, if one knocks down the lower level's four drop targets, hits two stationary targets positioned on the opposite side, and completes both return lanes, this awards a "super bonus" of 100,000 points (a large sum in those days) and lights the kickout saucer for the award of triple playfield scoring for 15 seconds. A great game all around!

Bally's game production reverted to single playfields after FG. Six games and almost a year later, their next multi-level offering, came in the form of ELEKTRA (Dec 1981) the first triple-level game! This game, even though it was the first triple-level, has always been overshadowed by its more popular counterpart—Gottlieb's HAUNTED HOUSE, released a few months later.

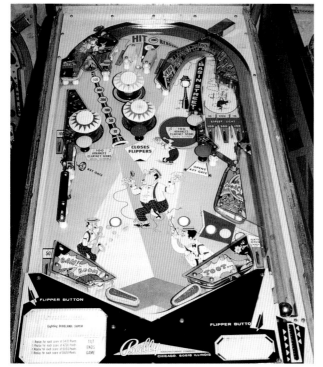

Bally's DIXIELAND (1968). This game is a good example of how designers came so close (yet so far) to multi-level playfields, long before BLACK KNIGHT. DIXIELAND featured an enclosed bagatelle style mini-playfield, accessible via a U-shaped laneway. Had this area been slightly elevated and accessed via a ramp, history would have been made 12 years sooner. *Courtesy of Graham McGuiness.* $425-500.

DIXIELAND playfield details.

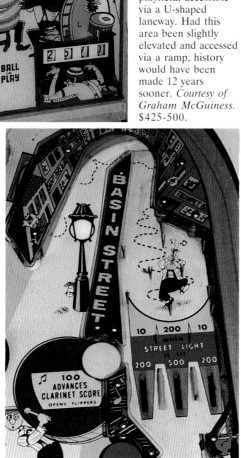

DIXIELAND playfield detail showing the enclosed mini "bagatelle" playfield.

DIXIELAND backglass detail.

of six flippers in all—two on the main playfield, two on the upper, and two on the lower. Four ramps give plenty of entries/exits to and from the upper level and it was also Bally's first multi-level game to include multiball. It was a pinball that for me took a lot of getting used to, due mainly to its scoring complexities, not to mention the lack of return lanes, but I liked it. Like FLASH GORDON, the game's final spoken comment is a memorable one; "You have been exposed to Elektra's radiation...will you return?"

Bally returned to a standard double-level layout in their next two multi-level games; VECTOR (Feb 1982) and BMX (Nov 1982), featuring a futuristic game of roller jai-alai and a BMX cyclo-cross theme (mountain bikes were still a few years away) respectively. VECTOR is a game jam-packed with features, including a breakaway plunger lane which terminated in a figure-8, kickout saucers within both outlanes for the unique Save-a-Ball feature, remote control targets (hitting upper targets in nominated se-

Bally's ELEKTRA (1981), the first triple-level pinball. This game has always been overshadowed by Gottlieb's HAUNTED HOUSE, partly because of the fact that the lower level on this game was self-contained and not connected in any way to the main playfield. *Courtesy of WMS industries Inc. All rights reserved.* $450-550.

ELEKTRA consists of double-level playfield layout similar to the previous Bally and Williams games, with the addition of a third "sunken" level, situated in the center of the main playfield between the slingshots, and visible through a transparent cover. One can be unquestionably correct in saying that ELEKTRA is a triple-level game, but saying that it is actually two pinballs wrapped into one is also correct, although this may prove confusing to those who have never played the game. The bottom level is not part of the general playfield layout where one can enter and leave at will during the course of a game. It is a self-contained playfield unit used as a bonus game once the ball drains to the outhole. Entry is awarded only if a certain amount of "Elektra" points were accumulated during normal play, usually 6 or 10 points (depending on the game setting) earned from the green 1-2-3 targets on the upper level. It boasts a total

-- 222 --

quence drops lower targets automatically one at a time) and even a ramp which measures the speed of the ball, with the readout appearing in an extra digital display embedded in the center of the playfield. Both VECTOR and BMX marked the start and end of 1982, with five single-level games between them making up the rest of that year. The playfield design for BMX was dusted off and re-used almost five years later (with slight modifications but still incorporating that previously mentioned outlane ball saver) on HARD BODY (Apr 1987).

Bally's multi-level VECTOR (1982), a game jam-packed with features. A breakaway plunger lane which ends in a figure-8, kickout saucers in both outlanes for the unique Save-A-Ball feature, remote control targets (hitting upper targets in nominated sequence drops lower targets automatically one at a time) and even a ramp which measures the speed of your ball, with the readout shown on an extra digital display embedded in the center of the playfield. *Courtesy of WMS industries Inc. All rights reserved.* $425-525.

Williams was first, Bally second, and third was Stern Electronics. Poor old Stern, always playing catch-up to the "Big Three" but hanging in there, if only just. LIGHTNING, their first multi-level game, was released in April 1981, five months after BK. It offers a near-symmetrical dual-level playfield, which some considered as Stern's version of BK. Each playfield has a set of flippers, (2" flippers for the upper level) and each flipper set has a pair of slingshots, which do not leave much room for bumpers anywhere on the game. The BLACK KNIGHT similarities continue with banks of three drop targets, a loop shot on the lower playfield and three-ball multiball, which was the main focus of the game. The digital displays include seven-digit scoring, which had just become the style of the times, though scores over 1 million on this game were rare. Like most pinballs built during this period, this game relies heavily on its multiball feature; without achieving this a score rarely reaches over 100,000 points. LIGHTNING was followed by SPLIT SECOND (Aug 1981) and IRON MAIDEN (Oct 1981), the latter of which was mostly distributed in Germany. IRON MAIDEN was the last multi-level game for Stern, and if not taking LAZERLORD (Oct 1984) into account (it only reached the prototype stage), it was only four games away from Stern's last pinball; ORBITOR 1 released in April 1982.

LIGHTNING (1981), Stern's first multi-level game. Parallels in playfield design to BLACK KNIGHT have always been commented, even so, the game strategies were quite unique and challenging. *Courtesy of Carl Heller.* $350-425.

Who else would enter into the world of multi-level pinballs? There were few big names remaining. Gottlieb was next with BLACK HOLE, unleashed as a counter attack on BLACK KNIGHT on October 1981.

The game theme for BLACK HOLE is that of the space phenomenon created by the collapse of a giant star. An object whose mass is so intensely concentrated, that the normal properties of space and time are so drastically altered that even light cannot escape its enormous gravitational pull. Heard all this before? Well almost everyone has heard of a black hole nowadays, but back in 1981 it was still a new and fascinating space thing.

German astronomer, Karl Schwarzschild predicted the existence of black holes as early as 1907, but it was not until sci-fi writers got ahold of the idea and preceded to mold it into televi-

sion and movie scripts that the general public became aware of such a thing.

The ever-popular television series *Star Trek*, appearing between 1966 and 1968, never featured the phenomenon; it was still too early. It was not until T.V serials like *Space 1999* and *Doctor Who*, shown in the early 1970s, that most of my generation got their science education (science fiction education actually) in the finer points of black holes (they were also sometimes known back then as black suns), space travel, time travel and general astrophysics. Later that decade, there was still enough room to exploit black holes even further, and so *Black Hole* the movie was produced by Walt Disney and released in 1979. I have always had a strange feeling that Gottlieb's pinball was somehow linked with the movie, even though they were two years apart.

BLACK HOLE, the pinball, is what I consider to be the first true multi-level game. Gottlieb was the first to use a "sunken" level; an additional play area below the main field, as was used later in Bally's ELEKTRA.

The multi-level layout of games like BLACK KNIGHT or FLASH GORDON consists of a standard playfield split in two, with no actual additional playfield surface area. BLACK HOLE, on the other hand, has the full area of a conventional game, plus approximately 25% more playfield underneath. The lower part of a normal playfield near the flippers and between the slingshots, which had always been left free of devices (this was the domain of bonus and bonus multiplier lights) was cut out on this game and covered with a blue tinted transparent cover. Through this window, one can see the lower playfield; the "Black Hole", in a darkened state, until one manages to get the ball down there, and then the area becomes illuminated. It was a brilliant idea.

This multi-level set out sure had some curious heads turning, and to add to that curiosity was the peculiarity of the sunken playfield sloping away from the player. It is like playing a pinball from the wrong end of the cabinet, with flippers flipping towards you, rather than away; this makes it appear more difficult to play than it really is. Once you become familiar with it, it is actually quite a refreshing way to play the game. Not so for some of the less coordinated players I used to know back then, that never got used to the idea, and it was quite comical to watch them play.

The most frequently asked question by anyone playing the game for the first time is "How do I get down there?" This is easily accomplished by shooting the ball all the way to the end of the left spinner lane, which ends in a U-turn. In the BLACK HOLE parlance it is called the "gravity tunnel". The game periodically encourages the player to "shoot the gravity tunnel" in its characteristic monotone voice. The entry itself is always available, only a silver spinner in the way. However, the question least asked, but more important to how one plays the game, is "How do I get back up?" The answer to that last question and more can be found on the instruction card, which, like any other new pinnie, is ignored until after a few games were played.

If one is not ready for the challenge of entering the "Black Hole" and does not know what to do when down there, then it is a sure-fire way of losing the ball. The lower playfield, due to its smaller area, is a lot faster to play, and only the most skilled players can keep the ball in play there for extended periods. To have the ball delivered safely back to the upper level, all one has to do is let it go down the guts; providing of course one meets the re-entry requirements that state "completing either lower target-bank opens gate". The gate in question is an outlane gate on the right side of the main playfield. The ball is shot up from the bottom through a tube that ends in front of the outlane. If the gate is open one keeps the ball, otherwise it will drain to the outhole with the dreaded announcement by the game's robotic voice; "Re-entry attempt... has failed!"

Close-up of the bottom playfield on BLACK HOLE. Notice the coil ramp on the top left hand corner of the viewing window; this is where the ball entered this lower level.

Center left & bottom left: Gottlieb's BLACK HOLE (1981). This game turned the multi-level concept upside-down, with an extra level below the main playfield—the first true multi-level game. It also featured six flippers, multiball, and an animated backglass with infinity lighting. *Mark Gibson collection.* $525-650.

The rest of BLACK HOLE boasted the usual pinball features of the time—multiball, speech (as just disclosed), etc etc. Classic games like this one always offer hidden attributes that only became apparent once the game is played; a complex multiball feature is one of them. In the name of fairness, as not all readers may be aware of the finer points of multiball, I have included a few paragraphs on this pinball at the end of Chapter Eleven, Part Two, a section that deals specifically with multiball. The other more unusual features worthy of mention are a total of six flippers, a digital bonus display, an animated backglass featuring a rotating disk, and backbox with infinity lighting.

Gottlieb's BLACK HOLE. A close look at the rotating disk animation unit behind the game's backglass.

Infinity lighting uses the same principle as when one stands between two mirrors and can see a "feedback" reflection running off into infinity. A circle of small lights around the inside edge of the backbox, placed between a reflective backglass further back and an extra glass cover in front, gives the same effect; the player able can see the lights running off into the distance. This type of lighting was first used on Bally's SPACE INVADERS (1980), and later on XENON (1980); it works best in dark surroundings.

Gottlieb, in the meantime, not happy with just two levels and six flippers, went on to build one with three levels and eight flippers! What could it be, but none other than...HAUNTED HOUSE!

If one was looking for a pinball with ambiance (the ambiance of an old Gothic mansion), then this was it. It was (and still is) a "one of a kind" pinball. As one might say; after they built it, they broke the mold!

The three levels are only part of its charm; its theme, its simple artwork with fleeing ghosts and great background sound and music (a different theme for each level in fact!), all add to the effect. The game relies on the age-old fascination of all things scary and bone chilling, but in an amusing way. It panders to that irresistible urge that all kids (not to mention adults) have had to explore the spook house at the seasonal amusement park.

The game consists of a lower playfield a la BLACK HOLE and a more conventional extra field, although somewhat smaller, situated on the top right hand corner of the main playfield. I found HAUNTED HOUSE a lot easier to play than BLACK HOLE (a pinball which I loved to hate, as I never seemed to have a good game on it) due mostly to the freedom of going from one level to another without losing the ball due to unaccomplished tasks. Most players (myself included) were relieved at this, as there was no danger of going "downstairs" with the possibility of never getting the ball back, as it was with BLACK HOLE.

One of my favorite images. An even closer look at the disk showing one of the doomed astronauts entering the black hole's event horizon.

Playfield of HAUNTED HOUSE.
See next page for caption.

Looking for a pinball with ambiance? Look no further than Gottlieb's HAUNTED HOUSE (1982). With its three levels, all interconnected, the game quickly became an arcade favorite. The theme, game name and playfield layout were a perfect match, and this lured even the non-pinball playing bystander to have a game. **See previous page for playfield.** *Courtesy of Jan J. Svach.* $625-750.

I will always remember HAUNTED HOUSE as the machine that handed out free games, not because it was too easy to play, but because of a slight problem that occurred with one particular game that resided in the Students Hall of the Tighes Hill Tech College in Newcastle, where I was a student back in 1982. The cost of a game in those days was 40 cents here in Australia (2 x 20-cent pieces), and depositing the coins into HAUNTED HOUSE produced a very distinctive creaking/buzzing sound. On this particular day, during my lunch break, I was playing the pinball with two other friends, one of who was nicknamed "Cookie". Cookie was a rough player, always tilting any machine at least once during a game, a true tilt-oholic. In the course of this game, Cookie slammed his fist down on top of the lock-down bar (the metal rail in front/top of the machine that holds the glass in place) with moderate force, following which the game rang out with that familiar buzzing sound. We all looked at each other for a moment, and without speaking a word we all knew what to do next—hit it again in the same manner, which Cookie did without hesitating. All eyes then focused on the credit display. We all skipped a few classes that afternoon.

As grandiose as HAUNTED HOUSE may have appeared, the game does lack certain contemporary features—speech and multiball. These two exclusions were, I believe, cost cutting measures implemented by Gottlieb in order to keep the game more attractive to distributors at a time when people were turning to video games. The game performed so well that, at first, players did not really notice that the two features had been omitted. Adding to the distraction, of course, are those numerous flippers. Eight flippers are situated as follows: two on the lower level (the cellar), two on the top level (the attic) and four on the main playfield. The four main flippers were wired separately from the others, controlled by a standard pair of flipper buttons. The rest (top and bottom playfields) are controlled by an extra pair of buttons situated slightly further up the cabinet in a similar fashion to the Magna Save buttons on BLACK KNIGHT. Here is where the fun

begins. Send the ball either "upstairs" or "downstairs", and one has to quickly change button positions. The same applies, of course, when the ball returns to the main field. The task is easily accomplished most of the time, but during those times when concentration is lacking, usually leads to a comedy of errors. The same applies of course to first time players, unaccustomed or unaware of the "flipper shuffle".

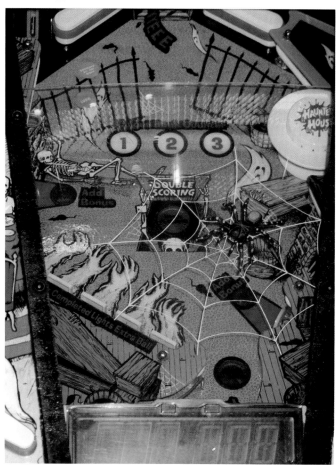

Lower playfield detail of HAUNTED HOUSE. Take a closer look. The owner of this machine decided to give his game an original touch, by placing a plastic spider on the decorative cobweb cover.

HAUNTED HOUSE upper playfield detail.

The artwork contained on the game's backglass features the "American Gothic" house made famous in Alfred Hitchcock's movie *Psycho*, along with a few tombstones situated in the front yard thrown in for good measure. Splashed across the bottom is the game name written in fresh...dripping...blood!

An eerie sight, HAUNTED HOUSE by night. *Photographs courtesy of Jan J. Svach.*

The only other triple-level game to be produced by Gottlieb was KRULL (Feb 1983). Its most striking feature is that of the lower playfield window, which incorporates a reducing lens. This gives the appearance that the lower playfield is very far away, and that the player is looking down a tube or some type of microscope. The ball and the flippers look very small down there, but all are standard size parts. KRULL was produced in such low quantities that it is virtually unknown to most players (myself included), other than what has been written about it in previous books. The failure of this game can be attributed to the decline of pinball popularity. Gottlieb was unable to support the production cost of the game due to poor market response as the company traversed a difficult period in its history. Only three of these games are believed to exist today.

The few games prior to KRULL were also produced in low quantities; one of them was SPIRIT (Aug 1982). A conventional multi-level game (only two levels, with the extra area above the playfield), it had a small production run of approximately 1200 units. It is a very attractive pinball, with a mystic phenomenon theme. The game brochure explains, "Encounter the SPIRIT in a Multi-level, Multiball Masterpiece from Gottlieb." Perhaps its most striking feature is the use of two extra two-inch flippers positioned at the bottom of each outlane. Just like Bally's "Flipsave", a well-timed flip will send the ball through a one-way gate and back into the return lane. One will find that very few people have had the honor of playing SPIRIT, especially those not living in the U.S.A at the time, myself included once again. A very collectible pinball indeed.

If a pinball manufacturer wanted to export merchandise to the opposite side of the globe, and that manufacturer happened to be Zaccaria (or A.M.I.), then the eastern coast of Australia (especially in either Melbourne or Sydney) would be a good place

to start. The exact opposite side of the globe from Bologna (Zaccaria's hometown, and pinball capital of Italy) is actually somewhere on the south island of New Zealand, but I am not sure they ever exported pinballs there.

Zaccaria's first multi-level game was PINBALL CHAMP 82 (March 1982). The pinball was a turning point for this company, a watershed, which put Zaccaria well and truly in the spotlight. It set the style for the games that were to follow, a style of pinball that comes to mind for most people even to this day when the name of Zaccaria is mentioned. Some may argue that the game was not all that popular; maybe so in the U.S.A, but the fact remains that it was successful enough for it to be re-released a year later as PINBALL CHAMP. The most noticeable features are an elevated plunger lane, a transparent upper playfield (more on those two later), a spring-hinged ball dropper which "dropped" the ball gently from the upper playfield, reducing wear on the lower playfield (a device that became a standard item in games to come) and finally, a headset jack positioned under the plunger where a player could plug in a pair of headphones, if one wished not to be disturbed by surrounding noise.

Italy's first multi-level game came in the form of Zaccaria's PINBALL CHAMP 82 (1982). It was their most popular game of all time and one which put Zaccaria well and truly into the spotlight. $375-425.

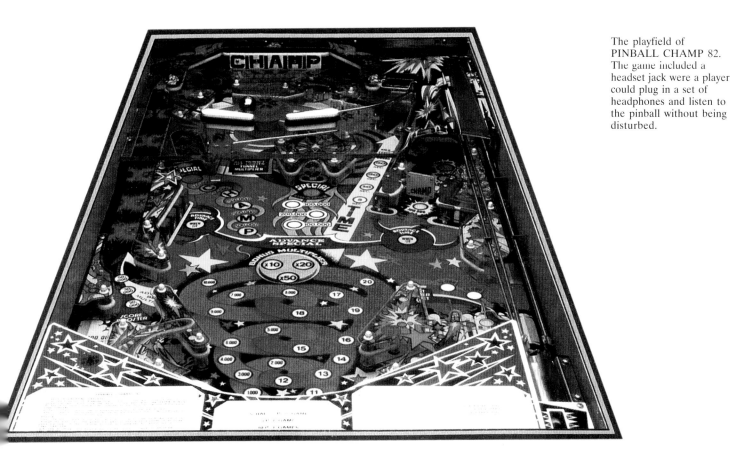

The playfield of PINBALL CHAMP 82. The game included a headset jack were a player could plug in a set of headphones and listen to the pinball without being disturbed.

The first Zaccaria pinball I ever played was SOCCER KINGS (Sep 1982), and as one may have guessed by now, it was their second multi-level game. As an Italian born Australian, I was quite surprised (but pleasantly so) to see an Italian pinball so far from home. Prior to that time, I did not even know there was such a thing as an Italian pinball!

The theme of SOCCER KINGS was, as the name suggests, that of soccer. A game popular in Europe, it was considered a minority sport in Australia and the U.S. at that time, which were the major overseas export markets for Zaccaria. Luckily, the word "soccer" was used in preference to football (a more common name for soccer in Britain), which of course would have created much confusion. "Football" in Australia can mean one of two things, either rugby league or Australian rules, and in the U.S. it is the common name for gridiron.

The next multi-level pinballs to follow in SOCCER KINGS' footsteps (not counting the re-release of PINBALL CHAMP 82) were FARFALLA (Sep 1983), DEVIL RIDERS (April 1984) and MAGIC CASTLE (Sep 1984).

il Flipper dei Campioni del Mondo

Zaccaria's SOCCER KINGS (1982). Zaccaria took advantage of Italy having just won the soccer world cup, held in Spain that same year. The Italian game brochure read, "The pinball of the World Champions." $325-375.

Flipper equipaggiato con il sensazionale dispositivo GAME TIME BONUS® *

FARFALLA is the pinball of love, with a seductive "Madam Butterfly" decorating the backglass. The backglass on DEVIL RIDERS, on the other hand, incorporates an animation unit featuring a motorcycling daredevil doing a "loop-the-loop", accompanied by the roar of a motorcycle, all of which commences every time the ball entered the upper level. On MAGIC CASTLE, Zaccaria reduced its multi-level style to an almost non-existent form. The upper level became nothing more than a sophisticated ramp with no flippers and three separate exits to the lower playfield. In hindsight, it was a sign of things to come. The name itself was a strange one for a pinball that incorporated a horror theme. It was slightly amusing however, as Zaccaria changed the names of famous horror characters Dr. Jekyll, Frankenstein and Dracula, to the playfield characters of Dr. Zekyll, Zankenstein and Zaccula.

DEVIL RIDERS, **see next page for caption.**

Above & top right: Zaccaria's FARFALLA (1983), the game of love. One of the best know multi-level pinballs to come out of Italy and probably one of the hardest names to pronounce—unless of, course, you speak Italian. Like SOCCER KINGS and PINBALL CHAMP, the upper level was transparent, and one could see a set of drop targets beneath. It was a great game to play, but the playfield artwork was not to my liking. $400-500.

Opposite page bottom right, this page top left, bottom left & top right: Zaccaria's DEVIL RIDERS (1984). Another multi-level game with a transparent upper level. Other features included on this game were almost standard equipment for Zaccaria pinballs. These included an elevated plunger lane, flipper save on the outlanes and a plastic molded backglass. Other things included were an animated backglass, featuring a motorcyclist doing a loop-the-loop accompanied by the roar of a motorcycle, all of which commenced every time the ball entered the upper level. The upper level was accessed by knocking down the targets in front of the ramps. The ramps would then lower a drawbridge to allow passage. *Courtesy of Edoardo Frola.* $400-475.

With the exception of MAGIC CASTLE, the additional upper playfields on all of Zaccaria's multi-level pinballs are transparent. Like BLACK HOLE, they can be considered true multi-level games, where the player is able to see the targets and bumpers located on the standard playfield directly beneath. One may also remember the disappearing platform on TIME MACHINE (1983), mentioned in Chapter Five. Although it possesses a moveable level, the game has never been considered multi-leveled.

Outhole view of Zaccaria's DEVIL RIDERS.

Zaccaria's MAGIC CASTLE (1984) reduced the multi-level concept to a minimum; it was a sign of things to come for the whole of the pinball industry. $350-425.

Incidentally, before continuing, I must point out how to correctly pronounce the name Zaccaria. I have found through experience that most people (particularly those unfamiliar with European languages) pronounce the "i" as in "eye", when it should sound like an "ee" as in "pea". The English spelling equivalent would therefore actually be "Zaccarea".

When one plays Zaccaria pinballs frequently, one knows what to expect. Some games have outlane flippers (see Chapter Two), others feature huge bonus multipliers (see Chapter Eleven) and multi-level games like DEVIL RIDERS, FARFALLA and MAGIC CASTLE have drawbridge-type ramps. Other game features that became standard on all Zaccaria pinballs around this time were the "game time bonus" and an elevated plunger ramp.

The bottom of the drawbridge ramps, unlike fixed ramps, could lift up and stop the ball from reaching the upper playfield until certain targets had been hit. The game time bonus is a timed feature much like that found on BLACK KNIGHT, but is available even while playing a single game. During the last ball one can accumulate extra play time (in seconds) by hitting playfield targets. For example, hitting a target awards a few seconds of extra play and the more targets one hits the more time is added, which is then displayed on the credit meter. At the end of the game, the ball returns to the plunger lane, the countdown will then commence and one plays continuously until the flippers lose power, signaling that the awarded time has elapsed.

The elevated plunger lane created by Zaccaria was constructed using a wire-formed conduit, which elevated the ball like a ramp, and transported it to the top of the playfield. The idea behind this was that with the plunger lane removed, the playfield could now be extended to the edge of the cabinet on the right-hand side. In order to achieve this, the conduit still runs along the right hand side of the cabinet, above the playfield, and because it was made of wire it does not obscure the extended playfield beneath it. A more elaborate form of this style can be found on Williams' STAR TREK T.N.G (1993).

Sadly, this is where it all ended, for the time being at least. At the risk of repeating myself ad nauseam, this was due to pinball companies scaling down production as they felt the pinch of video game popularity. The brighter side of the story is that when pinball popularity regained some of its lost ground, designers once again took on multi-level game construction. The history of multi-level pinballs has, in fact, two parts; part one was between 1980 and 1983/84, and part two is from 1986 up until the date of this publication. Let's then move on to part two.

From the introduction of the multi-level game, Williams' BLACK KNIGHT, to the last of such games like Zaccaria's MAGIC CASTLE, marking the end of part one, the percentage of multi-level pinballs built by the major manufactures made up about 25% of their total production. The figure for part two, once again taking into account only major manufacturers (the field now narrowed down substantially), is not quite as high, only about 10%.

This is not because the style of game has gone out of fashion, and once again such things cannot be easily explained and the answers pinpointed exactly, but the answer may be a simple one. Playfield design (not counting technological changes) is not quite the same as it was in 1980; the use of ramps has taken over the game.

The age of the ramp. Since the introduction of multi-level games, the ramp has become a integral part of the standard playfield. Not many pinballs have been built without them since the mid-1980s. Playfield detail from Williams' DRACULA (1993).

It seems that multi-level games left a lasting impression on players and designers, a three-dimensional feeling for pinballs. The playfields of old had only the two-dimensional properties of width and length, but no height; no contours. Simple ramps elevating the ball from the playfield became a simple and cheap way to satisfy that spacial addiction, mimicking a multi-level playfield and hence reducing their production numbers. If one adopts this view, it seems that Bally's XENON was ahead of its time. Released the same month as BLACK KNIGHT, it uses a ramp and a transparent tube to transport the ball from the right to the left-hand side of the playfield. While on that subject, one must not forget that ramps appeared on games built way back in the 1950s; one such game was Williams' NINE SISTERS (1953).

The Bony Beast! Some ramps have taken on very elaborate forms, as seen here on the playfield of Bally's SCARED STIFF (1996).

Williams' F-14 TOMCAT (1987) is a prime example of how the world of pinball had evolved since the beginning of that decade. Like silverball highway overpasses, a great deal had changed since simple ramps were used on games such Bally's XENON, and of course BLACK KNIGHT. *Mark Gibson collection.* $600-750.

Ramps have come in many forms. Many are short and straight with a dead end and a target (like a staircase to nowhere) as could be found on Williams' SPACE SHUTTLE (1984) or FIRE (1988), but some are like rollercoasters that transport the ball from the center of the playfield to one of the return lanes, which sets the player up for repetitive ramp shots, like Williams' CYCLONE (1988) or POLICE FORCE (1989). The latter increases the ramp's value after each successful repetition, starting from as low as 5000 points but reaching a maximum of one million points after several shots. However, the ramp will return back to its lower value if the sequence of repetitive shots is broken.

Ramps are everywhere, and designers seem to invent new ways of twisting and bending the clear plastic or wire-formed conduit from which they are made. One can become lost in the maze of spirals, loops and connections on games like Williams' TALES OF THE ARABIAN KNIGHTS (1996) for example. Games without ramps are very rare indeed these days. One such game is Bally's HARLEY DAVIDSON (1991), the last game produced by Bally with alphanumeric displays. Despite what would be considered an obvious design handicap for a pinball of the 1990s, the game became as much of a classic as the motorbike it was named after. Bally's reasons for not including any ramps is explained on the game's flyer which reads; "In honor of the Classic American Dream Machine, Midway Manufacturing Co. has captured the heart and soul of a Harley Davidson Softail Custom and built it into a straight-forward, back-to-basics Bally pinball."

Two multi-level pinballs that belong in this second part have already been mentioned in the previous paragraphs. One is Bally's HARD BODY (1987) and the other, William's BLACK KNIGHT 2000 (1989). Both these games are without doubt considered multi-level games. There have been other games built,

Ramps loop over in a figure-8 on Williams' TAXI (1988). *Courtesy of Gregory J. Corrigan.*

Williams' PINBOT (1986), a pinball that has undergone many reincarnations. First the sequel, THE MACHINE (1991), and then JACKBOT (1995). It included quite a large flipperless and transparent upper playfield, but most do not regard this as a multi-level game. *Courtesy of Ivo Vasella.* $450-575.

Williams' TALES OF THE ARABIAN KNIGHTS (1996). This game has both clear plastic and wire formed ramps. You can get lost in the maze of spirals, loops and connections. This game will probably be best remembered for its "magic lamp" spinning posts and the "shooting stars" cage-save, a game activated ball saver near each outlane. *Courtesy of WMS industries Inc. All rights reserved.*

however, where this is not as clear-cut. A raised playfield area with a player-controlled flipper is obviously an extra playfield level, but what about a raised level with no flippers, or an over-sophisticated ramp with a flipper or some form of player control? Three such

pinballs were Bally's MOTORDOME (1986), TRANSPORTER (1989) and Williams' NO FEAR (1995), all of which included a ramp flipper where the player could divert the course of the ball to an adjoining ramp and complete the game's skill shot feature. Multi-level or not? Who knows? Who cares, as long as the game is good fun to play! Another such game was Williams' PINBOT (1986). It features a small flipperless extra level on the right hand side of the playfield. The playfield is studded with small posts (like a miniature bagatelle game) but is transparent, where one could see the bumpers beneath on which it was mounted. The ball enters this level via the game's left ramp, which deposits the ball at the top end. The ball simply makes its way downfield bouncing off the posts, and it either falls down to the bumpers through a hole, or is channeled onto the right return lane. A similar design was used five years later on Williams' THE MACHINE-BRIDE OF PINBOT (1991) which was then followed by JACK-BOT in 1995, a remake of PINBOT with an almost identical playfield design.

Extra playfield or sophisticated ramp? You be the judge. Gottlieb's WIPE OUT (1993) has a snow sports theme (skiing, snow boarding, etc) where the player could participate in a down-hill slalom. During one of its many modes, a gate opens, allowing the ball to enter a ski-lift type conveyor belt (the game's patented eye-catching feature, pat #5335910, no joke), which elevates the ball to the top of a ramp, in this case the top of the downhill

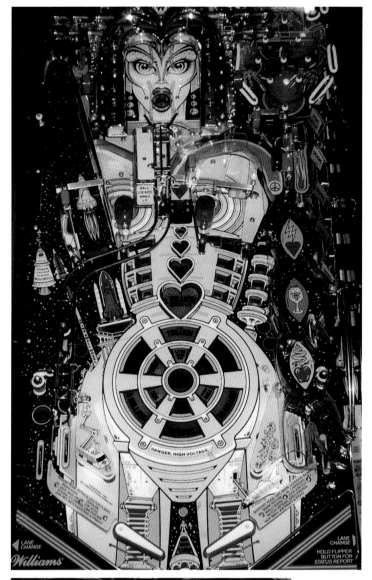

Gottlieb's WIPE OUT (1993). A game where you can go slalom skiing! The game is equipped with a ski lift which takes the ball to the top of a downhill course—a player-controlled ramp. The game featured background music, that of *Wipe Out* by the *Safaris* (1963), music more commonly associated with surfing than skiing, but it suited the game theme perfectly non the less. *Courtesy of Gottlieb Development LLC. All rights reserved.* $725-875.

Top left & bottom left: Playfield and detail of Williams' THE MACHINE: BRIDE OF PINBOT (1991). The last Williams game to feature alphanumeric displays, was the sequel to PINBOT, but far for an exact replica, although it did include some similarities, namely a flipperless and transparent upper playfield. *Courtesy of Jan J. Svach.*

course. Once at the top of the "hill" the ball is then held again by another gate until the end of a three-second countdown, executed in true competition style, before being released: beep... beep... beep... beeeep! The slalom course consists of a series of rollover lanes set up in pairs placed one after the other down a wide but gradual sloping ramp. The object of the slalom is to make the ball pass through the lit lane in each pair of lanes, with the assistance of a mechanism activated by the flipper buttons which shakes the entire ramp. If the ball were heading down the wrong lane, a touch of a button would shake the ramp and hopefully bounce the ball across to the other lane. Almost exactly the same set up (without the conveyor lift) was used on Williams' INDIANA JONES (1993). In this case, the ramp (or miniature playfield) can be inclined from left to right, shifting the ball from one side of the ramp to the other as it makes its way down towards the end. The player also has to deal with holes in the ramp where the ball can fall through.

Playfield detail from Williams' INDIANA JONES: a close-up of the tiltable playfield found on the upper left-hand corner.

Williams' INDIANA JONES (1993), a pinball that without a doubt will go down in history as one of the best games built in the 1990s. The extra wide playfield (630mm) was packed with excitement. It included a small upper playfield which could be tilted from side to side by using the flipper buttons. *Courtesy of Ivo Vasella.* $1150-1400.

Playfield toys from INDIANA JONES, in the form of a WWII German fighter aeroplane, a Messerschmitt if I am not mistaken. *Photos courtesy of Ivo Vasella.*

Williams reached a new level in pinball design with BANZAI RUN (1988), this time including an extra playfield in the backbox! This monster of a machine features a converted backbox that houses a near-vertical playfield that is almost of standard size. Unlike an animated backglass with flippers, as mentioned in Chapter Two, this playfield is connected to the standard playfield in the cabinet by a magnetic ball lift, which transports the ball from one area to the other. One can imagine the gravity of the situation when playing on this vertical upper level—very fast action indeed. The standard size backglass on this game was reduced to a much smaller version (which also housed a standard score display) and was situated above the vertical playfield, making the whole game very tall. The question remains: multi-level or not?

More conventional multi-level pinballs have emerged now and again from the production lines of the major companies, and some of their names and features will be mentioned briefly.

First off the rank was Bally's CITY SLICKERS (March 1987). Released one month before HARD BODY, it had a production run of only 300 units, which makes this a very rare game indeed. It features a small extra level on the top left-hand corner of the playfield, equipped with a solitary 2" flipper. It also features a strange captive ball ramp, again equipped with a solitary 2" flipper. Bally pinballs had me puzzled for quite some time during the late 1980s. The familiar Bally logo was always visible (Bally/Midway since 1983) on both backglass and playfield, as on all pinballs naturally, but what I could not understand was why the style of flipper had changed from the standard "fat" flipper with a rounded tip (much like Gottlieb's), to a thinner flipper resembling the type used by Williams. I later became aware that Midway Mfg. Co. had become a subsidiary of Williams. Two multi-level pinballs built during this time were ESCAPE FROM THE LOST WORLD (another questionable flipper/ramp game, but with a distinctly unique "Bridge of Gold" skill shot) and BLACKWATER 100, both released in 1988.

It seems like more than just coincidence that BLACKWATER 100, the last pinball built by Bally before the takeover, had the same motor-cross dirt bike theme which Williams used a few months later on BANZAI RUN, their next production. BLACKWATER 100 is far from normal; it utilized part of the playfield which up until now had been left untouched by designers. The area in question is the score card plate—found below the flippers, it covers the outhole and is used to display the game instruction card, and on older pinballs, the score card for the replay values. The standard playfield was lowered slightly and this entire area was completely restyled to accommodate an extra playfield, complete with a flipper. The game has three levels—the two just mentioned, plus an additional and more conventional one that one would expect in a multi-level game. With no room for the instruction card near the flippers, it was placed on the back wall of the playfield cabinet under the backbox.

Williams' BANZAI RUN was followed by more two more multi-level games that same year; SWORDS OF FURY (1988) and JOKERZ (1988), two of my favorite games of this period. The extra playfield on JOKERZ is one of these questionable types with no flippers, and is connected by two ramps, one on either side. Other game features include a suspenseful "double your score" shot, available on the last ball, and a small hidden ramp. A ramp hidden below the center of the playfield can be activated by a stationary target, which then raises the ramp to join another section of ramp that is otherwise inaccessible. This allows the player to activate the multiball feature.

SWORDS OF FURY is a pinball with a theme that is a cross between Greek mythology and Dungeons and Dragons. The game includes ramps, tunnels and an elevated playfield. This tricky little extra level gives the player the unwanted option of losing the ball via two exits. One is the obvious "down the guts" exit at the bottom of the playfield, but the other is a secret exit hidden behind what at first appears to be a standard drop target bank. Hitting a target or targets leaves a gap through which the ball can pass and fall into a passage, which eventually leads to the lower playfield.

The end of the decade was drawing near. Gottlieb produced

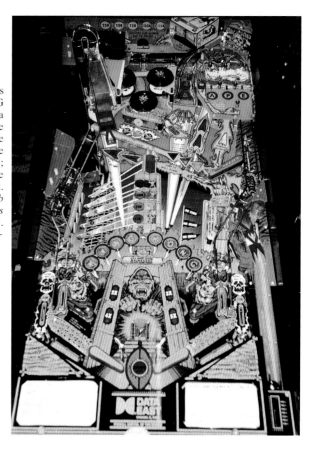

Data East's KING KONG (1990) was a multi-level game that never made it past the prototype stage; only 9 were produced. *Courtesy of Herb Silvers/Fabulous Fantasies.* $2000+

The playfield area is pushed to the limit on Bally's BLACKWATER 100 (1988). The scorecard plate was removed and an extra playfield added, which even included a flipper. A very unusual and eye-catching multi-level game. *Courtesy of WMS industries Inc. All rights reserved.* $575-675.

BONE BUSTERS in 1989, a game with four flippers and a theme that includes skeletons and skulls. It was a game that should not really be included here as there was no upper level. The fourth flipper is used as a "flipper switch gate", and is situated on a small upper ball holding level. A separate flipper button activates the gate. This was followed by a more conventional multi-level pinball; SUPER MARIO BROTHERS in 1992, approximately ten games later; the first machine by Gottlieb with a dot matrix display.

Mamma Mia! Gottlieb's SUPER MARIO BROS (1992). Gottlieb teamed up with Nintendo and gave one of the longest-lived video game characters his own pinball machine. It marked the return of the multi-level game for Gottlieb, and more importantly their first game to include a dot matrix display. *Courtesy of Gottlieb Development LLC and Nintendo of America Inc. All rights reserved.* $525-625.

The first multi-level pinball of the new decade arrived with the 50th birthday of a famous cartoon character; Bugs Bunny. Bally's BUGS BUNNY BIRTHDAY BASH (1991) is another unorthodox design featuring an inverted mezzanine-like playfield area on the left that almost splits the game in two, not top to bottom, but rather left to right. The game also introduced the first ever two-sided captive ball.

The year 1993 saw the release of Bally's POPEYE and TWILIGHT ZONE, Williams' WHITEWATER and Alvin G & Co's PISTOL POKER.

POPEYE's additional level consists of two flippers at the bottom end of a transparent playfield, similar in design to Zaccaria's DEVIL RIDERS, while the extra (and considerably smaller) level on TWILIGHT ZONE has player-controlled magnets, rather than

a set of flippers. Other game features included on TWILIGHT ZONE are a playfield gumball machine and a "power" ball—a ceramic ball, rather than a standard steel ball, which increases the speed of play.

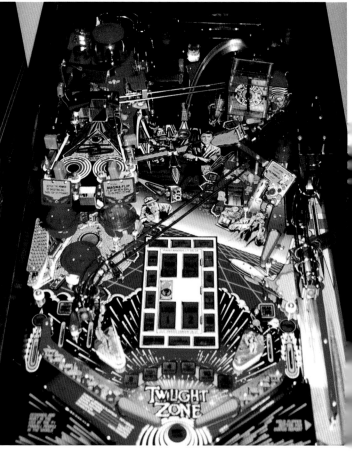

Bally's TWILIGHT ZONE (1993). Another successful game by Bally, which can be described as having a cult following world wide; not to mention the television series it was based on that has also gained that status over the years. The game included a variety of features, including a miniature gumball machine, a ceramic ball, and an additional upper level with Magna-flip flippers. *Courtesy of Mark Gibson.* $850-1000.

The very small upper playfield on TWILIGHT ZONE, known as the power field. The object is to defeat the "power" by shooting the ball though the top of the pyramid using magnets as flippers.

Bally's TWILIGHT ZONE playfield detail. Upper playfield detail showing a very sharp switchback ramp in the background, the "clock", and below that the "player piano" with moving target. *Photos courtesy of Mark Gibson.*

Backbox of Williams' WHITEWATER (1993), a game with plenty of ramps and rapids. *Courtesy of Dean Grover.* $900-1100.

Williams' WHITEWATER is a wickedly fast game which includes a "mini" upper playfield were there resides a single flipper and a furry little fellow called Big Foot, whose head spins around on various occasions. The plunger skill shot on this game is a close relative of that surprise entry found on BLACK KNIGHT that tricked many a player. The idea is to plunge the ball with the right force for it to make the upper playfield at a comfortable speed, in order to shoot for a ramp named "Insanity Falls" and collect the skill shot award. Plunging too softly leaves the ball in the plunger lane. Plunging too hard sends it down the "Spine Chiller" (another ramp) and hurtling towards the flippers.

Alvin's PISTOL POKER saw the return of a multi-level design reminiscent of those early years of the double-level game, which had occurred only just over a decade before, a period that seemed so far away for players like myself. The advertising slogan on the game's brochure stated that the game had "True multi-level play" and that "Alvin G. takes pinball to the next level!"

Alvin G & Co's PISTOL POKER (1993), a game design reminiscent of the early days of multi-level pinballs. As the brochure says, "True multi-level play!" This game was to be the last produced by this company. *Courtesy of Alvin J. Gottlieb. All rights reserved.* $600-725.

Data East released their first multi-level game on February 1994 with ROYAL RUMBLE, a game featuring the superstars of American wrestling at the time. The additional playfield is a small affair, comprised of two small flippers and one bank of three drop targets. This little level is instrumental for the start of the multiball feature. During a game, once the criteria for multiball is complete, one then shoots the ball onto this extra level to commence it. Multiball then starts on the lower playfield, and the player has to keep the balls in play on both levels.

Next came Bally's THE SHADOW, released on November 1994, one month short of BLACK KNIGHTS' 13th birthday. Like FLASH GORDON, the game's theme was based on the motion picture of the same name, which in this case starred Alec Baldwin. This game saw the introduction of yet another feature; I am not certain of its proper name but for this explanation I will call it the "slide" flipper. Residing on the extra level, the device is very different to that of a normal flipper. It consists of a bat that can be moved from left to right along the end of the playfield. The idea is to move the bat in the area of where the ball is heading at the right moment, hitting the ball almost at a tangent and slicing it back up the playfield. Personally it is much easier said than done. Other than the slide flipper, the game includes an extra pair of flipper buttons to activate two very elaborate ramp guides built in the form of Phur-bu daggers. The guides are placed at ramp junctions so the player can decide which way he/she wants the ball to go, just like a junction point on a railway.

Last but not least (hopefully not the last multi-level game we will see, I am sure) we come to Williams' CONGO, released on November 1995, a good cut-off point for this chapter. Yet another motion picture pin, but strangely enough, appearing a long time after the movie's release.

Data East's ROYAL RUMBLE (1994), the first multi-level pinball built by Data East. It featured the stars of championship wrestling and their voices could be heard while playing, especially that of Hulk Hogan. $825-1025.

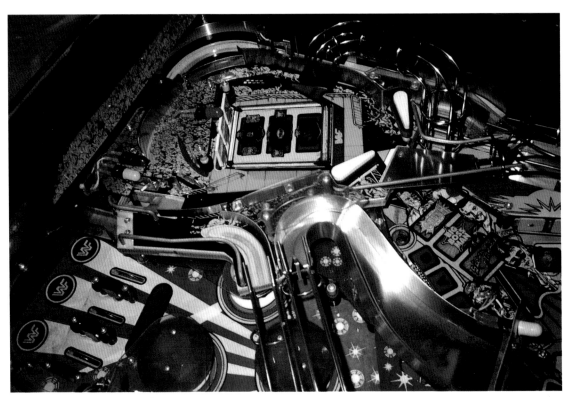

Close-up shot of the upper level on ROYAL RUMBLE.

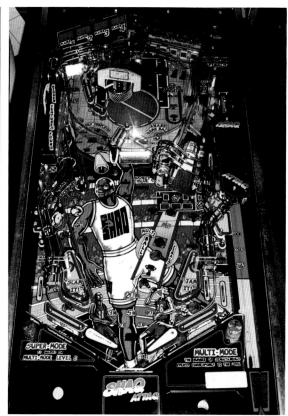

Gottlieb's SHAQ ATTAQ (1994) was not a multi-level game, although the top half of the playfield was kind of a mezzanine split level. The most interesting feature was the tiny jump ramp and basketball net. Yes, one could actually make the ball jump, fly though the air and land in the net— pretty neat. I bet it took the designers a while to get that to work just right.
Courtesy of Gregory J. Corrigan. $725-900.

Casting our minds back to the days of Bally's ELEKTRA, this game's extra playfield consists of a self-contained "sunken" level residing between the slingshots. Completing a number of shots on the upper playfield activates the level. The ball is then held on the upper playfield while the lower level commences play. The play strategy now concentrates on a set of five stationary C-O-N-G-O targets which have to be completed within a specified brief period of time, before the level is automatically disabled. The interesting feature is the use of an unorthodox set of flippers; the player uses the flipper buttons in order to have a little figurine of a gorilla bat the ball around with his hands!

Thus ends the lecture on multi-level games. If you are newly converted to this type of game and would like to buy one, be aware that some of the older games like BLACK HOLE, HAUNTED HOUSE or BLACK KNIGHT especially, are becoming quite expensive and will continue to rise in price as the years roll on and their legends grow.

SHAQ ATTAQ backglass detail. It's not over 'till the fat lady sings. The fat lady *is* singing, so let's move on to the next chapter.

In the previous ten chapters, the game of pinball has been dismantled into some of its major parts, the history and an analysis of game strategy for each has been explained. One unavoidable problem remains when something is pulled apart and categorized in such a fashion, and that is that we end up with bits and pieces, odds and ends. Here is a miscellaneous pile of pinball knowledge and history too big to be left out, though each individual subject is too small to be given its own chapter—hence the necessity for a chapter with the lot.

Part One: Add-a-Ball Pinballs

What are add-a-ball pinballs? Is it a completely different style of game that requires odd skills and strategies? Are add-a-ball pinballs still around? The answers to those questions and more will be answered here.

Warning sign on Genco's METRO (1940), informing players of the law requirements of the time. *Courtesy of Russ Jensen.*

Imagine a pinball where rather than receiving a free game when a certain score was reached, one was awarded with an additional ball. It is similar to receiving an "extended time" award when completing a lap within a specified time on a car racing video game, or the equivalent of the "extra man" awarded on most video games for reaching the designated score intervals to enable the player to keep playing. Well, that is the principle behind an add-a-ball pinball. Add-a-ball pinballs are no longer produced, the last of such games being SPEAK EASY and SPECTRUM, which were both produced by Bally in August 1982.

The first add-a-ball game, FLIPPER, was produced by Gottlieb on November 1960, in order to expand their U.S. pinball market into territories where pinballs awarding free games were still classed as prohibited gambling devices. The game of pinball had many problems with the concept of free play. Originally intended as a player incentive, a reward for skillful playing, it was seen as "something of value" in quite few U.S. states. Most of the blame

for this erroneous view can be placed on bingo machines, first used in 1951. As briefly stated earlier in Chapter Six, bingo machines were flipperless pinball look-alikes built to sidestep the gambling laws, while still allowing operators to award payouts. These machines awarded numerous free games (up to 999 in some cases) too many for anyone to be expected to play, so players were paid off in cash by operators. The operator would then clear the credit display. Although the playfields and the skill factors required were vastly different, pinball and bingo machines had almost identical cabinets, and so one can see how pinball was mistaken by some for a gambling game.

Bally's HI-FI (1954), a typical in-line bingo machine from that era. The first bingo machines were produced in 1951. This was a single card bingo but it also incorporated two extra "super" cards. It also incorporated a bump feature, a mechanical way to nudge the playfield to change the course of the ball before it fell into an undesired hole. The playfield was connected to two solenoids that shifted the playfield up (vertically), then back down to its original resting position. This was a violent movement. The bump feature was disconnected while the game was paying off, so as not to dislodge any balls in winning combinations. There were two buttons, one on each side of the cabinet (like flipper buttons) used to operate this, wired in parallel. **See next page for playfield.** *Courtesy of Rick Force.*

The add-a-ball feature brought down the law barriers which kept pinball out of certain states because the extra balls awarded were no longer seen as something of value but a form of game play extension.

FLIPPER was a big success for Gottlieb and so out came a string of similarly named games like FLIPPER PARADE (1961), FLIPPER FAIR (1961) and FLIPPER COWBOY (1962). On all these games, and others to follow, a player could accumulate up to ten extra balls to play. Williams jumped on the add-a-ball bandwagon by the end of 1961 with SKILL BALL (Sept 1961), then followed with more popular games like FRIENDSHIP 7 (1962) and VAGABOND (1962). SKILL BALL was originally named "Add-a-Ball", but there were concerns over Gottlieb having rights to that as a generic word for extra-ball/extended play type games, and that using it as a name for a specific pinball would cause legal problems. Apparently, a couple of games with the original "Add-a-Ball" backglass still exist.

Playfield of HI-FI. **See previous page for caption.**

Backglass of FLIPPER CLOWN. **See next page for caption.**

Bally's DIXIELAND (1980), not the pinball but another bingo machine. If you thought the inside of an EM game looked complicated, take a look at this monster! The inside of the cabinet was fitted with an electric fan to circulate the air within and stop the circuit motors from overheating! This was one of the last bingo machines built by Bally and was designed by Don Hooker, who designed almost all of the Bally's bingos since 1951. Approximately 100 in all! Landing a ball in a hole will light the corresponding number on the set of six cards shown on the backglass. Games are awarded, which are then redeemable for prizes or cash, when certain combinations are made; e.g. four numbers in a row. *Graham McGuiness collection.*

The small notice of "balls to play" rather than "ball in play", which appears on the backglass, is usually a dead give-away when it comes to identifying an old add-a-ball pinball.

The add-a-ball game was also welcomed in Italy, where pinball operation was governed by strict regulations and replay models were prohibited. Gottlieb began exporting pinballs there to join the already existing add-a-ball games manufactured by local companies such as Elettrocoin, based in the historic city of Florence.

By the mid 60s, manufacturers were turning out machines in both replay and add-a-ball versions. These pinballs would have the same playfield and art, but different names. One could be forgiven for experiencing a touch of *deja vu* when playing what may have appeared to be a new game, especially if one had just come home from a couple of weeks in Italy. Some of the replay models converted to add-a-ball were Gottlieb's CROSS TOWN (1966) became SUBWAY, ICE REVUE (1966) became ICE SHOW, Williams' MAGIC CITY (1967) became MAGIC TOWN and Gottlieb's EL DORADO (1975) became GOLD STRIKE, just to name a few.

Backglass of GOLD STRIKE.
See next page for caption.

Gottlieb's FLIPPER CLOWN (1962). After the success of FLIPPER (1960), the first add-a-ball pinball, Gottlieb produced several similarly named games to emphasize their add-a-ball appeal. These included FLIPPER FAIR (1961), FLIPPER COWBOY (1962), and of course this game. **See previous page for backglass.** *Courtesy of Ivo Vasella.* $750-900.

Gottlieb's FLIPPER FAIR (1961), one of the five pinballs in the so-called "flipper" series. *Jeff Grummel collection.* $725-875.

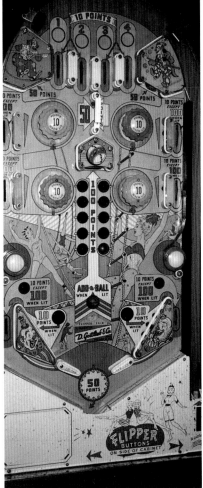

Williams' FRIENDSHIP 7 (1962). One of the best known add-a-ball pinballs built by Williams. The game was named after the *Mercury* space capsule which John H. Glenn navigated on Feb 20, 1962. It orbited the Earth three times and splashed down in the Atlantic Ocean after a five-hour flight. *Courtesy of Tim Van Blarcom.* $500-600.

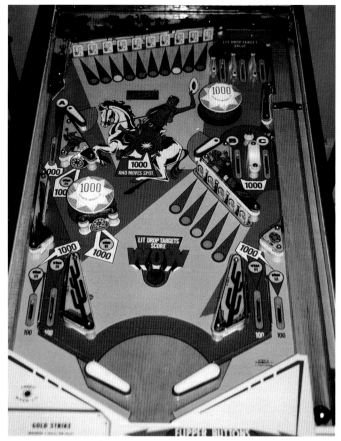

Gottlieb's GOLD STRIKE (1975), yet another remake of EL DORADO, this time in add-a-ball format. **See previous page for backglass.** *Courtesy of Mark Gibson.* $475-575.

By 1977 add-a-ball pinballs were becoming extinct as the gaming laws were revised in response to sociopolitical change. Add-a-ball games were no longer manufactured as separate models but incorporated in replay models as a convertible option. Standard replay models convertible to add-a-ball first appeared as early as 1967 in games like BEAT TIME by Williams, which featured a rock n' roll band called *The Bootless*—an obvious attempt to cash in on the wave of Beatlemania that was sweeping the world at the time.

Williams BLAST OFF (1967) was an add-a-ball version of APOLLO, also built in 1967. Both had the same artwork and playfield, only the name changed. Notice the vertical (pachinko style) bagatelle on the backglass. It shot a tiny ball from the top of the rocket which then bounced off the pins and jitterbugged its way down to land in one of five scoring slots. This took place at the end of every ball providing the 1 to 10 countdown (rollover buttons) was completed by hitting the specified "advance" targets and bumper. The game was built during the U.S. Apollo missions which first put man on the moon. *Courtesy of Tim Van Blarcom.* $500-600.

Backglass and upper playfield of MAGIC TOWN (1967), the add-a-ball version of MAGIC CITY. *Courtesy of Tim Van Blarcom.* $525-650.

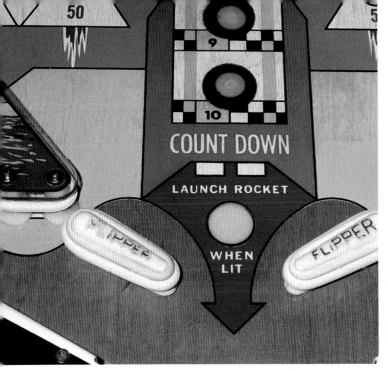

Summary

1960 First add-a-ball pinball built by Gottlieb.
1967 Replay pinballs have the option of add-a-ball conversion.
1979 Last EM replay pinball convertible to add-a-ball built by Gottlieb.
1982 Last add-a-ball pinballs built, Bally's SPEAK EASY and SPEC-TRUM.

Part Two: Multiball

The term "multiball" has been mentioned several times throughout this book without explanation beyond its obvious meaning. Here now all will be revealed in more detail—its history, its concept and the player strategies involved.

BLAST OFF upper and lower playfield details.

Playfield detail from Bally's FIREBALL (1972) featuring the god of multiball himself.

The last EM replay pinball convertible to add-a-ball was BLUE NOTE, produced by Gottlieb in 1979. Since then, the first and (up until now) last SS add-a-ball pinball was the previously mentioned SPEAK EASY, a failed attempt at re-introducing this particular style of game. SPEAK EASY was also released as a replay model for the German market. The convertible option to add-a-ball on replay models is still available on most modern machines.

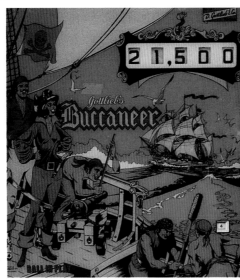

Gottlieb's BUCCANEER (1976) was also released in add-a-ball format as HIGH SEAS. *Courtesy of Mac.* $350-425.

One will not find the word "multiball" listed in the dictionary; it is a term exclusive to pinball, which describes the event of having more than one ball on the playfield at the same time. The multiball quantity changes from game to game. It can be as low as a two-ball multiball (the ordinary playfield ball plus an extra one) like on Bally's EMBRYON (1981) or as high as a staggering thirteen-ball multiball on Sega's APOLLO 13 (1996), but the most commonly used is the three-ball multiball.

Bally's EMBRYON (1981), was a wide body game which incorporated a two-ball multiball feature. *Courtesy of Tim Van Blarcom.* $425-500.

When a player engages the multiball feature on a pinball it is the start of a very different playing technique, literally a kind of juggling act. The interaction between balls makes for a very fast and unpredictable game, requiring the player to keep track of the entire playfield rather than focusing on just one ball. The longer one keeps the extra balls in play, the greater the scoring benefits, plus it increases the opportunity to complete high scoring features only available during multiball which cease as soon as all the additional balls are lost and normal play resumes.

How does one start this multiball action? Well, to specifically answer that question for each pinball would fill the pages of this book, so it is important to read the instruction card on any game before playing.

The first game to contain the multiball feature was Bally's BALLS-A-POPPIN produced in 1956. The term multiball had yet to be introduced so Bally named it the "wild balls" score booster feature. A player could receive up to six extra balls bouncing around the playfield at once, all shot automatically into play by the game's "wild balls bazooka"! The same basic game was re-released with minor playfield modifications a year later and named CIRCUS. It has been said that BALLS-A-POPPIN inspired Jim Patla to build a similar multiball feature when he designed CENTAUR for Bally in 1981.

The next revolutionary multiball pinball came from Williams, BEAT THE CLOCK in December 1963. This pinball featured a two-ball multiball play. To achieve multiball, a player had to lock (the common word used to this day) the first ball in one of the playfield kickout saucers. A second ball would then be made available and was put into play by using the plunger. If the second ball completed certain features, the first ball would be released to start multiball play. The modern multiball scenario was born. Bally went one step further that same month and released STAR JET, with a three-ball multiball. The concept was the same as BEAT THE CLOCK, except that any unused locked balls would remain captive and be carried over from game to game. This same feature would be repeated three years later on CAPERSVILLE, a very successful game which reached a production run of over 5000 units, big numbers for the 60s. Other EM multiball pinballs built by Bally were WIGGLER (1967), FOUR MILLION B.C. (1971) and FIREBALL (1972).

Detail of lock indicating light on the playfield of Sega's MAVERICK (1994). In this case one must lock all three balls before multiball can be achieved.

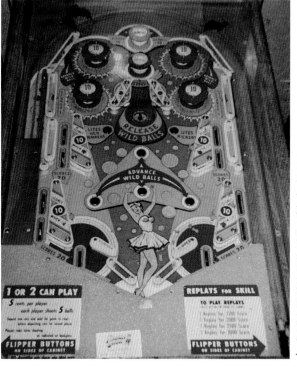

Bally's BALLS-A-POPPIN (1956). This game was not what one could call your typical game. For instance, it was a two-player game but with light-up scoring. It also incorporated a feature that was to become a standard inclusion on all pinballs 30 years later; multiball. *Courtesy of Russ Jensen.* $1075-1275.

introducing additional balls into the plunger lane and thus onto the playfield using the mechanical ball lift. On one of these regular five-ball games there was nothing stopping the player from pushing up all five balls at once, if for instance one was in a hurry to finish off a game. This practice did not improve the score or general play in any way, and was probably detrimental to the machine.

The faster scoring ability of electronic pinballs, plus their overall versatility, was ideally suited for multiball action, but surprisingly the first SS machine to incorporate multiball did not appear until March 1980, Williams' FIREPOWER. FIREPOWER, better known for introducing the lane change feature, had a three-ball multiball and was the industry's first big hit of the year. Williams re-used the same theme four years later when they released FIREPOWER 2 in January 1984. The first SS multiball offerings from other U.S. companies became Bally's XENON (Dec 1980), Stern's FLIGHT 2000 (Oct 1980) and Gottlieb's FORCE 2 (Jan 1981). Multiball is now a standard feature on all new pinballs, and has been so since about 1985. Prior to this, partly due to the pinball recession in the early 1980s, only about half of all SS games produced included multiball.

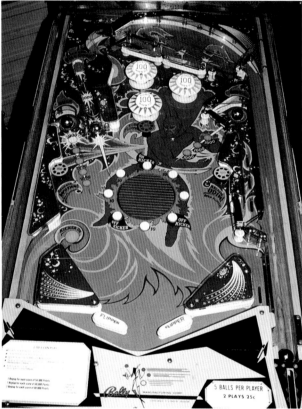

Bally's FIREBALL (1972), considered by many pinball enthusiasts to be the most collectible game ever made. A pinball book would not be complete without it. It combined a unique assortment of playfield features (two- or three-ball multiball being one of them), along with the eye catching artwork of Dave Christensen. Multiball can be hectic enough by itself without the added mayhem caused by the game's whirlwind spinner and zipper flippers. This has caused some division amongst players, many commenting that it became a game of luck rather than skill. *Rawdon Osborne collection.* $1400-1700.

Backglass detail of XENON (1980), Bally's first SS multiball game. *Photo courtesy of Peter Graabaek.*

During the EM era, there were very few pinball games built with the multiball feature. One of the reasons for this was linked with the deficiency in the EM scoring system, as explained in Chapter Three. Most of the scoring shots would not register if two or three different targets were to be hit simultaneously, therefore rendering a multiball, in most cases, a non-event scoringwise. On older EM games prior to the introduction of the ball return kicker (refer to Chapter Seven) one could create a multiball scenario by

Multiball has never been a compulsory feature that one had to complete during a game, but since its introduction, it has always played an important part in obtaining replay scores, especially in the older SS games. Unlike the new games of today (that boast an abundance of scoring options), their game play strategy was almost exclusively centered around achieving multiball. The rewards for reaching this stage have always been lucrative, but obviously only if one could keep the extra balls in play.

The first multiball incentives on SS games came as increased playfield scoring. If one achieved two-ball multiball then all playfield scores would be doubled, or tripled with three-ball multiball. To prevent any confusion to the reader, in the case of a target worth 900 points, it would be worth 1800 points and 2700 points for two- and three-ball multiball respectively. Without this type of incentive, during three-ball multiball, one could score three times faster than single ball play but not necessarily three times more. The need for multiplied scoring rewarded the player for the added risk and unpredictability involved with juggling more than one ball. If the scores remained the same between single and multiball plays, the player may well choose to stay with a single ball to achieve the same score, though it would take longer, because it was safer and more manageable. Either way it was applicable only as long as the extra balls were in play, and not all games were equipped with such a feature. Some games had no playfield multipliers at all, while others required the player to complete certain shots (during multiball of course) in order to increase their value. In the case of Stern's LIGHTNING (1981), these could be raised by shooting the ball through a small loop, which eventually increased the playfield values up to four times! On such pinballs one could easily amass enough points for a free game in one solid minute of multiball play with multiplied scoring, than would otherwise be accrued during a whole game without.

FATHOM playfield detail showing the double and triple playfield scores attainable during two-ball and three-ball multiball respectively.

FATHOM playfield detail of a locked ball. Locking the ball during play resets the in-line targets in front, while another ball is released into the plunger lane. Knocking down all three targets in front of the locked ball will release it and start two-ball multiball.

In 1986 the progressive jackpot feature was introduced on Williams' HIGH SPEED. A jackpot value is awarded during multiball if the player manages to make a difficult ramp shot (difficult under multiball conditions) with one of the balls. If the player fails, the jackpot value increases slightly, ready for the next multiball. If and when the jackpot is awarded, its value readjusts to a nominated base amount, ready again for the next multiball. It has become imperative to collect at least one jackpot value during a game, because the increased playfield scoring during multiball is no longer available. One has to do something during multiball rather than just keep the balls in play for as long as possible. The jackpot value will at times rise above the replay value of the game. For example, on Williams' JOKERZ (1988), the jackpot prize can reach a ceiling value of four million, which is approximately four times higher than the average replay value. A non-progressive jackpot value (one fixed at a certain value) is now a standard feature on all pinballs to date. On some pinballs the player can still increase the jackpot value (although only marginally) by completing or hitting certain targets or bouncing off the bumpers. These values automatically reset at the start of each new game. Jackpot values are now lesser in value, more relative to the replay scores than what they were back in the late 80s, unless of course one hits the super jackpot. The super jackpot is awarded when a second jackpot shot is made using the same multiball, and is (in some cases) double in value, though it is not available on all games.

Bally's FATHOM (1981). Multiball! Can you spot three balls in amongst the elaborate artwork? $525-625.

Before HIGH SPEED's jackpot feature set roots and grabbed the pinball world by the throat, other game designs featured slightly different multiball strategies. One pinball from Williams, strangely enough, incorporated a "Time Lock" feature. Found on ROAD KINGS (1986), which was built only a few months after HIGH SPEED, it gives the player the task of returning the balls back into the locks. The "Time Lock" is activated during the game's two-ball multiball, when one of the balls is returned into one of any three lock sites (two kickout holes and one ramp shot). This gives the player about ten seconds to re-lock the remaining ball in order to receive the "Time Lock" bonus. Once this is achieved the player has yet another chance to score, this time at the now lit "Mega Score" bonus by shooting under the left ramp. Pretty neat feature! If one cannot lock the remaining ball within the specified time for the "Time Lock" bonus, the first ball is re-released and the process starts over again. So long as one keeps both balls in play, one can continue in this attempt indefinitely.

The word multiball strikes fear into the hearts of pinball novices everywhere. For those of you intending to step into the world of the silverball, fear not, something is on your side—the ball saver. The feature is also known at times as the drain shield.

Introduced into pinballs at the start of the 1990s, it has also now become a standard playfield item. What the ball saver does is to give the player a honeymoon period at the start of each ball (approximately five to ten seconds), where if bad luck prevails and the ball is lost, it is returned to the plunger lane for a second chance. This also applies at the start of a multiball session, which can be a great relief for some, especially after having worked so hard to get there. Even if all the balls are lost within the first few seconds, they will be returned into play. In those early days before the ball saver was introduced, it was always disheartening to see a hard-earned multiball end in a matter of seconds.

The ball saver time limit, like most things, is set by the operator, and this means that it can also be turned off, so beware! One can gauge the amount of time left before the ball saver feature turns off by glancing at the playfield light situated between the flipper tips. This light has always been known as the "shoot again" extra ball light, which now has a second function. If the light is flashing on and off slowly, then there is plenty of time left. As the flashing becomes faster and turns into a rapid flicker, time is running out, only one or two seconds are left. It may sound like a crude timepiece to some, but for the experienced it is as good as a Swiss chronometer. The same type of indicating light was first used by Williams on their timed re-setting targets, like those on BLACK KNIGHT, as mentioned in Chapter Ten.

For every game, the multiball feature usually has a title in keeping with the overall theme. As previously explained, there are many ways of initiating multiball, and the most common way is by "locking" balls into traps. There have been games produced that have more than one area in which to lock balls, each pertaining to a different mode of multiball. One classic example is Williams' DRACULA (1992). It has three multiball modes: coffin multiball, castle multiball and mist multiball. The first two modes have separate lock sites, while the latter is a very original feature. When activated, a ball appears out of a side pocket of the playfield, and is pulled across to the opposite side by an underlying magnet, which travels on tracks. The object is to hit and dislodge the ball to begin two-ball multiball play before it disappears into the opposing pocket. Seeing the ball make its way across the playfield "no strings attached" always reminded me of the typical spooky séance, where objects move around by themselves. However, like all things, this particular mode has a couple of hidden surprises in store for the unwary (though not intentionally designed, I think). As the ball travels across the playfield, if one doesn't hit it hard enough with the first ball, both balls become stuck to the magnet, until one is released back into play as the other disappears into the opposing pocket. The other equally frustrating scenario is when the player's ball is successful in deflecting the trapped ball

from the magnet, but then becomes trapped in its place, because the initial strike occurred too quickly for the machine to detect and deactivate the magnet. One small consolation with this particular outcome is that the player still has a chance to shoot for the trapped ball with the now freed ball before it disappears once again on the opposing side.

Williams' DRACULA (1993), a game famous for its three different multiball modes, Coffin, Castle, and its most spectacular—the no-strings-attached Mist multiball. When one achieved two or even all three multiball modes at the same time, then one was awarded with Multi-Multiball, where any jackpots attained were doubled or tripled respectively. $800-975.

Multiball mode and jackpot multiplier indicating lights from Williams' DRACULA.

DRACULA playfield detail during Mist multiball. The silver trail is the ball making its way up the playfield; no strings attached!

Here now, as promised in the previous chapter, is where I'll explain how multiball worked on Gottlieb's BLACK HOLE, but first a small intro.

Attempting to control two or three balls at once on the same playfield is at times hard enough, without involving additional playfields! But that is the challenge one faces when playing multi-level games.

Williams' BLACK KNIGHT has a two- or three-ball multiball, depending on how many balls one manages to lock on the upper "extra" level, before releasing them by shooting for the kickout hole on the lower level with the free ball. Like Data East's ROYAL RUMBLE, multiball commences on the two separate levels. This takes the playing strategy one step further, as one has to extend one's field of view across both playfields. Anyone with chameleon-like eyesight would really excel at this point.

BLACK HOLE is no different, but it does give the player the option of keeping the multiball together on a single playfield, or spreading it out between levels. The game has two lock sites, one on each playfield. The lower playfield lock is always enabled, but the upper lock (on the main playfield) is enabled by hitting all four of the lit stationary targets on the lower right side of this same playfield. One may remember that the additional level on this game is situated below the main or "upper" playfield, and faces the opposite way. These targets are automatically reset after each ball, but the upper lock, once lit, remains lit. A ball locked on the lower level remains locked until multiball is activated or until the game ends, in which case it is released and drained to the outhole. A ball locked in the upper lock is released at the end of each ball, although the lock remains lit until multiball is complete, or the game ends. This is one of a few properties I dislike about the game. Having gone to all the trouble of locking the ball, it has to be re-locked if one loses the free ball. Are you with me so far?

After both locks have captured a ball, multiball starts by shooting the free ball into the "gravity tunnel", transferring it onto the lower level. This releases the lower locked ball only, so that the player starts with a two-ball multiball on the lower level. Once both balls are lost there, they are then launched one at a time back to the main upper playfield where, simultaneously, the upper playfield lock releases its ball. If the ball return gate is open, the player ends up with all three balls on the upper playfield, with the lower playfield remaining open. The fun really begins if the player can now man-

age to return a ball or two back to the lower playfield; then one of the truly unique features of BLACK HOLE becomes apparent. One ends up playing multiball on two levels in opposite directions simultaneously!

One final word of advice to conclude this part—the worst time to lose your cool is during multiball. Take a deep breath, and sound the trumpet. "The cavalry is coming...Charge!"

Summary

1956 First multiball feature used on Bally's BALLS-A-POPPIN.
1963 Williams' first multiball pinball built.
1980 First SS multiball pinball built by Williams.
1986 Jackpot feature introduced during multiball play to replace multiplied playfield scoring.

Part Three: The Tilt and The Bonus System

Every reasonably experienced pinball player knows the consequences of playing a game too rough. Shaking the machine too hard and too often will cause the machine to suddenly loose power. Lights go out, flippers don't work, the ball drains to the outhole and the word "TILT" is displayed on the backglass or on the score display. What has just been committed is a pinball no-no, and usually followed by comments from the participant claiming innocence like "Oh...no way, I didn't even touch the thing!"

Tilt, pinball's four letter word. Backglass detail from Genco's METRO, with the tilt sign displayed on the passing spaceship.

The tilt (pinball's four-letter word) is the anti-cheating mechanism, which stops players from using too much physical exertion in order to gain the upper hand on the laws of physics, namely gravity.

Tilting today's pinballs just stops players from being too aggressive. Overstepping the mark is occasionally just part of the game, however, a pinball will tilt long before anyone reaches a stage of cheating. After all, all that is really at stake is a free game. The penalty for tilting a pinball is losing the ball in play and the bonus.

The bonus is pinball's equivalent to a superannuation fund. For every significant point value scored or playfield feature completed, an additional score value is accumulated, and then added to the total score at the end of each ball. More about that later.

The pinball world of the penny arcade during the Great Depression was more of a casino than an innocent amusement center suitable for families and children. A lot of money was involved with

IMPROVED SPORTSMAN. See next page for caption.

-- 253 --

payout pinballs—desperate gamblers, shifty characters and very alert operators. There was too much to gain from cheating for players, and too much to lose for operators. Early pinballs were lightweight and easy to lift and shake, so before the tilt mechanism was invented, the only way that operators could discourage cheating was by nailing countertop games to the counter tops themselves.

O.D.Jenning's IMPROVED SPORTSMAN (1935) pay-out pinball. Like many games of that era, a "stool pigeon" tilt was used. To receive a payout one had to land balls in the matching holes (two rabbits, three pheasants etc.), but also land the ball in the "Skill Hole" at the top of the playfield (near the hunter). Regardless of what combinations were made, one could not receive a payout until the skill hole was made. In the case of multiple combinations achieved before the skill hole, only the highest combination paid, which was a good incentive to try and get the skill hole out of the way as early as possible. All one had to do then is pull the handle on the side and receive the reward. *Eugene Ricci collection.* $575-700.

When was the first tilt or anti-cheating mechanism built? This is a very tough question with no clear-cut answer. An anti cheating "device" can be any of a number of applications to stop the player from shaking or lifting the machine. Nailing the games down to the tabletop was one of them. Fixing the legs to the floor (I remember seeing that in an amusement center once) was another. Nothing new or high-tech about that; people have been "nailing" thing down since the day they invented nails, but an actual mechanism that "registered" the action of a game having been shaken and lifted?

Countertop games from the late 1920s contained rudimentary forms of tilt mechanisms. The earliest advertised tilts became commonplace in the early 1930s on games such as Gottlieb's BROKER'S TIP (June 1933) which described their feature as a "Novel anti-tilting device." Rockola's games such as WORLD'S FAIR JIGSAW (Aug 1933), described in Chapter Eight, displayed the words "Score void if tilted" on the game's advertisement.

The first successful mechanical tilt mechanism (or should I say the most documented) was invented by Harry Williams in 1933. It first appeared on Automatic Amusements' ADVANCE (Oct 1933) just as pinballs were about to became electric. Mr Williams' invention was known as a "stool pigeon" at first, but was later renamed by Harry after overhearing a frustrated player exclaim, "Damn! I tilted it" while he was getting a feel of player response to his new device on location in a drug store. The story is legendary, but as legends go, it was probably built on fiction rather than fact. An article in a men's magazine back in 1960 (*True* magazine, August 1960: "Ungunchable, Harry King of the Pins") written by J.P. Cahn, described how the stool pigeon changed its name to the "Tilt", but as one now knows, the word had already been associated with the device for some time.

This device, now known as the pedestal tilt, was comprised of a small metal pedestal on top of which sat a small metal ball. The

pedestal and ball were enclosed by glass inside a metal cup, which was visible to players near the front of the game. Shake or lift the machine on one side, and the ball would fall off and come to rest between the pedestal and cup edge. The pedestal tilt was not electric, it was just a visual indication of cheating to be used by the location owners (to check for cheating before making a manual payoff), or by other players to make sure their friends were playing fair. The ball was mechanically reset on top of the pedestal once a player inserted more money and pushed the coin slot in to start a new game.

In the following year Harry Williams invented the pendulum tilt or plum-bob tilt, the first electric tilt mechanism. This one consisted of a free-swinging, weighted chain suspended in the middle of a contact ring. The operating principle was simple; when the machine was moved or shaken, the weight would swing and come into contact with the ring, closing an electrical circuit and ending the game. This time the mechanism was housed inside the game and out of sight, so a dial was placed on the playfield to indicate the status. The same basic but refined system is still used today.

The anti-cheating devices found inside a pinball. This particular photo is from a pinball built in the early 1980s, but the principles of operation have been the same since 1935. At the top of the panel is a roll tilt where if one lifts the machine up from the front...Tilt! On the left is the pendulum tilt, and on the right is one of several slam switches.

The problems that players faced with the tilt device out of sight was that it was impossible to gauge just how close one had come to actually tilting the machine, until it was too late. Since the late 1980s, pinballs have been built with an early warning ability, advising the player with spoken comments or loud noises followed by a warning sign on the score display, to take it easy on the body English before the inevitable happens. These so-called "tilt warnings" are operator adjustable. They can be turned off so a player receives no warnings at all.

When multiple-player games arrived in 1954, a separate tilt mechanism was used for each player, but the tilt penalty was still the complete loss of a game rather than just the ball in play. The change came in 1964 with the resettable tilt. The new system meant that players did not have to fear losing a whole game even on the first of five balls, and could feel a little more relaxed knowing that less was at stake. The resettable tilt also meant that only one mechanism was needed for a multiple-player game, therefore reducing production costs.

In the same year Gottlieb came up with a revival of the bonus system on GIGI (Jan 1964). The bonus idea was conceived by game designer Harvey Heiss on Genco's METRO way back in 1940. The concept was then used on many a game, including such greats as Gottlieb's HUMPTY DUMPTY, were players could amass as much as 100,000 points, which they then had to try and collect at some stage during the game by landing the ball in the bottom kickout saucer. Also, almost all of United's games in the late 1940s included one or two of these bonus "build-up" kickout holes near the bottom of the playfield, as seen on games like MANHATTAN (1948). Even as close as 1961, on Williams' BOBO, could one find a bonus feature, which could be doubled, or even tripled! What Gottlieb introduced on GIGI was not new. It was a revived, revised and refined feature (the three R's), that was (and still is) instantly recognizable for what it means, even by the newer generation players of today. It was the new starting point for a feature that would dominate the pinball scene for the next 25 years.

The reason behind the bonus system was to give players added incentive not to tilt the game. If they did, valuable points (and even free games, in the case of GIGI) would be lost. The bonus system became a "good behaviour bond" collected at the end of the game. Pinballs with a bonus that could be collected at the end of each ball did not eventuate until the end of 1970, featured in Gottlieb's SNOW QUEEN (Nov 1970) and SNOW DARBY (Dec 1970). From then on the bonus became a commonplace feature, standard on all pinballs.

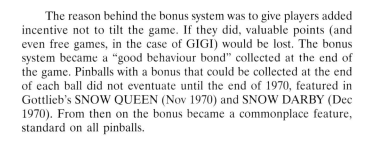

Playfield details from GIGI. Notice how the word "special" is spelt.

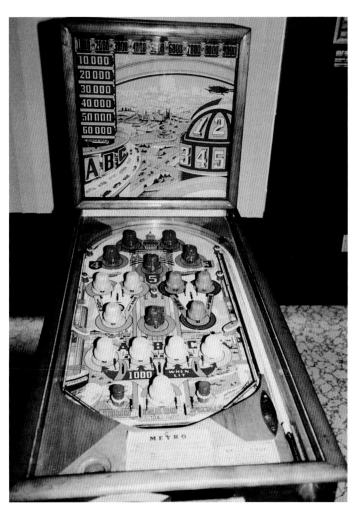

Genco's METRO (1940), were the word "bonus" was born. *Courtesy of Russ Jensen.*

Gottlieb's GIGI (1963). This pinball is best known for re-introducing the end-of-game bonus, a game feature first introduced in Genco's METRO (1940). The playfield design is reminiscent of those early flipperless playfields full of bumpers. The game rules are too good to be true; "lighting all of the red *or* yellow bumpers scores one advance" (another name for bonus in this case). Sure enough, once one starts playing it becomes apparent that things are not that simple. Lighting one of the seven numbered yellow bumpers causes the light of the corresponding red bumper to go out, and vice versa. All but three of the fourteen bumpers are thumpers. *Mark Jackson collection.* $775-950.

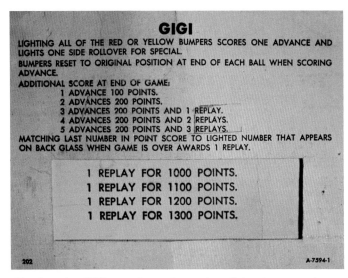

The deceptive GIGI game instruction card, outlining the game rules and the advance (bonus) awards.

On Gottlieb's TARGET ALPHA (1976), every drop target hit lights corresponding 1000 bonus light, the value of which is collected at the end of the ball. Bonus points count as double on the last ball.

Bonus points were normally displayed by a series of lit values arranged on the bottom part of the playfield, identical in function to backglass light-up scoring used in the '40s and '50s. A few Gottlieb pinballs of the 1980s went one step further and displayed the bonus score on a separate digital display located either on playfield or on the backglass. Two such examples are Gottlieb's HAUNTED HOUSE and SPIRIT. The bonus lit values on many SS pinballs, starting from the games of the late 1970s, could be stored in the machine's memory and recalled at the start of each new ball even after the bonus had been counted off at the end of the previous ball. This feature was called the bonus recall feature and it could be turned on or off at the operator's discretion. Ruthless operators usually turned this feature off, which made it harder for players to reach the replay value. Bonus values are no longer displayed on the playfield but can be accessed on the score display by using the status mode as described in Chapter Six.

Backglass and detail of Williams' CABARET (1969), a game with a few interesting features, one of which is the "super bonus". Bonus points are collected when making the center kickout saucer, but rather than the accumulated points being displayed on the playfield in the form of a bonus ladder (the standard format that was to follow), they are shown on a single reel in the center of the backglass. *Courtesy of Ivo Vasella.* $325-400.

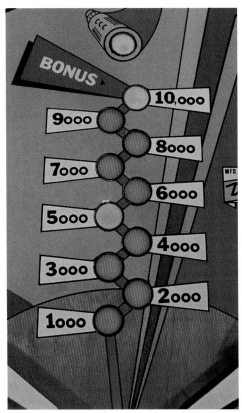

Bonus ladders. Here is one from Gottlieb's OUTER SPACE (1972).

CABARET backglass detail.

A feature that evolved with the increasing popularity of the bonus system is the bonus multiplier. A player can increase their little nest egg by a factor of 2x, then 3x, then 4x and even 5x, if one manages to complete nominated key playfield features, like the top rollover lanes, for example. The more times one completes them, the higher the multiplication factor, usually stopping at a factor of 5x, in the case of an average pinball built in between the late 70s and early 90s. EM games, lacking the technical superiority of the SS games that were to follow, were not as flexible when it came to bonus multipliers. Multiplication factors could reach as high as 3x as in the case of Williams' DEALERS CHOICE (1974) or Gottlieb's SURFER (1976), or even 10x as on Gottlieb's JACK IN THE BOX (1973) but for the most part remained a standard 2x. Even with JACK IN THE BOX having such a high multiplier, it was the only one in the game, unlike SS machines where usually four were available (2x, 3x, 4x, & 5x). As common with most EM games, any bonus obtained was counted as double on the last ball, or in some cases, filling all the bonus lights to maximum capacity, regardless of what ball one was on, awarded the same factor.

Backglass of CHARLIE'S ANGELS.
See next page for caption.

CABARET playfield details.

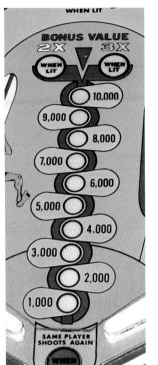

See previous page for backglass. *Courtesy of Rick Force.* $300-375.

CHARLIE'S ANGLES (1979), a typical Gottlieb machine from this era with typical features found on most pinballs, one of which was the bonus ladder. Standard on almost every pinball then and for years to follow. The usual array of bonus indicators, in this particular case 1,000 to 10,000, and bonus multipliers 2x, 3x, 4x & 5x. Playing a good ball let one amass a lot of bonus points, and a lot of bonus points led to a good score and a free game. Note: Not original Gottlieb flippers. **See previous page for backglass.** *Courtesy of Rick Force.* $300-375.

Yet another bonus ladder, this time from Gottlieb's SURFER (1976). Notice the 2x, but more importantly the 3x bonus multiplier, which was unusual for a Gottlieb EM machine. *Photo courtesy of Denis Bowler.*

There are many exceptions and variations to bonus multiplying features found on pinballs throughout the decades, and therefore I can only generalize, but one cannot go past mentioning the huge multiplication factors one could find on Zaccaria pinballs of the 1980s. A great example was CLOWN (1985), which had factors that were enormous; 20x, 40x, 60x and even 80x!

Bonus systems are still incorporated in the pinballs of today, but their value as a high scoring option has diminished. It still can turn out to be a nice little sum too big to be tilted away, especially if one is struggling for that free game.

Very rough players with tempers seem to take out their frustration on pinballs, shoving the machine back with force, lifting the front momentarily before dropping it and even kicking the cashbox door. This type of constant treatment can be detrimental to a pinball's health, and is definitely not welcomed by the operators. In addition to the standard pendulum tilt, pinballs since the 1960s have been fitted with anti-slam switches to deter such abuse. The penalty for slamming a pinball is the end of the game, or games. On multiple player pinballs, even if there is more than one person playing, everyone loses.

Slam switches, or slam tilts, are simpler in design than the pendulum tilt, simply because they do not have to be as delicate in sensing movement. A slam switch is made up of two switchblades, one of standard length, and one slightly longer. The longer blade is fitted with a weight at its end, which makes the blade "flick" if a sudden forceful movement is made on the pinball. Depending on the game's wiring, the action of the swinging weighted blade will cause it to make or break contact with the other switchblade. The result is the equivalent of turning the machine off

When the bonus ladder is completed on Zaccaria's MOON FLIGHT (1976), the player is awarded double bonus points at the end of that ball. In addition to this, making the left orbit lane awards increased point scoring or an extra ball, depending on the game setting.

A close look at a tiny slam switch, located on the inside of a cashbox door, for that dreaded kick in the guts.

and on very quickly, thus resulting in the loss of all games in play. Two slam switches can usually be found, one under the playfield or at the bottom of the cabinet, and one attached to the cashbox door, for that dreaded "kick in the guts".

Summary

1933 First successful tilt mechanism (the pedestal tilt) invented by Harry Williams.

1935 The pendulum tilt invented by Harry Williams.

1940 Genco's METRO introduces the bonus feature.

1964 Gottlieb produces GIGI, a game that reinstated the bonus feature as a integral part of the game strategy.

1964 Resettable tilt mechanisms first used.

1970 First pinballs built with the bonus feature collected at the end of each ball rather than at the end of the game.

Part Four: Pinball Oddities

Welcome to the world of pinball oddities of the late twentieth century! Readers of this book may have at times flicked through various sections while reading through others. If after having stopped to browse at the pinball list, you have come away a bit confused by comments in the remarks column such as, cocktail table style, 2-player head-to-head, or shakerball pinball, then these are the pages for you!

These oddities are the freaks of pinball nature, weird experiments in pinball design born out of the manufacturer's desire to break new ground in search of profit. Some species of pinballs have failed in their efforts to win over enough players to warrant their continued existence, and have therefore become extinct. Let us begin.

Cocktail Table Style Pinballs: Cocktail pinballs were small, inconspicuous games designed for sit-down play. The idea behind this style of game, first appearing in the 1930s but revived in 1978, was to build a pinball small enough to fit in where full size games could not be tolerated due to space restriction. Cocktail pinballs suited premises like nightclubs, restaurants and bars, where patrons felt more comfortable seated than standing up. They were inconspicuous because they had no backglass/backbox, the score displays neatly positioned in a group below the flippers. Throw a tablecloth over one and they would easily blend in with the surrounding furniture.

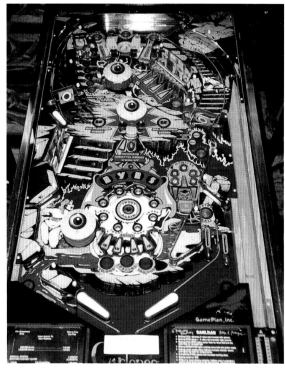

Game Plan's CYCLOPES (1985). Game Plan was a company that became experts at manufacturing cocktail style games. When they weren't building those, the built normal pinballs like this one. *Courtesy of Herb Silvers/ Fabulous Fantasies.* $1000+

The playfield sizes varied from game to game, but they were usually about two-thirds of a standard pinball area, while maintaining a similar width.

Approximately 25 of these games have been built between the years of 1978-1989. The most successful ones have come from companies like Game Plan and Allied Leisure. Because the cocktail pinball was targeted at older, over the legal age crowd, many carried advertising slogans. For instance, Game Plan's BLACK VELVET (1978) was actually the brand name of a light vodka, while CAMELIGHT (1978), again by Game Plan, advertised Camel cigarettes.

Shakerball Pinballs: In the history of the game, there have been only two shakerball pinballs built, and both by Allied Leisure. The first was SEA HUNT, built in 1972, then followed by SPOOKSVILLE (great name) in 1973. The games were housed in very large upright video game type cabinets; height 72", width 27" and depth 37", just to give an idea of the size. The flipper buttons were situated on top of two upright handles (predecessors of the joystick). These handles could be used to shake the playfield inside the cabinet, hence the name shakerball. The game play could also be converted to add-a-ball.

Allied Leisure's TAKE FIVE (1977). Sit down and enjoy a game of pinball, a cocktail table style pinball that is. *Jeff Grummel collection.* $275-350.

Allied Leisure's SPOOKSVILLE (1973), another great shakerball. Not your typical pinball cabinet; not your typical pinball, either. Only two such games were built, the other being SEA HUNT in 1972. $325-400.

Head-To-Head Pinballs: The two player head-to-head pinball broke away from the idea of man against machine, and instead pitted player against player. Imagine two pinball machines placed back-to-back. Remove the backbox, join the playfields together and one can get an idea of the concept of head-to-head pinballs. This double-ended machine had players facing each other, each controlling a set of flippers. The object of the game was to try and score a "goal" by sending the ball through the opposing player's flippers and into the outhole. The game can be easily linked to the table soccer games (foosball games) first developed in Switzer-land in the 1940s, which are still popular today in most European countries.

The origins of the first head-to-head game are still shrouded in mystery. The game design may have originated in France as early as 1964, the date of a magazine where an advertisement for one such game was found. The first American head-to-head ap-pears to have been built by Bally in 1967, BOOT-A-BALL. Only 100 BOOT-A-BALL games were built, and only one is known to exist today; the game was not found on American soil, but Italian! The pinball appears to have been built for the Italian/European market, as the game theme is that of a soccer match, a sport not very popular in the U.S.A back in those days.

Everyone knows that "It takes two to tango." The adage is applicable to these pinballs, their one and only drawback.

The most famous head-to-head pinball known among pin-ball-ologists has always been Gottlieb's CHALLENGER (1971).

CHALLENGER's playfield consists of eight flippers (4 each player), four bumpers, four slingshot kickers and little else, as the main objective of the game is to try and score goals rather than playfield points. Goal points for each player were tabulated on a small backbox, which was suspended between two posts above mid-playfield.

Alvin G. & Co's U.S.A FOOTBALL (1992), a typical two-player head-to-head game. Games of this style can be traced back to as early as 1964, but it is still uncertain who came up with the original idea. *Courtesy of Alvin J. Gottlieb. All rights reserved.* $650-800.

Above and opposite page top left: Gottlieb's CHALLENGER (1971), probably the best known head-to-head in the history of pinball. *Courtesy of Herb Silvers/Fabulous Fantasies.* $725-850.

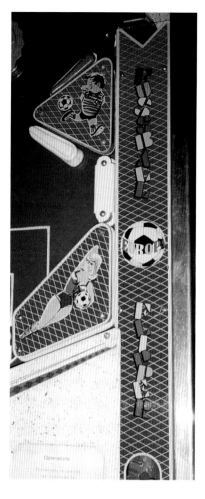

Playfield detail from FUSSBALL EUROPA FLIPPER. Such a long name for a pinball.

Playfield of CHALLENGER. **See previous page for caption.**

Lesser-known FUSSBALL EUROPA FLIPPER (c. 1967) by Forster also consisted of four bumpers and slingshot kickers, but when it came to flippers, it had twelve! Remotely similar in design to BOOT-A-BALL (which also had twelve flippers, but no bumpers), this was a completely goal-oriented game where the slingshots and bumpers did not score points, but were there simply to propel the ball. With no backbox for point scoring, the number of goals scored by each player was tallied by a progression of indicating lights on one side of the playfield. The first player to score ten goals won the game, which sadly also meant that the match was over. As previously mentioned in Chapter Two, this particular game also had 2.5" flippers, which seem to be the standard size for these types of games built in Europe. Other almost identical games included Elettrocoin's SELEN CUP (c. 1967), Artigiana Ricambi's BOWLING GIRL (c. 1973), possibly the only Italian head-to-head game not based on soccer, and Elettrogiochi's CALCIO ITALIA (c. 1967).

To date, 21 years after CHALLENGER, the last head to head game was built in 1992 by Alvin G. & Co. Alvin Gottlieb, son of David Gottlieb, founder of D. Gottlieb & Co., set up his own business in 1991. The company's first pinball was A.G. SOCCER BALL, a head-to-head game released on October 1991. The game was later re-released as A.G. FOOTBALL for the export markets on October 1992.

Forster's FUSSBALL EUROPA FLIPPER (1967), a rare find. It's unknown how many of these German games were built, or indeed how many are left, probably very few. This one made it all the way to Australia! Many of these early European head-to-head games had unusual 2.5" long flippers. *Jeff Grummel collection.* $625-725.

Alvin G. & Co's MYSTERY CASTLE (1993). The backglass is almost a remake of Zaccaria's MAGIC CASTLE (1984). It was hoped that this company would prosper, but unfortunately pinball times were hard, and 1993 was their last year in business. *Courtesy of Jan J. Svach.* $800-900.

Alvin G. & Co's U.S.A FOOT-BALL incorporated a very special type of flipper, one that works by itself! You no longer needed an opponent; you could play against the machine. The biggest drawback with head-to-head games had always been the need for two players. *Courtesy of Alvin J. Gottlieb. All rights reserved.*

As mentioned previously, the only drawback with head-to-head pinballs was that a minimum of two players is required. With A.G. SOCCER BALL, this was no longer necessary. With the help of a new invention, the "switch flipper", one player could play against the machine. The machine end of the game could sense an oncoming ball using a suspended wire arrangement held out in front of each flipper. Acting as a switch, the suspended wire/rod, hinged at both ends of the flipper, was lifted by the ball just before it actually hit the flipper. The flipper then activated, sending the ball (hopefully) back to the other side. Its design was also used to acknowledge ball possession. Each time a player hit the ball, and therefore lifted the switch, meant that the machine could register a "flipper hit".

Most enthusiasts hoped that Alvin G. & Co would bring new blood into the world of pinball, and maybe lift the popularity of the game to something comparable to the "good old days". Unfortunately, the company languished, their last pinball PISTOL POKER released in December 1993. The same could be said about Capcom. PINBALL MAGIC, their first pinball, was a real eye-opener. It was released in August 1995, but by the start of 1997, they had shut up shop.

Video Cabinet Style Pinball: "If you can't beat them, join them!" That was one strategy that some pinball manufacturers thought seriously about when the pinball market took a slide in the early 1980s. The idea was this: a lot of people wanted to play video games. The pinball manufacturers wanted them to play pinball instead, so they decided to build combination pinball/video games to win back some customers. The initial attraction of the video game drew players to play, and at some time during the game they had to play a pinball, whether they liked it or not. That may have been the plan. Like the shakerball pinballs of the 1970s, these games were built with upright cabinets (much smaller in size), this time to purposely blend in with the surrounding video games. The playfield of such a game was a small scaled-down version of a conventional pinball, with a video screen mounted vertically at eye level. Only two pinballs in this style have been produced to date, and both by Bally, BABY PAC-MAN (1982) and GRANNY AND THE GATORS (1983).

A similar style of pinball was built by Williams, this time minus the video game. Its name was VARKON. VARKON, built in 1983, was not popular with either pin-

Williams' VARKON (1982)—is a pinball in a video cabinet still a pinball? The internal playfield was projected vertically into the player's view by the use of mirrors, just like the ones used on the older style EM rifle games. *Courtesy of Herb Silvers/Fabulous Fantasies.* $775-1000.

ball or video game players and its like was never seen again. The game console was equipped with flipper buttons as well as two-way joysticks that would also control the flippers, to accommodate the video player, no doubt. Like BABY PAC-MAN, the playfield was relatively small, but this time it incorporated a small ramp on the left hand side, and a mini "sunken" playfield (yes, it was a multi-level game!) in the center of the main playfield which contained two small two-inch flippers and a separate ball. This lower playfield was activated when one completed a sequence of targets on the main playfield. No plunger was used on this game; instead, the ball was launched from between the flippers on the main playfield.

These type of pinball designs may have also been built by European countries around the same time, but as of yet, none have surfaced.

While on the subject of pinball/video combinations, Gottlieb's CAVEMAN (1982) and Red Baron's INVADER BALL (year unknown) cannot be overlooked. CAVEMAN was a conventional pinball in most aspects, with the exception of a small video screen embedded in the upper playfield. The monitor did not form part of the playfield as such, and the ball was not capable of rolling over the screen due to its inclination, in order to facilitate better viewing by the player. In similar fashion to the video mode on dot matrix displays, the pinball and video game (a kind of pac-man) were displayed alternatively, with the video action controlled by a joystick situated at the front of the cabinet. CAVEMAN certainly tested both pinball and video skills in one game.

Before CAVEMAN made an impression on players, Australia's Red Baron Amusements (Brisbane) unveiled INVADER BALL. My first impression upon seeing the game brochure was "Have they really built such a game?" I am unsure as to when this game was actually released; at a guess, it may have been around 1981-82. Without doubt, it is the strangest video game/pinball combination that I have ever seen. The playfield was of standard design for those times. The video monitor, along with a single standard digital score display (and digital credit display) was housed in the backbox. What makes the game so strange was that the video game was none other than *SPACE INVADERS*! It seems that old *SPACE INVADER* video games (which had gone out of popularity by that time) were used to construct the pinball as the monitor display features "player one" and "player two" score displays, when the pinball is obviously of one-player capacity. The monitor also displayed a credit meter at the bottom corner. I do not know if any INVADER BALL games still exist today, as I would definitely want to play one just to see how it all worked. Like so many other pinballs, they may all have found their way to the rubbish tip by now.

One will not see many playfields built like this; Gottlieb's CAVEMAN (1982), a video and pinball combination. *Courtesy of Jan J. Svach.* $375-450.

A very strange pinball/video hybrid is Red Baron's INVADER BALL (c. 1981). This Australian built pinball used a Space Invaders video screen mounted in the backbox. Perhaps spare parts from old out-of-date Space Invader games? Anyway, there you have it, "The one and only INVADER BALL, space pinball." $225-275.

WORLD CUP '90

THE PINBALL "CHAMPION OF THE WORLD" OF EARNINGS

A FIRST FROM THE INNOVATORS.

«WORLD CUP '90» is an industry first that will captivate pinball players everywhere. With a playing field and an integrated video game that offers players the action-packed, fast-paced excitement and competition of a real world cup soccer tournament.

Mr. GAME ON GOAL with WORLD CUP '90. The new and thrilling pinball game designed to attract and increase profits.

MISTER GAME s.r.l.
Vio Armoroli, 15
40012 Calderaro di Reno (BO) ITALY
Tel. (051) 72.23.81/82
Telefax (051) 72.04.69
Telex 520267 MRGAME I

Technology and winning fantasy

Mr. Game's WORLD CUP '90 (1990). This company only produced four pinballs during its short career; most of them included video and pinball action. The video games and pinball scores were displayed on a small screen in the backbox, a great concept first used in Japan during the late '70s on Universal's HAREM CAT (1979). Being an Italian firm, they obviously took advantage of the World Cup soccer tournament held in Italy that same year. $425-525.

Token-Pin Pinballs: The last "Token-Pin" pinball was released in 1996, Bally's SAFE CRACKER. At this moment, it may be too soon to tell whether any more like SAFE CRACKER will be built. To the reader, this statement may already be outdated.

To the skillful player, SAFE CRACKER awarded not only free games, but brass tokens also. The brass coins could not be exchanged for legal tender (legally), but were worth one game in value if inserted back into the machine. The way the game awarded coins was quite amusing. A coin slot situated just under the backglass would literally spit out the token(s) one at the time. The token would then land on the playfield's glass cover and roll down towards the player. Bally used the term "Token Pin" as a registered trademark for SAFE CRACKER, the first of such games. The dispensing of brass tokens for skillful play can be traced back to "payout pinballs" in the 1930s, which also dispensed tokens that could either be used to re-play the machine or be redeemed for cash or merchandise.

Bally's SAFE CRACKER (1996). The game dispensed tokens for completing certain tasks, the equivalent of a free game. Tokens could be deposited back into the machine in return for a game or kept as a souvenir. I think the later option was used more often. *Courtesy of WMS industries Inc. All rights reserved.* $1050-1300.

SAFE CRACKER included some other interesting features. First, the game was smaller in size than a standard pinball, making it look kind of cute. The second was the "timed play" rather than the conventional three- or five-ball play. In this case one could play continuously with an unlimited number of balls until the allotted time ran out—time that could be increased by completing certain scoring features. The same concept can be found on much older games like Williams' TRAVEL TIME (1973), Bally's BEAT THE CLOCK (1985) and Gottlieb's JAMES BOND (1980). The third and more unique feature was the backglass board game, which one played against the machine in order to reach the bank vault. Players spun and stopped a safe dial shown on the dot matrix display to determine how far to advance along the board; the machine (the guards) did the same by playing dice. Reaching the safe without getting caught earned a token award. Tokens quickly became game souvenirs. All had the game logo on one side, but on the other their depictions varied, showing game-associated icons—ten different tokens in all. All of this meant that there were more tokens coming out than going back in, which posed a question: what happens when the pinball runs out of tokens?

Game tokens have been around since the 1930s. Some arcade operators use tokens such as these even today as a means of reducing cash on premises or reducing staff numbers by their use of automatic token dispensing machines.

Williams' TRAVEL TIME (1973) used time units (up to 120 seconds) rather than a three- or five-ball game. Certain targets made the clock stop, while others re-started it, but once the time was up, the game was over. *Courtesy of Michael Tansell.* $325-400.

Speaking of game souvenirs, Stern's COSMIC PRINCESS (1979) and Playmatic's FLASH DRAGON (1980) took snapshots of players when the highest score was beaten. A Polaroid Instamatic camera positioned on top of and inside the backbox respectively would take a photo that would develop and be dispensed in seconds. At least in this case one had the proof to show friends that one really was a pinball wizard. The so-called "photomat" unit on COSMIC PRINCESS was an optional extra and so finding one still attached to the game is quite rare indeed. According to the manufacturer's game brochure, the unit greatly increased player appeal. Another interesting fact about COSMIC PRINCESS was that Stern apparently exported pinball components to Australia during the late 1970s, which were then assembled into complete pinballs by Leisure & Allied Industries (not to be confused with Allied Leisure); thus saving money on Australian import tax. The outcome was this particular game, one which was released only in Australia, and is virtually unknown elsewhere in the world. Say cheese!

Backglass of COSMIC PRINCESS. **See next page for caption.**

Souvenir game tokens from Bally's SAFE CRACKER (1996). Each coin had the game logo on one side and one of ten different game-associated icons on the other. Coins where awarded by the machine to only the best of players. Actual size of token is 1.25" in diameter.

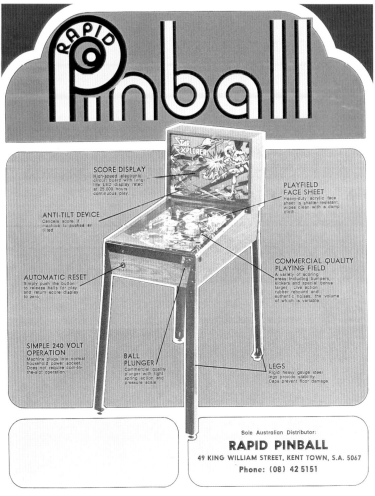

Stern's COSMIC PRINCESS (1979) was a pinball that was specifically built for the Australian market. To save money on import tax, Stern built the games in Australia with the help of Leisure & Allied Industries (not to be mistaken with Allied Leisure). One of the outstanding features of this game was the photomat unit (an optional component not shown here) which automatically took, and dispensed, a player's color photograph when the highest score to date was beaten. The manufacturers stated that "This optional unit greatly increases player appeal". Perhaps it did, but because it was optional, one is lucky to find this game with an original unit still intact. **See previous page for backglass.** *Denis Bowler collection.* $300-375.

STAR EXPLORER (1977), a non-commercial home pinball produced by Consolidated Industries. Here we see the game brochure from Rapid Pinball; the distributor of the game in Australia. Pinballs were unbelievably popular in the 70s and the home market for these pinballs became another avenue that manufacturers concentrated on. This was only successful for a few years because of the decline in pinball popularity due to video games and home video game units. These type of pinballs were about half the size of a coin-operated game. $50-75.

Non-Commercial Home Versions: Non-commercial home versions (NCHV), quite a mouthful I expect, if spoken at speed. A pinball in every sense of the word, description-wise, but not a true coin-operated pinball.

One will not find these kind of pinballs mentioned in the pinball list in Chapter Twelve; I have purposely left them out. My reason for doing so was simply because there has been such a wide variety of these games available in the past 20 years, ranging from near full-size pinballs, down to small countertop toy pinballs, making it very difficult to draw a line separating the two; especially when no visual confirmation between the two can be made.

The rise and fall of the larger kind of NCHV pinballs all occurred within a few years, 1976 to 1978/79. The start of this boom is speculative; the end is most certainly connected to the arrival of home video game systems.

Pinball was definitely the ultimate amusement machine, but a new SS game was too expensive for a average household to afford. There were pinball collectors back then too, snapping up the old EM pinnies as soon as they became affordable (which they did become, by the truck load, when SS games took over). Unless they knew how to fix them, there was no way parents were going to buy EM games as presents for their kids, for it would be financially risky if they broke down.

Wico's BIG TOP (1977). *Courtesy of Tim Van Blarcom.* $75-100.

Enterprising companies saw a hole in the market which they could fill. Their reasoning probably hinged on the idea that if they could build SS pinballs for home use at a substantially lower price, with the added benefit of a guarantee and warranty, then people would buy them.

Bally tried for a slice of the new market with game names that featured some of their best-known works of the time, including CAPTAIN FANTASTIC, EVEL KNIEVEL and FIREBALL. These scaled-down versions of the real thing, such as with CAPTAIN FANTASTIC, only had the name as a common factor; the playfield layout and artwork were both entirely different from the original.

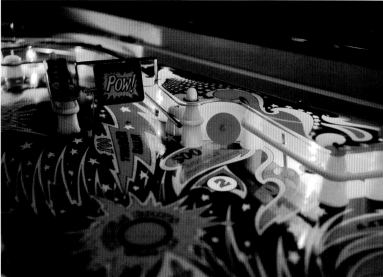

Playfield detail from FIREBALL (NCHV).

Home pinball prices averaged around $500 U.S. back then (still quite a bit of money in those days) which was approximately 3 to 4 times cheaper than buying a brand new coin-operated game.

Relatively unknown or non-existent companies came to the fore at this stage to cash in, with names like Mali, Consolidated Industries and Wico. Toy giant Mattel also produced home version pinballs such as LAS VEGAS in 1977.

The potential buyer should be aware of these games, to make sure that a game is actually a coin-operated machine, if that is what one wants or is paying for.

Here are some samples.

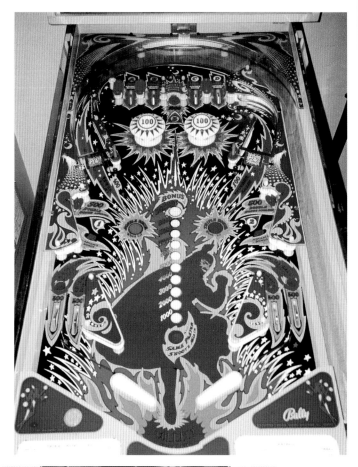

GAME NAME	COMPANY	YEAR
Alive	Brunswick	1978
Aspen	Brunswick	1976
Big Big	Mali	1977
Big Top	Wico	1977
Captain Fantastic	Bally	1977
Diamond Jim	Mali	1977
Evel Knievel	Bally	1978
Fireball	Bally	1976
Galaxy Ranger	Bally	1978
Las Vegas	Mattel	1977
Snow Bird	Mali	1977
Space Galaxy	Mali	1977
Star Explorer	Consol. Indust.	1977
Super Star	Brunswick	1976

Part Five: Woodrails And Wide Bodies

Can one judge a book by its cover? Can one judge a pinball by its cabinet? Books and pinballs are two very different things, but similarly one cannot judge how a pinball will play just by appearance. What can be ascertained, however, is its age. In fact, this is what this book in some way has been all about—dates, facts and changes in pinball design through the years.

Above left & left: Bally's FIREBALL (1976), the non-commercial home version. The backglass may look familiar (minus the EM scoring reels, replaced here by a single multi-player digital display) but the playfield layout is nothing like as used in the original game released in 1972. The increasing popularity of pinballs saw companies like Bally venture out of the coin-operated industry and into the home consumer market. Bally chose to market these games with the names of some of their previously popular games, such as CAPTAIN FANTASTIC and EVEL KNIEVEL. *Courtesy of Ray Johnson.* $75-125.

Imagine coming across a pinball for sale in the newspaper (as I'm sure a lot of us have done). Providing the name is given, you can easily determine its age by looking up the name in this book's list. You then can visualize what the game will look like once the date is known. The reverse applies when you are trying to date a game without the aid of a pinball list (the game may be an unknown), but know what the game looks like. With the information in this book you could probably date pinballs with an accuracy of plus or minus two to three years.

The term "woodrail", or "rail" in general, refers to the frame around the top of the playfield cabinet, placed there to hold the glass playfield cover; similar in function to a picture frame. Pinball cabinets have always been fabricated from wood or wood material, but unlike today's steel rails and steel legs; the only metallic materials used on those older pinball cabinets were the nuts and bolts.

A classic woodrail from Gottlieb; ROYAL FLUSH (1957). One may remember this pinball being mentioned in Chapter Eight. This was also one of the first pinballs to feature a roto-target. *Courtesy of Gary and Eric See.*

Playfield detail of ROYAL FLUSH, showing the game's top rollover lanes.

Perhaps the cheapest way to own a pinball is to win one in a competition. In this particular case, one could have won a Gottlieb's WORLD CHAMP (1957); a vintage woodrail, for the cost of a milkshake. *Courtesy of the Milk Marketing Pty Ltd, N.S.W, Australia.* $725-900.

In the next few paragraphs that form the last part of this chapter there will be no surprises, only more dates and more facts to add to the pinball dating equation, plus a few invigorating vibrations.

Backglass of CRISS CROSS. **See next page for caption.**

The 1950s are often referred to as "The golden age" of pinball. The introduction of the flipper in 1947 and the last use of wood rails in 1960 denote the start and end of this era. The last American woodrail game to be produced was Gottlieb's KEWPIE DOLL on October 1960.

The replacement of wood rails with steel rails was the last in a series of wood-to-metal changes. Steel legs replaced wooden legs around 1956. Steel cashbox doors started appearing around the same time and backbox steel door panels were introduced in 1958.

Since "The golden age", the width of a pinball has been pretty much standard, approximately 22". In November 1976, Atari unveiled THE ATARIANS, the industry's first wide body pinball. How wide was it? About 29 inches. THE ATARIANS was successful enough for Atari to continue building wide-bodied pinballs, and also successful enough for other companies to take notice. The first wide body games produced by other companies were Williams' CONTACT (1979), Bally's PARAGON (1979), Gottlieb's GENIE (1979), Stern's BIG GAME (1980), Hankin's HOWZAT (1980) and not to be forgotten, Sega's CHA CHA CHA (c.1978), which incidentally had the same lower playfield dual flipper configuration as Atari's TIME 2000 (1977).

The most popular wide body pinball built was Bally's SPACE INVADERS, which reached a production run of over 10,000 units. Despite their early popularity, wide bodies were slowly phased out of production. Approximately 35 to 40 such games were built between the years of 1976 and 1985.

Gottlieb's CRISS CROSS (1958). When this game came off the production line, one major difference from previous games was that it had a steel backbox door. Not a big deal to the player, but for manufacturers of pinball games it meant that construction materials were changing to cheaper, stronger and more durable materials. Steel was in, wood was out. Most CRISS CROSS games came equipped with steel legs (a change that began around 1956), but it seems a few missed out, like this one. **See previous page for backglass.** *Eugene Ricci collection.* $700-850.

SPOT-A-CARD (1960), one of Gottlieb's last woodrail pinballs. The last was KEWPIE DOLL, released two months after this game. *Mark Jackson collection.* $500-600.

Atari's AIRBORNE AVENGER (1977), another wide body classic. The backglass artwork by George Opperman is one of my favorites. *Courtesy of Midway Games Inc. All rights reserved.* $375-450.

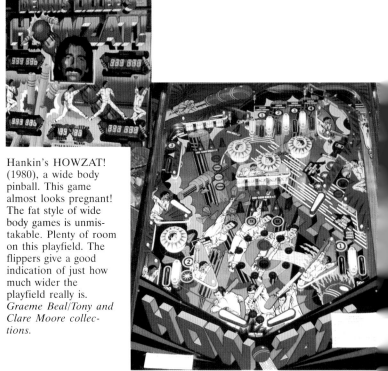

Hankin's HOWZAT! (1980), a wide body pinball. This game almost looks pregnant! The fat style of wide body games is unmistakable. Plenty of room on this playfield. The flippers give a good indication of just how much wider the playfield really is. *Graeme Beal/Tony and Clare Moore collections.*

Top left & bottom left: Atari's TIME 2000 (1977), a collector's item for those interested with anything remotely associated with the new millennium. It was Atari's second wide body pinball after the release of THE ATARIANS (1976). Both games may not have been a roaring success, but its new size registered a favorable response, so much so that other companies began to take notice. *Courtesy of Midway Games Inc. All rights reserved.* $375-450.

HOWZAT upper playfield detail.

HOWZAT game instruction
card, for those interested in
the game rules.

HOWZAT
PLAYER INSTRUCTIONS

3 BALLS — 20 CENTS PER PLAYER

★ COMPLETING ALL 'UPPER' DROP TARGETS,
1st TIME SCORES 10,000, LIGHTS UPPER POP BUMPERS
2nd TIME SCORES 20,000
3rd TIME SCORES 50,000
4th TIME AWARDS SPECIAL

★ COMPLETING ALL 'LOWER' DROP TARGETS
1st TIME INCREASES VALUE OF EJECT HOLE TO 10,000, LIGHTS
STAR ROLLOVERS
2nd TIME LIGHTS SPIN TARGETS
3rd TIME INCREASES VALUE OF EJECT HOLE TO AWARD AN
EXTRA BALL.

★ COMPLETING ROLLOVERS '1', '2' AND '3' INCREASES BONUS
MULTIPLIER TO '3X'.

★ COMPLETING ROLLOVERS '1', '2', '3' AND '4' INCREASES BONUS
MULTIPLIER TO '5X'.

★ TILT PENALTY — BALL IN PLAY.

Williams, Bally and Data East built a range of slightly wider
pinballs (not actually true wide bodies) during 1993 and 1994. The
cabinet width measured at 25", approximately halfway between a
standard cabinet and a wide body. These games included some
previously mentioned pinballs like Williams' DEMOLITION MAN
(1994) and INDIANA JONES (1993), and Data East's ROYAL
RUMBLE (1994), to name just a few.

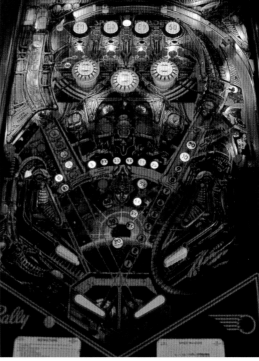

Bally's SPACE
INVADERS
(1980);the pinball.
Although it was
Atari that
introduced the
wide body
concept, it was
Bally who
produced the most
successful pinball
in that category
(this game) with a
production run of
approximately
11,400 units.
SPACE INVAD-
ERS contained a
unique mix of
images. Firstly, it
was named after
the successful
video game, the
little icons from it
appear scattered
around the cabinet
and playfield.
Secondly, the
monster on the on
the backglass is
none other than
the alien from the 1979 movie *Alien* which starred Sigourney Weaver.
Last but not least is the playfield art drawn by Paul Faris, which he
based on the artwork style of H.R Geiger. *Courtesy of Peter Graabaek.*
$400-475.

Playfield of Hankin's THE EMPIRE STRIKES BACK (1981). This
game would be the ultimate show piece for any collector of *Star Wars*
merchandise. All of Hankin's games have become collector's items
"Down Under". Hankin pulled out all stops on this game, even going as
far as obtaining a photo of Mark Hamil (Luke Skywalker) with the
machine for the promotional brochure. *Courtesy of A. Hankin & Co.*
$525-625.

It seems that Atari liked to build things big, and so before they dropped out of pinball production they offered the world HERCULES (1979). HERCULES is huge! The game uses a cue ball instead of a normal steel ball. The playfield size (39" wide) and playfield components (flippers, bumpers etc.), all increased in relative proportions to the ball. The game stands approximately seven feet high and was also around eight feet long!

Another oversized pinball is Innovative Concepts' THE FLINTSTONES (1994), not to be confused with Williams' game with the same name and year of manufacture. This pinball, based on the popular cartoon, is not quite as big as HERCULES in size, but was designed especially for children. A special platform in front of the game allows children to step up and view the playfield. Also, rather than having them stretch their little arms to grasp the flipper buttons on each side of the cabinet, a smaller cabinet front was mounted on the end of the machine.

Wooden cabinets, wide cabinets, what about vibrating cabinets? Ever held on to the handlebars of a motorcycle (or even a lawnmower) and felt the vibrations of the motor run up your arms? Well, one can receive the same sensation while playing Williams' EARTHSHAKER (1989). The cabinet vibrates only at certain times, like at the start of multiball, for example. The vibrations are supposed to simulate an earthquake, which is the pinball's theme.

I had my first game on EARTHSHAKER in a quiet little cafe/bar while visiting Luzern, Switzerland. I got quite a surprise at the start of my game when the machine did what it was built to do. There were only two pinballs in that establishment, the other was Data East's TIME MACHINE (1988). Having never played either of the two but only having enough spare change for one, it was a toss-up decision. Both pinballs were less than two years old at that stage, so I considered my chances of coming across both games again in my travels quite high. As my "pinball luck" would have it, I have come across EARTHSHAKER numerous times since then, but as for TIME MACHINE... I never saw it again. It appears that for me, it was the one that got away!

Backglass of EARTHSHAKER. **See next page for caption.**

Pink flowers, man-eating cats and seductive women—it's all there in Stern's CHEETAH (1980). CHEETAH was Stern's next wide body pinball to be built after BIG GAME (1980). *Courtesy of Rawdon Osborne.* $375-425.

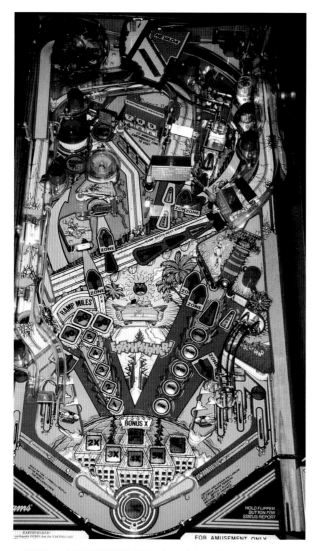

Williams' EARTHSHAKER (1989) included a simple mechanism inside the cabinet that turned the whole machine into one big vibrating mass. It was a great accompaniment to the game's theme. **See previous page for backglass.** *Courtesy of Jan J. Svach.* $650-800.

Other vibrating pinballs have been Bally's HARLEY DAVIDSON (1991), Data East's TALES FROM THE CRYPT (1993) and ROYAL RUMBLE (1994), Gottlieb's GLADIATORS (1993), Williams' ROAD SHOW (1994) and last of all, Sega's THE LOST WORLD (1997). The game that I believe used this novelty to its best effect was HARLEY DAVIDSON. At the start of each ball one could "rev-up" the hog to their heart's content by using the flipper buttons. Brroom...Brroom!

Summary

1956-58 Steel cabinet components replace wooden components—legs and doors, for example.
1960 Last American wood rail produced, Gottlieb's KEWPIE DOLL.
1976 First wide body pinball produced, Atari's THE ATARIANS.
1989 Williams' EARTHSHAKER, first pinball with a vibrating cabinet.

Center right & bottom right: Williams' ROAD SHOW (1994). This game seems jam-packed with every pinball gimmick known to man; and sure enough, it also featured a vibrating cabinet. The vibrating mechanisms on games like these were put to good use, usually synchronized with certain targets or features, giving an added sensory experience. *Courtesy of Ivo Vasella.* $1400-1700.

Chapter Twelve

The Pinball List

The pride and joy of past pinball books has always been the mandatory pinball list featured at the conclusion of the book. This book is no exception.

Although I started the list on my own—years before acquiring my first pinball book, or having even the slightest notion of ever writing this book—the following list would never have reached the stage at which it is now without certain invaluable references. They are listed in the bibliography.

The listed games from around the world number about 3000. I cannot be totally sure that every pinball ever built is named here, nor can I estimate how complete the list is. There are most probably quite a few games still missing, but I am quietly confident that it is at least over 95% complete within the specified time period.

There are certain parameters to which the list has been restricted. First, there has always been a fine line in the early 1930s between countertop games/bagatelles and pinballs. I have decided to start the list at 1933 simply to try and avoid having to encompass games that could very well date back to the 1800s, the world of the bagatelle. Bagatelles and countertop games are something that most pinball players/collectors respect as being the ancestors of the modern game but not something that they would prefer to acquire over games of the last 40 or 50 years, especially when a game is bought more for the entertainment value than just another piece in the collection. The total time frame of the list is between 1933 and 1998.

Other exclusions include payout pinballs and bingo (in-line) machines that were not built for what one would call amusement, but rather for gambling. Non-commercial games, sometimes called home-versions, are not shown here as explained in Chapter Eleven, although a small list is included there. Finally, baseball games or pitch and bat games, as they are sometimes known, have also been excluded. At first glance, one may mistake a baseball machine for a pinball game because of their similarity in size and shape, but that similarity soon disappears upon closer inspection of the playfield. The games simulated (the term is used in the past tense as these games are no longer built) the popular American game of baseball and did not achieve popularity outside the United States, except in Japan where the sport was widely followed. I have made every attempt to check the information on each game listed and I apologize in advance if any of these excluded games have found their way into the list by mistake.

In addition to normal pinball games, the list will also include conversion kit pinballs and pinballs that were produced only as prototypes and never released or mass-produced. Conversion kit pinballs as described previously, are virtually "new from old" games, and although there will possibly be nothing wrong with them, if one comes across one of these games with the intention of buying, one will at least know what one is getting. Prototype pinballs which never made it to full production runs are very rare games indeed. Only a small number of these games will appear on the list and only the better-known ones at that.

The list is comprised of six columns: company name or trade name, game name, year of manufacture, player capacity, country of manufacture and a remarks column.

Manufacturer's name and game name will always be listed, although production year and player capacity may not always be known, in which case the letters N/A (not available) and U (unknown) will be shown respectively. As more than 80% of all games listed originate from the U.S.A, a blank space in the country column will signify that the game was built in the U.S.A unless noted otherwise. Finally a remarks column will outline certain playfield features, or other features of each game in abbreviated form, such as how many flippers (if more than a standard set of two) for example, or how many drop targets, and so on. At a glance this is obviously the most incomplete part of the list. For most of the American games from the 1970s and onwards, I have been able to obtain this type of information, but of course older games and those built outside the U.S.A are harder to find.

Short of having a photo of each game (an almost impossible undertaking) this is a short and exact way of describing certain playfield features. A number of these features in pinball design have become standard over the years; all pinballs now have flippers, for example, and include speech. Such features will not be shown in the remarks column unless a reasonable difference exists. There are, of course, many of these items scattered throughout the long history of pinball and the little bit of knowledge that you have picked up while reading through the previous chapters will go a long way.

Abbreviations

AB: Animated backglass.
ADB: Add-a-ball pinball.
AN: Alphanumeric display.
B: Bumpers - plus number of.
BFF: Back-to-front flippers.
BI: Buy-in option at end of game.
BO: Backbox ornament.
CB: Captive ball or messenger ball.
DB: Disc bumpers - plus number of (bumper without solenoid).
DL: Double level playfield.
DM: Dot matrix display.
DRS: Drum reel scoring (abbreviation found between years 1953 to 1960).
DT: Drop targets – plus number of.
EM: Electromechanical pinball (only shown on games between 1976-1979).
EP: Electronic plunger.
F: Flipper–plus number of.
FD: Flipper drain (opening between certain in-line flippers).
FS: Flipper save available.
FT: Flyaway targets.
HS: Horseshoe loop.
IDT: In-line drop targets.
KB: Outlane kickback.
KO: Kickout hole or saucer–plus number of.
LC: Lane change available.
LIC: Licensed theme (T.V show/movie).
LUS: Light-up scoring (Abbreviation found between years 1953 to 1960).
MB: Multiball–plus number of.
MG: Magna save available (mostly on Williams pinballs).
MOL: Multiple outlanes (more than two).
MRL: Multiple return lanes (more than two).
MT: Moving target.
MUSB: Mushroom bumpers–plus number of.
NF: No flippers (only shown from 1947 onwards).
NLC: No lane change available.
NOL: No outlanes.
NRL: No return lanes (only shown on pinballs from 1965 onwards).
NV: Non talking/voice pinball.
OG: Outlane gate/return gate.
PBG: Photographic backglass.
PR: Production run.
RS: Ramp/Ramps on playfield.
RT: Roto target.
RW: Roulette wheel.
S: Spinner/spinning target.
SP: Spinning posts.
SS: Solid state pinball (only shown on games between 1976-1979).
TL: Triple level playfield.
TP: Timed play, rather than three- or five-ball play.
TRL: Top rollover lanes–plus number of.
TS: Turret Shooter.
UP: Game or player activated post (up post) near flippers.
V: Voice/talking pinball.
VC: Vibrating cabinet.
VID/P: Video/pinball combination.
VM: Video mode available.
VT: Vari-target.
WB: Wide body pinball.
WR: Woodrail (abbreviation found only between 1957 & 1960).
WWS: Whirlwind spinner.
ZF: Zipper flippers.

Manufacturer	Game Name	Year	Players	Country	Remarks
Gottlieb	300	1975	4		AB, S, 2B, PR-7925, 2TRL
Genco	400	1952	1		
Playmec Flippers	15 Pool	1976	U	Italy	
Gottlieb	2001	1971	1		20DT, 5KO, 2-Inch Flippers, 2B, PR-2200
Inder	250 Cc	1992	4	Spain	
Williams	3 Jokers	1970	1		ADB, 5TRL, 5B, 1KO, NRL, UP
Williams	3-D	1958	1		LUS
Bally	3-In-Line	1963	4		PR-1000
Bally	41 Derby	1941	1		
Genco	42nd Street	1933	1		
Atari	4x4	1983	4		Prototype Only Produced, WB, 8CB, 8DT, 3B, S
Gottlieb	A Nightmare On Elm Street	1994	4		3F, CB, MB, KB, UP Type Clawsave Device, PR-2800
Alvin G. & Co	A.G Football	1992	2		Export Version Of A.G Soccer-Ball, PR-500
Alvin G. & Co	A.G Soccer-Ball	1991	2		Two-Player Head-to-Head, 6F, 3MB, AN, PR-500, 4S.
Gottlieb	A-B-C Bowler	1941	1		
Gottlieb	Abracadabra	1975	1		10DT, 2B, MRL, 4TRL, PR-2825
Gottlieb	Ace High	1957	1		LUS, WR, PR-2100
Williams	Aces & Kings	1970	4		SP, 3B, 3TRL, UP
Bally	Aces High	1965	4		4TRL, 5MUSB, NRL, 4B, PR-1275
Auto Bell Novelty	Acey Ducy	1960	1		Cocktail Table Style
United	Across The Board	1952	1		
Bally	Action	1934	1		
Automatic Amusements	Action	1935	1		
Chicago Coin	Action	1969	1		
Bontempi	Action	N/A	U	Italy	
Williams	Add-A-Ball	1961	1		
Bally	Addams Family	1992	4		RS, DM, 4F, MB, 4B, LIC, BO
Bally	Addams Family Collectors Edition	1994	4		PR-1000
Genco	Admiral	1933	1		
Automatic Amusements	Advance	1933	1		
Genco	Advance Roll	1945	1		
Data East	Adventures Rocky And Bullwinkle	1993	4		AB, KB, 5DT, RS, 3TRL, 3B, EP
Zaccaria	Aerobatics	1977	1	Italy	EM
Wico	Af-Tor	1984	1		
Game Plan	Agents 777	1985	4		PR-400
Williams	A-Go-Go	1966	4		3B, RW, MOL, NRL, PR-5100
Bally	Air Aces	1975	4		4F, 10DT, 2B, PR-3085
Exhibit	Air Circus	1942	1		
Western Equipment	Air Derby	1937	1		
Bally	Air Force	1940	1		
Capcom	Airborne	1996	4		PR-1350
Atari	Airborne Avenger	1977	4		WB, 2TRL, 3B, MOL, S, 2OG, CB, 2KO, PR-350
Exhibit	Airliner	1939	1		
Genco	Airport	1939	1		
Gottlieb	Airport	1969	2		2VT, NRL, 4B, 6TRL, PR-1900
Bally	Airway	1933	1		
Bally	Airway	1937	1		
Bally	Aladdin's Castle	1976	2		S, 3B, EM, 4TRL, 3F, PR-4155
Bergmann & Co	Alarm	1958	1	Germany	LUS
Interflip	Alaska	1978	4	Spain	11DT, 3B, 2KO, 2TRL, 1P EM Version Released In 1977
Arco	Alert	1943	1		
Williams	Algar	1980	4		WB, 3B, 3CB, PR-349
Stern	Ali	1980	4		NV, LIC, 3KO, 6DT, 3B, PR-2971
Stoner	Ali Baba	1940	1		24B
Gottlieb	Ali Baba	1948	1		
Sega	Ali Baba	1976	2	Japan	
Gottlieb	Alice In Wonderland	1948	1		
Williams	Alien Poker	1980	4		V, 3F, LC, 5DT, S, 4B, 3KO, MB, 4TRL, PR-6000
Gottlieb	Alien Star	1984	4		2MB, 4TRL, 3B, S, 1KO, PR-1065
A.A Amusements	All American Odd Ball	1988	1		
Williams	All American Quarterback	1952	1		
A.B.T Mfg	All Stars	1934	1		
Gottlieb	All Stars	1972	1		
Bally	Alligator	1968	1		Released Only In Germany, ZF, NRL, 3B, 3TRL, 5MUSB
Gottlieb	All-Star Basketball	1952	1		
Nasco	Aloha	1949	1		Conversion Kit Pinball
Gottlieb	Aloha	1961	2		PR-1700
C.E.A.	Alpha 2001	1977	1	Italy	
Williams	Alpine Club	1965	1		4B, 2KO, 3DB, 4F, NRL, PR-1200
Alvin G. & Co	Al's Garage Band World Tour	1992	4		3MB, WWS, DM, VM, EP, PR-1000
Gottlieb	Amazon Hunt	1983	4		PR-1515
Gottlieb	Amazon Hunt 2	1987	4		Conversion Kit Pinball, MRL, 3B, 10DT, 3TRL, PR-781
Stoner	Ambassador	1933	1		
Williams	Amber	1947	1		NF
Juegos Populares	America	1986	4	Spain	
G.B Daval	American Beauty	1934	1		
Bally	Amigo	1974	4		2TRL, 1KO, 3B, S, PR-4325
Stoner	Anabel	1940	1		
Game Plan	Andromeda	1985	4		PR-500
Bontempi	Angels	N/A	U	Italy	
Playmatic	Antar	1979	4	Spain	SS, 3F, 1B, S, 10DT
Nordamatic	Antares	1979	4	Italy	SS, 3F, S, 2B, 4TRL, 4DT, MRL
Glickman	Anti Aircraft	1944	1		Conversion Kit Pinball
Playmatic	Apache	1975	1	Spain	
Jeutel	Apocalypse	1985	4	France	PR-500
Williams	Apollo	1967	1		AB, 1DB, 4B, NRL, Bagatelle In Backglass, PR-1300
Sega	Apollo 13	1995	4		13MB, 3F, RS, DM, VM, LIC
United	Aquacade	1949	1		
Juegos Populares	Aqualand	1986	4	Spain	
Gottlieb	Aquarius	1970	1		5KO, 3B, NRL, 2-Inch Flippers, PR-2025
Gottlieb	Arabian Knights	1953	1		LUS
Bally	Arcade	1938	1		
Williams	Arcade	1951	1		
Glickman	Archery	1944	1		Conversion Kit Pinball
Gottlieb	Arena	1987	4		PBG, 3MB, RS, AN, PR-3099
Genco	Argentine	1941	1		
Williams	Argosy	1977	4		EM, S, 2B, DT, 1KO, PR-2052
United	Arizona	1943	1		Conversion Kit Pinball 12DB
Bally	Arlington	1943	1		
Stoner	Armada	1941	1		
Rock-Ola	Army & Navy	1935	1		
Victory Games	Army And Navy	1944	1		Conversion Kit Pinball
Williams	Army Navy	1953	1		MOL, 3B, 2KO, DRS
Stoner	Around The World	1937	1		
Gottlieb	Around The World	1959	2		DRS, PR-800
Williams	Arrow Head	1957	1		LUS
Bally	Arrowhead	1938	1		
Keeney	Arrowhead	1963	2		
Victory Games	Artists & Models	1944	1		Conversion Kit Pinball
Western Equipment	Ascot Derby	1938	1		
Brunswick	Aspen	1979	4		
Gottlieb	Asteroid Annie And The Aliens	1980	1		10DT, 2B, S, 4TRL, 1KO, PR-210
Universal	Asteroid Killer	1980	4	Japan	

Manufacturer	Name	Year	#	Country	Notes
Gottlieb	Astro	1971	1		ADB, PR-500
Segasa / Sonic	Astro- Flite	1974	1	Spain	
Chicago Coin	Astronaut	1969	2		UP
Bally	Atlantic City	1938	1		
Bergmann & Co	Atlanticus	1960	1	Germany	
Gottlieb	Atlantis	1975	1		9DT, 2B, 3TRL, PR-2225
Nordamatic	Atlantis	1978	1	Italy	E M
Bally	Atlantis	1989	4		3MB, RS, V, AN, S, 4DT, 3B
Gottlieb	Atlas	1959	2		PR-950
Inder	Atleto	1991	4	Spain	
Playmatic	Attack	1980	4	Spain	
Bally	Attack From Mars	1995	4		RS, DM, 3B, VM
Bally	Attention	1940	1		
Exhibit	Attention	1940	1		
Game Plan	Attila The Hun	1984	4		PR-500
Stoner	Auroran	1937	1		PR-10150
Genco	Auto Derby	1937	1		
Gottlieb	Auto Race	1956	1		LUS
Gottlieb	Auto Race	1969	1		
A.B.T Mfg	Autobank	1934	1		
A.B.T Mfg	Autocount	1933	1		
A.B.T Mfg	Autodart	1935	1		
A.B.T Mfg	Autowhirl	1934	1		
Exhibit	Avalon	1939	1		
Gottlieb	Awards	1937	1		
Williams	Aztec	1976	4		EM, S, 3B, 3TRL, SS Prototype Produced In 1977
Segasa / Sonic	Baby Doll	1975	1	Spain	
United	Baby Face	1948	1		
Pacific Amusement	Baby Lite- A- Line	1935	1		
Bally	Baby Pac-Man	1982	1		Video Cabinet Style, VID/P, S, 2KO, 5DT, PR-7000
Data East	Back To The Future	1990	4		RS, 1KO, AN, V, LIC, MB
Williams	Bad Cats	1989	4		RW, RS, AN, V, AB, VT -Type Linear Target, 3TRL
Gottlieb	Bad Girls	1988	4		2MB, 3F, RS, AN, 7DT, 3B, PR-2500
Gottlieb	Baffle Ball	1935	1		
Gottlieb	Baffle Card	1946	1		
Mills Novelty	Balance	1935	1		
Bally	Bali-Hi	1973	4		
Stoner	Ball Fan	1935	1		
Stoner	Ball Fan	1937	1		
Bally	Ballerina	1948	1		
Bally	Balls A Poppin	1956	2		LUS, 7MB, PR-750, 4B, 2DB, 1KO
Bally	Bally Booster	1937	1		
Bally	Bally Entry	1938	1		
Bally	Bally Entry	1947	1		
Bally	Bally Hoo	1969	4		3B, NRL, UP, 2KO, 3TRL, MUSB, 3-Inch Flippers, PR-2115
Bally	Bally Reserve	1938	1		
Bally	Bally Rocket	1947	1		
Bally	Bally Royal	1939	1		
Bally	Bally Stables	1937	1		
Bally	Bally Supreme	1939	1		
Bally	Bally View	1938	1		
Bally	Ballyhoo	1947	1		NF
Bally	Bambino	1938	1		
Keeney	Band Leader	1949	1		
Genco	Band Wagon	1940	1		
Williams	Band Wagon	1955	1		DRS
Bally	Band Wagon	1965	4		3B, 4MUSB, 3TRL, NRL, OG, PR-1840
Genco	Bang	1939	1		
Recel	Bang! Bang!	1974	2	Spain	
Buckley	Banjo	1936	1		
Exhibit	Banjo	1948	1		BFF, 4F, 7DB, 2KO
Rock-Ola	Bank Nite	1936	1		EM, ADB, PR-730
Gottlieb	Bank Shot	1976	1		TS, No Bumpers, 6KO
Gottlieb	Bank-A-Ball	1950	1		AB, 3B, 5TRL, PR-3400
Gottlieb	Bank-A-Ball	1965	1		
Bally	Banker	1935	1		
Williams	Banzai Run	1988	4		Vert. Playfield In Backbox, RS, V, 6F, UP, AN, MB
Gottlieb	Barb Wire	1996	4		PR-1000
Gottlieb	Barnacle Bill	1948	1		
Williams	Barracora	1981	4		3MB, 3B, S, 3TRL, 2KO, 8DT, PR-2350
Western Products	Barrage	1941	1		
Allied Amusements	Barrel Roll	1935	1		
Chicago Coin	Base Hit	1935	1		
Genco	Base Hit	1935	1		
Genco	Baseball	1934	1		
Genco	Baseball	1935	1		
G.B Daval	Baseball	1937	1		
Stoner	Baseball	1940	1		
Marvel	Baseball	1944	1		Conversion Kit Pinball
Victory Games	Baseball	1946	1		Conversion Kit Pinball
Chicago Coin	Baseball	1947	1		NF
Gottlieb	Baseball	1970	1		3TRL, 2VT, 2B, 2-Inch Flippers, PR-2350
M.A.M	Basket Ball	1967	1	Spain	4B, 5DB, NRL, 3MB
Giuliano Lodola	Basket World Trotter	1979	4	Italy	
Chicago Coin	Basketball	1947	1		
Gottlieb	Basketball	1949	1		
Chicago Coin	Basketball Champ	1949	1		
Data East	Batman	1991	4		DM, RS, 3MB, 3B, BO
Sega	Batman Forever	1995	4		3F, DM, MB, LIC, 4DT, 3TRL, 3B, MRL, VM
Genco	Batter Up	1937	1		
Gottlieb	Batter Up	1970	1		PR-560
Gottlieb	Batting Champ	1939	1		
Bally	Battle	1935	1		
Sega	Bay Watch	1995	6		MB, VM, DM, 4F, LIC, 3TRL, 3DT, MRL, 3B
Nasco	Bazaar	1949	1		Conversion Kit Pinball
Bally	Bazaar	1966	1		ZF, PR-2925
Exhibit	Be Pop	1950	1		
Nasco	Beach Club	1949	1		Conversion Kit Pinball
Rally	Beach Games	1962	2	France	4F, 5B
Bally	Beach Queens	1960	1		NF, 10B, 1KO, LUS, WR, PR-950, One ball play
Stoner	Beacon	1935	1		
Chicago Coin	Beam Lite	1935	1		
Chicago Coin	Beamlite Of 37	1937	1		
Exhibit	Beano	1936	1		
Western Equipment	Beat' Em	1937	1		
Williams	Beat The Clock	1963	1		PR-2100
Bally	Beat The Clock	1985	4		3F, 3B, TP, 4TRL, 2KO, 7DT, PR-500
Williams	Beat Time	1967	2		5B, 4TRL, NRL, PR-2082
Chicago Coin	Beatnicks	1967	2		
Bally	Beauty	1940	1		
Bally	Beauty Contest	1960	1		NF, ONE BALL PLAY, LUS, PR-750
Bally	Beauty Queens	1960	1		NF, LUS, PR-950
Gottlieb	Bell Ringer	1990	4		
Gottlieb	Belle Hop	1941	1		

Manufacturer	Name	Year	#	Country	Notes
California Games	Bells	1935	1		
Exhibit	Bells	1935	1		
Staal	Ben Hur	1977	4	France	SS, MRL, 5DT, 3TRL, 1B, 3F
Chicago Coin	Bermuda	1947	1		
Chicago Coin	Bermuda Roll Down	1948	1		
Westerhaus	Big 3	1945	1		Conversion Kit Pinball
Capcom	Big Bang Bar	1996	4		Prototype Only Produced, PR-14
G.B Daval	Big Ben	1936	1		
Hawtins	Big Ben	1946	1	Britain	
Williams	Big Ben	1954	1		
Segasa / Sonic	Big Ben	1975	1	Spain	
Williams	Big Ben	1975	1		
G.B Daval	Big Bertha	1934	1		
Bensa	Big Brave	1974	1	Italy	
Gottlieb	Big Brave	1974	2		Same As Big Injun & Big Indian, VT, 5DT, 2B, 3TRL, PR-3450
Gottlieb	Big Broadcast	1933	1		
G.B Daval	Big Brother	1934	1		
Gottlieb	Big Casino	1961	1		PR-1600
Alben	Big Champ	1958	1	France	
Williams	Big Chief	1965	4		3TRL, 3B, NRL, PR-2950
Genco	Big Chief	1940	1		
Williams	Big Daddy	1963	1		6TRL, 2KO, 3B, 6TRL, 1DT, PR-1050
Bally	Big Day	1964	4		4TRL, 6MUSB, 3B, PR-2075
Williams	Big Deal	1963	1		PR-1350
Williams	Big Deal	1977	4		EM, HS, 4TRL, 2B, DT?, PR-7300
Europlay	Big Dryver	1979	4	Italy	EM & SS Versions Released
Mondialmatic	Big Dryvers	1979	1	Italy	
Chicago Coin	Big Flipper	1970	2		5-Inch Flippers
Rock-Ola	Big Game	1935	1		
Stern	Big Game	1980	4		NV, WB, 3F, NLC, 2S, 3B, 9DT, 4F, 3TRL, PR-2713
Segasa / Sonic	Big Guns	1987	4	Spain	Built Under License From Williams
Williams	Big Guns	1987	4		RS, UP, 4F, 3MB, V, AN, AB, KB, 6DT
Exhibit	Big Hit	1946	1		
Chicago Coin	Big Hit	1952	1		
Gottlieb	Big Hit	1977	1		EM, 10DT, 2B, 2VT, 4F, Run Reels, No Plunger, PR-2200
Maresa	Big Horse	1966	1	Spain	
Gottlieb	Big House	1989	4		3MB, AN, RS, 3TRL, 3B, PR-1977
A.M.I	Big Hunt	1976	1	Italy	EM, 3B, 4DT, MRL
Gottlieb	Big Hurt	1995	4		3F, CB, DM, MB, LIC, RS, 3DT, 2B, Catchers Mitt, PR-1985
Gottlieb	Big Indian	1974	4		Also Marketed As Big Injun & Big Brave, PR-8030
Gottlieb	Big Injun	1974	4		Also Marketed As Big Indian & Big Brave
Gottlieb	Big Jack	1968	1		PR-1725
Sega	Big Kick	1977	1	Japan	SS
Genco	Big League	1940	1		
Bally	Big League	1946	1		
Chicago Coin	Big League Baseball	1955	4		
Exhibit	Big Parade	1941	1		
Exhibit	Big Parade	1941	1		
United	Big Parade	1946	1		
Keeney	Big Parley	1947	1		
Western Products	Big Prize	1940	1		
California Games	Big Shot	1936	1		
Exhibit	Big Shot	1936	1		
Gottlieb	Big Shot	1974	2		PR-2900
Gottlieb	Big Show	1940	1		
Bally	Big Show	1974	2		PR-1000
Keeney	Big Six	1939	1		
Williams	Big Star	1972	1		NRL, UP, 4B, 3TRL, 1DT, 1KO, PR-1130
Williams	Big Strike	1966	1		ADB, 5B, NRL, 1DB, PR-3600
Keeney	Big Ten	1938	1		
Evans	Big Ten Basketball	1935	1		
Mills Novelty	Big Three	1941	1		
Baker Novelty	Big Time	1941	1		
Sega	Big Together	1977	1	Japan	SS
Pioneer	Big Top	1945	1		Conversion Kit Pinball
Genco	Big Top	1949	1		BFF, 2B, 3KO, 14DB
Gottlieb	Big Top	1964	2		ADB, 1TRL, 4B, 2DB, 4F, PR-750
Genco	Big Town	1940	1		
Playmatic	Big Town	1978	4	Spain	
Bally	Big Valley	1970	4		PR-2500
Sleic	Bike Race	1995	4	Spain	DM
Shyvers Mfg	Billiard Flash	1934	1		
Nasco	Bingo Bango	1951	1		
Segasa / Sonic	Bird Man	1978	1	Spain	
Baker Novelty	Birdic	1940	1		
Genco	Black Beauty	1933	1		
Keeney	Black Dragon	N/A	1		
Playmatic	Black Fever	1980	4	Spain	3F, 1B, 5DT, 1KO, MRL
Playmatic	Black Flag	1975	4	Spain	
Genco	Black Gold	1949	1		
Williams	Black Gold	1975	1		PR-55
Giuliano Lodola	Black Hole	1980	4	Italy	Copy Of Gottlieb's Black Out
Gottlieb	Black Hole	1981	4		V, DL, NLC, 6F, 3MB, 5D, 16DT, 3TRL, OG, PR-8774
Williams	Black Jack	1960	1		
Bally	Black Jack	1978	4		EM & SS Versions Released, 3B, S, 4TRL, 1KO, PR-4883
Williams	Black Knight	1980	4		DL, RS, V, MS, 4F, 3MB, 1B, 12DT, S, PR-13075
Williams	Black Knight 2000	1989	4		DL, V, MS, 3F, AN, 3MB, 3B, KB, 3TRL, 6DT
Recel	Black Magic	1980	1	Spain	2CB, 6DT
Bally	Black Pyramid	1984	4		MT, PR-2500
Inder	Black Reed	1975	1	Spain	
Giuliano Lodola	Black Rider	1981	4	Italy	
Bally	Black Rose	1991	4		RS, DM, 3F, 3MB, VM, TS
Astro Games	Black Sheep Squadron	1979	4		4TRL, 3B, S
Game Plan	Black Velvet	1978	4		Cocktail Table Style
Bally	Blackbelt	1986	4		4F, RS, AN, PR-600
Zaccaria	Blackbelt	1986	4	Italy	RT
Williams	Blackout	1980	4		V, LC, 6DT, 3B, 2S, 3TRL, PR-7050
Stoner	Blackstone	1933	1		Manufactured For Chicago Coin
Bally	Blackwater 100	1988	4		5F, 3MB, DL, AN, PR-3000
Williams	Blast Off	1967	1		ADB, 1DB, 4B, AB, NRL, Bagatelle In Backglass, PR-4635
Brunswick	Block A Shot	1976	4		
Playbar	Bloddy Roller	1987	4	Spain	
Genco	Blondie	1940	1		
Chicago Coin	Blondie	1956	1		LUS
Geiger	Bloody China	1985	4	Germany	Conversion Kit Pinball
Williams	Blue Chip	1976	1		EM, 2B, 2S, 2KO, PR-2150
Bally	Blue Grass	1941	1		
Chicago Coin	Blue Max	1975	4		2S, 2B, 3TRL
Gottlieb	Blue Note	1979	1		EM, PR-229
Bally	Blue Ribbon	1933	1		
Bally	Blue Ribbon	1939	1		
Bally	Blue Ribbon	1965	4		4TRL, 3B, NRL, 8MUSB, OG, PR-875
United	Blue Skies	1948	1		
Deluxe Amusements	Blue Star Double	1933	1		

Manufacturer	Title	Year		Country	Notes
G.B Daval	Blue Streack	1934	1		
Bally	Bmx	1982	4		4F, DL, RS, DT, PR-406
Williams	Bobo	1961	1		3DB, 3B, LUS, PR-400
Exhibit	Bobs	1936	1		
Chicago Coin	Bola Way	1941	1		
United	Bolero	1951	1		
Victory Games	Bomb The Axis Rats	1944	1		Conversion Kit Pinball
P & S Machine Co	Bombardier	1943	1		Conversion Kit Pinball
Victory Games	Bombardier	1944	1		Conversion Kit Pinball
Hannover	Bombenfeurer	1936	1	Germany	
Rock-Ola	Bomber	1935	1		
Chicago Coin	Bomber	1943	1		Conversion Kit Pinball
Chicago Coin	Bomber	1951	1		
Bally	Bon Voyage	1974	1		CB, S, 2B, 3TRL, 1KO, PR-1585
Exhibit	Bonanza	1934	1		
Williams	Bonanza	1947	1		NF
Gottlieb	Bonanza	1964	2		3B, 3DB, 4TRL, PR-2640
Gottlieb	Bone Busters	1989	4		4MB, V, 4F, DL, AN, PR-2000
Genco	Bone Head	1948	1		
Bally	Bongo	1964	2		4TRL, 3B, PR-1050
Bally	Bonus	1936	1		
Allied Leisure	Boogie	1976	4		
G.B Daval	Boo-Hoo	1937	1		
Bontempi	Book Makers	N/A	U	Italy	
Bally	Boomerang	1974	4		1B, 2CB, PR-2585
Bally	Boot A Ball	1967	i		Two Player Head-To-Head, 12F, PR-100
Gottlieb	Border Town	1940	1		
Genco	Bosco	1941	1		
Williams	Boston	1949	1		
Exhibit	Bounty	1938	1		
Gottlieb	Bounty Hunter	1985	4		WB, 3F, AN, PR-1200
Bally	Bow And Arrow	1975	4		EM, 4B, 2KO, 2S, SS Prototype Produced In 1976, PR-7360
Williams	Bowl-A-Strike	1965	1		ADB, PR-1400
Gottlieb	Bowling Alley	1940	1		
Chicago Coin	Bowling Alley	1949	1		
Gottlieb	Bowling Champ	1949	1		
Salmon	Bowling Flipper	1961	2	France	
Artigiana Ricambi	Bowling Girl	N/A	2	Italy	Two Player Head-To-Head
Gottlieb	Bowling League	1947	1		NF
Gottlieb	Bowling Queen	1964	1		MOL, 4B, 2TRL, PR-2650
Bally	Bowl-O	1970	1		3TRL, 3B, UP, NRL, 3-Inch Flippers, PR-1050
G.B Daval	Box Score	1939	1		
Gottlieb	Box Score	1947	1		NF
Williams	Box Score	1947	1		
Maresa	Boxing	1967	1	Spain	
Inder	Brave Team	1985	4	Spain	
United	Brazil	1943	1		Conversion Kit Pinball
Capcom	Breakshot	1996	4		3TRL, 3B, 3F, 6DT, 3CB, PR-1000
Bergmann & Co	Brilliant Torero	1938	1	Germany	21B
Gottlieb	Bristol Hills	1971	2		PR-110
Stoner	Brite Spot	1940	1		
Gottlieb	Brite Star	1958	2		DRS
Bally	Broadcast	1941	1		
Pacific Amusement	Broadway	1936	1		
Bally	Broadway	1951	1		
Gottlieb	Brokers Tip	1933	1		
Exhibit	Broncho	1937	1		
Genco	Broncho	1947	1		NF
Chicago Coin	Bronco	1963	2		4B, 4TRL, 2KO
Gottlieb	Bronco	1977	4		EM, 3B, 3TRL, 3DT, 2KO, Same Play As Mustang, PR-9160
Genco	Bubble	1939	1		
Genco	Bubbles	1947	1		
Gottlieb	Buccaneer	1948	1		
Gottlieb	Buccaneer	1976	1		EM, 5B, S, 5TRL, PR-3650
Gottlieb	Buck Rogers	1979	4		NV, CB, 2B, 8DT, 4TRL, PR-7410
Mambelli	Buck Rogers	1979	U	Italy	
Chicago Coin	Buckaroo	1939	1		
Gottlieb	Buckaroo	1965	1		AB, 3DB, 3B, 5TRL, RT, NRL, PR-2600
Chicago Coin	Budget	1936	1		
Gottlieb	Buffalo Bill	1950	1		
Bally	Bugs Bunny Birthday Ball	1991	4		V, AN, DL, 3F, 3TRL, S, 3DT, CB
Exhibit	Build Up	1948	1		
G.M Laboratories	Builder Upper	1935	1		
Bally	Bull Fight	1965	1		3TRL, 3B, NRL, 7MUSB, PR-825
Bally	Bulls Eye	1965	1		PR-80
Bally	Bull's Eye	1935	1		
Grand Products	Bullseye 301	1986	4		Conversion Kit Pinball
Pinstar	Bullseye 301	1986	4		
Bally	Bumper	1937	1		
G.B Daval	Bumper Bowling	1937	1		3TRL, 1B, PR-1250
Gottlieb	Bumper Pool	1969	1		4TRL, 3B, 6MUSB, PR-825
Bally	Bus Stop	1964	2		
Inder	Bushido	1993	U	Spain	
Segasa / Sonic	Butterfly	1977	4	Spain	EM
G.B Daval	Buttons	1936	1		
Exhibit	Buttons	1938	1		
Gottlieb	Buttons And Bows	1949	1		
Rock-Ola	Buzzer	1935	1		
Bally	C.O.D	1935	1		LUS
Williams	C.O.D	1953	1		UP, 5B, 4TRL, 1KO, NRL, PR-3852
Williams	Cabaret	1969	4		
Recreativos Franco	Cabaret	1972	1	Spain	
Gottlieb	Cactus Jack	1991	4		V, RS, 2MB, AN, PR-1900
Playmatic	Caddie	1975	1	Spain	
Genco	Cadillac	1940	1		
Elettrogiochi	Calcio Italia	1967	2	Italy	12F, 4B, Two Player Head-To-Head
Genco	Camel Caravan	1949	1		
Game Plan	Camelite	1978	4		Cocktail Table Style
Bally	Camelot	1970	4		PR-1865
Exhibit	Campus	1950	1		
Bally	Campus Queen	1966	4		PR-1125
Williams	Can Can	1955	1		LUS, 4TRL, 3B, 6DB, AB
Gottlieb	Canada Dry	1977	4		EM, 4F, 2B, 15DT, 2TRL, PR-2885
Genco	Canasta	1950	1		
Inder	Canasta 86	1986	4	Spain	
Segasa / Sonic	Cannes	1976	4	Spain	EM
Mills Novelty	Cannon Fire	1934	1		
Shyvers Mfg	Cannon Fire	1934	1		
Bally	Capersville	1966	4		3MB, ZF, 6MUSB, 3B, 2KO, PR-5120
Chicago Coin	Capri	1956	1		
Gottlieb	Captain Card	1974	1		ADB, PR-675
Bally	Captain Fantastic	1976	4		4F, 3TRL, 5DT, FD, OG, EM, PR-16155
Genco	Captain Kidd	1941	1		
Gottlieb	Captain Kidd	1960	2		PR-900

Manufacturer	Title	Year	#	Country	Notes
Game Plan	Captin Hook	1985	4		PR-450
Gottlieb	Car Hop	1990	4		PR-1060
Genco	Caravan	1949	1		
Genco	Caravan	1949	1		
Williams	Caravan	1952	1		
Playmatic	Caravan	1974	1	Spain	
Williams	Caravelle	1961	4		RT, PR-425
Nordamatic	Card Castle	1977	1	Italy	EM
Gottlieb	Card King	1971	1		PR-2340
Gottlieb	Card Trix	1970	1		ADB, PR-1750
Europlay	Card Whiz	1976	1	Italy	EM
Gottlieb	Card Whiz	1976	2		EM, PR-3250
Genco	Cargo	1937	1		
United	Caribbean	1948	1		
International	Caribbean Cruise	1989	4		Cocktail Table Style, 4F, MSL, 2B, PR-377
Genco	Carnival	1937	1		
Marvel	Carnival	1947	1		NF
Bally	Carnival	1948	1		
Alben	Carnival	1960	1	France	
Sega	Carnival	1976	1	Japan	EM, 3B, UP, 3TRL, NRL
Playmatic	Carnival	1977	2	Spain	
United	Carolina	1949	1		
Keeney	Carousel	1947	1		
Maresa	Carrusel	1967	1	Spain	
Williams	Casanova	1966	2		3TRL, 3B, NRL, Bagatelle In Backglass, PR-3575
Acme	Casba	1948	1		
Segasa / Sonic	Casbah	1972	1	Spain	
Chicago Coin	Casino	1936	1		
Pacific Amusement	Casino	1936	1		
Williams	Casino	1958	1		
Elettrocoin	Casino	1967	1	Italy	ADB, 3B, 5TRL, 1DB
Chicago Coin	Casino	1972	4		2WWS
Bill Port	Casino 2000	1977	1	Spain	
Segasa / Sonic	Casino Royale	1976	4	Spain	EM, 1KO, 3B, Lit Roulette Wheel Feature
Exhibit	Castle Lite	1935	1		
Stern	Catacomb	1981	4		AB, MB, V, 3F, 9DT, 2B, S
Marvel	Catalina	1943	1		Conversion Kit Pinball
Chicago Coin	Catalina	1948	1		
Recel	Cavalier	1979	4	Spain	
Gottlieb	Caveman	1982	4		V, VID/P, 4F, 3B, NRL, 8DT, PR-1800
Bally	Centaur	1981	4		5MB, V, CB, IDT, 12DT, LC, 3B, PR-3700
Bally	Centaur 2	1983	4		5MB, V, CB, IDT, 12DT, LC, 3B, PR-1550
Gottlieb	Centigrade 37	1977	1		EM, 3B, 3TRL, 4DT, 1KO, MRL, PR-1600
Gottlieb	Central Park	1966	1		4B, NRL, 2TRL, PR-3100
Playmatic	Cerberus	1982	4	Spain	
Sega	Cha Cha Cha	1978	2	Japan	SS, 4F, WB, 2B, CB
Pacific Amusement	Chain A Lite	1935	1		
Sullivan & Nolan	Challenger	1943	1		Conversion Kit Pinball
Gottlieb	Challenger	1971	2		Two Player Head-To-Head, 8F, 4B, PR-210
Geiger	Challenger	1981	4	Germany	
Game Plan	Challenger 1	1979	4		
Bally	Champ	1974	4		2B, S, 1KO, 2TRL, 2CB, PR-4070
Bally	Champion	1939	1		
Chicago Coin	Champion	1949	1		
Nordamatic	Champion	1975	1	Italy	EM, 3B, 3TRL, 2KO
Barni	Champion 85	1985	4	Spain	
Genco	Champion Baseball	1955	2		
Bally	Champion Pub	1998	4		
Genco	Champs	1936	1		
Playmatic	Chance	1978	4	Spain	SS
Gottlieb	Charlies Angles	1979	4		EM & SS Versions Released, 2B, 8DT, 4TRL, PR-7950
Bally	Charm	1940	1		
Recel	Check	1975	2	Spain	
Recel	Check Mate	1975	4	Spain	
Data East	Checkpoint	1991	4		DM, V, 3MB, EP, RS
Genco	Cheer Leader	1935	1		
Stern	Cheetah	1980	4		WB, 3F, 14DT, MRL, 3S, 3B, MB, PR-1223
Interflip	Cherokee	1977	4	Spain	EM
Segasa / Sonic	Cherry Bell	1978	4	Spain	EM
Automatic Amusements	Chevron	1935	1		
Bally	Cheyron	1939	1		
Gottlieb	Chicago Cubs Triple Play	1985	4		AN, 4F, PR-1365
G.B Daval	Chicago Express	1935	1		
G.B Daval	Chicago Express	1938	1		
Exhibit	Chico	1948	1		
Exhibit	Chico	1935	1		
Chicago Coin	Chico Baseball	1938	1		
Chicago Coin	Chico Derby	1937	1		
Chicago Coin	Chico Races	1937	1		
Exhibit	Chief	1939	1		
Pacific Amusement	Chieftain	1935	1		
Gottlieb	Chinatown	1952	1		
Jennings	Chocolate Drop	1935	1		
Segasa / Sonic	Chorus Line	1978	4	Spain	
Stoner	Chubbie	1938	1		
Game Plan	Chuck A Luck	1978	4		Cocktail Table Style
Gottlieb	Cinderella	1948	1		
Chicago Coin	Cinema	1976	4		EM
Fascination Game	Circa 1933	1979	2		Cocktail Table Style
Genco	Circus	1939	1		
Exhibit	Circus	1948	1		
Bally	Circus	1957	2		LUS, 4B, 2DB, 1KO, PR-3550
Bally	Circus	1973	4		
Zaccaria	Circus	1977	4	Italy	EM, 2B, 2S, 1KO, 3TRL
Brunswick	Circus	1980	4		
Gottlieb	Circus	1980	4		WB, 5F, NV, 2B, 4TRL, PR-1700
Century Games	Circus Circus	1978	1		Cocktail Table Style
Williams	Circus Wagon	1955	1		DRS
Bally	Cirqus Voltaire	1997	4		S, 3B, HS, MB, RS, VM, DM, 2KO, CB, Disappearing Bumper
Bally	Citation	1949	1		
Bally	City Slicker	1987	4		2MB, 5F, AN, DI, 4B, PR 300
Gottlieb	Class Of 1812	1991	4		V, RS, 3MB, AN, 8DT, 3TRL, PR-1670
Gottlieb	Classy Bowler	1956	1		LUS
Marvel	Cleopatra	1948	1		
Gottlieb	Cleopatra	1977	4		EM & SS Versions Released, 5TRL, 3B, 5DT, 2KO, PR-8900
Mondialmatic	Cleopatra	1979	1	Italy	
Keeney	Click	1947	1		NF
Stoner	Clipper	1939	1		
Bergmann & Co	Clipper	1954	1	Germany	
Gottlieb	Close Encounters	1978	4		SS, 4F, 5DT, RT, 2B, S, 3TRL, PR-10420
Stoner	Close Finish	1936	1		
Zaccaria	Clown	1985	4	Italy	3B, 4DT
Inder	Clown	1988	4	Spain	
Bally	Club House	1937	1		

Manufacturer	Name	Year	Players	Country	Notes
Williams	Club House	1958	1		LUS
Bell Games	Cobra	1987	4	Italy	
Playbar	Cobra	1987	4	Spain	
Exhibit	Co-Ed	1947	1		
Gottlieb	College Days	1949	1		
Gottlieb	College Football	1936	1		
Gottlieb	College Queens	1969	4		2VT, 6TRL, 4B, NRL, PR-1725
Treff Automaten	Colorado (Or Treff Colorado)	1957	1	Germany	
Keeney	Colorama	1963	2		
Williams	Colors	1954	1		LUS
Glickman	Combat	1944	1		Conversion Kit Pinball
Zaccaria	Combat	1977	4	Italy	EM & SS Versions Released
Automatic Amusements	Combination	1933	1		
Comptoir Industrial	Come Back	1988	4	France	
Williams	Comet	1985	4		RS, V, PR-8100
Unidesa	Comet	1986	4	Spain	Built Under License From Williams
Rally	Comics	1968	4	France	SP, UP, 5TRL
Genco	Commander	1933	1		
Chicago Coin	Commodore	1939	1		
Petaco	Comodin	1975	1	Spain	VT, 3B, 5TRL
Exhibit	Coney Island	1937	1		
Game Plan	Coney Island	1979	4		PR-3000
Exhibit	Congo	1940	1		
Williams	Congo	1995	4		LIC, VM, DM, MB, DL, 3F
Exhibit	Conquest	1939	1		
Playmatic	Conquest 200	1976	4	Spain	Released In Two Sizes
Pacific Amusement	Contact	1934	1		
Exhibit	Contact	1939	1		
Exhibit	Contact	1948	1		Remake Of 1939 Pinball
Williams	Contact	1978	4		SS, WB, 4F, UP, 3B, NRL, FD, Dual Action Flippers, MT, PR-2502
Gottlieb	Contention	1940	1		
Keeney	Contest	1941	1		
Gottlieb	Contest	1958	4		
Gottlieb	Continental Cafe	1957	2		
Williams	Control Tower	1951	1		BFF, 3KO, 4DB, 3B, 2TRL
Gottlieb	Convention	1940	1		
Williams	Coquette	1962	2		
Gottlieb	Coronation	1952	1		
Gottlieb	Corral	1961	1		6B, 1DB, MOL, PR-2000, RT
The Best	Corsair	1976	U	Italy	
Inder	Corsario	1990	4	Spain	
Bally	Corvette	1994	4		RS, 3F, MB, BI, VM, 3B, 3TRL, KB
Bell Games	Cosmic Flash	1984	4	Italy	
Nsm	Cosmic Flash	1985	4	Germany	
Williams	Cosmic Gunfight	1982	4		3MB, NV, PR-1008
Stern	Cosmic Princess	1979	4		Released Only In Australia, MRL, 3B, 2S, 5DT, 5TRL, 1KO
Coffee Mat	Cosmic Wars	1978	4		Cocktail Table Style
Bell Games	Cosmodrome	1980	4	Italy	
Bally	Cosmos	1969	4		3B, MUSB, NRL, PR-2160
Exhibit	Cossfire	1947	1		NF
Novamatic	Count Down	1970	1	Italy	
Gottlieb	Count Down	1979	4		4F, NV, 16DT, 1B, 1KO, PR-9899
Gottlieb	Counter Force	1980	4		WB, NV, 4F, 2B, 7DT, 6TRL, MRL, PR-3870
Keeney	Cover Girl	1947	1		7F
Gottlieb	Cover Girl	1962	1		TRL, 3B, 2KO, PR-2100
Gottlieb	Cow Poke	1965	1		AB, ADB, PR-1256, 5TRL, 3DB, 3B, RT, NRL
Keeney	Cowboy	1939	1		
Chicago Coin	Cowboy	1970	4		
Century Mfg	Crack Shot	1934	1		
Chicago Coin	Cracker Jack	1936	1		
Chicago Coin	Crazy Ball	1948	1		
Sega	Crazy Clock	1976	2	Japan	
Recel	Crazy Race	1978	4	Spain	
Bally	Creature From The Black Lagoon	1993	4		DM, VM, RS, 2MB, Playfield Hologram
Gottlieb	Crescendo	1970	2		5DT, 5B, 5TRL, NRL, Same Play As Groovy, PR-1175
Genco	Criss Cross	1934	1		
Genco	Criss Cross	1935	1		Electric Version
Gottlieb	Criss Cross	1958	1		LUS, WR, 5B, 1TRL
Recel	Criterium 2000	1975	4	Spain	
Recel	Criterium 75	1975	4	Spain	2B, 3CB, S, UP
Recel	Criterium 75	1978	4	Spain	SS
Recel	Criterium 80	1975	1	Spain	
Giorgio Massiniero	Crocket	1976	1	Italy	
Jennings	Cross Country	1936	1		
Bally	Cross Country	1963	1		PR-500
Gottlieb	Cross Roads	1952	1		
Gottlieb	Cross Town	1966	1		AB, 4TRL, 4B, 2DB, NRL, PR-2765
Bally	Crossline	1937	1		
Bally	Crossline	1941	1		
Williams	Crossword	1959	1		3B, 6DB, LUS, 3KO
Taito	Crown Soccer Special	N/A	2	Japan	Two Player Head-To-Head
Bally	Crusader	1933	1		
Chicago Coin	Cue	1936	1		
Stern	Cue	1983	4		Prototype Only Produced
Williams	Cue Ball	1956	1		LUS
Gottlieb	Cue Ball Wizard	1992	4		14DT, 3MB, RS, 3B, VM, DM, EP, HS
Bally	Cue Tease	1963	2		3TRL, 4B, 2DB, PR-500
Williams	Cue Tee	1954	1		
Williams	Cue-T	1968	1		ADB, PR-2800
Rally	Curling	1965	2	France	
Bally	Cybernaut	1985	4		3F, RS, NV, 4DT, PR-900
Gottlieb	Cyclone	1935	1		
Williams	Cyclone	1947	1		NF
Gottlieb	Cyclone	1951	1		
Williams	Cyclone	1988	4		AB, RS, 1DT, V, AN, Ferris Wheel
Williams	Cyclops	1980	U		Prototype Only Produced
Game Plan	Cyclops	1985	4		3F, 3B, 2S, 2TRL, 8DT, 1KO, PR-400
Williams	Daffie	1968	1		ADB, ZF, PR-2453
Williams	Daffy Derby	1954	1		
Bally	Daily Dozen	1937	1		
Gottlieb	Daily Races 1937	1936	1		
Gottlieb	Daisy May	1954	1		LUS
Mr Game	Dakar	1988	4	Italy	
Maresa	Dakota 2	1966	1	Spain	
Williams	Dallas	1949	1		
Gottlieb	Dancing Dolls	1960	1		6B, 1DB, 2KO, LUS, WR, PR-1150
Gottlieb	Dancing Lady	1966	4		AB, NRL, RT, 4B, 4TRL, PR-2675
Bally	Dandy	1940	1		
Bally	Dark Horse	1940	1		
Geiger	Dark Rider	1985	4	Germany	Conversion Kit For Bally's Star Trek
Bell Games	Dark Shadow	1986	4	Italy	
Segasa / Sonic	Darling	1973	2	Spain	
Williams	Darling	1973	2		2B, CB, NRL, 2TRL, PR-3677
Williams	Darts	1960	1		LUS

Stoner	Davy Jones	1939	1		
Stoner	Daytona	1937	1		
Gottlieb	Deadly Weapon	1990	4		PR-803
Automatic Amusements	Dealer	1935	1		
Williams	Dealer	1953	1		
Segasa / Sonic	Dealers Choice	1974	4	Spain	
Williams	Dealers Choice	1974	4		4F, FD, 3B, 2TRL, PR-8850
Pin-Ball	Death Dealer	1976	1		
Genco	Defence	1945	1		
Williams	Defender	1982	2		MB, 3F, PR-369, 2B, 4TRL, 5DT
Baker Novelty	Defense	1940	1		
Williams	De-Icer	1949	1		
Bally	Delta Queen	1974	1		PR-1575
Gottlieb	Deluxe Jumbo	1954	4		DRS
Gottlieb	Deluxe Sluggin Champ	1955	1		LUS
Deluxe Amusements	Deluxe Twins	1933	1		
Brunswick	Demolition Classic	1979	4		
Williams	Demolition Man	1994	4		3F, RS, MB, CB, Flipper Handles, BI, 3TRL
Bally	Derby	1935	1		
Chicago Coin	Derby	1951	1		
Elettrocoin	Derby	1970	1	Italy	Conversion Kit Pinball
A.M.I	Derby	1975	1	Italy	
Victory Sales	Derby 1947	1947	1		
Bally	Derby 41	1941	1		
Keeney	Derby Champ	1938	1		
Western Products	Derby Clock	1939	1		
Gottlieb	Derby Day	1956	1		LUS
Williams	Derby Day	1967	2		AB
Western Products	Derby King	1938	1		
Great Lakes	Derby King	1947	1		
United	Derby Roll	1955	1		
Western Products	Derby Time	1938	1		
Western Products	Derby Winner	1941	1		
Nordamatic	Devil	1978	1	Italy	EM
Tecnoplay	Devil King	1987	4	San Marino	
Zaccaria	Devil Riders	1984	4	Italy	DL, 4F, RS, FS, AB, 6DT, V
Gottlieb	Devils Dare	1982	4		3MB, V, WB, 3F, 3B, KB, 2S, MRL, PR-3832
Williams	Dew-Wa-Ditty	1948	1		
Gottlieb	Diamond Jack	1967	1		ADB, RT, 3B, 4TRL, PR-650
Gottlieb	Diamond Lady	1988	4		AN, RS, MB, 3B, 2S, 14DT, PR-2700
Gottlieb	Diamond Lill	1954	1		6DB, 1B, BFF, MOL, 2KO, LUS, PR-700
Llobregat	Dig-A-Star	1966	U	Spain	ZF, 4B, 4TRL, NRL
Gottlieb	Dimension	1971	1		ADB, 20DT, 5KO, 2-Inch Flippers, PR-490
Williams	Diner	1990	4		RS, MB, AB, AN, 3B, 3TRL, 6DT
Williams	Ding Dong	1968	1		5TRL, 3B, HS, NRL, PR-1850
Alvin G. & Co	Dinosaur Eggs	1993	1		
Williams	Dipsy Doodle	1971	4		5B, CB, 1KO, NRL, UP
Williams	Dirty Harry	1995	4		TS, 3F, MB, BI, 3TRL, LIC
Stern	Disco	1977	2		PR-815
Allied Leisure	Disco 79	1979	4		Cocktail Table Style, NRL, 3B, 3TRL, 2DT
Williams	Disco Fever	1978	4		BF, 2TRL, HS, 2B, 5DT, PR-6000
Bally	Discoteck	1965	2		MUSB, 3B, NRL, PR-730
Pacific Amusement	Discovery	1935	1		
Williams	Disk Jockey	1952	1		
Rock-Ola	Ditto	1936	1		
Chicago Coin	Dixie	1940	1		
Bally	Dixieland	1968	1		ZF, 3B, 4MUSB, 2TRL, NRL, ÖG, PR-1800
Western Equipment	Do Or Dont	1935	1		
Exhibit	Do Re Me	1941	1		
Bally	Doctor Who	1992	4		3F, RS, VM, 3MB, LIC, EP, BO
Gottlieb	Dodge City	1965	4		AB, PR-3175, 6TRL, 3B, 4DB, MOL, NRL, 2KO
Bally	Dogies	1968	1		ZF, PR-3670
Marvel	Dolly	1947	1		
Bally	Dolly Parton	1979	4		LIC, NV, IDT, 3B, S, 4DT, PR-7350
Chicago Coin	Dolphin	1974	2		3CB, 2B, NRL, 1TRL
Williams	Domino	1952	1		3TRL, BFF, 3B, 3KO
Gottlieb	Domino	1968	1		RT, 4B, NRL, 2KO, 6TRL, PR-2650
Keeney	Domino Bowler	1953	1		
Recel	Don Quijote	1979	4	Spain	
Sleic	Dona Elvira 2	1996	4	Spain	
Williams	Doodle Bug	1971	1		UP, CB, 1KO, OG, 5B
Williams	Doozie	1968	1		ADB, ZF, 5B, 4TRL, NRL, PR-2150
Genco	Double Action	1952	1		MT, 2B, 3DB, 2TRL, 2KO, NOL, 2-Slot Kickers
Gottlieb	Double Action	1958	2		
Bally	Double Barrel	1946	1		
Williams	Double Barrel	1961	2		PR-700
Bally	Double Feature	1939	1		
Stoner	Double Feature	1940	1		
Victory Sales	Double Feature	1946	1		
Bally	Double Feature	1948	1		
Gottlieb	Double Feature	1950	1		
Exhibit	Double Play	1941	1		
Keeney	Double Score	1936	1		
Gottlieb	Double Shuffle	1949	1		
Southwestern	Double Shuffle Twin	1933	1		
Genco	Double Track	1938	1		
G.B Daval	Double Treasure	1939	1		
Bally	Double Up	1970	1		4B, 3-Inch Flippers, NRL, 2KO, 2MUSB, 4TRL, PR-55
Baker Novelty	Doughboy	1940	1		
Bally	Dr Dude	1991	4		2MB, RS, V, AN
Stern	Dracula	1979	4		3F, NV, PR-3612
Williams	Dracula	1993	4		DM, VM, RS, EP, 3B, MB, LIC, 1DT
Interflip	Dragon	1977	4	Spain	EM, 3B, 4TRL, 1KO, Remake of Dragoon
Gottlieb	Dragon	1978	4		EM & SS Versions Released, 2VT, S, 4TRL, PR-7057
Gottlieb	Dragonette	1954	1		LUS
Stern	Dragonfist	1982	4		
Recreativos Franco	Dragoon	1974	1	Spain	
Bally	Draw Bell	1936	1		
Williams	Dreamy	1950	1		
Exhibit	Drop Kick	1934	1		
Gottlieb	Drop-A-Card	1971	1		2-Inch Flippers, 2B, 13DT, NRL, 2TRL, PR-2600
Gottlieb	Drum Major	1940	1		
Playmatic	Ducks	1975	1	Spain	
Genco	Dude Ranch	1940	1		
Bally	Duet	1940	1		
Gottlieb	Duette	1955	2		DRS, 3B, 4DB, BFF, 3TRL, PR-326
Gottlieb	Duette Delux	1955	1		Larger Version of Duette
Bally	Dungeons And Dragons	1987	4		BO, 3MB, RS, V, AN, LIC, 3F, IDT, PR-2000
Gottlieb	Duotron	1974	2		PR-2525
Exhibit	Duplex	1940	1		
Roy Mcginnis	Dust Whirls	1944	1		Conversion Kit Pinball
Chicago Coin	Dux	1937	1		AB
Williams	Dynamite	1946	1		
Allied Leisure	Dyn-O-Mite	1975	2		SS, 4DT, 1B, 3TRL, OG

Williams	Eager Beaver	1965	2		4B, 1DB, NRL, PR-1301
P & S Machine Co	Eagle Squadron	1943	1		Conversion Kit Pinball
Williams	Earth Shaker	1989	4		VC, MB, RS, V, AN, 3F,CB, S, 3B
Zaccaria	Earth Wind & Fire	1981	4	Italy	
Gottlieb	Easy Aces	1955	1		LUS, PR-1100
Glickman	Easy Pickin	1944	1		Conversion Kit Pinball
Rock-Ola	Easy Steps	1938	1		
Gottlieb	Eclipse	1982	4		19DT, 4B, 4F, Single-Level Version of Black Hole, PR-1300
Gottlieb	Egg Head	1962	1		5B, 4DB, PR-2100
Williams	Eight Ball	1952	1		
Bally	Eight Ball	1977	4		PR- 20230, SS, 4TRL, 3B, S, KB
Williams	Eight Ball (8 Ball)	1966	2		PR-3250
Bally	Eight Ball Champ	1985	4		3F, 2B, 3TRL, S, 5DT, PR-1500
Bally	Eight Ball Classic	1984	4		
Bally	Eight Ball Deluxe	1981	4		3F, V, IDT, NLC, 12DT, 1KO, PR-8250
Bally	Eight Ball Deluxe Le	1982	4		3F, V, IDT, NLC, 12DT, 1KO, PR-2388
Gottlieb	El Dorado	1975	1		4F, 2B, 15DT, 2TRL, PR-2875
Europlay	El Dorado	1976	1	Italy	F M
Gottlieb	El Dorado	1984	4		WB, 3F, PR 905
Williams	El Paso	1948	1		
Keeney	El Rancho	1962	1		
Playmec Flippers	El Tigre	1975	U	Italy	
Exhibit	El Toro	1938	1		
Williams	El Toro	1963	2		2DT, 4B, 3TRL, RT, PR-1850
Bally	El Toro	1972	1		3TRL, 3B, 3MU5B, NRL, PR-2065
Exhibit	Electro	1934	1		
Stoner	Electro	1938	1		
Electro B.D	Electro Black Diamond	1933	1		
Bally	Elektra	1981	4		6F, TL, CB, V, 2MB, RS, 2KO, PR-2950
Gottlieb	Elektra Pool	1965	1		
Keeney	Eleven Belles	1958	1		
Gottlieb	Elite Guard	1968	1		PR-4000
T & M Sales	Elmer	1949	1		Conversion Kit Pinball
Bally	Elvira And The Party Monsters	1989	4		3MB, V, RS, AN
Bally	Embryon	1981	4		2MB, 4F, WB, 3CB, 4B, 3TRL, FS, 7DT, 1KO, PR-2250
Bally	Entry	1941	1		
Bally	Equalite	1937	1		
Erich Buttner	Erbu Ball	1933	1	Germany	Horse Racing Theme
Erich Buttner	Erbu Ball	1933	1	Germany	Workforce Theme
Erich Buttner	Erbu Rennen	1935	1	Germany	
Fascination Game	Eros 2	1979	2		
Fascination Game	Eros One	1979	2		Cocktail Table Style
Jac Van Ham	Escape	1987	4	Holland	
Royal	Escape	1988	U	Holland	
Bally	Escape From The Lost World	1988	4		4F, 2MB, DL, V, AN, PR-1500
Stoner	Esquire	1934	1		
Bally	Eureka	1938	1		
Bally	Eureka	1948	1		
Aisch & Melchers	Euromat	1960	1	Germany	Countertop Game, NF, LUS
Aisch & Melchers	Euromat Deluxe	1964	1	Germany	Countertop Game, NF
Aisch & Melchers	Euromat Super	1964	1	Germany	Countertop Game, NF
Aisch & Melchers	Euromat Super 2	1964	1	Germany	Countertop Game, NF
Forster	Europa Flipper	1967	2	Germany	Two Player Head-To-Head
Bally	Evel Knievel	1977	4		EM & SS Versions Released, 5DT, 2S, 3B, 2DB, PR-14155
Playmatic	Evil Fight	1980	4	Spain	
Jeutel	Evolution	1986	4	France	PR-180
Jeutel	Excalibur	1981	4	France	Prototype produced only
Gottlieb	Excalibur	1988	4		2MB, 4F, RS, AN, PR-1710
G.B Daval	Excel	1936	1		
Nordamatic	Explorer	1976	1	Italy	EM, MRL, 2B, 1KO
Sega	Explorer	1976	2	Japan	EM, 3B, NRL, UP, 1KO
Williams	Expo	1969	2		5TRL, 5B, NRL, UP, 1KO, OG, 3-Inch Flippers
Chicago Coin	Exposition	1938	1		
Bally	Expressway	1971	1		UP, NRL, 6MUSB, 3B, 2KO, PR-1555
Gottlieb	Extra Inning	1971	1		ADB, PR-350
Gottlieb	Eye Of The Tiger	1978	2		EM, PR-730, Same Play As Sinbad
Hankin	FJ	1978	4	Australia	2TRL, 3B, 3KO, 2S
Bell Games	F1 Grand Prix	1987	4	Italy	
Williams	F-14 Tomcat	1987	4		4MB, RS, 4F, V, AN
Viza Manufacturing	Fabulous 50's	1978	2		
Segasa / Sonic	Faces	1976	4	Spain	EM, 2S, 2B, 1KO
Juegos Populares	Faeton	1985	4	Spain	
Genco	Fair	1936	1		
Gottlieb	Fair	1939	1		
Recel	Fair Fight	1978	4	Spain	
Gottlieb	Fair Lady	1956	2		DRS
Buckley	Fairplay	1936	1		
Williams	Fairway	1953	1		LUS
Playmatic	Fairy	1975	1	Spain	
Gottlieb	Falstaff	1957	4		DRS
Game Plan	Family Fun	1978	4		Cocktail Table Style
Stoner	Fan	1935	1		
Glickman	Fan Dancer	1944	1		Conversion Kit Pinball
Playmatic	Fandango	1976	1	Spain	
Williams	Fan-Tas-Tic	1972	4		RW, 4B, NRL, 2KO, KB, OG, PR-5680
Peyper	Fantastic World	1985	4	Spain	
Stoner	Fantasy	1940	1		
Playmatic	Fantasy	1976	4	Spain	
Bell Games	Fantasy	1982	4	Italy	Conversion Kit Pinball
Stoner	Fantasy Jackpot	1940	1		
Gottlieb	Far Out	1974	2		10DT, 2B, 1KO, 3TRL, Same Play As Out Of Sight, PR-4820
Zaccaria	Farfalla	1983	4	Italy	V, DL, FS, 6F, 17DT, 3TRL, 4B, RS
Bally	Farimont	1941	1		
Gottlieb	Fashion Show	1962	2		7TRL, 3B, 2DB, PR-2675
Exhibit	Fast Ball	1946	1		
Gottlieb	Fast Draw	1975	4		3B, MRL, DT, 3TRL, PR-8045
Sullivan & Nolan	Fast Track	1943	1		Conversion Kit Pinball
Bally	Fathom	1981	4		V, 3F, 15DT, 2IDT, S, LC, 3MB, 3B, 2KO, PR-3500
Bally	Fatima	1933	1		
Bergmann & Co	Favorit	1939	1	Germany	NF
Keeney	Favorite	1948	1		
Western Equipment	Feed Bag	1938	1		
Chicago Coin	Festival	1966	4		
Recel	Fiery 30's	1974	4	Spain	
Chicago Coin	Fiesta	1938	1		
Exhibit	Fiesta	1946	2		
Williams	Fiesta	1959	2		RT
Playmatic	Fiesta	1976	4	Spain	EM, 2B, 1TRL, 1KO
Inder	Fifteen	1974	1	Spain	
Bally	Fifth Inning	1939	1		
G.M Laboratories	Fifty Fifty	1935	1		
Bally	Fifty Fifty (50/50)	1965	2		3B, 4TRL, NRL, 6MUSB, PR-580
Automatic Games	Fifty Grand	1933	1		
Chicago Coin	Fighting Irish	1950	1		

Manufacturer	Name	Year	#	Country	Notes
Nasco	Fight'n Phils	1950	1		
Nasco	Film Cavalcade	1949	1		Conversion Kit Pinball
Chicago Coin	Finance	1936	1		
Williams	Fire	1987	4		UP, RS, V, 3MB, AN
Gottlieb	Fire Alarm	1939	1		
Keeney	Fire Ball	1937	1		
Williams	Fire Champagne Edition	1987	4		UP, RS, V, 3MB, AN
Gottlieb	Fire Chief	1935	1		
Keeney	Fire Cracker	1938	1		
Chicago Coin	Fire Cracker	1963	2		
Bally	Fire Cracker	1971	4		PR-2800
Zaccaria	Fire Mountain	1980	4	Italy	
Gottlieb	Fire Queen	1977	2		EM, 2B, 4TRL, 9DT, Same Play As Vulcan, PR-970
Bally	Fireball	1972	4		PR- 4,700, ZF, WWS, 3MB, KB, 3B, NRL, CB, 3MUSB, PR-3815
Centromatic	Fireball	1972	1	Spain	Copy of Bally's Fireball
Coinomatic	Fireball	1972	1	Spain	Copy of Bally's Fireball
Bally	Fireball 2	1981	4		3F, 3MB, V, 11DT, 3B, 2TRL, UP, PR-2300
Bell Games	Fireball 2	1981	4	Italy	Identical To Bally Game Of Same Name
Bally	Fireball Classic	1985	4		WWS, 3MB, KB, 3B, NRL, CB, V, 3MUSB, PR-2000
Williams	Firepower	1980	4		V, LC, 3MB, 4B, PR-17410
Williams	Firepower Ii	1984	4		2MB, PR-3400, 4TRL, 4B, S, RS
Gottlieb	Firestone	1933	1		
Williams	Fish Tales	1992	4		BO, RS, 3MB, S, 1DT, EP, DM, VM, CB
Exhibit	Fishin'	1943	1		
Stoner	Five & Ten	1935	1		
Gottlieb	Five And Ten	1941	1		
Gottlieb	Flag Ship	1957	2		
Exhibit	Flagship	1940	1		
Allied Leisure	Flame Of Athens	1978	4		
Williams	Flamingo	1947	1		NF
Exhibit	Flash	1939	1		
Williams	Flash	1979	4		NV, 3F, 4TRL, S, 3B, 7DT, 1KO, PR-19505
Playmatic	Flash Dragon	1980	4	Spain	Camera Takes Photo of High Scoring Player
Bally	Flash Gordon	1981	4		3F, DL, V, LIC, 10DT, 3B, IDT, 1KO, PR-10000
Bell Games	Flash Gordon	1981	4	Italy	Identical To Bally Game of Same Name
Rock-Ola	Flash Lite	1935	1		
Mills Novelty	Flasher	1937	1		
Sportmatic	Flashman	1984	U	Spain	
Williams	Flat Top	1945	1		Conversion Kit Pinball
Bally	Fleet	1934	1		
Bally	Fleet	1937	1		
Bally	Fleet	1940	1		
Exhibit	Fleet Review	1938	1		
Bally	Flicker	1934	1		
Bally	Flicker	1941	1		
Bally	Flicker	1975	2		1B, 2CB, S, 1KO, PR-1585
Aisch & Melchers	Flick-Flack	1971	1	Germany	
Aisch & Melchers	Flick-Flack	1972	2	Germany	
Exhibit	Flight	1938	1		
Stern	Flight 2000	1980	4		WB, 3MB, V, 2B, MRL, 8DT, 4TRL, 2S, PR-6300
Bally	Flip Flop	1974	4		4F, 2B, 2KO, PR-5350
Gottlieb	Flip-A-Card	1970	1		6TRL, 3B, 1KO, ADB, 2-Inch Flippers, PR-1800
Gottlieb	Flipper	1960	1		ADB, 8TRL, 3B, 2DB, NOL, 2KO, DRS, PR-1100
Bontempi	Flipper	N/A	U	Italy	
Gottlieb	Flipper Clown	1962	1		ADB, RT, 4B, 4TRL, AB, PR-1550
Gottlieb	Flipper Cowboy	1962	1		ADB, 5TRL, RT, 3DB, 3B, PR-1000
Gottlieb	Flipper Fair	1961	1		ADB, 4TRL, 4B, 2DB, PR-1150
Gottlieb	Flipper Football	1966	6		PR-750
Petaco	Flipper Game	1900	U	Spain	2B, CB, 2T, 8DT, E
Gottlieb	Flipper Parade	1961	1		ADB, 5TRL, 5B, 2KO, PR-1500
Gottlieb	Flipper Pool	1965	1		AB, ADB, PR-700
Inder	Flip-Vi	1991	4	Spain	
Genco	Floating Power	1948	1		BFF, 2KO, 2B, 10DB
Rally	Flower's Child	1968	1	France	Prototype Only Produced, PR-30
Geiger	Fly High	1985	4	Germany	Conversion Kit For Bally's Supersonic
Genco	Flying Aces	1956	2		DRS
Gottlieb	Flying Carpet	1972	1		4TRL, 3B, NRL, PR-3170
Western Products	Flying Champ	1941	1		
Gottlieb	Flying Chariots	1963	2		PR-3410
Gottlieb	Flying Circus	1961	2		4B, CB, 2KO, 6TRL, PR-2050
Genco	Flying Colors	1935	1		
Gottlieb	Flying High	1953	1		LUS
Centromatic	Flying High	1978	4	Spain	EM & SS Versions Released
Genco	Flying Saucers	1950	1		
Genco	Flying Scott	1939	1		
Gottlieb	Flying Trapeze	1947	1		NF
Gottlieb	Flying Trapeze	1934	1		
Gottlieb	Flying Trapeze Junior	1934	1		
Midway	Flying Turns	1963	2		TS, AB
Genco	Follies Of 1940	1939	1		
Victory Games	Follies Of 46	1946	1		Conversion Kit Pinball
G.B Daval	Follow Up	1939	1		
Chicago Coin	Football	1949	1		
Jennings	Football	1934	1		
Genco	Football 1937	1937	1		
Gottlieb	Force Ii	1981	4		WB, 2MB, 4F, 14DT, 3B, S, PR-2000
Bally	Fore	1973	1		PR-80
Westerhaus	Foreign Colors	1945	1		Conversion Kit Pinball
Genco	Formation	1940	1		
Recel	Formula One	1980	4	Spain	
Rock-Ola	Fortune	1936	1		
Keeney	Fortune	1941	1		
Petaco	Fortune	1976	4	Spain	EM
Mills Novelty	Forward March	1937	1		
Century Mfg	Forward Pass	1934	1		
Gottlieb	Foto Finish	1961	1		7DB, 4TRL, 2B, 1KO, PR-1000
Genco	Four Aces	1942	1		
Williams	Four Aces (4 Aces)	1970	2		4F, SP, MOL, No Plunger , Similar To Aces & Kings
Gottlieb	Four Belles (4-Belles)	1954	1		LUS, PR-400
Williams	Four Corners	1952	1		
Keeney	Four Diamonds	1941	1		
Gottlieb	Four Horsemen	1950	1		4F, 5TRL, 4B, 2DB, UP
Bally	Four Million B.C	1971	4		ZF, 3MB, KB, 3B, 2MUSB, PR-3550
Bally	Four Queens (4 Queens)	1970	1		3B, 3TRL, 4MUSB, ZF, 2KO, NRL, PR-1256
A.B.T Mfg	Four Roses	1936	1		
Genco	Four Roses	1940	1		
Williams	Four Roses (4 Roses)	1962	1		2DB, 3B, 2KO, 1TRL, PR-1250, RT
Gottlieb	Four Seasons	1969	4		PR-1500
Gottlieb	Four Square (4 Square)	1971	1		2-Inch Flippers, 3B, 4TRL, PR-2200
Williams	Four Star (4 Star)	1958	1		LUS, WR
Gottlieb	Four Stars	1952	1		4B, LUS, 4F
Baker Novelty	Four-Five-Six	1940	1		
Chicago Coin	Fox Hunt	1940	1		
Game Plan	Foxy Lady	1978	2		Cocktail Table Style

Sega	Frankenstein	1994	4		3F, MB, EP, DM, RS, 1KO, S, 3B, KB, LIC
Western Equipment	Free Play	1936	1		
Keeney	Free Races	1937	1		
Bally	Freedom	1976	4		EM & SS Versions Released, 2S, 5DT, 4B, 2KO, PR-6580
Gottlieb	Freefall	1974	1		ADB, Same Play As Sky Jump, PR-650
Stern	Freefall	1981	4		3MB, V, LC, PR-1300
Williams	Freshie	1949	1		
Williams	Friendship 7	1962	1		ADB, RT, 4B, 4DB, 2TRL, PR-800
Marvel	Frisco	1946	1		Conversion Kit Pinball
Bally	Frisky	1935	1		
Bally	Frisky	1949	1		
Bontempi	Frog Man	N/A	U	Italy	Conversion Kit Pinball
Bally	Frontier	1980	4		6DT, IDT, S, 3B, 3TRL, 1KO, PR-1850
Bell Games	Frontier	1981	4	Italy	Identical To Bally Game Of Same Name
Gottlieb	Frontiersman	1955	1		LUS, PR-1000
Interflip	Full	1975	1	Spain	
Williams	Full House	1966	1		3B, NRL, 3TRL, Slot Machine On Playfield, PR-2900
Bally	Fun Cruise	1966	1		6B, NF, 8MUSB, PR-675
Genco	Fun Fair	1957	1		LUS, AD, 3D, 2DB
Gottlieb	Fun Fair	1968	1		PR-2601
Williams	Fun Fest	1973	4		NRL, UP, 5B, MT, OG, KB, PR-6025
Williams	Fun House	1956	4		DRS
Williams	Fun House	1990	4		3MB, RS, V, AN, 2 Plungers, Dummy's Head On Field
Gottlieb	Fun Land	1968	1		4TRL, 3B, NRL, 2S, PR-3100
Gottlieb	Fun Park	1968	1		PR-580
Bally	Fun Spot 63	1962	1		
Bell Games	Future Queen	1987	4	Italy	
Bally	Future Spa	1979	4		WB, NV, IDT, KB, 5B, 2S, 6TRL, PR-6400
Zaccaria	Future World	1979	4	Italy	
Bally	Futurity	1951	1		
Victory Games	G.I.Joe	1944	1		Conversion Kit Pinball
Bally	Galahad	1970	2		4TRL, 4B, 2KO, NRL, UP, PR-791
Gottlieb	Galaxie	1971	1		20DT, ADB, 5KO, 2B, 2-Inch Flippers, PR-1279
The Best	Galaxie	N/A	U	Italy	
Sega	Galaxy	1976	1	Japan	EM, UP, 3B, 3TRL, NRL
Stern	Galaxy	1980	4		NV, 3B, S, 4DT, MRL, 4TRL, PR-5150
Cic Play	Galaxy Play	1986	4	Spain	
Cic Play	Galaxy Play 2	1987	4	Spain	
Pacific Amusement	Galloping Ghost	1935	1		
Pinstar	Gamatron	1985	4		Conversion Kit Pinball
Segasa / Sonic	Gamatron	1986	4	Spain	
Bally	Game Show	1990	4		2MB, RS, V, AN, 3TRL, 3B
Bally	Gator	1969	4		ZF
Gottlieb	Gaucho	1963	4		RT, 4DB, 5B, 2TRL, PR-5350
Williams	Gay 90's	1970	4		2DB, 3B, UP, 3-Inch Flippers, NRL, 1KO
Bally	Gay Cruise	1965	1		PR-60
Williams	Gay Paree	1957	4		
Genco	Gay Time	1938	1		
Playmatic	Geisha	1974	1	Spain	
Gottlieb	Gemini	1978	2		EM, PR-300, 8DT, 2B, 4TRL
G.B Daval	Gems	1939	1		
Gottlieb	Genesis	1986	4		AN, MB, RS
Gottlieb	Genie	1979	4		WB, 5F, 11DT, 3B, 4TRL, 1KO, S, NV
Williams	Georgia	1950	1		
Allied Leisure	Getaway	1978	4		
Exhibit	Giant	1935	1		
Gottlieb	Gigi	1964	1		5DB, 3B, PR-3575
Bally	Gilligans Island	1991	4		DM, 2MB
Chicago Coin	Gin	1974	1		
Gottlieb	Gin Rummy	1949	1		
Chicago Coin	Ginger	1936	1		
Williams	Ginger	1947	1		NF
Victory Games	Girls Ahoy	1944	1		Conversion Kit Pinball
Giuliano Lodola	Giuone	1978	1	Italy	EM, Copy Of Gottlieb's Poseiden
Williams	Gizmo	1948	1		
Gottlieb	Gladiator	1956	2		DRS, PR-1200
Gottlieb	Gladiators	1993	4		4F, RS, VC, MB, DM, 3DT, PR-1995
Gottlieb	Glamor	1951	1		
Victory Games	Glamor Girls	1943	1		Conversion Kit Pinball
Bally	Glamour	1940	1		
Jack Rogers	Glamour Lites	1959	1	France	
Genco	Glider	1949	1		
Game Plan	Global Warfare	1981	4		4F, FD, 3B, S, 4KO, 9DT, PR-10
Gottlieb	Globe Trotter	1937	1		
Rock-Ola	Globe Trotter	1937	1		
Gottlieb	Globe Trotter	1951	1		5TRL, 4B, 4F, BFF, 1KO
Tura	Glokenbomber	1938	1	Germany	16B
Keeney	Go Cart	1963	1		
Genco	Goal Kick	1934	1		
Chicago Coin	Gobs	1942	1		
Sega	Godzilla	1998	4		
Gottlieb	Goin' Nuts	1983	4		Limited Production Run, PR-10
Rock-Ola	Gold Award	1935	1		
Bally	Gold Ball	1983	4		NV, 3B, S, 4TRL, PR-1750
Bally	Gold Cup	1948	1		
Marvel	Gold Mine	1948	1		
Keeney	Gold Nugget	1947	1		
Chicago Coin	Gold Record	1975	4		SP, 3B, 3TRL
Rock-Ola	Gold Rush	1935	1		
Bally	Gold Rush	1966	1		AB, MUSB, PR-1750
Williams	Gold Rush	1971	4		
Gottlieb	Gold Star	1940	1		
Gottlieb	Gold Star	1940	1		
Gottlieb	Gold Star	1954	1		LUS
Giorgio Massiniero	Gold Star	1976	1	Italy	
A.M.I	Gold Star	1977	1	Italy	
Gottlieb	Gold Strike	1975	1		PR-675
Gottlieb	Gold Wings	1986	4		AN, BO, 4F, 2MB, PBG, PR-3260
Chicago Coin	Goldball	1947	1		NF
Alben	Golden	1958	1	France	
Royal Novelty	Golden Arrow	1934	1		
Giuliano Lodola	Golden Arrow	1978	4	Italy	
Gottlieb	Golden Arrow	1978	1		EM, 3B, 2S, 4TRL, PR-1530
Williams	Golden Bells	1959	1		LUS
Sega	Golden Cue	1998	4		
Sega	Golden Eye	1995	4		RS, MB, 3TRL, 3B, Eject Or Die Feature, LIC, VM
Exhibit	Golden Gate	1934	1		
Exhibit	Golden Gate	1939	1		
Chicago Coin	Golden Gloves	1949	1		
Williams	Golden Gloves	1960	1		3B, MOL, WR, 3TRL, LUS
Genco	Golden Nugget	1953	1		
Exhibit	Gondola	1949	1		
Gottlieb	Gondolier	1958	2		
Elettrocoin	Good Year	1969	1	Italy	Conversion Kit Pinball

Williams	Gorgar	1979	4		V, 3B, 6DT, 3TRL, 1KO, PR-14000
Williams	Granada	1972	1		ADB, PR-875
Chicago Coin	Grand Award	1949	1		
United	Grand Canyon	1943	1		Conversion Kit Pinball
Fisher & Coe	Grand Central	1933	1		
Williams	Grand Champion	1953	1		
Western Equipment	Grand Derby	1938	1		
Williams	Grand Lizard	1986	4		MS, 3MB, 4F, RS, AN, PR-2750
Williams	Grand Prix	1976	4		EM, 2S, 2B, 3KO, PR-10554
Keeney	Grand Slam	1936	1		
Gottlieb	Grand Slam	1953	1		5DB, 3B, NOL, LUS
Gottlieb	Grand Slam	1972	1		2B, RT, 3KO, 4TRL, Run Reels, PR-3600
Bally	Grand Slam	1983	4		Released in Australia as a 2-Player 3F, NV, 5FT, PR-1000
Bontempi	Grand Slam	N/A	U	Italy	
Bally	Grand Stand	1950	1		
Bally	Grand Tour	1964	1		S, 3B, 4MUSB, 1TRL, PR-1310
Gottlieb	Grande Domino	1968	1		PR-4000
Bally	Granny And The Gators	1984	2		Video Cabinet Style VID/P
Alben	Great Circus	1958	2	France	4B, 5TRL, 2KO
Keeney	Great Guns	1937	1		
Gottlieb	Green Pastures	1954	1		LUS
Genco	Grid Iron	1934	1		
Gottlieb	Gridiron	1978	2		No Plunger, 2VT, 4F, 2FD, 2B, 6TRL, NRL, Point Reels, PR-1025
Gottlieb	Groovy	1970	4		5DT, 5B, 5TRL, NRL, Same Play as Crescendo, PR-1355
Williams	Guardian	1983	U		Prototype only Produced
Williams	Gulfstream	1973	1		5TRL, 3B, 2KO, PR-4175
Segasa / Sonic	Gulfstream	1974	U	Spain	
G.B Daval	Gun Club	1939	1		
Genco	Gun Club	1941	1		
Williams	Gun Club	1953	1		DRS
Staal	Gun Men	1977	4	France	SS, 2B, 8DT
Chicago Coin	Gun Smoke	1968	2		
Playmatic	Gunner	1974	1	Spain	
Data East	Guns & Roses	1994	4		RS, 3F, MB, DM, VM, EP, CB, 2 Plungers
Williams	Gusher	1958	1		4DB, 3B, 1KO, WR, Disappearing Bumper
Gottlieb	Guys And Dolls	1953	1		LUS, 9DB, NF?
Gottlieb	Gypsy Queen	1955	1		LUS, 2DB, 3B, PR-1400
Keeney	Hacienda	1962	1		
Rally	Hairy Singers	1964	4	France	
Juegos Populares	Halley Comet	1986	4	Spain	
Exhibit	Handicap	1938	1		
Williams	Handicap	1952	1		AB, 2BFF, 6B, 8TRL, WR
Bally	Hang Glider	1976	4		EM, 5DT, S, 3B, 1KO, PR-2325
Segasa / Sonic	Hang On	1988	4	Spain	
Playmatic	Hangers	1977	4	Spain	
Gottlieb	Happy Clown	1964	4		6TRL, 4B, MOL, 2KO, PR-3235
Genco	Happy Days	1936	1		
Gottlieb	Happy Days	1952	1		LUS
Rally	Happy Papeete	1963	2	France	
Bally	Happy Tour	1964	1		PR-250
Gottlieb	Happy-Go-Lucky	1951	1		
Gottlieb	Harbor Lites	1956	1		LUS
Bally	Hard Body	1987	4		4F, DL, RS, AN, PR-2000
Playmatic	Harem	1974	1	Spain	
Universal	Harem Cat	1979	6	Japan	Score Displayed On Video Monitor
Exhibit	Hare-N-Hound	1937	1		
Bally	Harlem Globetrotters	1979	4		LIC, 3F, FD, NV, 3S, 3B, IDT, OG, 2KO, PR-14550
Bally	Harley Davidson	1991	4		V, FC, 5MB, 7C4, 3B, 2S, 0DT, 3TRL
Gottlieb	Harmony	1967	1		PR-2000
Bally	Harvest	1964	1		3B, 5MUSB, 3TRL, OG, PR-1075
Bally	Harvest Moon	1935	1		
Gottlieb	Harvest Moon	1948	1		
Genco	Harvest Time	1950	1		
Williams	Harvey	1951	1		
Gottlieb	Haunted House	1982	4		TL, NV, 8F, 4B, RS, 8DT, PR-6835
United	Havana	1947	1		NF
United	Hawaii	1947	1		NF
Gottlieb	Hawaiian Beauty	1954	1		7DB, 3B, NOL, LUS
Gottlieb	Hawaiian Isle	1966	1		PR-500
Centromatic	Hawk Black	1974	1	Spain	
Bally	Hawthorn	1939	1		
Bally	Hay Ride	1964	1		ADB Version of Harvest, PR-250
Williams	Hayburners	1951	1		BFF, 6B, 3TRL, AB
Williams	Hayburners 2	1968	2		AB, TS, ZF
Bally	Headliner	1939	1		
Gottlieb	Hearts And Spades	1969	1		ADB, PR-615
Inder	Hearts Gain	1971	1	Spain	
Allied Leisure	Hearts Spades	1978	2		Cocktail Table Style
Williams	Heat Wave	1964	1		AB, 5B, 1DT, 2MT
Bally	Heat Wave	1967	1		
Bally	Heavy Hitter	1948	1		
Bally	Heavy Metal Meltdown	1987	4		5MB, RS, AN, 3B, 2KO, PR-1600
Chicago Coin	Hee-Haw	1973	4		
Universal	Hercules	1977	2	Japan	EM, 3B, 2TRL
Atari	Hercules	1979	4		Oversize Game With Cue Ball Size Ball
Western Equipment	Hey Day	1938	1		
Tecnoplay	Hi Ball	1988	4	San Marino	
Pacific Amusement	Hi De Lo	1937	1		
Bally	Hi Deal	1975	1		S, 3B, 1KO, PR-1047
Gottlieb	Hi- Diver	1959	1		AB, LUS, WR
Gottlieb	Hi Dolly	1965	2		RT, 3B, 6DB, 5TRL, PR-1600
Genco	Hi Hat	1941	1		
Exhibit	Hi-Ball	1938	1		
Chicago Coin	Hi-Flyer	1974	2		
Williams	High Ace	1974	4		
Gottlieb	High Dive	1941	1		
Genco	High Fly Baseball	1956	2		
Bally	High Hand	1935	1		
Gottlieb	High Hand	1973	1		16DT, 1B, 2TRL, PR-4950
Chicago Coin	High Lo	1935	1		
Chicago Coin	High Low	1936	1		
Western Equipment	High Pockets	1934	1		
Chicago Coin	High Score Pool	1971	2		
Gottlieb	High Seas	1976	1		EM, ADB, S, 5B, 5TRL, PR-380
Unidesa	High Speed	1986	4	Spain	Built Under License From Williams
Williams	High Speed	1986	4		3MB, V, RS, AN, 3F, KB, 3B, BO, 3S, PR-17080
Stoner	High Stepper	1941	1		
G.B Daval	High-Lite	1939	1		
G.B Daval	High-Lite	1939	1		
Williams	Highways	1961	1		PR-600
Williams	Hi-Hand	1957	1		
Western Equipment	Hi-Lite	1935	1		
Genco	Hi-Lo	1938	1		
Gottlieb	Hi-Lo	1969	1		4B, 5TRL, PR-5000

Bally	Hi-Lo Ace	1973	1		4B, 5TRL, PR-2500
E.A.S	Hippye	1970	4	Germany	
Keeney	Hi-Ride	1947	1		
Gottlieb	Hi-Score	1967	4		RW, 4F, 4B, 1DB, PR-1900
Keeney	Hi-Straight	1960	1		
Genco	Hit And Run	1938	1		
Genco	Hit And Run	1951	1		
Playmatic	Hit Line	1974	1	Spain	
Gottlieb	Hit N Run	1952	1		
Keeney	Hit Number	1938	1		
Pacific Amusement	Hit Or Miss	1935	1		
Marvel	Hit Parade	1948	1		
Chicago Coin	Hit Parade	1951	1		
Gottlieb	Hit The Deck	1978	1		EM, 3B, 6TRL, 2KO, PR-375
Victory Games	Hit The Japs	1943	1		Conversion Kit Pinball
Pin-Ball	Hit To Score	1979	1		
Gottlieb	Hit-A-Card	1967	1		PR-1600
Chicago Coin	Hockey	1941	1		
Rally	Hockey Girl	1964	2	France	
Allied Leisure	Hoe Down	1978	1		
Bally	Hokus Pokus	1975	2		3S, 2B, 4TRL, OG, PR-3086
Stoner	Hold 'Em	1936	1		
Stoner	Hold Over	1940	1		
Western Products	Hold Tight	1939	1		
Chicago Coin	Holiday	1948	1		
Marvel	Hollywood	1945	1		
Williams	Hollywood	1961	2		PR-550
Chicago Coin	Hollywood	1976	2		
Gottlieb	Hollywood Heat	1986	4		PBG, AN, 3MB, RS, 4F, NV, PR-3400
Robbins	Home Run	1936	1		
Chicago Coin	Home Run	1937	1		
Chicago Coin	Home Run	1940	1		
Chicago Coin	Home Run	1941	1		
Gottlieb	Home Run	1971	1		PR-580
Genco	Home Stretch	1937	1		
A.B.T Mfg	Homestrech	1935	1		
Exhibit	Honey	1937	1		
Genco	Honey	1947	1		NF
Williams	Honey	1972	4		PR-6300, UP, 5B, 3TRL, NRL, OG, 3DT, 3KO
Williams	Hong Kong	1952	1		
Data East	Hook	1992	4		RS, DM, 3MB, LIC, EP
Gottlieb	Hoops	1991	4		3MB, AN, PR-879
Bally	Hootenanny	1963	1		4TRL, 3B, PR-1051
Gottlieb	Horoscope	1941	1		
Williams	Horse Feathers	1952	2		
Williams	Horse Shoes	1951	1		
Western Products	Horseshoes	1939	1		
Inder	Hot And Cold	1978	4	Spain	
Williams	Hot Diggity	1956	1		LUS
Bally	Hot Doggin	1980	4		WB, 3F, MRL, IDT, 1KO, S, 10DT, 3TRL, 4B, PR-2050
Nsm	Hot Firebirds	1985	4	Germany	
Stern	Hot Hand	1979	4		NV, Spinning Flipper, PR-4117
Williams	Hot Line	1966	1		5B, 1DB, 2TRL, NRL, PR-3651
A.M.I	Hot Race	1976	4	Italy	16DT, 3B, 5TRL, EM
Bally	Hot Rod	1949	1		NF
Gottlieb	Hot Shot	1973	4		1DB, 14DT, PR-9000
Gottlieb	Hot Shots	1989	4		2MB, RS, AN, PR-2342
Gottlieb	Hot Springs	1937	1		
Keeney	Hot Tip	1937	1		
Keeney	Hot Tip	1947	1		NF
Williams	Hot Tip	1977	4		EM & SS Versions Released, CB, 6DT, S, 1B
Zaccaria	Hot Wheels	1979	4	Italy	
Zaccaria	House Of Diamonds	1978	4	Italy	
Hankin	Howzat	1980	4	Australia	WB, PR-350, 4F, 4B, 9DT, 4TRL, NLC, 1KO, 2S
Chicago Coin	Hula-Hula	1965	2		AB
Gottlieb	Humpty Dumpty	1947	1		PR- OVER 6,500, 6BFF
Gottlieb	Hurdy Gurdy	1966	1		ADB, 4B, MOL, NRL, PR-3186
Williams	Hurricane	1991	4		DM, 3MB, RS, Ferris Wheels
Gottlieb	Hyde Park	1966	1		PR-951
Petaco	Icarus	1977	4	Spain	EM
Gottlieb	Ice Fever	1985	4		PR-1585
I.D.I.	Ice Mania	1985	4	Italy	
Gottlieb	Ice Revue	1965	1		1DB, 5TRL, 4B, 2KO, NRL, PR-2050
Gottlieb	Ice Show	1966	1		1DB, 5TRL, 4B, 2KO, NRL, ADB, PR-400
United	Idaho	1944	1		Conversion Kit Pinball
Jentzsch & Meerz	Imo Bomber	1936	1	Germany	14B
Jentzsch & Meerz	Imo Diamant	1938	1	Germany	
Jentzsch & Meerz	Imo Rennen	1936	1	Germany	
Jentzsch & Meerz	Imo Spurt	1952	1	Germany	18DB
Jentzsch & Meerz	Imo Weltflug	1937	1	Germany	16B
Mills Novelty	Impact	1935	1		
Interflip	Impact	1975	4	Spain	
Jack Rogers	Imperator	1960	2	France	
Williams	Indiana Jones	1993	4		DL, 3MB, 4DT, EP, DM, VM, RS, CB, LIC, 4TRL
Bally	Indianapolis 500	1995	4		3F, BI, EP, 3B, DM, VM
Automatic Amusements	Indicator	1934	1		
Sega	Indipendence Day	1996	4		LIC, RS, MB, 3F, 3B, 3TRL
Red Baron Amusements	Invader Ball	1980	1	Australia	8DT, 2B, CB, 4TRL, VID/P
Genco	Invaders	1954	1		
Westerhaus	Invasion	1943	1		Conversion Kit Pinball
Komputer Dynamics	Invasion Strategy	1976	2		
Sleic	Io Moon	1996	4	Spain	
Unidesa	Iron Balls	1986	4	Spain	
Stern	Iron Maiden	1981	4		DL, 13DT, RS, S, 4F
Bally	Island Queens	1960	U		
Nasco	Ivanhoe	1950	1		Conversion Kit Pinball
Keeney	Ivory Golf	1935	1		
Bally	Jack And Jill	1933	2		Two Playfields Side By Side
Gottlieb	Jack And Jill	1948	1		
Century Mfg	Jack Rabbit	1934	1		
Williams	Jackbot	1995	4		Similar Playfield As Pinbot, DM
Gottlieb	Jack-In-The-Box	1973	4		4F, 10DT, 2B, NRL, 3TRL, 2KO, PR-8300
Williams	Jackpot	1971	4		PR-6303
B.E.M	Jackrabbit	N/A	U	Italy	
Gottlieb	Jacks Open	1977	1		EM, 9DT, 3B, 4TRL, PR-2975
Gottlieb	Jacks To Open	1984	4		9DT, PR-2350
Segasa / Sonic	Jai Alai	1978	4	Spain	Prototype Only Produced
Recel	Jake Mate	1974	1	Spain	
Interflip	Jalisco	1976	1	Spain	
Williams	Jalopy	1951	1		AB
Exhibit	Jamboree	1948	1		
Gottlieb	James Bond	1980	4		NV, TP, 2FD, 13DT, 3B, 3TRL, 4F, PR-3625
Exhibit	Jeanie	1950	1		
Gottlieb	Jet Spin	1977	4		EM, RT, VT, 2B, 3TRL, PR-4761

Manufacturer	Name	Year	#	Country	Notes
Rock-Ola	Jig Joy	1937	1		
Williams	Jig Saw	1957	1		3B, 4DB, 10TRL, WR, LUS
Scientific Machine	Jimmy Valentine	1936	1		
Genco	Jitter Bug	1938	1		
Western Equipment	Jitters	1936	1		
Williams	Jive Time	1970	1		AB, 5B, NRL, UP, 2KO
A.B.C Coin	Jockey Club	1933	1		
Standard Mfg	Jockey Club	1933	1		
Bally	Jockey Club	1941	1		
Gottlieb	Jockey Club	1954	1		LUS
Bally	Jockey Special	1947	1		
Bally	Jockey Special	1948	1		
Williams	Johnny Mnemonic	1995	4		BI, MB, 3TRL, 3B, DM, VM, LIC
Gottlieb	Joker	1950	1		
Playmatic	Joker	1974	1	Spain	
Gottlieb	Joker Poker	1978	4		EM & SS Versions Released, 3F, 2B, 3TRL, 14DT, PR-10100
Midway	Jokers Wild	1960	1		
Segasa / Sonic	Joker's Wild	1977	4	Spain	
Venture Line	Joker's Wild	1978	4		Cocktail Table Style
Williams	Jokerz	1988	4		V, RS, 2MB, AN, DL
Chicago Coin	Jolly	1940	1		
Rally	Jolly Captain	1965	2	France	
United	Jolly Joker	1955	1		
Mondialmatic	Jolly Joker	1979	1	Italy	
Williams	Jolly Jokers	1962	1		ADB, PR-700
Playmatic	Jolly Ride	1974	1	Spain	
Williams	Jolly Roger	1968	4		RT, NRL, 4TRL, 4B, PR-3502
Bally	Joust	1969	2		ZF, 3B, 4MUSB, PR-1050
Williams	Joust	1983	2		Two Player Head-To-Head, PR-402, 2S, 16DT
Gottlieb	Jubilee	1955	4		DRS, PR-500
Williams	Jubilee	1973	4		2CB, NRL, 2B, 2TRL, PR-7303
Bally	Judge Dread	1993	4		RS, 4F, MB, VM, EP, CB, DM, BI, BO, LIC
Exhibit	Judy	1950	1		
Chicago Coin	Juke Box	1976	4		Same Play as Sound Stage
Exhibit	Jumper	1939	1		
Williams	Jumpin' Jacks	1963	2		PR-1500
Gottlieb	Jumping Jack	1973	2		4F, 10DT, 2B, NRL, 3TRL, 2KO
Genco	Jungle	1938	1		
Williams	Jungle	1960	1		AB, 4TRL, 5B, LUS
Gottlieb	Jungle	1972	4		1B, S, OG, 3TRL, Same Play as Wild Life, PR-5775
Rock-Ola	Jungle Ball	1933	1		
Exhibit	Jungle Hunt	1935	1		
Gottlieb	Jungle King	1973	2		ADB, PR-825
R.M.G	Jungle King	1973	1	Italy	
Gottlieb	Jungle Life	1973	1		1B, S, OG, 3TRL, Same Play as Wild Life, PR-2730
Williams	Jungle Lord	1981	4		MB, MS, V, DL, 4F, Enclosed Mini Playfield, 11DT, RS, PR-6000
Gottlieb	Jungle Princess	1977	2		EM, 4F, 10DT, 3B, 3TRL, 2KO, Same Play as Jungle Queen
Gottlieb	Jungle Queen	1977	4		EM, 4F, 10DT, 3B, 3TRL, 2KO, Same Play as Jungle Princess
Genco	Junior	1934	1		
Bally	Junk Yard	1996	4		RS, DM, MB, VM, EP, Suspended Captive Ball
Data East	Jurrasic Park	1993	4		MB, DM, 3F, VM, RS, EP, LIC, CB, 3B
Gottlieb	Just 21	1950	1		TS, 4DB
Peo Mfg	Justice	1936	1		
Gottlieb	K.C.Jones	1949	1		
Bally	Karate Fight	1986	4		4F, RS, AN
Rally	Karting	1962	2	France	
Gottlieb	Keen-A-Ball	1939	1		
Keeney	Keen-O	1937	1		
Gottlieb	Keep Em Flying	1943	1		
Gottlieb	Kelly Pool	1935	1		
Bally	Kentucky	1941	1		
Bally	Kentucky	1949	1		
Bally	Kentucky Star	1949	1		
Inder	Keops	1978	4	Spain	
Gottlieb	Kewpie Doll	1960	1		WR, DRS, PR-950
Bally	Key Lite	1939	1		
Williams	Kick Off	1958	1		LUS
Williams	Kick Off	1967	1		ADB
Bally	Kick Off	1976	4		EM, 4F, 7DT, 3B, 4TRL, S, PR-1655
Chicago Coin	Kicker	1966	1		5TRL, 3CB, 3B, NRL
Gottlieb	Kicker	1977	1		EM, ADB, PR-380
Shyvers Mfg	Kickers	1937	1		
Chicago Coin	Kilroy	1947	1		NF
Gottlieb	King Arthur	1949	1		
Maresa	King Ball	1967	1	Spain	
Gottlieb	King Cole	1948	1		
Genco	King Fish	1935	1		
Petaco	King Game	1974	1	Spain	
Data East	King Kong	1990	4		Prototype Only Produced
Gottlieb	King Kool	1972	2		4TRL, 4F, 2FD, 3B, NRL, PR-3325
Gottlieb	King Of Diamonds	1967	1		4TRL, 3B, RT, PR-3200
Chicago Coin	King Pin	1951	1		
Williams	King Pin	1962	2		PR-1250
Gottlieb	King Pin	1973	1		4F, 2B, 10DT, 2KO, PR-4350
Bally	King Rex	1969	1		ADB, PR-275
Gottlieb	King Rock	1972	4		4TRL, 4F, 2FD, 3B, NRL, PR-4000
Bally	King Tut	1969	1		PR-800
Capcom	Kingpin	1996	4		Prototype Only Produced
Genco	Kings	1935	1		
Williams	Kings	1957	1		LUS
Gottlieb	Kings & Queens	1965	1		7TRL, 3B, 2DB, NRL, 4KO, PR-2875
Bally	Kings Of Steel	1984	4		3F, NV, 6DT, 3B, OG, 1KO, PR-2900
P & S Machine Co	Kismet	1945	1		Conversion Kit Pinball
Williams	Kismet	1961	4		PR-700
Bally	Kiss	1979	4		LIC, OG, NV, 5TRL, 4B, 4DT, 2S, PR-17000
Genco	Klever Lite	1935	1		
Genco	Klick	1938	1		
Williams	Klondike	1971	1		5B, NRL, 3KO, UP, 2TRL, 3RT Resembling A Slot Machine
Stoner	Knicker Bocker	1934	1		
Chicago Coin	Knickerbocker	1934	1		
Gottlieb	Knock Out	1950	1		5DB, 2B Animated Playfield
Exhibit	Knock Out	1941	1		
Victory Games	Knock Out The Japs	1943	1		Conversion Kit Pinball
Automatic Amusements	Knockout	1935	1		
Bally	Knockout	1975	2		PR-2085
Treff Automaten	Komet (Or Treff Komet)	1954	1	Germany	
Gottlieb	Krull	1983	4		TL, 7F, LIC, 3B, RS, PR-10
Playmatic	Kz-26	1984	4	Spain	
Stoner	L	1934	1		
K.C.Tabart	L' Hexagone	1986	4	France	Conversion Kit Pinball, 2B, 11DT, 3TRL, NRL, 3F, S, CB
Geiger	La Retata	N/A	U	Germany	
Geiger	Lady Death	1985	4	Germany	Conversion Kit For Bally's Mata Hari
Gottlieb	Lady Luck	1954	1		LUS, PR-700
Williams	Lady Luck	1968	2		NRL, 4B, PR-3020

Recel	Lady Luck	1976	4	Spain	EM, 4B, 4TRL, CB
Bally	Lady Luck	1986	4		3F, PR-500
Gottlieb	Lady Robin Hood	1948	1		
Game Plan	Lady Sharpshooter	1985	4		PR-1200
Chicago Coin	Lagionaire	1941	1		
Exhibit	Lancer	1940	1		
Gottlieb	Lancer	1961	2		7TRL, 4B, PR-1700
Trankner & Wietfeld	Landerkampf	1935	1	Germany	
Rally	Landing On Venus	1964	1	France	
Exhibit	Landslide	1940	1		
Inder	Lap By Lap	1986	4	Spain	RS, 2S, 3B, 3TRL
Nasco	Lariat	1949	1		Conversion Kit Pinball
Gottlieb	Lariat	1969	2		ADB, PR-150
Llobregat	Las Vegas	1967	1	Spain	
Dama	Las Vegas	1970	1	Italy	Conversion Kit Pinball
Chicago Coin	Las Vegas	1972	1		
Williams	Laser Ball	1979	4		NV, 3F, WB, 3B, 5TRL, 2S, 3KO, PR-4500
Williams	Laser Cue	1984	4		NV, 4F, PR-2800, 5DT, 3B, S, 3TRL
Data East	Last Action Hero	1993	4		RS, DM, EP, MB, BO, 2CB, LIC
Playmatic	Last Lap	1974	4	Spain	
Williams	Laura	1945	1		Conversion Kit Pinball
Gottlieb	Lawman	1971	2		10DT, 2B, 3TRL, Same Play as Sheriff, PR-1750
Data East	Lazer War	1987	4		PBG, RS, AN, 3MB, V, 3B, KB, BO
Stern	Lazerlord	1984	4		Prototype Only Produced
Williams	Lazy Q	1955	1		
K C Tabart	Le Grande 8	1985	1	France	Conversion Kit Pinball, 4F, 12DT, 2D, S
Jeutel	Le King	1983	4	France	4TRL, 4DT, S, 2B, PR-500
Bally	Lead Off	1940	1		
Exhibit	Leader	1940	1		
Marvel	Leap Year	1948	1		
Stern	Lectronamo	1978	4		SS, 3B, 8DT, S, 1KO, PR-2423
Chicago Coin	Leland	1933	1		
Data East	Lethal Weapon	1992	4		DM, VM, RS, 3MB, EP, LIC
G.B Daval	Liberty	1939	1		
Gottlieb	Liberty	1943	1		Conversion Kit Pinball
Bally	Liberty	1944	1		
Williams	Liberty Bell	1977	2		EM, 1KO, 2B, 2S, NRL, 2DT, PR-3000
Gottlieb	Liberty Belle	1962	4		PR-2950
Centromatic	Libra	1974	1	Spain	
Exhibit	Lightning	1934	1		
Exhibit	Lightning	1938	1		
Marvel	Lightning	1947	1		
Stern	Lightning	1981	4		DL, V, 4F, 3MB, 9DT, S, PR-2350
Gottlieb	Lightning Ball	1959	1		LUS, WR
Gottlieb	Lights Camera Action	1989	4		V, 3F, AN, PR-1708
Bally	Lights Out	1939	1		
Bally	Lime Light	1940	1		
Bally	Line Up	1937	1		
Western Equipment	Line-O	1936	1		
Baker Novelty	Line-Up	1940	1		
Lin Up	Lin-Up	1933	1		
Pacific Amusement	Lite Aline	1935	1		
Evans	Lite-A-Basket	1936	1		
Gottlieb	Lite-A-Card	1960	2		4F, 3B, 2DB, 4TRL, LUS, WR, PR-850
Gottlieb	Lite-O-Card	1939	1		
Williams	Little Chief	1975	4		2B, 1KO, 3TRL, PR-6300
Chicago Coin	Little Dandy	1939	1		
Bally	Little Joe	1972	4		6TRL, 4B, 1KO, NRL, 3MUSB, UP, PR-2080
Exhibit	Live Power	1942	1		
Chicago Coin	Live Wire	1937	1		
Game Plan	Lizard	1981	4		PR-1400
Game Plan	Loch Ness Monster	1985	4		Prototype Only Produced
Zaccaria	Locomotion	1981	4	Italy	
Lone Eagle	Lone Eagle	1933	1		
Exhibit	Lone Star	1940	1		
Genco	Long Beach	1937	1		
Exhibit	Long Champ	1940	1		
Forster	Long Island	1966	2	Germany	
Victory Sales	Longacres	1949	1		
Bally	Loop The Loop	1966	2		3TRL, Spinning Bumper, 3MUSB, NRL, 1KO, PR-1055
Juegos Populares	Lortium	1987	4	Spain	3F
Sega	Lost In Space	1998	4		WWS, LIC, EP
Bally	Lost World	1978	4		CB, 2KO, 3B, 2TRL, S, PR-10330
Gottlieb	Lot-O-Fun	1939	1		
Gottlieb	Lot-O-Smoke	1939	1		
Williams	Love Bug	1971	1		ADB
Gottlieb	Lovely Lucy	1954	1		LUS, 7DB, 3B, NOL
Mondialmatic	Lovers	1979	1	Italy	
Chicago Coin	Lucky	1939	1		
Williams	Lucky Ace	1974	1		4F, 3B, FD, 2TRL, PR-2809
Segasa / Sonic	Lucky Ace	1975	1	Spain	
Gottlieb	Lucky Card	1977	1		EM, ADB, PR-455
Micro Games	Lucky Draw	1978	1		
Zaccaria	Lucky Fruit	1975	1	Italy	EM, ADB, PR-610
Gottlieb	Lucky Hand	1977	1		EM, ADB, PR-610
Nordamatic	Lucky Man	1976	2	Italy	E M
Williams	Lucky Seven	1977	4		EM, SS Version Produced In 1978, 2DT, S, 2B, 4TRL, PR-4252
C.E.A.	Lucky Shot	1978	1	Italy	
Inder	Lucky Smile	1976	4	Spain	NF
Gottlieb	Lucky Star	1947	1		
Genco	Lucky Stars	1935	1		
Genco	Lucky Strike	1940	1		
Williams	Lucky Strike	1965	1		AB, PR-1800
Gottlieb	Lucky Strike	1975	1		ADB, PR-1013
Deluxe Amusements	Lucky Twins	1933	1		
Williams	Lulu	1954	1		
Williams	Lunar Shot	1967	1		Released Only In Italy
Mr Game	Mac Attack	1989	4	Italy	Pistol Grip Flipper Buttons
Maguinas / Mac Pinball	Mac Jungle	1987	4	Spain	Conversion Kit Pinball
Elettrocoin	Macao	N/A	1	Italy	MID 1960, 4B, 5TRL, NRL
Inder	Mach 2	1993	4	Spain	
Maguinas / Mac Pinball	Mac's Galaxy	1986	4	Spain	
Data East	Mad	1993	4		Prototype Only Produced
Stoner	Mad Cap	1936	1		
Playmatic	Mad Race	1984	4	Spain	
Bally	Mad World	1964	2		4TRL, 3B, 2MUSB, PR-2050
Nasco	Madam Butterfly	1949	1		Conversion Kit Pinball
Gottlieb	Mademoiselle	1959	2		DRS, 6B, 5DB
Gottlieb	Madison Square Garden	1950	1		2B, BFF
Exhibit	Magic	1948	1		
Playmatic	Magic	1974	1	Spain	
Stern	Magic	1979	4		NV, 3TRL, 2S, 3B, 3DT, PR-2466
Zaccaria	Magic Castle	1984	4	Italy	11DT, DL, RS, FS, 3B, 4F, AB
Bally	Magic Circle	1965	1		3B, 6MUSB, 3TRL, PR-580

Manufacturer	Name	Year	#	Country	Notes
Williams	Magic City	1967	1		4B, 5TRL, NRL, PR-2675
Bill Port	Magic City	1977	4	Spain	
Williams	Magic Clock	1960	2		MT
Keeney	Magic Lamp	1937	1		
Jack Rogers	Magic Lites	1959	1	France	
Arkon	Magic Picture Pin	1982	4	Germany	
Bell Games	Magic Picture Pin	1982	4	Italy	
Williams	Magic Town	1967	1		ADB, 4B, 5TRL, NRL, PR-3950
Gottlieb	Magic Wizard	1971	1		
Gottlieb	Magnotron	1974	4		3TRL, 3B, HS, 1KO, PR-6550
Gottlieb	Maisie	1947	1		NF
Gottlieb	Majestic	1957	4		RT, WR, 5B, 4TRL
Allied Amusements	Majik Keys Kicker	1934	1		
Pacific Amusement	Major League	1934	1		
United	Major League Baseball	1948	1		
Williams	Majorettes	1952	1		5B, 2DB, LUS
Gottlieb	Majorettes	1964	1		ADB, 6TRL, 2KO, 4B, 6DB, PR-425
Chicago Coin	Majors	1939	1		
Chicago Coin	Majors Of 41	1941	1		
Chicago Coin	Majors'49	1949	1		
Pacific Amusement	Make Or Break	1937	1		
Exhibit	Mam'selle	1947	1		NF
G.B Daval	Man On The Moon	1935	1		
Nasco	Mandalay	1950	1		
United	Manhattan	1948	1		
Gottlieb	Marathon	1955	2		DRS, PR-750
Gottlieb	Marble Queen	1953	1		LUS, 4B, 6DB
A.B.T Mfg	Marbl-Jax	1933	1		
Genco	Mardi Gras	1948	1		
Williams	Mardi Gras	1962	4		4B, MOL, 5TRL, 2RT, PR-1100
Bally	Mariner	1971	4		2TRL, 3MUSB, 3B, NRL, OG, UP, PR-2000
Westerhaus	Marines	1944	1		Conversion Kit Pinball
Westerhaus	Marines At Play	1945	1		Conversion Kit Pinball
Gottlieb	Mario Andretti	1995	4		PR-1120
Gottlieb	Mario Brothers Mushroom World	1992	4		Children's Pinball
Gottlieb	Marjorie	1947	1		NF
Chicago Coin	Mars	1937	1		
Gottlieb	Mars - God Of War	1981	4		V, WB, 3MB, RS, 4F, PR 5240
Segasa / Sonic	Mars Trek	1977	4	Spain	
Chicago Coin	Marvel	1930	1		
Williams	Maryland	1949	1		
Bally	Mascot	1940	1		
Gottlieb	Masquerade	1966	4		AB, 4F, NRL, 4B, 2TRL, 1DB, PR-3662
Recel	Master Stroke	1977	1	Spain	
Pacific Amusement	Masterpiece	1933	1		
Bally	Mata Hari	1978	4		EM & SS Versions Released, 4B, 8DT, 1KO, TRL, PR-16340
Genco	Match Em	1937	1		
Bally	Match The Dial	1935	1		
Peo Mfg	Mat-Cha-Score	1933	1		
Sega	Maverick The Movie	1994	4		17DT, KB, 3F, RS, CB, 4TRL, 3B
Gottlieb	Mayfair	1966	2		3B, 5TRL, PR-2120
Jeutel	Maze	1986	U	France	
Williams	Medieval Madness	1997	4		3B, RS, DM, EP, 2TRL, MB, Castle and Draw Bridge
Bally	Medusa	1981	4		4F, ZF, V, 11DT, 4B, PR-3250
Playmatic	Megaaton	1984	4	Spain	
Bally	Melody	1948	1		
Gottlieb	Melody	1967	1		ADB, PR-550
Gottlieb	Melody Lane	1960	2		
Bally	Melody Roll	1948	1		
Stern	Memory Lane	1978	4		SS, PR-2624
Unidesa	Mephisto	1987	4	Spain	Built Under License From Williams
Bally	Mercury	1937	1		
Genco	Mercury	1950	1		
Gottlieb	Mermaid	1951	1		
Gottlieb	Merry Go Round	1934	1		
Exhibit	Merry Go Round	1940	1		
Genco	Merry Widow	1948	1		
Williams	Merry Widow	1963	4		PR-2150
Gottlieb	Merry-Go-Round	1960	2		NOL, 3B, 4TRL, DRS, PR-750
Rally	Messalina	1965	2	France	
Inder	Metal Man	1992	4	Spain	
Stern	Meteor	1979	4		NV, 3F, 1B, 2DB, 15DT, S, PR-8362
Genco	Metro	1940	1		
Williams	Metro	1961	1		4DB, 2B, 2KO, Disappearing Bumper, PR-700
Pacific Amusement	Metropolitan	1933	1		
United	Mexico	1947	1		NF
Elettrocoin	Mexico	1970	1	Italy	Conversion Kit Pinball
Zaccaria	Mexico 86	1986	4	Italy	AN, 3B, 7DT
Chicago Coin	Miami	1938	1		
Gottlieb	Miami Beach	1941	1		
Gottlieb	Mibs	1969	1		PR-2200, 2TRL, 4B, NRL, 2-Inch Flippers
Data East	Michael Jordan	1992	4		Limited Production Run
Micropin Corp.	Micropin	1980	4		Countertop Game, SS
Atari	Middle Earth	1978	4		WB, 10DT, 4F, 2B
Bally	Midget Racer	1946	1		11DB
G.B Daval	Midway	1939	1		
United	Midway	1942	1		Conversion Kit Pinball
Bally	Mike And Ike	1933	2		Two Playfields Side By Side
Game Plan	Mike Bossy	1982	4		
Sega	Mikoshi	1978	2	Japan	SS
Williams	Millionare	1987	4		3F, MB, RW, AN, V, 3B, PR-3500
Exhibit	Mimi	1948	1		
Gottlieb	Mini Cycle	1970	2		3B, 5TRL, VT, PR-885
Gottlieb	Mini Pool	1969	1		ADB, 3TRL, 1B, PR-500
Bally	Mini Zag	1968	1		PR-1172
Gottlieb	Minstrel Man	1951	1		UP, 6DB, 1B, 2KO
Stoner	Miss America	1937	1		
Victory Games	Miss America	1944	1		Conversion Kit Pinball
Gottlieb	Miss America	1947	1		NF
Gottlieb	Miss Annabelle	1959	1		DRS, AB
Sega	Miss Nessie	1978	4	Japan	
M.A.M	Miss Spy	1967	1	Spain	
R.M.G	Miss Theresine	1970	1	Italy	
Inder	Miss Universo	1972	1	Spain	
Geiger	Miss World	1985	4	Germany	Conversion Kit For Bally's Kiss
Recreativos Franco	Mississippi	1973	1	Spain	
Williams	Miss-O	1969	1		PR-2351
Bally	Missouri Mules	1947	1		
Segasa / Sonic	Monaco	1977	4	Spain	
Data East	Monday Night Football	1989	4		RS, V, AN,
Dama	Mondial Bank	1970	1	Italy	
Bally	Monicker	1941	1		
Chicago Coin	Monopolee	1936	1		

Williams	Monster Bash	1998	4		
Bally	Monte Carlo	1964	1		5TRL, 5B, 5MUSB, PR-1050
Bally	Monte Carlo	1973	4		NRL, 3B, 2KO, UP, PR-5254
Nordamatic	Monte Carlo	1976	1	Italy	
Gottlieb	Monte Carlo	1987	4		RW, AN, 3MB, RS, PR-4315
Sega	Monte Rosa	1977	4	Japan	SS
United	Monterray	1948	1		
Atari	Monza	1979	U		Prototype Only Produced, Cocktail Table Style
Zaccaria	Moon Flight	1976	1	Italy	EM, 3B, 4TRL
United	Moon Glow	1948	1		
Inder	Moon Light	1987	4	Spain	RS, 3B, 5TRL
Chicago Coin	Moon Shot	1969	4		
Bally	Moon Shot	1963	1		4B, 5TRL, PR-1250
Exhibit	Morocco	1948	1		
Jennings	Motor Drome	1936	1		
Mr Game	Motor Show	1989	4	Italy	Pistol Grip Flipper Buttons, VID/P
Bally	Motordome	1986	4		4F, RS, AN, 3B, 3TRL, 1KO, S, PR-2000
Williams	Moulin Rouge	1965	1		6DB, 3B, 1TRL, 3KO, NRL, PR-1325
Bally	Mousin Around	1990	4		3MB, 3B, RS, AN, 3TRL
I.D.I.	Movie Master	1984	4	Italy	
Bally	Mr & Mrs Pac-Man	1982	4		3F, 11DT, 2B, 1KO, PR-10600
Genco	Mr Chips	1939	1		
Recel	Mr Doom	1979	4	Spain	
Recel	Mr Evil	1978	4	Spain	
Keeney	Muli-Free-Races	1938	1		
Bally	Multiple	1936	1		
Chicago Coin	Multiple	1936	1		
Inder	Mundial 90	1990	4	Spain	
Williams	Music Man	1960	4		Disappearing Bumper
Chicago Coin	Mustang	1964	2		3B, Revolving Target Feature
Gottlieb	Mustang	1977	2		EM, 3B, 3TRL, 3DT, 2KO, PR-2225
Bally	Mysterian	1984	4		Prototype Only Produced
Exhibit	Mystery	1947	1		NF
Alvin G. & Co	Mystery Castle	1993	4		DM, KB, RS, 3F, PR-500
Pacific Amusement	Mystic	1937	1		
Bally	Mystic	1941	1		
Bally	Mystic	1980	4		2TRL, 3B, 2S, 1KO, CB, 9DT, PR-3950
Home Novelty	Mystic Ball	1933	1		
Gottlieb	Mystic Marvel	1954	1		LUS
Zaccaria	Mystic Star	1986	4	Italy	Conversion Kit Pinball
Chicago Coin	Nags	1938	1		
Williams	Nags	1951	1		
Williams	Nags	1960	1		5TRL, MOL, 6B, Bumper Turntable, WR
Maresa	Nairobi	1966	1	Spain	
Williams	Naples	1957	2		
Genco	Natural	1939	1		
Zaccaria	Nautilus	1977	1	Italy	EM
Playmatic	Nautilus	1984	4	Spain	
A.M.I	Navajo	1976	4	Italy	
Bally	Nba Fastbreak	1997	4		3F, AB, RS, MB
G.B Daval	Neck N Neck	1935	1		
Mills Novelty	Neighbors	1936	1		
Peyper	Nemesis	1986	4	Spain	
Pacific Amusement	Neontact	1935	1		
Gottlieb	Neptune	1978	1		EM, PR-270
Atari	Neutron Star	1981	4		Prototype Only Produced
United	Nevada	1947	1		NF
Genco	New Century Special	1933	1		
Exhibit	New Contact	1948	1		
Exhibit	New Jeep	1940	1		
The Field	New Moon	1933	1		
Bally	New Rapid Fire	1941	1		
Bell Games	New Wave	1985	4	Italy	Conversion Kit Pinball, 2B, 3TRL, MT, IDT, OG, 3DT
Playmatic	New World	1976	4	Spain	EM, 2S, 2B
Gottlieb	New York	1976	2		EM, ADB, PR-300
E.G.S.	New York	1981	4	Italy	
Gottlieb	Niagara	1951	1		6DB, 4B, 4KO, NOL
Segasa / Sonic	Night Fever	1979	4	Spain	
Gottlieb	Night Hawk	1981	4		Prototype Only Produced
International	Night Moves	1989	4		Cocktail Table Style
Bally	Night Rider	1977	4		EM & SS Versions Released, PR-11155
Stern	Nine Ball	1980	4		3MB, 12DT, 2B, S, HS, PR-2279
Glickman	Nine Bells	1944	1		Conversion Kit Pinball
Williams	Nine Sisters	1953	1		One Flipper Only, DRS, 4DB, 3B, Spiral Ramp
Bally	Nip-It	1973	4		ZF, 4B, 2KO, NRL, 1MUSB, PR-4580
Chicago Coin	Nippy	1939	1		
Bally	Nitro Groundshaker	1980	4		4DT, 3B, 2KO, S, 2TRL, PR-7950
Treff Automaten	Nixe (Or Treff Nixie)	1954	1	Germany	
Williams	No Fear (Dangerous Sports)	1995	4		BI, 3F, DM, EP, VM, DL
Williams	No Good Golfers	1997	4		3F, WWS, 2S, 3B, RS, CB, Mini Jump Ramp
Bergmann & Co	Nordexpress	1955	1	Germany	
Gottlieb	North Star	1964	1		5TRL, 5B, 2DB, 2KO, PR-2525
Sega	Nostalgia	1977	2	Japan	SS
Bontempi	Novelty	N/A	U	Italy	
Gottlieb	Now	1971	4		8DT, 4TRL, 3B, NRL, PR-1125
Gottlieb	Nudge It	1990	4		
Bally	Nudgy	1947	1		NF
Stern	Nugent	1978	4		SS, 3TRL, 3B, S, 6DT, 3F, 1KO, PR-2671
California Games	Numbers	1934	1		
Jentzsch & Meerz	Nurburgring	1939	1	Germany	15B
Bontempi	O.K Corral	N/A	U	Italy	
Exhibit	Oasis	1950	1		
Chicago Coin	O-Boy	1939	1		
Chicago Coin	Ocean Park	1939	1		
G.B Daval	Odd Ball	1938	1		
G.B Daval	Odd Ball Junior	1938	1		
Bally	Odds & Evens	1973	1		UP, 3B, 2KO, NRL, PR-2570
Peyper	Odin	1985	4	Spain	
Segasa / Sonic	Odin Deluxe	1985	4	Spain	
Peyper	Odisea Paris Dakar	1987	4	Spain	
Genco	Official Baseball	1934	1		
Williams	Oh Boy	1964	2		3DB, 6B, 1KO, PR-1700
Gottlieb	Oh Johnny	1940	1		
United	Oklahoma	1944	1		Conversion Kit Pinball
United	Oklahoma	1949	1		
Gottlieb	Oklahoma	1961	4		
Bally	Old Chicago	1976	4		EM, 5B, 5DT, 2TRL, NRL, S, 2KO, PR-7155
Gottlieb	Old Faithfull	1949	1		
Universal	Old Hilltop	1951	1		
Keeney	Old Plantation	1961	1		
Jeutel	Olympic Games	1984	4	France	CB, 3F, 2B, 3TRL, 5DT, PR-500
Williams	Olympic Hockey	1972	2		AB, 5B, 1DB, NRL, UP, PR-2555
California Games	Olympic Pins	1935	1		
Williams	Olympics	1952	1		BFF, 4B, 4KO

Manufacturer	Name	Year	#	Country	Notes
Gottlieb	Olympics	1962	2		4TRL, 5DB, 4B
Chicago Coin	Olympics	1975	2		
Juegos Populares	Olympus	1986	4	Spain	
Bally	On Beam	1969	1		4TRL, 4B, 1KO, 4MUSB
Baker Novelty	On Deck	1940	1		
Victory Games	On The Deck	1944	1		Conversion Kit Pinball
Mills Novelty	One Two Three	1940	1		
Genco	One,Two,Three	1948	1		
Peo Mfg	One-Two-Three	1935	1		
R.M.G	Only Star	1971	1	Italy	ZF
Bally	Op Pop Pop	1969	1		Prototype Only Produced
Data East	Operation Desert Storm	1992	4		AN, WWS, 3F, 3MB
Gottlieb	Operation Thunder	1992	4		
Marvel	Opportunity	1946	1		
Gottlieb	Orbit	1972	4		VT, 3B, S, 3RTL, Same Play as Outer Space, PR-3200
Hankin	Orbit 1	1978	4	Australia	3B, VT, 4TRL, S
Stern	Orbitor 1	1982	4		V, 2MB, Uneven Playfield, Spinning Bumpers, PR-889
Marvel	Oscar	1947	1		NF
Kozak	Our Aristocrat	1933	1		
Gottlieb	Out Of Sight	1975	2		Same Play As Far Out, PR-1750
Gottlieb	Outer Space	1972	2		VT, 3B, S, 3RTL, OG, Same Play As Orbit, PR-2350
Stoner	Oval Ten	1933	1		
G.B Daval	Over And Under	1936	1		
Glickman	Over The Top	1944	1		Conversion Kit Pinball
Mills Novelty	Owl	1941	1		
Mills Novelty	Owl	1942	1		Conversion Kit Pinball
Williams	Oxo	1973	4		3B, 6TRL, PR-7053
Western Equipment	Paddles	1937	1		
Chicago Coin	Paddock	1937	1		
Williams	Paddock	1969	1		3TRL, 5B, 3 Inch Flippers, PR 1952
Gottlieb	Palace Guard	1968	1		ADB, 5TRL 4B, NRL, MOL, MT, PR-625
Williams	Palisades	1953	1		
Bally	Palm Beach	1952	1		
Bally	Palm Springs	1938	1		
Llobregat	Palma	1966	U	Spain	
Williams	Palooka	1964	1		ADB, 1DT, 3B, 2DB, PR-700
Bally	Pan American	1941	1		
G.B Daval	Panama	1936	1		
Gottlieb	Panthra	1980	4		NV, NLC, 12DT, 2B, 4TRL, S, PR-5220
Jeutel	Papillon	1984	4	France	PR-600
G.M Laboratories	Par Golf	1935	1		
Chicago Coin	Par Golf	1965	1		
Glickman	Parade Leader	1944	1		Conversion Kit Pinball
Gottlieb	Paradise	1940	1		
United	Paradise	1948	1		
Gottlieb	Paradise	1965	2		4TRL, 4B, 4KO, PR-2100
Petaco	Paradiso (Or Paraiso)	1967	2	Spain	
Bally	Paragon	1979	4		WB, 4F, NV, 4B, IDT, S, 7DT, 2KO, FD, PR-9120
Williams	Paratrooper	1952	1		
P & S Machine Co	Paratroops	1943	1		Conversion Kit Pinball
Bally	Pari-Mutual	1936	1		
Playmatic	Party	1979	4	Spain	SS, 2B, 2TRL, 4B, MRL
Bally	Party Animal	1987	4		3F, 3MB, RS, V, AN, 3B, IDT, 3DT, 1KO, PR-2250
Bally	Party Zone	1991	4		DM, 2MB, RS
Exhibit	Pass Kick	1934	1		
Keeney	Pastime	1938	1		
Williams	Pat Hand	1975	4		3F, 2B, 5DT, PR-6500
Gottlieb	Paul Bunyan	1968	2		3TRL, 3B, NRL, 6 2-Inch Flippers, PR-1900
Buckley	Pay Day	1936	1		
Glickman	Peacherino	1944	1		Conversion Kit Pinball
Chicago Coin	Peachy	1938	1		
Jennings	Pedal Pushers	1938	1		
Bally	Pennant	1933	1		
Micropin Corp.	Pentacup	1979	4		
Chicago Coin	Peppy	1938	1		
Williams	Perky	1956	1		LUS
Juegos Populares	Petaco	1984	4	Spain	6DT, CB, 2B
Juegos Populares	Petaco 2	1985	4	Spain	
Williams	Peter Pan	1955	1		LUS, 5TRL, 2B, 2DB
Pacific Amusement	Phantom	1937	1		
Data East	Phantom Of The Opera	1990	4		AN, RS, 3MB, V, KB, 3B, 3TRL
Playmatic	Phantom Ship	1980	U	Spain	DL, V, MB, MS, 4F, RS, PR-2500
Williams	Pharaoh	1981	4		
Williams	Phoenix	1948	1		
Williams	Phoenix	1978	4		SS, 5TRL, 3B, S, 10DT, PR-6198
Universal	Photo Finish	1949	1		
Williams	Piccadilly	1956	2		DRS
The Field	Pick Up	1933	1		
Bally	Pickem	1939	1		
Gottlieb	Picnic	1958	2		4B, RT, 5TRL
Maresa	Picnic	1967	1	Spain	
Peo Mfg	Pigskin	1934	1		
Victory Sales	Pimlico	1946	1		
Recel	Pin Ball	1984	4	Spain	
Bell Games	Pin Ball Pool	1983	4	Italy	Conversion Kit Pinball
Chicago Coin	Pin Bowler	1949	1		
Gottlieb	Pin Up	1975	1		ADB, 2KO, 10DT, 4F, 2B, PR-715
Gottlieb	Pin Wheel	1953	1		LUS, 4F
Stern	Pinball	1977	4		EM & SS Versions Released, 3B, S, 2KO, PR-2288
Bell Games	Pinball	1983	4	Italy	Conversion Kit Pinball
Inder	Pinball	1987	4	Spain	
Joctronic	Pinball	1987	4	Spain	
Zaccaria	Pinball Champ	1983	4	Italy	Same Play as Pinball Champ 82
Assa	Pinball Champ	1986	4	Spain	
Zaccaria	Pinball Champ 82	1982	4	Italy	DL, 4F, S, 1B, 7DT
Capcom	Pinball Magic	1995	4		DM, 1B, RS, 5DT, PR-1200
Gottlieb	Pinball Pool	1979	4		NV, 14DT, CB, 2B, 2KO, PR-7200
Williams	Pinbot	1986	4		DL, V, 2MB, RS, AN, BO, 3DT, 3B, 3KO, PR-12000
Unidesa	Pinbot	1987	4	Spain	Built Under License From Williams
Gottlieb	Pink Panther	1981	4		3F, 4B, 7DT, 4TRL, NV, WB, 3MB, PR-2840
Williams	Pinky	1950	1		
Gottlieb	Pioneer	1976	2		EM, 8DT, MRL, 3B, 3TRL, 1KO, PR-3625
Chicago Coin	Pippin	1935	1		
Chicago Coin	Pirate Gold	1969	1		
Alvin G. & Co	Pistol Poker	1993	4		DM, RS, DL, 2B, 3F, PR-200
Williams	Pit Stop	1968	2		NRL, 3B, LAP REELS, PR-2000
Williams	Planets	1971	2		
Exhibit	Play Ball	1938	1		
Bally	Play Ball	1941	1		
Victory Games	Play Ball	1944	1		Conversion Kit Pinball
Chicago Coin	Play Ball	1951	1		
Gottlieb	Play Ball	1971	1		Run Reels, 2VT, 3B, No Plunger, PR-3076
Chicago Coin	Play Boy	1947	1		
Gottlieb	Play Pool	1972	1		PR-2339

Manufacturer	Title	Year		Country	Notes
Playmatic	Play Time	1974	1	Spain	TP, 2B
Bontempi	Play Time	N/A	U	Italy	
Rally	Playboy	1967	2	France	Digital Scoring, SP, 5TRL, 1B, UP?
Bally	Playboy	1978	4		LIC, 4TRL, 5DT, 3B, PR-18250
Data Fast	Playboy 35th Anniversary	1989	4		3MB, RS, AN, V, 3B, 4TRL.
Bontempi	Player	N/A	U	Italy	
Exhibit	Playland	1950	1		
Baker Novelty	Playmate	1940	1		
Gottlieb	Playmates	1968	1		ADB, PR-500, RT, 4B, 6TRL, NRL
Exhibit	Playtime	1949	1		
Chicago Coin	Playtime	1968	2		
Gottlieb	Pleasure Isle	1965	1		
Gottlieb	Plus And Minus	1935	1		
Bally	Pockets	1936	1		
Gottlieb	Poker Face	1953	1		LUS
Keeney	Poker Face	1963	1		4DB, 1B, 1KO
Recel	Poker Plus	1978	4	Spain	EM & SS Versions Released
Williams	Pokerino	1978	4		WB, CB, 3B, 5DT, 4F, 2FD, NRL, S, Dual Action Flippers
Segasa / Sonic	Pole Position	1987	4	Spain	
Williams	Police Force	1989	4		3MB, RS, V, AN, BO, RS, 1KO
Western Equipment	Policy	1936	1		
Chicago Coin	Polo	1940	1		
Gottlieb	Polo	1970	4		2-Inch Flippers, 3B, 5TRL, VT, PR-1140
Western Equipment	Ponies	1936	1		
Bontempi	Ponies	N/A	U	Italy	
Genco	Pontiac	1934	1		
Zaccaria	Pool Champion	1985	4	Italy	
Manilamatic	Pool Rabbit	N/A	U	Italy	
Bally	Pool Sharks	1990	4		RS, CB, V, AN
Gottlieb	Pop-A-Card	1972	1		ADB Version Of Drop-A-Card, PR-825
Bally	Popeye Saves The Earth	1993	4		DL, 4F, DM, BI?
Gottlieb	Poseiden	1978	1		EM, PR-530
Williams	Post Time	1969	1		ADB, 3-Inch Flippers, PR-2002
Jennings	Power Play	1937	1		
Bally	Power Play	1978	4		4F, UP, 3B, 1KO, 8DT, PR-13750
Genco	Powerhouse	1940	1		
Northwest	Premier	1933	1		
Gottlieb	President Junior	1934	1		
Williams	Pretty Baby	1965	2		
Western Equipment	Preview	1937	1		
Gottlieb	Preview	1962	2		
Gottlieb	Pro Football	1973	1		No Plunger, 2VT, 4F, 2FD, 2B, 6TRL, NRL, Point Reels
Gottlieb	Pro Pool	1973	1		ADB, 1B, 14DT, 3TRL, 1KO, PR-800
P & S Machine Co	Production	1943	1		Conversion Kit Pinball
Mills Novelty	Proffesional Baseball	1934	1		
Western Equipment	Programe	1937	1		
Robbins	Progress	1933	1		
Bally	Progress	1940	1		
Segasa / Sonic	Prospector	1977	4	Spain	EM
Gottlieb	Psychedelic	1970	1		PR-1800
Genco	Puddin'head	1948	1		
Genco	Punch	1939	1		
Chicago Coin	Punchy	1950	1		
Alvin G. & Co	Punchy The Clown	1993	1		PR-100
Gottlieb	Punk	1982	4		4F, MB, 3TRL, 5B, 6DT, 2 Outholes, PR-960
Joctronic	Punky Willy	1986	4	Spain	
Exhibit	Pylon	1940	1		
Gottlieb	Pyramid	1939	1		
Gottlieb	Pyramid	1977	2		EM, 3B, 2KO, 5TRL, 5DT, Same Play As Cleopatra
Gottlieb	Q-Berts Quest	1983	4		4F, WB, PR-884
Western Products	Qualified	1938	1		
Bally	Quarterback	1976	2		PR-1050
Gottlieb	Quartette	1952	1		LUS
M.A.M	Que Bueno	1967	1	Spain	
Gottlieb	Queen Of Diamonds	1959	1		LUS
Gottlieb	Queen Of Hearts	1952	1		LUS
Alben	Queen Of Hearts	1957	U	France	
Zaccaria	Queen's Castle	1978	1	Italy	EM
Silver Star	Question Mark	1933	1		
Gottlieb	Quick Draw	1975	2		3TRL, MRL, 3B, DT, PR-2660
Western Equipment	Quick Silver	1935	1		
Keeney	Quicksilver	1935	1		
Stern	Quicksilver	1980	4		NV, NLC, 7DT, 4TRL, 4B, 2S, 1KO, PR-1200
Western Equipment	Quinella	1938	1		
Gottlieb	Quintette	1953	1		LUS
Pacific Amusement	Quintuplet	1935	1		
Bontempi	Race Day	N/A	U	Italy	
Sullivan & Nolan	Race King	1943	1		Conversion Kit Pinball
Geiger	Race Stars	1979	4	Germany	
Williams	Race The Clock	1955	4		DRS
Gottlieb	Race Time	1959	2		
Midway	Race Way	1963	2		
Playmatic	Racers	1974	1	Spain	
Western Equipment	Races	1936	1		
Pacific Amusement	Races	1937	1		
Stoner	Races	1937	1		
Jennings	Racing Club	1937	1		
Gottlieb	Rack-A-Ball	1962	1		PR-2700
Gottlieb	Rack'em Up	1983	4		3B, 4TRL, 7DT, MRL, S, PR-1762
Bally	Radical	1990	4		4F, 2MB, RS, V, AN
California Games	Radio Station	1934	1		
Williams	Rag Mop	1950	1		
Genco	Ragtime	1938	1		
Playmatic	Raid (Or The Raid)	1984	4	Spain	
Keeney	Rainbow	1936	1		
Williams	Rainbow	1948	1		
Gottlieb	Rainbow	1956	1		LUS
Dama	Rally	1970	1	Italy	
Rally	Rally Girl	1966	4	France	Digital Scoring, 5TRL, 5B
United	Ramona	1949	1		
Bally	Ramp Worrior	1988	4		
Bally	Rancho	1948	1		
Gottlieb	Rancho	1965	1		AB, ADB
Williams	Rancho	1977	2		EM, NRL, S, 2B, DT, 3TRL, KO
Bally	Ranger	1935	1		
Exhibit	Ranger	1947	1		NF
Chicago Coin	Rapid Transit	1935	1		
Williams	Rat Race	1983	4		Prototype Only Produced
Gottlieb	Raven	1986	4		PBG, AN, PR-3550
Chicago Coin	Rawhide	1977	4		EM
Gottlieb	Ready, Aim, Fire	1983	4		5B, 1TRL, PR-390
Game Plan	Real	1978	4		Cocktail Table Style
California Games	Rebound	1934	1		
Exhibit	Rebound	1934	1		

Exhibit	Rebound	1939	1		
Chicago Coin	Rebound	1948	1		
Bally	Record Time	1940	1		
Genco	Recorder	1938	1		
Europlay	Red Arrow	1978	1	Italy	EM
Midway	Red Ball	1959	1		
Chicago Coin	Red Baron	1975	2		Same Play As Blue Max
Barni	Red Baron	1985	4	Spain	
Bally	Red Max	1972	1		PR-70
G.B Daval	Red N Blue	1937	1		
Pacific Amusement	Red Sails	1936	1		
United	Red Shoes	1950	1		
Zaccaria	Red Show	1975	4	Italy	
Success	Red White & Blue	1941	1		
Glickman	Redheads	1944	1		Conversion Kit Pinball
Williams	Reflex	1982	U		Prototype Only Produced
Williams	Regatta	1955	1		LUS
Stoner	Regent	1933	1		
Gottlieb	Register	1956	4		DRS, 4B, 6DB, BFF
Gottlieb	Register (Junior & Senior Versions)	1934	1		
Gottlieb	Relay	1934	1		
Williams	Reno	1957	1		LUS
Keeney	Repeater	1940	1		
Chicago Coin	Replay	1937	1		
Exhibit	Request	1938	1		
Gottlieb	Rescue 911	1994	4		3F, RS, MB, CB, DM, PR-4000
Williams	Reserve	1961	1		3B, 2DB
Exhibit	Review	1938	1		
United	Revue	1947	1		
Bergmann & Co	Revue	1957	1	Germany	
Petaco	Rey De Diamantes	1967	1	Spain	Copy of Gottlieb's King of Diamonds
Jumaci	Rey Del Oeste	N/A	1	Spain	
Stoner	Riccochet	1937	1		
Jocmatic	Rider's Surf	1986	4	Spain	7DT, 2B, 3TRL
Genco	Rink	1939	1		
United	Rio	1947	1		NF
United	Rio	1949	1		
Playmatic	Rio	1977	4	Spain	EM, 2B, 3F, CB Mini Playfield
Game Plan	Rio	1978	4		Cocktail Table Style
Genco	Rip Snorter	1949	1		
Stoner	Ritz	1938	1		
Williams	River Boat	1964	1		1TRL 5B, MT
Williams	River Boat Gambler	1990	4		AB, AN, RS, 2MB, Backglass Roulette Wheel
United	Riviera	1946	1		Conversion Kit Pinball
Alben	Riviera	1958	2	France	
Chicago Coin	Riviera	1973	4		UP, 4F, 3B, NRL, 5TRL, KB
Bontempi	Road	N/A	U	Italy	
Williams	Road Kings	1986	4		V, RS, MB, AN, KB, 4B, 2TRL, 3KO, PR-5500
Gottlieb	Road Race	1969	1		3B, 4TRL, NRL, Rotating Arrow Bumper, PR-1425
Geiger	Road Racer	1985	4	Germany	Conversion Kit For Bally's Evel Knevel
Atari	Road Runner	1979	4		Prototype Only Produced, 3F, 2S, 5DT, 3CB, 2B
Williams	Road Show	1994	4		4F, MB, RS, 2 Plungers, BI, 3B, MRL, VC, DM
G.B Daval	Robin Hood	1938	1		
Sega	Robin Hood	1976	1	Japan	
Pin-Ball	Robin Hood	1978	1		
Gottlieb	Robo War	1988	4		MB, AN, PR-2130
Data East	Robocop	1990	4		RS, V, AN, LIC, MB
Zaccaria	Robot	1985	4	Italy	
Gottlieb	Rock	1985	4		AN, PR-1875
Playmatic	Rock 2500	1985	4	Spain	
Gottlieb	Rock Encore	1986	4		AN, PR-245
W##illiams	Rock N Roll	1970	1		ADB, AB, 5B, 2KO, NRL, UP
Allied Leisure	Rock On	1975	4		
Gottlieb	Rock Star	1979	1		EM, PR-268, 3TRL, 5B, 2S, 1KO
Bally	Rockelite	1935	1		
Genco	Rocket	1950	1		
Williams	Rocket	1959	1		LUS, WR
Bally	Rocket Iii	1967	1		ZF, Spinning Bumper, PR-2603
Bally	Rocket Of 38	1938	1		
Gottlieb	Rocket Ship	1958	1		LUS, WR, RT, 4DB, 2B
Gottlieb	Rocketter	1950	1		
Bally	Rockmakers	1968	4		PR-2420
Gottlieb	Rocky	1982	4		5F, 4B, 11DT, S, WB, PR-1504
Giuliano Lodola	Rocky Girl	1979	1	Italy	EM, Copy of Gottlieb's Rock Star
Exhibit	Rodeo	1935	1		
United	Rodeo	1953	1		
Midway	Rodeo	1964	2		TS, 4B
Sega	Rodeo	1977	2	Japan	EM
Bally	Rogo	1974	4		2KO, 2B, HS, 1TRL, NRL, PR-3075
Chicago Coin	Rola Score	1936	1		
Chicago Coin	Roll Down	1947	1		
Gottlieb	Roller Coaster	1971	2		PR-1550
Bally	Roller Derby	1939	1		
Gottlieb	Roller Disco	1980	4		WB, 4F, NV, NLC, 10DT, 3B, 1KO, 4TRL, PR-2400
Williams	Roller Games	1990	4		3MB, 3F, RS, V, AN, S
Bally	Rolling Stones	1980	4		LIC, 5DT, 4TRL, 3B, PR-5700
Genco	Rollover	1937	1		
Genco	Roly Poly	1936	1		
United	Rondevoo	1948	1		
Elettrocoin	Rose & Can Can	1968	1	Italy	
Chicago Coin	Rose Bowl	1937	1		
Gottlieb	Rose-Bowl	1951	1		
Genco	Rotation	1936	1		
Stoner	Rotation	1940	1		
Midway	Rotation Viii	1978	4		Cocktail Table Style, 3F, 3B, S
Williams	Roto	1969	2		5TRL, 5B, 1KO, 3-Inch Flippers, NRL
Gottlieb	Roto Pool	1958	1		WR, LUS, 4B, RT
Pacific Amusement	Rotolite	1935	1		
Gottlieb	Round Up	1948	1		
Bally	Round Up	1971	2		PR-70
Chicago Coin	Roxy	1940	1		
Chicago Coin	Royal Flash	1964	2		
Jac Van Ham	Royal Flippers	1987	4	Holland	LUS, 4DB, 3B, RT, 3TRL,WR
Gottlieb	Royal Flush	1957	1		EM, 9DT, 1KO, 1B, OG, 5TRL, PR-12250
Gottlieb	Royal Flush	1976	4		PR-2044
Gottlieb	Royal Flush Deluxe	1983	4		4B, 5TRL, NRL, MT, PR-2900
Gottlieb	Royal Guard	1968	1		EM
Europlay	Royal King	N/A	1	Italy	3B, Same Play as Top Card, PR-1480
Gottlieb	Royal Pair	1974	1		4F, DL, DM, VC, RS, VM, 7DT, CB, 3TRL, 3B, BI, EP
Data East	Royal Rumble	1994	4		
Chicago Coin	Rugby	1936	1		
Inder	Running Horses	1976	1	Spain	
Genco	Running Wild	1937	1		
Bally	Safari	1968	2		4B, 3TRL, 4MUSB, PR-1100

Manufacturer	Title	Year	#	Country	Notes
Bally	Safe Cracker	1996	4		Token-Pin Pinball, TP, 3F, RS, SP, DM, AB, 3B
Scientific Machine	Safety Zone	1934	1		
K.C.Tabart	Sahara Love	1984	4	France	Conversion Kit Pinball, CB, 4F, 9DT, S, 1B
Glickman	Sailorettes 42	1942	1		Conversion Kit Pinball
Chicago Coin	Sally	1948	1		
Rally	Saloon	1965	4	France	
Baker Novelty	Salute	1941	1		
Exhibit	Samba	1948	1		
Alben	Samba	1961	2	France	WR, RT, 3B, 2DB, 4F
Williams	San Francisco	1964	2		2TRL, 3B, 5DB, 2KO, PR-2000
Bally	Santa Anita	1940	1		
United	Santa Fe	1943	1		Conversion Kit Pinball
Sega	Sapporo	1976	1	Japan	EM, 3B, 3TRL, UP, NRL, Slalom Ramp
Stoner	Sara- Suzy	1940	1		
Williams	Saratoga	1948	1		
Williams	Satellite	1958	1		LUS
C.E.A.	Satellite	1978	4	Italy	
Williams	Satin Doll	1975	2		4F, FD, 2B, NRL, PR-2400
Nordamatic	Saturn	1977	1	Italy	E M
Bell Games	Saturn 2	1985	4	Italy	Conversion Kit Pinball
Elettrocoin	Scala Reale	1970	1	Italy	
Glickman	Scandals 42	1943	1		Conversion Kit Pinball
Bally	Scared Stiff	1996	4		AB, DM, RS, MB, 3TRL, 3B, Jumping Frog Targets
Gottlieb	School Days	1941	1		
Rally	Schuss	1968	1	France	ADB
Bally	Scoop	1939	1		
Gottlieb	Score Board	1933	1		
Chicago Coin	Score Board	1948	1		
Gottlieb	Score Card	1940	1		
Keeney	Score Champ	1940	1		
Gottlieb	Score-A-Line	1940	1		
Gottlieb	Score-Board	1956	4		DRS
Game Plan	Scoring Machine	1982	4		Cocktail Table Style
Williams	Scorpion	1980	4		WB, LC, 4F, 2MB, S, 11DT, MRL, 3TRL, 3B, 2KO
Genco	Scotty	1936	1		
Tecnoplay	Scramble	1987	4	San Marino	
Rock-Ola	Screamo	1935	1		
Williams	Screamo	1954	1		
Inder	Screech	1978	4	Spain	
Genco	Screw Ball	1948	1		
Bally	Scrimmage	1935	1		
Gottlieb	Scuba	1970	2		3B, 4TRL, 2-Inch Flippers
Gottlieb	Sea Belles	1956	2		DRS
Bally	Sea Biscuit	1939	1		
United	Sea Breeze	1946	1		
Gottlieb	Sea Hawk	1941	1		
Allied Leisure	Sea Hunt	1972	1		Shakerball Pinball
Chicago Coin	Sea Isle	1947	1		NF
Williams	Sea Jockey	1951	1		AB
Bally	Sea Ray	1971	2		PR-1300
Victory Games	Sea Rider	1945	1		Conversion Kit Pinball
Recel	Sea Scare	1978	1	Spain	
Gottlieb	Sea Shore	1964	2		RT, 4B, 4DB, 2TRL, PR-1780
Gottlieb	Sea Side	1967	2		PR-900
Williams	Sea Wolf	1959	1		LUS, DB, Disappearing Bumper, WR, 4F
Stern	Seawitch	1980	4		NV, 4F, S, 3B, 11DT, PR-2503
Data East	Secret Serice	1988	4		3F, RS, AN, 3MB, 3TRL, 3B, S
Bally	See Saw	1970	4		2KO, 4B, 4TRL, UP, NRL, OG, 2MUSB, PR-1517
Gottlieb	Select-A-Card	1950	1		TS, 4DB
Elettrocoin	Selen Cup	N/A	2	Italy	12F, 4B, Two Player Head-To-Head
Chicago Coin	Sensation	1934	1		
Chicago Coin	Sensation Of1937	1937	1		
G.B Daval	Sequence	1936	1		
United	Serenade	1948	1		
Alben	Serenade	1957	2	France	4F, 4B
Williams	Serenade	1960	2		
Playmatic	Serenade	1974	1	Spain	
Genco	Set Up	1934	1		
Williams	Set Up	1969	1		ADB
Keeney	Seven Eleven	1935	1		
Western Products	Seven Flashes	1941	2		
Gottlieb	Seven Seas	1959	2		DRS, WR
Genco	Seven Up	1941	1		
Williams	Seven Up	1969	1		4B, NRL, 4F, UP, 3-Inch Flippers
Inder	Seven Winner	1973	1	Spain	
Pinball Vision	Sexy Girl	1978	4		
Bell Games	Sexy Girl	1979	4	Italy	
Ranco	Sexy Girl	1980	4	Switzerland	Conversion Kit Pinball
Arkon	Sexy Girl	1981	4	Germany	Conversion Kit Pinball
Arkon	Sexy Girl Deluxe	1983	4	Germany	
Jack Rogers	Sexy Lites	1959	2	France	
Williams	Shamrock	1956	2		DRS
Inder	Shamrock	1977	4	Spain	
Chicago Coin	Shanghai	1948	1		
Gottlieb	Shangri-La	1943	1		
P & S Machine Co	Shangri-La	1943	1		Conversion Kit Pinball
Williams	Shangri-La	1967	4		4B, NRL, PR-4900
Exhibit	Shantytown	1949	1		
Gottlieb	Shaq Attaq	1994	4		4F, RS MB, Basketball Net, VT, WWS, S, 5DT
Hankin	Shark	1980	4	Australia	4F, 3B, WB, 8DT, MRL, 3TRL, HS, S, PR-200
Gottlieb	Sharpshooter	1949	1		
Game Plan	Sharpshooter	1978	4		4B, 7DT, 3TRL, S, PR-4200
Game Plan	Sharpshooter 2	1984	4		PR-600
Bally	Sheba	1965	2		PR-825
Gottlieb	Sheriff	1971	4		10DT, 2B, 3TRL, Same Play As Lawman, PR-2900
Barni	Shield	1985	4	Spain	
Gottlieb	Shindig	1953	1		LUS, 6DB, 3B, BFF
Rock-Ola	Ship Ahoy	1935	1		
Gottlieb	Ship Ahoy	1976	1		EM, ADB, 5B, S, 5TRL, ADB, PR-1150
Gottlieb	Ship Mates	1964	4		6TRL, 4B, 2KO, RT, PR-5115
Williams	Shoo Shoo	1951	1		
G.M Laboratories	Shoot The Chutes	1936	1		
Williams	Shoot The Moon	1951	1		
Ema	Shooting	N/A	1	Germany	Early 1950s
G.B Daval	Shooting Star	1934	1		
P & S Machine Co	Shooting Stars	1947	1		NF
Zaccaria	Shooting The Rapids	1979	4	Italy	
Stoner	Short Sox	1936	1		
Exhibit	Short Stop	1940	1		
Exhibit	Short Stop	1948	1		
Chicago Coin	Show Boat	1934	1		
Chicago Coin	Show Boat	1941	1		
United	Show Boat	1949	1		
Genco	Show Boat	1957	1		LUS, 6B, 3TRL

Manufacturer	Name	Year	#	Country	Notes
Gottlieb	Show Boat	1961	1		6B, 1DB, 4F, PR-1950
Williams	Show Girl	1946	1		
Automatic Amusements	Showdown	1935	1		
Chicago Coin	Showtime	1974	4		
Baker Novelty	Shuffle	1940	1		
Chicago Coin	Shuffle Board	1948	1		
Exhibit	Shuffle Bowl	1948	1		
Chicago Coin	Shuffle King	1948	1		
G.B Daval	Side Kick	1938	1		
Bally	Signal	1934	1		
Automatic Amusements	Signal	1935	1		
Gottlieb	Silver	1957	1		LUS, 4B, 2DB, RT
Genco	Silver Chest	1953	1		
Genco	Silver Cup	1933	1		
Bergmann & Co	Silver Cup	1968	2	Germany	
Genco	Silver Flash	1937	1		
A.B.T Mfg	Silver Gate	1933	1		
The Field	Silver Horseshoe	1933	1		
Bally	Silver Skates	1941	1		
Williams	Silver Skates	1953	1		LUS, 4F, 3B, 2DB
Gottlieb	Silver Slugger	1990	4		AN, 3S, VT, 3B, 4DT, 4TRL, PR-2100
Baker Novelty	Silver Spray	1941	1		
Bally	Silver Streak	1947	1		
Bally	Silverball Mania	1980	4		3B, 4DB, PR-10350
Gottlieb	Sinbad	1978	4		SS, 2FD, 4F, 10DT, 4TRL, NRL, PR-12950
Bell Games	Sinbad	1979	4	Italy	
Gottlieb	Sing Along	1967	1		PR-3300, 4B, 4KO, 4TRL, NRL
United	Singapore	1947	1		
G.M Laboratories	Sink Or Swim	1935	1		
Victory Games	Sink The Japs	1942	1		Conversion Kit Pinball
Peyper	Sir Lancelot	1994	4	Spain	
Mondialmatic	Sisters	1979	1	Italy	
Gottlieb	Sittin Pretty	1958	1		LUS, WR, RT, 4B, 4DB
Bally	Six Million Dollar Man	1978	6		UP, LIC, 2S, 3B, 1KO, 5DT, PR-10320
Bally	Six Shooter	1966	6		NRL, 6MUSB, 2KO, 2TRL, Spinning Bumper, OG
Bally	Six Six Six	1935	1		
Bally	Six Sticks	1966	6		3TRL, 3B, 5MUSB
Glickman	Sixty Grand	1944	1		Conversion Kit Pinball
Globe	Sixty-Six	1934	1		
Inder	Skate Board	1980	4	Spain	
Bally	Skateball	1980	4		4F, LC, NV, 3B, S, 11DT, PR-4150
Williams	Ski Club	1965	1		ADB, PR-550
Genco	Ski Hi	1937	1		
Zaccaria	Ski Jump	1978	1	Italy	SS
Williams	Skill Ball	1961	1		ADB, MT, 4DB, 3B, PR-650
Bally	Skill Circle	1935	1		
Bally	Skill Derby	1960	1		
Mills Novelty	Skill Feature	1940	1		
Bell Games	Skill Flight	1986	4	Italy	3F, RS, S, MB
Williams	Skill Pool	1963	1		1DB, 4B, 2KO
Gottlieb	Skill Roll	1936	1		
Bally	Skill Score	1960	1		
Keeney	Skill Time	1937	1		
Gottlieb	Skill-Pool	1952	1		
Auto Bell Novelty	Skilro	1962	1		
Gottlieb	Skipper	1969	4		4B, NRL, 2-Inch Flippers, 2VT
Pacific Amusement	Skooky	1937	1		
Exhibit	Sky Blazer	1941	1		
Exhibit	Sky Chief	1942	1		
United	Sky Chief	1945	1		
Gottlieb	Sky Dive	1974	1		3B, 7DT, 4TRL, Same Play as Sky Jump, PR-2260
Bally	Sky Divers	1964	1		4TRL, 3B, 3MUSB, PR-2250
Europlay	Sky Fly	1978	4	Italy	
Gottlieb	Sky Jump	1974	1		3B, 7DT, 4TRL, PR-4200
Petaco	Sky Jump	1974	1	Spain	
Bally	Sky Kings	1973	1		2B, S, 1KO, 2CB, 2TRL, PR-2000
Keeney	Sky Lark	1941	1		
Gottlieb	Sky Linc	1965	1		NRL, 5B, 6TRL, MOL, 1DB, PR-2000
Keeney	Sky Ray	1941	1		
Victory Games	Sky Rider	1944	1		Conversion Kit Pinball
Chicago Coin	Sky Rider	1974	4		3B, S, 4TRL
Bally	Sky Rocket	1971	2		PR-545
Europlay	Sky Star	1974	1	Italy	
I.D.I.	Sky Warrior	1983	4	Italy	
Williams	Skylab	1974	1		PR-3650
Chicago Coin	Skyline	1940	1		
Bally	Skyscrapre	1934	1		
Jennings	Skyway	1934	1		
Williams	Skyway	1954	1		One Flipper Only, LUS
Unidesa	Slalom Code 0.3	1988	4	Spain	
Victory Games	Slap The Japs	1943	1		Conversion Kit Pinball
Bally	Slapstick	1976	1		4F, 2B, PR-85
Sleic	Sleic Pin-Ball	1994	4	Spain	
Gottlieb	Slick Chick	1963	1		4DB, 5B, NOL, PR-4550
Williams	Slugfest	1952	1		
Gottlieb	Slugger	1938	1		
United	Slugger	1950	1		
Genco	Sluggers	1941	1		
Gottlieb	Sluggin Champ	1955	1		LUS, PR-950
Victory Games	Smack The Japs	1943	1		Conversion Kit Pinball
Williams	Smart Set	1969	4		3-Inch Flippers, UP, 4B, NRL, 3KO?, PR-4500
Williams	Smarty	1946	1		
Williams	Smarty	1968	1		5TRL, 3B, HS, NRL, ADB, PR-2200
Williams	Smoke Signal	1955	1		2B, 2DB, 1TRL, 1KO, LUS
Exhibit	Smokey	1947	1		NF
Williams	Snafu	1955	1		LUS
Chicago Coin	Snappy	1938	1		
Chicago Coin	Snappy	1941	1		
Stoner	Snooks	1939	1		
Williams	Snooks	1951	1		
Pacific Amusement	Snooky	1937	1		
Gottlieb	Snow Derby	1970	2		Same Play as Snow Queen, PR-1050
Gottlieb	Snow Queen	1970	4		3B, 4KO, 2S, 2-Inch Flippers, PR-1480
Genco	Soccer	1936	1		
Williams	Soccer	1964	2		PR-2850
Gottlieb	Soccer	1975	2		AB, 3B, 2S, 2KO, OG, PR-2900
Zaccaria	Soccer Kings	1982	4	Italy	V, DL, MT, 5F
Western Equipment	Sokit	1936	1		
Gottlieb	Solar City	1977	2		EM, 4F, 2B, 15DT, 2TRL, PR-2525
Williams	Solar Fire	1981	4		MB, MS, DL, 4F, CB, RS, 13DT, PR-782
Gottlieb	Solar Ride	1979	4		EM & SS Versions Released, 3F, 5DT, 3B, 4TRL, FD
Segasa / Sonic	Solar Wars	1986	4	Spain	
Williams	Solids & Stripes	1971	2		6KO, 5B, NRL, 3TRL
Gottlieb	Solitare	1967	1		

Williams	Sorcerer	1985	4		2MB, 3F, V, 2S, 3B, 3DT, 4TRL, RS, PR-3700
Chicago Coin	Sound Stage	1976	2		2B, EM, 2TRL, 1KO, PR-3000
Chicago Coin	South Pacifc	1964	2		
Genco	South Pacific	1950	1		
Genco	South Paw	1941	1		
United	South Seas	1945	1		Conversion Kit Pinball
Gottlieb	Southern Belle	1955	1		4TRL, 4B, 2DB, 2KO, LUS, PR-1000
Zaccaria	Space City	1979	1	Italy	
Micro Games	Space Fantasy	1977	U		
Playmatic	Space Gambler	1978	4	Spain	2B, S, 2MUSB, 2TRL- Light Tunnel In Backglass
Bell Games	Space Hawks	1985	4	Italy	3F, RS, NV, 4DT, Conversion Kit Pinball
Bally	Space Invaders	1980	4		WB, 4F, HS, 3B, 4DB, 3TRL, CB, S, 4DT, NLC, NV, PR-11400
Sega	Space Jam	1996	4		DM, RS, EP, LIC, 3DT, CB, 3B, VM
Williams	Space Mission	1976	4		Same play as Space Odyssey, PR-11652
Williams	Space Odyssey	1976	2		EM, 3TRL, S, 2B, NRL, MT, 2KO, HS, PR-4300
Gottlieb	Space Orbit	1972	1		3B, VT, 5TRL, PR-2100
R.M.G	Space Orbit	1972	1	Italy	
Maguinas / Mac Pinball	Space Panther	1988	4	Spain	Conversion Kit Pinball
Recel	Space Race	1977	4	Spain	EM, 10DT, 2B, MRL, 2TRL
Geiger	Space Rider	1981	4	Germany	
Atari	Space Riders	1978	4		WB, 3CB, 2S, MRL, 2KO, 3DT, 4TRL, 2B
Williams	Space Ship	1961	1		LUS, 3B, 4TRL, 2KO, PR-800
Unidesa	Space Ship	1986	4	Spain	
Zaccaria	Space Shuttle	1980	4	Italy	4B, 9DT, S, 3TRL, 1KO
Williams	Space Shuttle	1984	4		UP, RS, V, MB, 3TRL, 4DT, OG, 3B, 2KO, PR-7000
Unidesa	Space Shuttle	1986	4	Spain	Built Under License From Williams
Williams	Space Station	1988	4		RS, 3MB, AN
Tecnoplay	Space Team	1988	4	San Marino	
Bally	Space Time	1972	4		UP, 4B, NRL, Tunnel Feature on Playfield, PR-5000
Bensa	Space Time	1973	1	Italy	
Maguinas / Mac Pinball	Space Train	1987	4	Spain	Conversion Kit Pinball, AN, RS, 3B, 3TRL
Gottlieb	Space Walk	1979	2		PR-217, EM Version of Countdown
Geiger	Space Wars	1985	4	Germany	Conversion Kit For Bally's Eight Ball
Giuliano Lodola	Space Woman	1979	4	Italy	Copy of Gottlieb's Solar Ride
Williams	Spacelab	1974	1		PR-30
Playmatic	Spain 82	1982	4	Spain	
Williams	Spanish Eyes	1972	1		HS, ADB, 4B, 5TRL, NRL, PR 3905
Segasa / Sonic	Spanish Eyes	1973	1	Spain	
Williams	Spark Plugs	1951	1		AB, BFF, 6B, 7TRL
Stoner	Sparky	1941	1		
Bally	Speak Easy	1982	2		3B, 5TRL, 5FT, RW, S, ADB
Bally	Speak Easy 4	1982	4		Released Only In Germany
Playmatic	Speakeasy	1977	4	Spain	Same play as The 30'S
Bally	Special Entry	1947	1		NF
Bally	Special Force	1986	4		AN, RS, 3MB, 3B, 5DT, IDT
Bally	Special Force Girls	1986	4		Released In Germany - Copy of Special Force
A.B.T Mfg	Special-Jax	1933	1		
Valley	Spectra Iv	1978	4		Cocktail Table Style
Bally	Spectrum	1982	4		V, 2S, 12DT, 5KO, NOL, PR-994
G.B Daval	Speed	1937	1		
Bally	Speed Ball	1941	1		
Keeney	Speed Demon	1940	1		
Gottlieb	Speed King	1936	1		
Playmec Flippers	Speed Rush	1975	1	Italy	
Gottlieb	Speedway	1933	1		
Keeney	Speedway	1940	1		
Williams	Speedway	1948	1		
Exhibit	Speedy	1939	1		
Chicago Coin	Spellbound	1946	1		
Gottlieb	Spiderman	1980	4		2B, 4F, FD, 8DT, S, NV, NLC
Petaco	Spin A Card	1969	1	Spain	Copy Of Gottlieb's Spin-A-Card
Gottlieb	Spin Out	1975	1		5TRL, 2B, RT, PR-2850
Gottlieb	Spin Wheel	1968	4		5KO, 3B, NRL
Gottlieb	Spin-A-Card	1969	1		5TRL, 4B, 2KO, 2-Inch Flippers
Chicago Coin	Spinball	1948	1		
G.B Daval	Spinner	1938	1		
Bally	Spinner	1963	1		
Gottlieb	Spirit	1982	4		DL, 6F, 3MB, RS, FS, 6DT, 1B, 3KO
Micro Games	Spirit Of 76	1975	2		PR-125
Gottlieb	Spirit Of 76	1976	4		EM, 8DT, MRL, 3B, 3TRL, 1KO, PR-10300
Genco	Spit Fire	1935	1		
Williams	Spit Fire	1954	1		
Genco	Splash	1938	1		
Coincraft	Split Second	1935	1		
Stern	Split Second	1981	4		3MB, V, 4F, DL, S, 11DT, 2B, MRL, 3TRL
Chicago Coin	Spokes	1938	1		
Zaccaria	Spookey	1987	4	Italy	
Allied Leisure	Spooksville	1973	1		Shakerball Pinball
Unidesa	Sport 2000	1988	4	Spain	
Bally	Sport Event	1940	1		
Bally	Sport King	1940	1		
Chicago Coin	Sport Parade	1940	1		
Jennings	Sportland	1936	1		
Chicago Coin	Sports	1939	1		
Gottlieb	Sports Parade	1937	1		
Genco	Sportsman	1951	1		
Williams	Sportsman	1952	1		
Jennings	Sportsman Deluxe	1937	1		
Chicago Coin	Sporty	1940	1		
Gottlieb	Spot Bowler	1950	1		
G.B Daval	Spot- Lite	1935	1		
Gottlieb	Spot Pool	1941	1		
Gottlieb	Spot Pool	1955	1		LUS
Williams	Spot Pool	1959	1		LUS, WR
Gottlieb	Spot Pool	1976	1		EM, ADB
Gottlieb	Spot-A-Card	1941	1		
Gottlieb	Spot-A-Card	1960	1		3B, 2DB, MOL, 4KO, WR, DRS
Rex Mfg	Spot-Cha	1945	1		Conversion Kit Pinball
Bally	Spottem	1939	1		
Gottlieb	Spring Break	1987	4		4MB, 4F, AN, 9DT, 3B, 3TRL, RS
Genco	Spring Time	1952	1		
Chicago Coin	Springtime	1937	1		
Bally	Sprint	1937	1		
A.M.I	Sprint Girl	1976	1	Italy	
Bally	Spy Hunter	1984	4		4F, CB, NV, PR-2300
Rock-Ola	Squadron	1935	1		
Gottlieb	Square Head	1963	1		ADB, 5B, 4DB, PR-975
Chicago Coin	St Moritz Alps	1938	1		
Williams	St Louis	1949	1		
Chicago Coin	St Moritz	1938	1		
Keeney	Stable Mate	1938	1		
Chicago Coin	Stadium	1951	1		
Como	Stadium	1951	1		
Gottlieb	Stage Coach	1954	1		LUS, PR-650

Manufacturer	Name	Year	#	Country	Notes
Chicago Coin	Stage Coach	1968	4		3B, 3KO, NRL, UP, 2-Inch Flippers
Gottlieb	Stage Door Canteen	1946	1		PR - 7500
Rock-Ola	Stampede	1935	1		
Stern	Stampede	1977	2		EM, S, 2B, CB, 2KO, PR-1100
Williams	Star Action	1974	1		3B, SP
Chicago Coin	Star Attraction	1941	1		
Century Games	Star Battle	1978	2		Cocktail Table Style
Williams	Star Fighter	1983	U		Prototype Only Produced
Playmatic	Star Fire	1985	4	Spain	
Stern	Star Gazer	1980	4		NV, 3B, 3S, 9DT, NRL, PR-869
Zaccaria	Star God	1980	4	Italy	
Proma	Star Guard	1985	U		
Bally	Star Jet	1963	2		3B, 2DB, 2KO, 3TRL, 3MB, PR-1050
Williams	Star Light	1984	4		3B, 3TRL, S, 2MB
Recreativos Garcia	Star Light	1986	4	Spain	
Exhibit	Star Lite	1935	1		
Williams	Star Pool	1954	1		
Williams	Star Pool	1974	4		3B, SP, 4DT, OG
Gottlieb	Star Race	1980	4		WB, NV, 4F, 2B, 2VT, 4TRL, 7DT
Allied Leisure	Star Shooter	1979	4		Cocktail Table Style
Gottlieb	Star Trek	1971	1		3B, 2-Inch Flippers
Bally	Star Trek	1979	4		LIC, NV, 1KO, 3B, 4DT, 2TRL, PR-16842
Data East	Star Trek 25th Anniversary	1991	4		EP, DM, VM, V, RS, 3MB, LIC, KB, MT
Williams	Star Trek T.N.G.	1993	4		3F, MB, S, KB, 1DT, RS, DM, VM, EP, TS, BI, LIC
Game Plan	Star Trip	1978	4		Cocktail Table Style
Segasa / Sonic	Star Wars	1987	4	Spain	
Data East	Star Wars	1992	4		DM, VM, RS, EP, 3MB, KB, LIC, PR-10400
Sega	Star Wars Trilogy	1997	6		4B, VM, TS, 4DT, 3D Backglass, EP
United	Stardust	1948	1		
Williams	Stardust	1972	4		2KO, 5B, NRL, UP
Williams	Starfire	1956	1		LUS
Gottlieb	Stargate	1995	4		LIC
Glickman	Starlight	1944	1		Conversion Kit Pinball
Exhibit	Starlite	1940	1		
Exhibit	Starlite	1947	1		
Williams	Starlite	1953	1		
Exhibit	Stars	1941	1		
Stern	Stars	1978	4		SS, 6DT, 2S, 1B, PR-5127
Exhibit	Stars Jeep	1942	1		
Zaccaria	Stars Phoenix	1987	4	Italy	
Sega	Starship Troopers	1997	4		
Keeney	Startime	1961	1		
Genco	State Fair	1947	1		NF
United	Steeple Chase	1952	1		
Williams	Steeplechase	1957	1		LUS
Geiger	Stellar Airship	1980	4	Germany	
Williams	Stellar Wars	1979	4		WB, NV, CB, MRL, 5B, 4TRL, 7DT, 2S
Genco	Step Up	1934	1		
Genco	Step Up	1946	1		
Keeney	Stepper Upper	1938	1		
Williams	Still Crazy	1984	U		Prototype Only Produced
Stern	Stingray	1977	4		SS, 3B, 2KO, S, 5DT, PR-3006
Gottlieb	Stock Car	1970	1		ADB
G.B Daval	Stock Exchange	1936	1		
Genco	Stop And Go	1947	1		
Genco	Stop And Go	1951	1		
Genco	Stop N Go	1938	1		
Williams	Stop N Go	1964	2		
Playmatic	Stop Ship	1985	4	Spain	
Segasa / Sonic	Storm	1979	4	Spain	Similar To Williams As 'Flash'
Pacific Amusement	Stormy	1937	1		
Williams	Stormy	1948	1		
Gottlieb	Straight Flush	1957	1		LUS, WR
Williams	Straight Flush	1970	1		ADB, 3-Inch Flippers, UP, 5B, 1KO, NRL, 5TRL
Gottlieb	Straight Shooter	1959	1		LUS
G.B Daval	Strand	1937	1		
Bally	Strange Science	1986	4		3F, 5MB, RS, V, AN, PR-2350
Gottlieb	Strange World	1978	1		EM, 3B, NRL, 4TRL
Williams	Strato-Flite	1974	4		
Chicago Coin	Strat-O-Liner	1940	1		
Bally	Streamline	1934	1		
United	Streamliner	1944	1		Conversion Kit Pinball
Gottlieb	Street Fighter 2	1993	4		DM, 3MB, 3F, RS, Spinning Flipper
R.M.G	Strike	1973	1	Italy	
Zaccaria	Strike	1978	1	Italy	
Williams	Strike Zone	1970	2		4B, 4TRL, UP, OG, NRL
Gottlieb	Striker	1982	4		WB, 6F, 4B, 3TRL, 10DT, 2S, 2 OUTHOLES
Bally	Strikes And Spares	1978	4		PR-12820
Williams	Struggle Buggies	1953	1		DRS, 7DB, 1B, NOL
Williams	Student Prince	1968	4		ZF
Genco	Subway	1934	1		
Gottlieb	Subway	1966	1		Released Only In Italy, AB, NRL, ADB, 4B, 2DB
Genco	Subway Special	1934	1		
Elettrocoin	Summer Time	1970	1	Italy	Conversion Kit Pinball
Williams	Summer Time	1973	1		
Gottlieb	Summertime	1940	1		
United	Summertime	1948	1		
Exhibit	Sun Beam	1941	1		
United	Sun Valley	1942	1		Conversion Kit Pinball
Chicago Coin	Sun Valley	1962	2		
Rally	Sunday On Ice	1962	2	France	
Williams	Sunny	1947	1		
Giorgio Massiniero	Sun's Cruise	1976	1	Italy	
Gottlieb	Sunset	1962	2		MOL, CB, 4B, 2DB, 2TRL
Gottlieb	Sunshine	1958	1		LUS, WR
Stoner	Super 8	1934	1		
Gottlieb	Super Bowl	1969	1		
Bell Games	Super Bowl	1984	4	Italy	Conversion Kit Pinball
Inder	Super Bowling	1974	2	Spain	
Keeney	Super Charger	N/A	1		
Stoner	Super Chubbie	1941	1		
Gottlieb	Super Circus	1957	2		WR, 3B, 5TRL, DRS
Gottlieb	Super Duo	1967	1		
A.A Amusements	Super Flip	1987	1		VIDEO PINBALL IN PINBALL CABINET
Chicago Coin	Super Flipper	1975	1		
Chicago Coin	Super Hockey	1949	1		
Gottlieb	Super Jumbo	1954	4		DRS, 4B, 7TRL, NOL, PR-500
Gottlieb	Super Mario Brothers	1992	4		DM, VM, 3MB, DL, 3F, EP, UP
Game Plan	Super Nova	1982	4		PR-1000
Gottlieb	Super Orbit	1983	4		
Allied Leisure	Super Picker	1977	2		
Chicago Coin	Super Score	1946	1		
Williams	Super Score	1956	1		LUS
Gottlieb	Super Score	1967	2		RW, 4B, 1DB, NRL, MOL, 4F

Keeney	Super Six Of 40	1939	1		
Gottlieb	Super Soccer	1975	4		AB, 4TRL, 2S, 3B, 2KO, OG, Same Play as Soccer
Genco	Super Special	1933	1		
Gottlieb	Super Spin	1977	2		EM, Same Play as Jet Spin
Williams	Super Star	1972	1		NRL, UP, 4B, 3TRL, 1DT, 1KO
Chicago Coin	Super Star	1975	4		
Segasa / Sonic	Super Straight	1977	4	Spain	EM
C.E.A.	Super Tris	1979	1	Italy	
Playmatic	Super Win	1980	1	Spain	
Stoner	Super Zeta	1938	1		
Allcoin	Superbowl	1984	4		
Williams	Super-Flite	1974	2		
Gottlieb	Superliner	1946	1		
Atari	Superman	1979	4		WB, MRL, 5DT, 2S, 4TRL, 4B, NV
Zaccaria	Supersonic	1977	U	Italy	EM
Bally	Supersonic	1979	4		3B, S, OG, NV, 5TRL, 1KO, PR-10340
Buckley	Sure Shot	1936	1		
Gottlieb	Sure Shot	1976	1		EM, 5TRL, 3B, 2KO
Gottlieb	Surf And Safari	1991	4		V, 3MB, RS, AN
Gottlieb	Surf Champ	1976	4		EM, 5DT, 1KO, 4TRL, S, 2B
Bally	Surf Queens	1946	1		
Williams	Surf Rider	1956	4		
Gottlieb	Surf Side	1967	2		3B, NRL, RT, 2TRL, 4F
Gottlieb	Surfer	1976	2		EM, 5DT, 1KO, 4TRL, S, 2B
Bally	Surfers	1967	1		ZF, 3B, NRL, PR-908
Sega	Surfing	1976	1	Japan	
Bally	Suspense	1938	1		
Williams	Suspense	1946	1		
Williams	Suspense	1969	2		RW, 5B, NRL, 2KO, 2TRL, 4F
Exhibit	Swanee	1949	1		
Recel	Swashbuckler	1979	4	Spain	
Williams	Sweepstakes	1952	1		
Gottlieb	Sweet Add-A-Line	1955	1		LUS, PR-800
Gottlieb	Sweet Hearts	1963	1		5TRL, 5B, PR-4450
Alben	Sweet Sioux	1959	2	France	
Gottlieb	Sweet Sioux	1959	4		
T & M Sales	Sweet Sue	1948	1		Conversion Kit Pinball
Houston Showcase	Sweetheart	1933	1		
Williams	Sweetheart	1950	1		BFF, 2B, 2DB, 10KO, NOL
Houston Showcase	Sweetheart Double	1933	1		
Glickman	Sweethearts	1944	1		Conversion Kit Pinball
Chicago Coin	Swing	1938	1		
Gottlieb	Swing Along	1963	2		5TRL, 4B, 3S
Genco	Swing Time	1937	1		
Williams	Swing Time	1963	1		ADB, 5TRL, 3B, 2DB, 1KO
Williams	Swinger	1973	2		UP, NRL, 5B, 1KO, MT, OG, KB
Williams	Swords Of Fury	1988	4		DL, V, 4F, RS, AN, MB, HS
Chicago Coin	System	1936	1		
Allied Leisure	T.N.T.	1976	4		
Stoner	Tackle	1935	1		
Gottlieb	Tag Team Pinball	1985	4		WB, 3MB, 3F, AN
Nsm	Tag Team Pinball	1986	4	Germany	
Chicago Coin	Tahiti	1949	1		
Jack Rogers	Tahiti	1961	2	France	
Victory Games	Tail Gunner	1944	1		Conversion Kit Pinball
Bingo Novelty	Tailspin	1933	1		
Mondialmatic	Take A Card	1979	1	Italy	
Allied Leisure	Take Five	1977	2		Cocktail Table Style
Data East	Tales From The Crypt	1993	4		MB, VC, CB, EP, RS, DM, LIC, KB, S
Williams	Tales Of The Arabian Knights	1996	4		SP, Cage Save, MB, RS, BI, DM, 2CB, 3B
Exhibit	Tally Ho	1947	1		NF, 4KO
United	Tampico	1949	1		
Playmatic	Tam-Tam	1974	1	Spain	3B, 4F, 2TRL
Europlay	Tanga	1975	1	Italy	
Evans	Tango	1935	1		
Harry Hoppe Corp	Taps	1939	1		AB
Gottlieb	Target Alpha	1976	4		EM, 4F, 2B, 15DT, 2TRL
Gottlieb	Target Pool	1969	1		3TRL, 1B
Baker Novelty	Target Skill	1941	1		
Inder	Tasty Samba	1976	4	Spain	
Williams	Taxi	1988	4		V, AN, RS, 3MB, 6DT
Williams	Teachers Pet	1965	1		4KO, 3B, 2DB, 2DT, NRL, OG, PR-1600
Gottlieb	Team One	1977	1		EM, ADB, 10DT, MRL, 2B, 4TRL
Gottlieb	Tee'd Off	1993	4		CB, 3F, RW, MB, RS, 3DT, BO
Data East	Teenage Mutant Ninja Turtles	1991	4		WWS, RS, DM, CB, 3MB, EP, LIC
Star Machine	Teezer	1933	1		
Gottlieb	Telecard	1949	1		
Gustav Husemann	Tempo Tempo	1955	1	Germany	LUS
Chicago Coin	Temptation	1948	1		
Sega	Temptation	1977	1	Japan	
Bally	Ten Pin	1969	1		
Genco	Ten Spot	1941	1		
Williams	Ten Spot	1961	1		3B, MT, PR-900
Zaccaria	Ten Stars	1976	1	Italy	EM, Also Released as 2- and 4- Player
Gottlieb	Ten Up	1973	1		2KO, 10DT, 4F, 2B
Zaccaria	Ten Up	1974	4	Italy	
Llobregat	Tenis	1966	U	Spain	
Williams	Tennessee	1948	1		
United	Tenth Inning	1948	1		
Williams	Terminator 2 Judgment Day	1991	4		EP, DM, 3MB, RS, 3B, 1DT, KB, VM, TS, PR-15000
Marisel	Terry's	1968	1	Spain	
Alben	Texan	1960	4	France	
Gottlieb	Texan	1960	4		Also Released As A 2-Player Version
Gottlieb	Texas Mustang	1941	1		
Gottlieb	Texas Ranger	1972	1		
Playmatic	The 30's	1977	1	Spain	EM, AB, 3B, 5KO, Slot Machine Feature
Atari	The Atarians	1976	4		WB, 4F, FD, 7KO, 3B, 2OG
Mondialmatic	The Best Jump	1979	1	Italy	
Gottlieb	The Champ	1940	1		
Hankin	The Empire Strikes Back	1981	4	Australia	WB, 4F, 4DT, 2S, 4TRL, 4B, 2KO
Fascination Game	The Entertainer	1979	2		
Innovative Concepts	The Flinstones	1994	1		Oversize Children's Pinball DM, 3F, BFF, RS
Williams	The Flinstones	1994	4		3F, MB, EP, RS, DM, BI, LIC
Gottlieb	The Games	1984	4		4TRL, 4B, CB, 1KO
Nsm	The Games	1985	4	Germany	Copy of Gottlieb's game with same name
Williams	The Getaway-High Speed 2	1992	4		RS, 3MB, 3F, DM, VM, EP, Turbo Charger, KB
Recel	The Godfather	1974	4	Spain	
Bell Games	The Hunter	1980	4	Italy	3B, 5DT, 4TRL
Gottlieb	The Incredible Hulk	1979	4		NV, S, 2B, 4RTL, 7DT, PR-6150
Alben	The King	1959	4	France	
Bell Games	The King	1978	4	Italy	SS
Sega	The Lost World - Jurrasic Park	1997	4		VC, 2S, 4MB, SF, RS
Williams	The Machine Bride Of Pinbot	1991	4		V, MB, DL, AN, RS, S, Spinnning Ball Lock
Gottlieb	The New Champ	1941	1		

Bally	The President	1933	1		
Bally	The Shadow	1994	4		DM, VM, 3F, DL, MB, RS, Slide Flipper, BI, LIC
A.M.I	The Shark	1976	1	Italy	
Data East	The Simpsons	1990	4		V, RS, MB, AN, 3B, 8DT, LIC, S, 3KO
Chicago Coin	The Thing	1951	1		
Sega	The X-Files	1997	6		
Bally	Theatre Of Magic	1995	4		RS, DM, VM, CB, 1KO, S, MS, MB, BI, 3B
Segasa / Sonic	Third World	1978	4	Spain	
Bally	Thistledows	1938	1		
Gottlieb	Thoro-Bred	1965	2		2TRL, 6B, 1DB
Victory Sales	Thorobreds	1946	1		
C.E.A.	Three Aces	1979	4	Italy	
Williams	Three Coins (3 Coins)	1962	1		PR-1100
Williams	Three Deuces	1955	1		LUS
Genco	Three Feathers	1949	1		BFF, 1B
Grand Products	Three Hundred	1986	4		
Bally	Three In Line	1935	1		
Gottlieb	Three Musketeers	1949	1		
Chicago Vending	Three Point	1934	1		
Gottlieb	Three Score	1940	1		
Pacific Amusement	Three Star Special	1937	1		
Stoner	Three Up	1941	1		
Chicago Coin	Thrill	1948	1		
Chicago Coin	Thriller	1936	1		
Keeney	Thriller	1939	1		
Arco	Thumbs Up	1942	1		
Williams	Thunderball	1983	4		Prototype Only Produced
Williams	Thunderbird	1954	1		
Bally	Thunderbolt	1938	1		
Allied Leisure	Thunderbolt	1977	4		
Europlay	Tic & Toc	1974	1	Italy	
Stoner	Tick A Lite	1935	1		
Pacific Amusement	Ticket	1935	1		
Williams	Tic-Tac-Toe	1959	1		
Alben	Tierce	1964	2	France	
Gottlieb	Tiger	1975	1		
Bell Games	Tiger Rag	1984	1	Italy	Conversion Kit Pinball
I.D.I.	Tiger Woman	1982	4	Italy	
Chicago Coin	Tigers	1939	1		
Williams	Tim-Buc-Tu	1956	1		LUS
Pacific Amusement	Time	1935	1		
Atari	Time 2000	1977	4		WB, 4F, 2B, 2KO, NRL
Williams	Time Fantasy	1982	2		5TRL, 3B, HS, Bonus Timed Play, PR-608
Gottlieb	Time Line	1980	4		WB, NV, 4F, 14DT, 3B, MRL
Zaccaria	Time Machine	1983	4	Italy	V, Disappearing Bumper Platform
Data East	Time Machine	1988	4		RS, AN, 3MB, V
Bally	Time Tunnel	1972	4		
Williams	Time Warp	1979	4		BF, 3TRL, 5B, 8DT, NV, 2KO, PR-8875
Bally	Time Zone	1973	2		Same Play as Space Time, PR-2500
Chicago Coin	Times Square	1935	1		
Williams	Times Square	1953	1		6B, 4F, LUS
C.E.A.	Timothy	1977	4	Italy	SS
Chicago Coin	Tit For Tat	1935	1		
Gottlieb	Title Fight	1990	4		
Gottlieb	Tivoli	1968	1		
Gottlieb	Tko	1979	1		PR-125, EM, 3B, 2KO
Rock-Ola	TNT	1935	1		
Heinrich Santelmann	Toby Ball	1933	1	Germany	
Williams	Toledo	1976	2		EM, PR-3000
Williams	Tom Tom	1963	2		2MT, NOL, 4B, 1DB, 2TRL, PR-1300
Data East	Tommy	1993	4		3F, MB, CB, RS, DM, VM, Flipper Blinders, PR-3500
Gottlieb	Top Card	1974	1		3B, same play as Royal Pair
Western Equipment	Top' Em	1936	1		
Williams	Top Hand	1966	1		RT, 3B, 3TRL, NRL
Gottlieb	Top Hand	1973	1		16DT, 1B, 2TRL, same play as High Hand
R.M.G	Top Hand	1973	1	Italy	
Stoner	Top Hat	1935	1		
Williams	Top Hat	1958	2		
A.B.T Mfg	Top It	1936	1		
Bally	Top Notcher	1941	1		
Bell Games	Top Pin	1988	4	Italy	Conversion Kit Pinball
Recel	Top Racer	1976	1	Spain	EM
Gottlieb	Top Score	1975	2		AB, S, 2B, 2TRL
Recel	Top Speed	1975	4	Spain	
Chicago Coin	Top Ten	1975	2		Same play as Gold Record
Inder	Topaz	1979	4	Spain	
Bally	Topic	1941	1		
Chicago Coin	Topper	1939	1		
Gottlieb	Torch	1980	4		NV, RT, 10DT, 2B, 2TRL
Williams	Torchy	1947	1		NF
Gottlieb	Toreador	1956	2		DRS
Williams	Tornado	1947	1		NF
Recel	Torneo	1978	1	Spain	Single Ball Play, SS
Rally	Toro	1963	2	France	
Jennings	Torpedo	1936	1		
Keeney	Torpedo	1936	1		
Petaco	Torpedo	1976	1	Spain	EM, VT
Data East	Torpedo Alley	1988	4		3F, 3MB, AN, V, 3TRL, 3B, RS
P & S Machine Co	Torpedo Patrol	1943	1		Conversion Kit Pinball
Genco	Total Roll	1945	1		
Rock-Ola	Totalite	1936	1		
G.B Daval	Totalizer	1937	1		
Gottlieb	Totem	1979	4		NV, VT, 6DT, 2B, 1KO, 4TRL, MRL
Inder	Touch	1973	1	Spain	
Chicago Coin	Touch Off	1936	1		
Williams	Touchdown	1967	1		5B, 2DB, NRL, PR-2253
Gottlieb	Touchdown	1984	4		
Mills Novelty	Tournament	1937	1		
Gottlieb	Tournament	1955	2		BFF, 3B, 4DB, DRS, PR-600
Exhibit	Track Meet	1937	1		
Gottlieb	Track Record	1939	1		
Chicago Coin	Track Stars	1937	1		
United	Trade Winds	1945	1		Conversion Kit Pinball
Genco	Trade Winds	1948	1		
Williams	Trade Winds	1962	1		3B, 4TRL, PR-1250
Bally	Traffic Model	1935	1		
Bally	Trail Drive	1970	1		3B, NRL, 2KO, 4MUSB
Playmatic	Trailer	1985	4	Spain	
Bally	Trailways	1941	1		
Williams	Tramway	1974	4		
Rock-Ola	Trans-Atlantic	1936	1		
Bally	Transporter	1989	4		V, AN, 6DT, RS, 3F, KB, 3B
Rock-Ola	Trap Shot	1936	1		
Gottlieb	Trapeze	1940	1		

Manufacturer	Title	Year		Country	Notes
Exhibit	Trapper	1936	1		
Peo Mfg	Travel	1935	1		
Giorgio Massiniero	Travel Agency	1976	1	Italy	
Segasa / Sonic	Travel Time	1973	1	Spain	Same play as Williams' game of same name
Williams	Travel Time	1973	1		TP, 3B, 1KO, NRL, PR-3450
Exhibit	Treasure Chest	1947	1		
Regama	Trebol 1	1986	U	Spain	
Treff Automaten	Treff-Gloria	1953	1	Germany	Water Ski Theme, 6BFF, 8DB, 1KO, LUS
Treff Automaten	Treff-Gloria	1953	1	Germany	Speed Boat Theme, 6BFF, 8DB, 1KO, LUS
Genco	Tri Score	1951	1		BFF, 5KO, 2B
Williams	Tri Zone	1979	4		NV, PR-7250, 3B, S, 4DT, 2TRL
Genco	Tri-A-Lite	1933	1		
Atari	Triangle	1976	4		WB?
Genco	Tricks	1936	1		
Stern	Trident	1979	4		NV
Exhibit	Trigger	1951	1		
Chicago Coin	Trinidad	1948	1		
Bally	Trio	1965	1		
Genco	Triple Action	1948	1		
Segasa / Sonic	Triple Action	1974	1	Spain	
Williams	Triple Action	1974	1		3B, SP, PR-3828
Genco	Triple Play	1938	1		
Glickman	Triple Play	1944	1		Conversion Kit Pinball
Williams	Triple Strike	1975	1		PR-3376
G.B Daval	Triple Threat	1939	1		
Gottlieb	Triplets	1950	1		
Bally	Triumph	1940	1		
Rock-Ola	Trojan	1935	1		
Chicago Coin	Trophy	1938	1		
Bally	Trophy	1948	1		
Williams	Tropic Fun	1973	1		Same play as Gulfstream, PR-1100
Gottlieb	Tropic Isle	1962	1		4B, 5TRL
Bally	Tropic Queens	1960	U		NF, 10DB
United	Tropicana	1948	1		
Glickman	Tropics	1944	1		Conversion Kit Pinball
Gottlieb	Troubadour	1967	1		
Bally	Truck Stop	1988	4		4F, 2MB, RS, V, AN
Exhibit	Tumbleweed	1949	1		
Tura	Tura Ball	1933	1	Germany	
Tura	Tura Derby	1934	1	Germany	
Bergmann & Co	Turf	1957	1	Germany	
Williams	Turf Champ	1958	1		WR, 6B, NOL, 6TRL, animated playfield, LUS
Bergmann & Co	Turf Derby	1958	1	Germany	
Chicago Coin	Turf King	1937	1		
Bally	Turf King	1941	1		
Chicago Coin	Turf Queens	1938	1		
Gottlieb	Turn Table	1935	1		
Jentzsch & Meerz	Turnier	1935	1	Germany	
Williams	Tuscon	1949	1		
Genco	Twentieth Century	1933	1		
Williams	Twenty Grand	1952	1		
Gottlieb	Twenty One	1937	1		
Rock-Ola	Twenty-One	1935	1		
Mc And D	Twenty-One	1948	1		
Williams	Twentyone (21)	1960	1		WR, 4TRL, 2KO, 3B, 2DB
Rock-Ola	Twenty-One-Thousand (21,000)	1936	1		
Bally	Twilight Zone	1993	4		4F, DL, DM, RS, power ball, LIC
Gottlieb	Twin Bill	1955	1		LUS, PR-800
Recel	Twin Gain	1977	1	Spain	EM, 2B, 2VT, 2TRL
Keeney	Twin Six	1941	1		
Victory Games	Twin Six	1946	1		Conversion Kit Pinball
Bally	Twin Win	1974	2		4F, 2KO, 2B, 4MUSB, WWS, no plunger
Baker Novelty	Twinkle	1939	1		
Chicago Coin	Twinky	1967	2		3B, 2KO, NRL
Bally	Twist	1962	1		
Rally	Twist	1963	2	France	4F, 4B, 2KO, 3TRL
Sega	Twister	1996	4		WWS, RS, DM, MB, LIC, 2S
C & S Novelty	Two Bells	1945	1		Conversion Kit Pinball
Pacific Amusement	Two Five Twenty	1935	1		
Bally	Two In One (2 In 1)	1964	2		PR-1060
Gottlieb	Tx-Sector	1988	4		3F, V, 2MB, AN
Bally	U.S.A	1958	1		LUS, WR, NF
Alvin G. & Co	U.S.A Football	1992	2		Two Player Head-To-Head, 6F, AN, 4S.
Bell Games	U-Boat 65	1988	4	Italy	
Playmatic	Ufo-X	1984	4	Spain	
Stoner	Ump	1941	1		
Recel	Underwater	1976	4	Spain	EM
Universal Novelty	Universe	1933	1		
Gottlieb	Universe	1959	1		DRS, WR, AB, 3B, 6TRL, 4F
Zaccaria	Universe	1977	4	Italy	EM
Keeney	Up And Up	1939	1		
Inder	Up Away	1975	1	Spain	
United	Utah	1949	1		
Pin-Ball	Utran	1977	1		
Bally	Vacation	1940	1		
Williams	Vagabond	1962	1		ADB, 1DT, 4B, PR-600
Williams	Valencia	1976	4		EM
Williams	Valiant	1962	2		4F, 2MT, 4KO, PR-1050
Jeutel	Valkyrie	1982	4	France	PR-100
Bally	Vampire	1971	2		UP, NRL, 3B, PR-799
Exhibit	Vanities	1947	1		NF
Gottlieb	Varasity	1935	1		
Bally	Variety	1939	1		
Williams	Varkon	1982	2		Video cabinet style, PR-90
Bally	Vector	1982	4		4F, DL, V, 3MB, 9DT, 4KO, RS, PR-3500
Game Plan	Vegas	1979	4		
Gottlieb	Vegas	1990	4		RT, 3B, 5DT, 2KO, 2TRL, PR-1500
Pinstar	Velocity Ball	1986	4		
Keeney	Velvet	1936	1		
Keeney	Velvet	1941	1		
Chicago Coin	Venus	1941	1		
Jolux	Venus	1969	4	France	
Recreativos Franco	Venus 5	1973	1	Spain	
Westerhaus	Victorious 1943	1943	1		Conversion Kit Pinball
Westerhaus	Victorious 1944	1944	1		Conversion Kit Pinball
Westerhaus	Victorious 1945	1945	1		Conversion Kit Pinball
Genco	Victory	1941	1		
Gottlieb	Victory	1987	4		PBG, 4F, RS, AN, PR-3315
Bally	Victory	1939	1		
Bally	Victory Special	1946	1		
Bally	Viking	1980	4		1DT, 7DT, S, 2KO, 4B, PR-2600
Williams	Vikings	1960	2		
Stern	Viper	1981	4		3MB, 3F, WB
Sega	Viper - Night Driving	1998	6		
Williams	Virginia	1948	1		
Stoner /	Vogue	1938	1		
Bally	Vogue	1939	1		

Manufacturer	Name	Year	Players	Country	Notes
Gottlieb	Volcano	1981	4		WB, MB, 3F, V, 10DT, 4B, PR-3655
Gottlieb	Volley	1976	1		EM, 3B, 15DT, 3TRL, PR-2900
Bally	Voltan	1979	4		3B, 2S, 4TRL, NV, PR-365
Gottlieb	Vulcan	1977	4		EM, 2B, 4TRL, 9DT, same play as Fire Queen, PR-3575
Alben	Wagon Train	1960	1	France	
Gottlieb	Wagon Train	1960	1		RT, WR, 3B, 1TRL, DRS
United	Wagon Wheels	1945	1		Conversion Kit Pinball
Stoner	Waldorf	1933	1		
Joctronic	Walkaria	1986	4	Spain	
Viza Manufacturing	War	1978	2		Cocktail Table Style
Williams	Warlok	1983	4		PR-412, 3B, 3TRL, S, 6DT
Gottlieb	Watch My Line	1951	1		NF, Bingo Style Pinball
Gottlieb	Water World	1995	4		LIC, PR-1500
Rally	West Club	1967	2	France	Digital Scoring
A.M.I	West Show	1976	1	Italy	
Exhibit	West Wind	1941	1		
Globe	Westbound	1935	1		
Gottlieb	Western	1969	2		
Dama	Western	1970	1	Italy	Conversion Kit Pinball
Western Equipment	Wheel Of Fortune	1936	1		
Midway	Wheels 2	1975	4		
Peerless Products	Whiffle	1935	1		
Exhibit	Whirl Pool	1935	1		
Gottlieb	Whirl Wind	1958	2		DRS, WR
Roy Mcginnis	Whirlaway	1943	1		Conversion Kit Pinball
Victory Games	Whirlaway	1943	1		Conversion Kit Pinball
Victory Sales	Whirlaway	1943	1		Conversion Kit Pinball
Williams	Whirlwind	1990	4		AN, BO, 3F, 3MB, WWS, RS
Unidesa	White Force	1987	4	Spain	
Bally	White Sails	1939	1		
Bell Games	White Shark	1980	4	Italy	Conversion Kit Pinball
Williams	White Water	1993	4		3MB, RS, 3F, DL, DM, BO
Genco	Whizz	1946	1		Vertical Pinball
Chicago Coin	Whizz Kids	1952	1		
Bally	Whodunit A Murder Mystery	1995	4		RS, MB, Slot Machine on Playfield
Williams	Whoopee	1964	4		4B, 1DB, 5CB, PR-2075
Bally	Wiggler	1967	4		3MB, ZF, 3B, 3TRL, 2KO, NRL, 3MUSB, PR-3410
Bensa	Wild Boy	1974	1	Italy	
Williams	Wild Card	1977	1		EM, 2B, 3KO, PR-901
Keeney	Wild Cargo	1934	1		
Keeney	Wild Fire	1941	1		
Stern	Wild Fyre	1978	4		S, 3B, 3DT, 4KO, MRL, 7DT, PR-2400
Gottlieb	Wild Life	1972	2		1B, S, 3TRL, OG, PR-3875
Gottlieb	Wild West	1951	1		
Bally	Wild Wheels	1966	2		4TRL, 7MUSB, OG, 3B, RT, NRL, PR-580
Gottlieb	Wild Wild West	1969	2		5B, NRL, 2VT, PR-1350
Geiger	Wildschutz	1980	4	Germany	Also released as a 2 Player game
Exhibit	William Tell	1936	1		
Alben	Win A Card	1964	2	France	
Western Equipment	Windjammer	1938	1		
Buckley	Windy City	1933	1		
Williams	Wing Ding	1964	1		AB, ADB, 5TRL, 3KO, 3B, MOL
Chicago Coin	Wing Lite	1935	1		
Rock-Ola	Wings	1933	1		
Exhibit	Wings	1940	1		
A.B.T Mfg	Winner	1934	1		
Western Equipment	Winner	1937	1		
Universal	Winner	1950	1		
Williams	Winner	1972	2		TS, 4F
Sega	Winner	1976	1	Japan	3B, 5TRL, NRL, 1KO
Zaccaria	Winter Sports	1978	4	Italy	SS
Gottlieb	Wipe Out	1993	4		RS, DL, MB, DM, PR-2150
United	Wisconsin	1948	1		
Gottlieb	Wishing Well	1955	1		LUS, 4TRL, 3B, PR-1050
Genco	Wizard	1937	1		
Gottlieb	Wizard	1971	1		Released only in Italy, 3B, NRL, 5TRL
Bally	Wizard	1975	4		PR-10005, 3B, S, flip flag feature
Peyper	Wolf Man	1987	4	Spain	2CB, 4DT, 3B
Williams	Wonderland	1955	1		LUS
Zaccaria	Wood's Queen	1976	1	Italy	EM, also released as 2- and 4-Player
Gottlieb	World Beauties	1960	1		LUS, WR
Gottlieb	World Challenge Soccer	1994	4		DM, 3F, MD, R5, 4KO, 10DT, PR-1470
Gottlieb	World Champ	1957	1		WR, LUS
Williams	World Cup	1978	4		SS, 3TRL, 2B, S, NRL, 2KO, PR-6253
Mr Game	World Cup 90	1990	4	Italy	Pistol Grip Flipper Buttons
Bally	World Cup Soccer	1994	4		KB, S, MS, MB, RS, DM, Spinning Ball, BI, 3B, MT
Bell Games	World Defender	1984	4	Italy	Conversion Kit Pinball
Gottlieb	World Fair	1964	1		5TRL, 5DB, 5B, PR-4650
Victory Games	World Series	1944	1		Conversion Kit Pinball
Gottlieb	World Series	1972	1		ADB, PR-775
Bontempi	World Star	N/A	U	Italy	
Bally	World's Fair	1938	1		
Rock-Ola	World's Fair Jig-Saw	1933	1		PR- 70,000
Rock-Ola	World's Series	1934	1		
Stoner	Wow	1941	1		
Tecnoplay	X Force	1986	4	San Marino	
Bally	Xenon	1980	4		2MB, V, RS, S, 2KO, 4DT, PR-11000
Bally	X's And O's	1984	4		PR-3300
Chicago Coin	Yacht Club	1940	1		
Inder	Yale	1974	1	Spain	
Marvel	Yankee Doodle	1943	1		Conversion Kit Pinball
Chicago Coin	Yanks	1942	1		
Williams	Yanks	1948	1		
Llobregat	Yazine	1967	1	Spain	
Williams	Yukon	1971	1		ADB, 5B, 5DT same play as Klondike, PR-30
United	Yuma Arizona	1950	1		
Zaccaria	Zankor	1986	4	Italy	
G.B Daval	Zenith	1936	1		
Bally	Zephyr	1938	1		
Bally	Zephyr Junior	1938	1		
Stoner	Zeta	1938	1		
Treff Automaten	Ziel	1954	1	Germany	
Genco	Zig Zag	1941	1		
Williams	Zig Zag	1964	1		PR-1675
Williams	Zingo	1944	1		Vertical Pinball
Genco	Zip	1938	1		
Exhibit	Zip	1939	1		
Bally	Zip-A-Doo	1970	2		UP, 4TRL, 4B, NRL, 1KO, PR-1083
Stoner	Zipper	1938	1		
Playmatic	Zira	1980	4	Spain	
Williams	Zodiac	1971	2		4F, SP, NRL, PR-704 -
Exhibit	Zombie	1940	1		
Stoner	Zoom	1935	1		
Giuliano Lodola	Zoser	1981	4	Italy	Copy of Williams' Pharaoh

Chapter Thirteen

Silverball Statistics

What can one do with over 3000 pinball names, dates, 180 companies, and ten different countries? Most will know for certain that the majority of pinballs have been built in the U.S.A, but what percentage exactly? With the aid of a computer and a database of information like the previous list, one can extract such information at the touch of a button or two. Seven graphs (or graph types to be precise) have been drawn to give a visual representation of the most obvious questions you may have had.

All information on each of the graphs has been obtained from Chapter Twelve, and therefore, is only as accurate as the list itself. As briefly mentioned in the previous chapter, one can only estimate this accuracy. I know for certain that it is not 100% complete within itself (approximately 1% of pinballs listed have no date of manufacture, for example), and absolutely positive that it does not list every pinball that has ever been built. I am quite certain of this because, during the course of compiling this book, I have had to update the list several times. Like the old story goes, just when one thinks one has everything covered...!

Most of the graphs will be easy to understand at a glance, though some will be better understood with a bit of explanation. One thing common to all the graphs, however, is that none will include any prototype pinballs shown, which counts for approx 1% of games on the list. Another common, and more important factor, is the use of "game name" quantities only, and not total production run quantities. This is because the production runs for a large percentage of pinballs shown on the list are not known, and therefore it is obvious that graphs cannot be drawn. Although these types of graphs would provide a better representation of the pinball world and its history, it is unlikely that such complete information is ever going to surface for a large majority of games. Production quantities have become something of a Holy Grail, treasured as important information among pinball collectors.

GRAPH ONE: World Pinball Production 1933-1998. A simple graph showing the percentage split between pinballs built in the U.S.A and the rest of the world. This graph leads on to Graph Two.

GRAPH TWO: "Other Countries" Pinball Production. A percentage per country split of the total number of pinballs built outside the U.S.A.

GRAPH THREE: The Pinball Trade Timeline. A slightly unconventional graph showing 42 of the better-known and longest-lived companies, covering their life span in the field of pinball production. The data shown for each company represents the period of time from the first listed pinball to the last. With the exception of Sega, the companies chosen were those with pinball production spanning four years and over.

GRAPH FOUR: The Silverball Merchants. Another pie graph, this time showing the percentage distribution of the number of pinballs produced by each company. The top 17 biggest manufacturers (Data East and Sega counted as one) are represented against the rest of the companies appearing on the list. One can clearly see the "big three" (Bally, Gottlieb, and Williams) making up almost 50% of the total.

GRAPH FIVE: The Pinball Decades. The last of the pie graphs showing the percentage split of pinballs produced within each decade. One can see the drastic cuts in game production during the last three decades, almost reducing by half each time, taking into account that the last decade is still not complete. A breakup of each decade is shown in bar graph form in Graph Six.

GRAPH SIX: Average Yearly Pinball Production (A.Y.P.P.). The best has been left for last. Undoubtedly my favorite graph, one which I spent more time on than any other. It shows the average yearly pinball production at any particular point in time between 1935 and 1999 (plotted at two-year intervals) and also

reflects, to some extent, the relative ups and downs in game popularity. For example, it clearly shows the rise and fall of the game during the late 1970s. Unfortunately, this, and the entire graph, would have been more pronounced and visually correct if it had the benefit of total production run volumes rather than just the number of game types/names produced. The graph is basically a simple timeline where one can see how many new games were produced each year, or more importantly how many new games one would have expected to see and play in the course of that year. Included in the graph are twenty event markers, detailing historical occurrences relating to pinball. You may wish to add your own! Their contents are as follows.

1) January 1937: The coil bumper is introduced on Bally's BUMPER.

2) September 1939: World War II begins.

3) August 1945: World War II ends.

4) October 1947: The flipper is introduced on Gottlieb's HUMPTY DUMPTY.

5) October 1948: Powered thumper bumpers introduced.

6) 1951: Bingo machines introduced by United Manufacturing and Bally to fill the void left by the banning of all payout pinballs. The slide in production from 1949 to 1951 extending to 1955 was due to the withdrawal of companies like Bally, Chicago Coin, United, Genco and Exhibit, who halted pinball production (due to market saturation) to concentrate on building other arcade machines like baseball games, bowling machines and, of course, bingos.

7) October 1953: First appearance of drum reel scoring on pinballs, introduced by Williams.

8) October 1954: Gottlieb releases SUPER JUMBO, the first multiple-player pinball game.

9) October 1960: Gottlieb introduces the add-a-ball pinball concept on FLIPPER.

10) December 1963: Williams and Bally introduce the modern form of multiball play (BEAT THE CLOCK and STAR JET respectively), where the player is required to "lock" balls on the playfield.

11) August 1968: The first use of 3" flippers on American pinballs.

12) April 1969: British rock group *The Who* releases *Tommy*, an album that features a rock opera about a deaf, dumb, and blind kid. The most popular song of that album was Pinball Wizard, which is now considered one the top rock'n'roll songs of all time.

13) 1972: Nutting industries produces *COMPUTER SPACE*, the first coin-operated video game. The video game army is beginning to form.

14) Mid-1975: Micro industries produces SPIRIT OF 76, the first non-relay based solid state pinball using microchip technology. By looking at the graph at this point in time, it seems that a pinball boom had commenced approximately two years prior. This is contrary to the belief that the pinball boom of the 70s had started with the introduction of SS technology.

15) October 1978: Midway manufacturing introduces *SPACE INVADERS*, the coin-operated video game that took the world by storm and signaled the decline in pinball popularity. There was even a song on the pop charts!

16) November 1980: Midway manufacturing unveils *PAC-MAN*, the game that became the most popular game in the history of coin operated amusement machines. It, too, had a song on the charts at the time. **December 1980:** Williams builds BLACK KNIGHT, one of the most successful pinballs during the period, but as one can see, the downward trend had already started.

17) May 1985: Alphanumeric displays first used on Gottlieb's CHICAGO CUBS TRIPLE PLAY. The downward trend finally stops.

18) February 1991: The dot matrix display is first introduced on CHECKPOINT by Data East.

19) February 1992: ADDAMS FAMILY by Bally becomes the biggest selling game in the history of postwar pinball with a production run of over 21,000 units.

20) Mid 1996: Gottlieb, longtime pinball manufacturer, produces its last pinball. A sad end to the graph and to a company that for many years was the driving name behind the game.

GRAPH 1: WORLD PINBALL PRODUCTION 1933 TO 1998

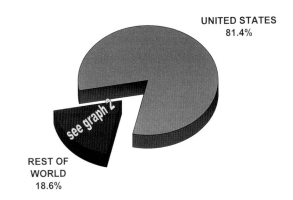

World pinball production 1933 to 1998. Graph does not include prototype pinballs from list. Graph volume equals 3057 units.

GRAPH 2: REST OF WORLD PINBALL PRODUCTION

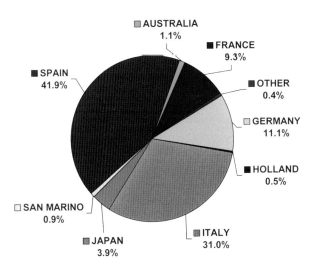

Rest of world pinball production. Graph does not include prototype pinballs from list. Graph represents the percentage split of 568 pinballs, which is 18.6% of the total world production.

GRAPH 4: THE SILVERBALL MERCHANTS

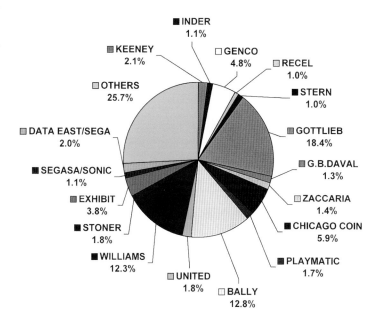

The silverball merchants. Graph represents the percentage split of the top 17 major companies (totaling production of 1% and over) against the "other" 173 manufacturers who have produced pinballs between 1933 and 1998.

GRAPH 5: THE PINBALL DECADES

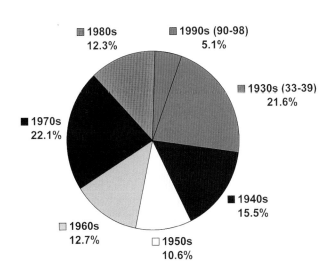

The pinball decades. Graph represents the percentage of pinballs produced in each decade from a total 2897 units out of a possible 2925 (28 games listed with unknown date). Graph does not include prototype or conversion kits, which total 156 units. Graph does not represent actual production run volumes.

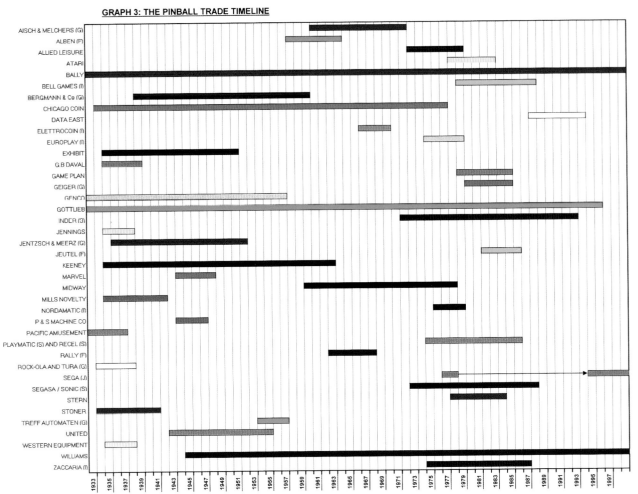

The pinball trade timeline. All companies listed are from the U.S.A., unless noted as follows: France (F), Italy (I), Germany (G), Spain (S) and Japan (J).

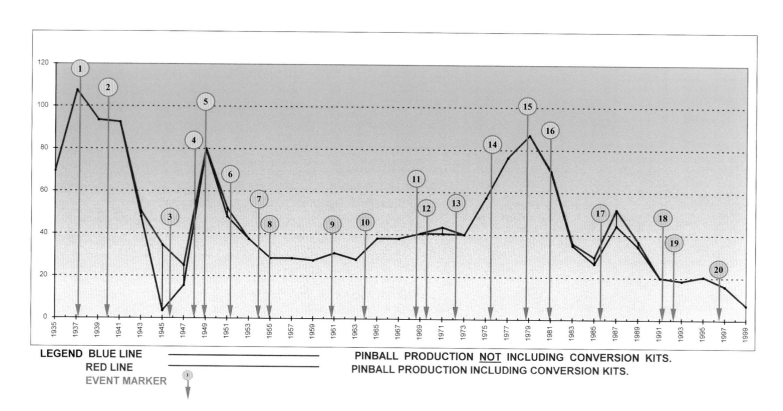

LEGEND **BLUE LINE** ——————————— PINBALL PRODUCTION **NOT** INCLUDING CONVERSION KITS.

RED LINE ——————————— PINBALL PRODUCTION INCLUDING CONVERSION KITS.

EVENT MARKER

This graph represents the average yearly pinball production between the start of 1935 and the end of 1998, calculated at two-year intervals. Graph uses 2897 listed pinballs out of a possible 2925 (28 pinballs listed with unknown date) for the blue line. An additional 131 listed conversion kits are used for the red line. Graph does not include prototype pinballs from list. Graph represents the average yearly number of pinball types produced and not the total production run volume.

Which is considered to be the world's best-known pinball to this day? Is it Gottlieb's HUMPTY DUMPTY? Within the world community of pinball fans maybe, but outside of that it is doubtful. It could be Bally's ADDAMS FAMILY or Williams' TERMINATOR II. They have certainly had good player response, well known movie tie-ins, and have been in many locations worldwide. I think we are getting close, it is hard to say exactly. If we decided to broaden our field to encompass video and computer pinball games, then there is no question as to which is the world's best known (or should we say most played) pinball game at this point in time; Maxis' Space Cadet 3D pinball which was included as a free game on Microsoft's Windows 95 Microsoft Plus software packages.

Computers these days are everywhere, at work or at home; if you don't have one yourself, then you know someone who does. Since its release in 1995, even if just the English speaking world is taken into consideration, how many millions of people have had some form of exposure to this particular game if only just to play it once? Ten million; twenty million?

It is ironic that the video/computer games, which almost drove the pinball industry into the ground, have in this case introduced pinball to so many people, that it would have been otherwise impossible for actual pinball manufacturers to achieve the same exposure for one of their own games. People who own a computer and have never played a real pinball before can at least become familiar with the game by playing the equivalent of a pinball simulator. Unknowingly, 3D pinball on Microsoft Plus has become a kind of tribute to the 20th Century's ultimate amusement machine.

1972 was the year when the first coin-operated video games were introduced into the arcade scene. These video pioneers, with their black and white T.V. monitors, as primitive as they seem today, astounded both players and by-standers alike (by-standers like mum and dad for instance, who considered themselves too old to play those sort of games). An appealing aspect of those first games, now long forgotten, was the ability to interact with the images on a T.V. No longer was the king of household appliances just the "sit down and watch" version, a different kind of T.V.— where one controlled the action—could be found at the local pinball parlor!

The first big hit at the start of the video game age in 1972 (like the song "The dawning of the age of Aquarius" by the Fifth Dimension) was Atari's *PONG. PONG*, like the name suggests, was a bat and ball Ping-Pong game where opposing players could make a ball (which was actually square) bounce off a long rectangular bat which was under their control. With the use of a knob on the console, one could move the bat only up or down the T.V. screen. Other companies soon produced their own pong-style games; like Williams' *PRO TENNIS* and *PADDLE BALL* and Allied Leisure's *PADDLE BATTLE*.

The lack of diversity with these first "T.V. games" made their popularity slide a fraction between 1973 and 1975, in comparison to the remarkable increase in appeal of pinballs. Video game popularity decreased even further when SS pinballs were introduced

Allied Leisure's SUPER SOCCER (1973). Don't let the name fool you, it was just another PONG-style game. After the success of Atari's PONG in 1972, other major companies came out with their own versions. They were all basically clones of the original, with slight modifications and attention-grabbing names.

between 1976 and 1978. The change in fortunes for both pinballs and video games came in October 1978 with the release of the video game *SPACE INVADERS*, and the rest is history.

Between *PONG* and *SPACE INVADERS* the video game was in no man's land. In amusement arcades where prime floor space was reserved for banks of pinball machines, the video game, still barely holding on to its novelty status, could be found in amongst the iron claw machines, electromechanical rifle games and driving games. It was during this time that the video pinball emerged. One could say that the video material used on these early video pinnics was taken from games like *PONG*. The bats in *PONG* were rearranged to some extent into flippers, but the square ball remained the same. By adding a few simple scoring devices like a bumper or two and then a plunger perhaps, the pinball simulator was born.

Chicago Coin's
TV PINGAME
one or two players

It's the industry's most revolutionary new game.

Let TV PINGAME start gathering crowds for you. It's a game with long and lasting drawing power! From start to finish, it was designed with the operator in mind.

- ADJUSTABLE for free game or extra ball.
- 25¢ play. Adjustable for two games 25¢. Also three games for two quarters.
- 5 BALLS—adjustable to three balls per game.
- GAME plays itself to attract attention when not in use.
- COMPACT cabinet.
- TV PINGAME can be operated anywhere, even in locations where pin balls are not.
- BALL changes speed and direction. No two games play alike—just like regulation flipper game.

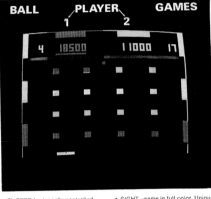

- FLIPPER horizonally controlled, rebounds ball right, left, or straight up.
- 16 BUMPERS. Knock them out and score 100 points each. Knock them all out for a bonus of 8000 points. Game continues with 16 new bumpers.
- 9 POCKETS. Hit pockets and score 100 points or lose ball in lower corner pockets.
- MOVING TARGET moves across top of screen. Hit it and score 2000 points.
- BALL COUNT and GAME CREDITS, as well as DIGITAL SCORES, displayed on screen.

- SIGHT—game in full color. Unique color overlay on standard TV screen.
- SOUND—has real chimes plus realistic pin ball electronic sounds.

DIMENSIONS:
Height: 61" Width: 23"
Depth: 24" Weight: 225 lbs.

WARRANTY:
Six months—logic board.
Three months—TV monitor.

Chicago Coin
1725 West Diversey Chicago, Illinois 60614

Chicago Coin's TV PINGAME (1973). Despite the name and the advertising hype, this game was nothing more than a one-player version of PONG with targets. Pinball simulators still had a long way to go.

Chicago Coin's
ONE-PLAYER
SUPER FLIPPER

PIN GAME PLAY WITH REAL FLIPPER BUTTONS AND BALL SHOOTER --
FAST, HIGH-SCORING ACTION --
TV SIGHT, SOUND AND MOTION --
ALL IN A HANDSOME PIN GAME CABINET . . .

AND YOU CAN OPERATE IT ANYWHERE!

SCORING OPPORTUNITIES ALL OVER THE SCREEN!

PLAYER INFORMATION IN DIGITAL READOUTS ON COLORFUL BACKGLASS.

5 BALLS. Convertible to 3-Ball Play, Add-a-Ball or Replay.

25¢ PLAY, Adjustable to 2/25¢ or 3/50¢.

ALL SOLID STATE!
WARRANTY:
Logic Board—6 Months
TV Monitor—3 Months

Shipping Dimensions and Weights:		
Height:	50"	127 CM
Length:	30"	76.6 CM
Width:	27"	68.5 CM
Weight:	241 LBS.	109.32 KG

Chicago Coin
1725 West Diversey/Chicago, Illinois 60614

Where Exclusive Guarantees and Quality Control Protect Your Profits

Chicago Coin's SUPER FLIPPER (1975), a video pinball in a pinball cabinet with flipper buttons and a real plunger. Chicago Coin took a step in the right direction by housing the game in a pinball cabinet, but the gameplay itself was still primitive and very unpinball like.

One of the first out of a very few video pinballs designed as arcade machines was Chicago Coin's *SUPER FLIPPER*, built in 1975. *SUPER FLIPPER* was, in appearance, unlike any other recognizable video game. From a distance it could easily be mistaken for a somewhat smaller pinball. It had a backbox and backglass, cabinet, plunger and even flipper buttons, but the playfield, upon closer inspection, was a large black and white T.V monitor. A light blue overlay was used to give the monitor a bit of color. The playfield layout had very primitive physics, which gave the game a "no-where-near" sense of reality, and the flippers were mere horizontal lines that would slide from one position to another (left to right) with a press of the flipper buttons. *SUPER FLIPPER* also had a digital score display with SS circuitry throughout (obviously), but because of its video game stigma, it has never been recognized as one of the first SS pinballs, and perhaps rightly so. Atari would make a much better job at a video pinball three years later with their game (appropriately titled) *VIDEO PINBALL*.

Atari's version of video pinball came housed in an ordinary-looking video game cabinet, with minor modifications. It was very nicely done considering the technology available at the time. This game incorporated a mirror over a black and white T.V monitor that gave the impression of a real 3D playfield. Like *SUPER FLIPPER*, a real plunger was mounted on the front of the console that merely activated a switch to tell the computer to send the ball into play. The flipper buttons were on either side of the console panel, which was spring-hinged so that it would move slightly with some pressure. Moving or nudging the console caused the game to shake or nudge the playfield and in due course adjust the path and speed of the ball appropriately. Too many nudges caused the game to tilt. In all, a very fun game to play.

The video game finally caught up to pinball on Atari's VIDEO PIN-BALL (1978). The game was light-years ahead of anything that had come before it, considering the technology available at the time. A worthy substitute for a pinball, at last. *Jeff Grummel collection.*

It is easy to comment when one has the benefit of hindsight, but it seems quite logical now that games like *SUPER FLIPPER* were destined never to succeed. In those early days of video pinballs one can just imagine the lack of realism associated with the game. So why would anyone (apart from having his/her first game to satisfy curiosity) continue to play a pinball simulation when the real thing was close at hand? Video games went on to conquer the world, but for the video pinball, the amusement arcade became out of bounds; it could not co-exist side by side with its real counterpart.

Around the same time that *SPACE INVADERS* was released, there was another video game boom happening, this time at home. Department stores were running hot with home video game units like the *CHANNEL F* by Fairchild (1976), the *INTELLIVISION* by Mattel (1979) and the famous *ATARI 2600* by Atari (1980). Even Bally produced their own home game unit in 1978, which was called the *PROFESSIONAL ARCADE* at first, but because of market pressure it was apparently withdrawn. Not to be outdone, Bally re-released it some time later, updated and re-named the *ASTROCADE*.

For the general population of the late 70s and early 80s, a real pinball was still considered outside the realms of everyday acquisitions and commodities, but a video game cartridge containing a pinball game was most definitely not. The video pinball had found a new home. All of the previously mentioned companies who produced home game units, also produced a video pinball game to suit. A typical comment one may have found on the back of a pinball video game cartridge box could have been "like playing a pinball in your own home" or advertised in the store as "a real pinball at a fraction of the price!" Fraction of the price, yes, but also a fraction of the realism and feel. The pinball cabinet built

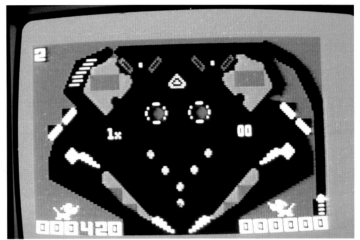

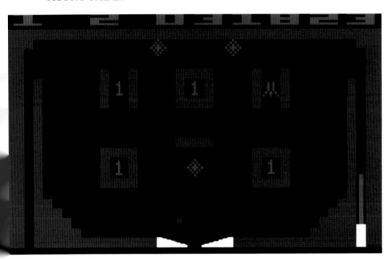

An artist's version of Atari's VIDEO PINBALL (1981), not the arcade game, but the version available on the *Atari 2600* home entertainment unit. The game was about as primitive as a pinball simulator could get, and was nothing like its arcade twin. *Courtesy of Sharon Postlethwaite Buzek B.A.V.A.*

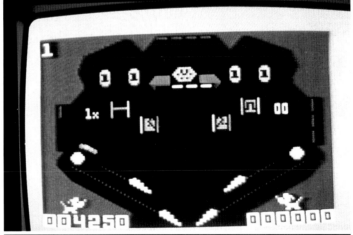

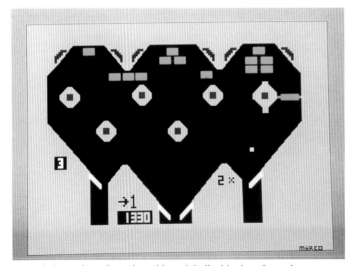

An artist's version of another video pinball, this time from the *ASTROCADE*, Bally's first home video game unit. The screen shot shown here was one of two video pinballs available on the same cartridge. *Courtesy of Sharon Postlethwaite Buzek B.A.V.A.*

Three screen shots from Mattel Electronics' PINBALL (1981), on the Intellivision home game system. A weird playfield setup with those four flippers; does it bring back any memories? What about those cute puppy dogs! *Courtesy of Sharon Postlethwaite Buzek B.A.V.A.*

around *SUPER FLIPPER*'s television playfield was a great bonus for the game, but removing that and replacing it with a hand-held joystick for the home market was like discarding the last true link to that famous arcade machine. All there was left now was a two-dimensional image resembling a pinball playfield, and at this stage, an image still quite primitive.

The home video game boom lasted a few years up until 1984, when its popularity crashed probably due to market saturation. Within those few prosperous years, hundreds of different video games were produced in cartridge form for home video units, by dozens of different companies some of which have never been heard of since. The percentage of video pinballs produced among these was very small, less than 1%. Despite this low figure it still meant that there were people in the industry willing to revive the video pinball every time game technology improved.

By the start of the 1990s, the teenagers who had played on units like the *ATARI 2600* had themselves become adults. With those old games now way out of fashion (not to mention left behind by technology), a new generation of teenagers took to department stores in search of newer games. The home video game boom was back on, this time led by firms like Nintendo and Sega.

Speaking from my own experience, typical teenagers of the late 1970s and early 1980s knew how to play pinball as well as video games. They felt as comfortable grabbing a set of flipper buttons on the side of a cabinet as with a joystick on a video game console—a breed apart from teenagers of the late 1980s and early 1990s. Having grown up on nothing but video games even at an early age, by the time they turned into teenagers they were already old hands at video games, but unfortunately pinballs were never part of their diet. They knew pinball, but they never really understood the game strategy. There are always exceptions of course, but for the majority this was an unfortunate truth.

This reminds me of a story my brother once told me, about a time when he was playing pinball at the local amusement center. Two younger lads were playing another pinball beside him, and he noticed that they obviously did not know how to play. Both were uncoordinated with the flippers (the term we use for such a person is a "Terry-two-flicks"; it describes the action when both flippers are activated at the same time to hit the ball when only one flipper is needed), and general knowledge, like lane-change for instance, was lacking. What gave their video game upbringing away was when one turned to the other and said "you've only got one man left" rather than saying "you've only got one ball left." A dead giveaway.

By 1992, increasingly more and more sophisticated video pinballs could be bought for home usage. This allowed the video game generation to play a pinball that was much closer to the real thing, and more importantly, in a hand-held control/joystick format to which they were accustomed. From here emerged two quite separate pinball players/connoisseurs. One was strictly devoted to real pinball, occasionally playing the other style if the opportunity presented itself, but not altogether approving of such games as worthy pinball substitutes. The other, devoted to video games in general, preferred to play a video pinball on T.V. or computer at home rather than seeking out amusement arcades or going as far as buying a real one for home use. These two different groups are still part of today's modern pinball world.

The graphics created by these newly arrived games were in a simple 3-D format, and in some cases, the playfield was viewed in a perspective similar to that of standing in front of a real pinball. The game's programming was also better. The all-important component in all pinballs; the ball, not only looked more real but performed more as such. The biggest drawback with the older games was the way the ball behaved as it bounced around; it lacked the fluid, unpredictable motion of its real-life model. These newer games were a vast improvement; all that was really missing was the feel of a cabinet and flipper buttons in between your hands.

Despite the huge steps forward, one could still come across minor deficiencies both in programming, and in the fact that the game could not be nudged like a real pinball. Video pinballs did (and still do) incorporate a nudge button on the controls or keyboard, but it was not the same; it did not allow for natural body

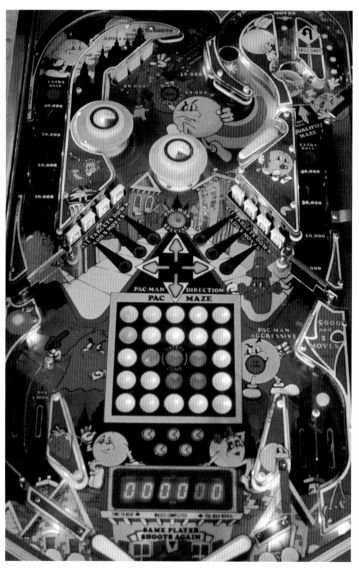

Bally's MR & MRS PAC-MAN (1982). Not exactly a video pinball, but a video game reincarnated as a pinball. The *Pac-Man* video game was still running hot in the arcades, so if Bally could not beat them, they did certainly join them. *Courtesy of Ivo Vasella.* $525-650.

English during play. A typical example of a program deficiency in those days could be found Kaze's *SUPER PINBALL*, produced and released by Nintendo in 1993 for use on the Super Nintendo game unit. During multiball play, when three balls were played at once, interaction between these balls did not exist. In other words, the balls could not bounce off each other, and could occupy the same space as if no other ball was on the playfield. The game cartridge contained three pinball tables; "Jolly Joker", "Blackbeard and Ironmen" and "Wizard". The playfields were very similar in design/strategy and all had great background music, but each varied in difficulty.

Video pinballs on CD-ROM have now been available for a few years, but despite their arcade quality, it may still be some time before any such full scale arcade machine makes its way, once again, to sit side by side with a real pinball.

Nintendo's SUPER PINBALL (1993). This game cartridge contained three pinball tables: "Jolly Joker", "Blackbeard and Ironmen" and "Wizard". The playfields were very similar in design and all had great background music, but each varied in difficulty. *Courtesy of Nintendo of America Inc. All rights reserved.*

Bottom left & bottom right: Two of the five video game pin-tables available on BALLS OF STEEL (1997) designed by Wildfire Studios. Things have come a long way since the humble beginnings of home computer games like Atari's VIDEO PINBALL back in 1981. *Courtesy of Joel Finch/Wildfire Studios.*

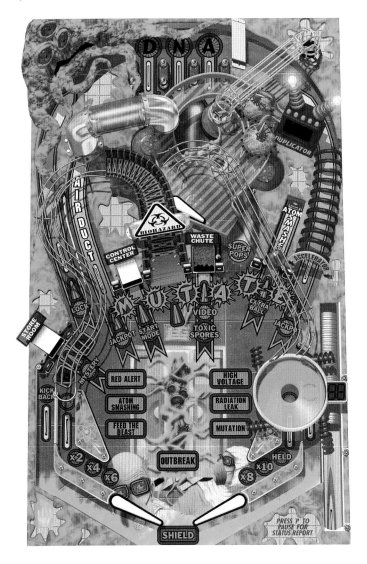

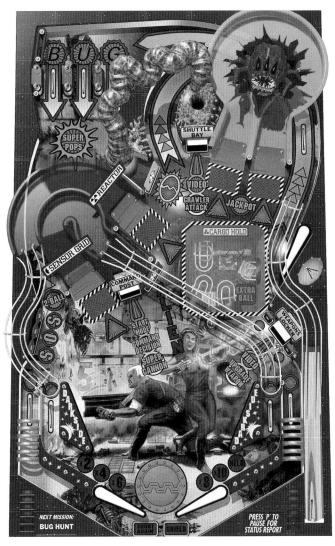

It is hard to predict the future for a game that has endured so many ups and downs. Computer technology may not be able to save the conventional pinball, but there is hope that it may immortalize it some way.

The few pinball companies still operating today may, for some unforeseeable reason, cease production in the near future. At this point in time I know for certain that even if this does occur, the pinball game will not die out easily. I would be lying if I said that I did not want to see pinballs regain the popularity that they once had, but my dilemma is that there are too many older pinballs that I still have not played yet. I blame it all on nostalgia, seeing illustrations of pinballs that I have not played in years, and some that I have never played at all; takes me back to my past; my childhood and my teenage years. I know that in ten years time I will probably be thinking the same way about games that have just been released. By then enthusiasts may be able to play their favorite pinball, from days gone by, on their computer, the technology for which already exists. A good example of such was produced by Amtex (a company no longer in business) in the early 1990s. If one was a great fan of Gottlieb's ROYAL FLUSH (1976) or Bally's EIGHT BALL DELUXE (1981), then both games could be purchased in computer game format. These simulations were an exact copy of the original games, giving the player that nostalgic arcade feel. Even more recently, software giant Microsoft produced *PINBALL ARCADE* (1998), a real treat for pinball fans. This computer package featured seven of the Gottlieb all time classics from the 1930s to the 1990s; BAFFLE BALL (1932), HUMPTY DUMPTY (1947), KNOCK OUT (1950), SLICK CHICK (1963), SPIRIT OF 76 (1976), HAUNTED HOUSE (1983) and CUE BALL WIZARD (1993); all digitally reproduced in all their glory.

My wish for the future is to be able to play virtual reality pinball, if the real thing cannot be found. Imagine a virtual reality pinball were one can pick out their favorite pinball from any era, just like songs on a jukebox. Insert the money, step up onto the game arena, pick the pinball and put the visor on. The game arena will comprise of a front section of pinball cabinet so that the player can grab a set of flipper buttons. For the total pinball experience, the game chosen could come with the surroundings from that era. Choose a pinball with its release date; say Gottlieb's CROSS TOWN from 1966, then choose the venue and the city; say a coffee bar in London, and that's where you would end up. The ultimate nostalgia trip with all the sights, sounds and fashions from that year.

For those of you who are reading this book 20 or so years after its publication, having found it on dad's old bookshelf, or worse, gathering dust in the attic; you alone will know if my wish came true.

For the reader's perusal, starting on page 311 is a list of over 70 different video pinball games that have been manufactured over the years, from 1974 to 1998. It is not a complete list by far, but it will give an indication of the games that were, and still are, available.

Gottlieb's ROYAL FLUSH (1976), a classic game in more ways than one. It was re-released as CARD WHIZ (1976) in a two-player format, and yes, it was reincarnated in the mid-1990s as a video pinball simulation. Amtex produced the video version, which was an exact replica of the original—drop targets, score reels, the lot. It was later included in a pinball video package named PINBALL DELUXE, released by Softkey, which also included a simulation of Bally's EIGHT BALL DELUXE (1981). *Courtesy of Mark Gibson.* $375-475.

ROYAL FLUSH playfield detail.
Courtesy of Jeff Grummel.

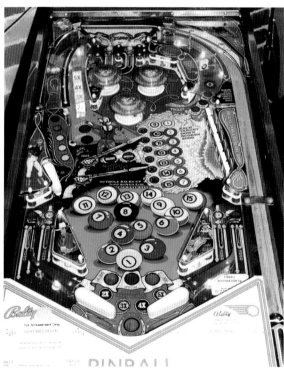

Bally's EIGHT BALL DELUXE (1981), like Gottlieb's ROYAL FLUSH (1976), was released in computer game version by Amtex in the-mid 90s. *Rawdon Osborne collection.*

Gottlieb's PIONEER (1976) was the two-player version of the four-player SPIRIT OF 76 (1976). If you cannot afford either one of these classic pinballs, or have no room in the house for such a game, do not despair. Microsoft's *PINBALL ARCADE* (1998) CD-ROM package included six Gottlieb pinballs, from the '30s through to the '90s; SPIRIT OF 76 was one of them. *Courtesy of Mac.* $350-425.

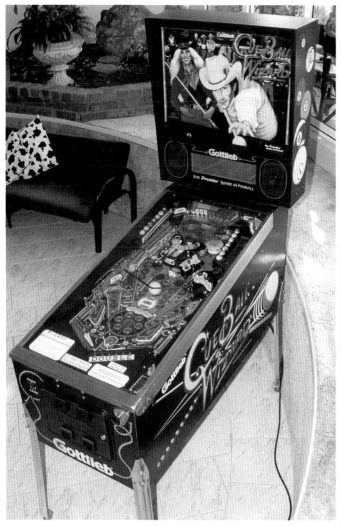

Gottlieb's CUE BALL WIZARD (1992) was immortalized on CD-ROM on Microsoft's *PINBALL ARCADE*. Computer technology may be advancing at an accelerated rate, but there is not one vidpin (video pinball) around that can beat the real feel of a pinball—not yet anyway. This was easily put to the test with this game, as even in 1998 (when *PINBALL ARCADE* was released), you could still find a real CUE BALL WIZARD pinball at the local pool hall. *Courtesy of Darryl Moore*. $625-775.

Backglass and detail of Gottlieb's SLICK CHICK (1963). Playboy Enterprises, Inc. opened up the first of its Playboy Clubs in Chicago in 1960. The clubs offered male entertainment and featured female staff members as "bunnies", dressed in revealing rabbit outfits with ears and cotton tails. Although no direct association has been made, the outfits the two ladies are wearing are definitely Playboy material. The computer game version on *PINBALL ARCADE* was so authentic that one could hear the buzzing sound of the flipper coils as the flippers were energized. *Courtesy of Jan J. Svach*. $775-950.

Video Pinball List

MANUFACTURER	GAME NAME	OPERATING SYSTEM	YEAR
Sierra	3d Ultra Pinball	PC	1995
21st Century	Absolute Pinball	PC	Late '90s
Sears	Arcade Pinball	Atari 2600	1981
Gaga Communications	Babe Watch	Saturn/Playstation	1996
Pinball Wizards	Balls Of Steel	PC	1997
Electronic Arts	Crue Ball-Heavy Metal Pinball	Sega Megadrive	1993
Star Play	Crystal Caliburn	PC	1993
B & N Software	Deep Sea	PC	1998
Sega	Digital Pinball	Sega Saturn	1995
Tegen	Dragon's Revenge	Sega Megadrive	1993
Amtex	Eightball Deluxe	PC	Early '90s
B & N Software	Enigma	PC	1998
Epic Megagames	Epic Pinball	PC	1994
Electronic Arts	Extreme Pinball	Sony Playstation	1995
Gaga Communications	Extreme Sports	Saturn/Playstation	1996
Maxis/Cinematronix	Full Tilt! 2 Pinball	PC	1996
Maxis/Cinematronix	Full Tilt! Pinball	PC	1995
Tradewest	High Speed	Super Nintendo	1991
Virgin Interactive	Hyper 3d Pinball	PC	Late '90s
Nintendo	Kirby's Pinball Land	Nintendo Gameboy	1993
Kaze	Last Gladiators	Sega Saturn	1996
Gaga Communications	Law And Justice	Saturn/Playstation	1996
Star Play	Loony Labyrinth	PC	1996
Atari	Midnight Magic	Atari 2600	1981
Rumatic	Mini Flipper	Arcade Game	1986
Kaze	Necronomicon	Sega Saturn	1996
Bally	Pinball	Astrocade	1978
Mattel Electronics	Pinball	Mattel Intellivision	1982
Zellers	Pinball	Atari 2600	1981
Expert Software	Pinball 2000	PC	1996
Expert Software	Pinball 4000	PC	1996
21st Century	Pinball Arcade	PC	1995
Microsoft	Pinball Arcade	PC	1998
Fairchild	Pinball Challenge	Channel F	1976
Softkey	Pinball Deluxe	PC	Early '90s
21st Century	Pinball Dreams	PC	Early '90s
21st Century	Pinball Fantasies	PC	1995
21st Century	Pinball Fantasies Deluxe	PC	1996
21st Century	Pinball Illusions	PC	1996
Atari	Pinball Jam	Atari Lynx	1989
Encore Software	Pinball Madness	PC	Early '90s
21st Century	Pinball Mania	PC	1995
Jaleco	Pinball Quest	Super Nintendo	1990
Softkey/Mondadori	Pinball Warriors	PC	1995
Kingsoft	Pinball Wizard	Unknown	Late '80s
Ikarion	Pinball Wizards 2000	PC	Late '90s
21st Century	Pinball World	PC	1996
Mattel Electronics	Pinbot	Super Nintendo	1991
Kaze	Power Rangers	Sony Playstation	1996
Empire Interactive	Pro Pinball	Sega Saturn	1994
Empire Interactive	Pro Pinball! Timeshock	PC	Late '90s
Codemasters	Psyco Pinball	Sega Megadrive	1993
Hal Laboratories	Rollerball	Super Nintendo	1988
Amtex	Royal Flush	PC	Early '90s
Sidam	Rugby	Arcade Game	Unknown
High Voltage Software	Ruiner Pinball	Atari Jaguar	1996
Epic Megagames	Silverball Pinball	PC	Late '90s
Liquid Designs	Slam Tilt	PC	1996
Maxis / Cinematronix	Space Cadet	PC	1995
Milton Bradley	Spinball	Vectrex	1983
General Admission Software	Sports Baseball	PC	1996
General Admission Software	Sports Basketball	PC	1996
General Admission Software	Sports Football	PC	1996
General Admission Software	Sports Hockey	PC	1996
Interplay	Star Trek Pinball	PC	1997
Chicago Coin	Super Flipper	Arcade Game	1975
Kaze	Super Pinball Behind The Mask	Super Nintendo	1993
Kaze	Super Pinball 2 The Amazing Odyssey	Unknown	1994
Eletro Plastic	Super Video Pinball	Unknown	1988
Exidy	T.V Pinball	Arcade Game	1974
Sierra	Take A Break Pinball	PC	Late '90s
Tdk	Tdk Pinball Machine	PC	1995
Gaga	The Viking Tales	Sony Playstation	1996
Magnavox	Thunderball	Odyssey 2	1978
21st Century	Total Pinball 3d	PC	Late '90s
Amtex	Tristan Pinball	PC	1993
Ocean Software	True Pinball	Sega Saturn	1995
Model Racing	U.F.O	Arcade Game	1978
Gt Interactive	Ultimate Pinball	PC	Early '90s
Atari	Video Pinball	Atari 2600	1981
Atari	Video Pinball	Arcade Game	1978
Atari	Video Pinball	Atari C-380	1976

The Video Modes

APOLLO 13 (Sega 1995) Land the lunar module on the surface of the moon by using the left and right flipper buttons as thruster controls. Press both buttons simultaneously to activate vertical thrusters.

ATTACK FROM MARS (Bally 1995) The player is in control of a constantly shooting cannon. Try to hit and destroy the flying saucers before they land.

BATMAN FOREVER (Sega 1995) Guide the batwing plane over rooftops. Dodge obstacles whilst attempting to collect bonus point markers.

BAY WATCH (Sega 1995) Go water skiing. Avoid floating junk and head for the jump ramps to collect bonus points.

BLACK ROSE (Bally 1991)
1) **Walk the plank:** After being forced to walk off the plank, and going overboard, you come face to face with a shark. Press the flipper buttons in rapid succession in order to outswim the shark and reach safety to collect your reward. If you are old enough to remember playing a video game called HYPER OLYMPICS in the early 1980s, you will know exactly what I mean about hitting buttons in rapid succession.
2) **Swing from the riggings:** Let go of the rope at the right moment so the pirate can land safely on the other ship to claim the prize, or fall to his death.
3) **The knife throw:** Make the pirate let go of the knife at the right moment as he swings his arm. Hit the target to collect the prize.

CHAMPION PUB (Bally 1998)
1) **Poker night:** Poker night is a simple five-card draw video poker game. The display will present five cards the player can keep or discard any cards. Flipper buttons move the selection box left or right. The plunger button discards, and both flipper buttons depressed at the same time collects the prize. Prizes are awarded according to the nature of the hand.
2) **Spitting gallery:** The spitting gallery is an amusing video mode where the player must move a large spittoon left or right across the bar using the flipper buttons in order to catch the the customers' spit. Catch 10 before missing three to win.

CIRQUS VOLITARE (Bally 1997) Enter the circus sideshow! Help Roonie, the tricycle-riding kangaroo, jump over a collection of objects. Press both flippers in at once to make him jump.

CONGO (Williams 1995) Take a leisurely boat trip down an uncharted river but try to avoid the rocks and hippos.

CORVETTE (Bally 1994) Buckle up the seat belt and prepare for a drag race. Left flipper button accelerator, right button gear shifter. Good luck!

CREATURE FROM THE BLACK LAGOON (Bally 1993) Use the left and right flipper buttons to throw punches at a peeping tom. Hit him about 15 times in as many seconds to win while he tries to dodge the punches.

CUE BALL WIZARD (Gottlieb 1992) Catch falling pool balls by moving a pocket either left or right—but you have to be quick!

DOCTOR WHO (Bally 1992) Help the doctor by making him jump over obstacles while running to the tardis, otherwise he will be caught by the Daleks.

DRACULA (Williams 1993) Shoot dead the advancing wolves before they reach you, and eat you. Beware, there are only a limited number of bullets available.

FISH TALES (Williams 1992) Shoot as many boats and waterskiers as possible with your torpedoes. Take care with the shots and hurry, as there are limited amounts of time and torpedoes available.

GOLDEN EYE (Sega 1995) Shoot soldiers using the plunger trigger while the ball is still in play. The pinball will advise when the mode is about to begin by saying, "Shoot to kill." Completing this mode successfully will light the "Eject or die" feature on both outlanes. When the ball is lost down either one of the outlanes, the ball is shot back automatically through the flippers for a second chance. One has ten seconds to hit a specified target otherwise the flippers loose power and the ball is again lost.

GUNS N' ROSES (Data East 1994) Dodge cars and other traffic while riding a motorbike. Do try and hit the pedestrians as they are worth extra points.

INDIANA JONES (Williams 1993)
1) **The mine cart:** Steer the mine cart through a series of tunnels making sure to stay on the right track by avoiding boarded up entrances at tunnel junctions.
2) **Choose wisely:** Keep an eye on the Holy Grail while it's being mixed up and repositioned very quickly among other Holy Grail look-alikes. Once this has finished one must try to choose wisely for a reward.
3) **Find the medallion:** Move the gunsight left and right with the flipper buttons in order to shoot the bad guys at the bar and find the medallion.

INDIANAPOLIS 500 (Bally 1995) Steer a racing car around obstacles scattered on the famous track, but try to run over bonus point markers. Clear 30 obstacles to reach the end of the mode.

JOHNNY MNENONIC (Williams 1995) Play a Pac-Man style video game where one moves a round cursor in order to catch smaller moving objects. Try to clear the area within the allotted amount of time. Note; use the extra flipper buttons for the up and down movement of the cursor.

JUDGE DREAD (Williams 1993) This is a good combination of simultaneous pinball play and video mode. On the dot matrix display, a freeway chase is taking place. The car in front is swerving all over the road, and you must try to shoot it down with a missile. Trap the ball with the flipper and shoot for the ramp at the moment the car swerves in front of Dread's motorbike.

JUNK YARD (Bally 1996) has two video modes, both involving the junkyard guard dog; Spike.
1) Run from Spike: Press the flippers in rapid succession in order to outrun Spike and reach safety.
2) Shoot Spike: Shoot pieces of toast at Spike with a toaster gun. Spike is chasing a girl back and fourth between two door openings. Try not to hit the girl. A limited amount of toast is available, as well as time.

JURASSIC PARK (Data East 1993) Shoot Dinosaurs as they move across the gunsight, while the ball is still in play. Once again the pinball will advise the player (indirectly) when the mode is about to begin.

LETHAL WEAPON 3 (Data East 1992)
1) Uzi shootout: Shoot the bad guy using the plunger trigger while the ball is still in play, a Data East/Sega trademark. Easier said than done.
2) Fist fight: Outpunch the opponent (the pinball) by pressing the flipper buttons in rapid succession.

NO FEAR, DANGEROUS SPORTS (Williams 1995) Go motorcycle riding. Head for the jumps and collect bonus point markers.

ROYAL RUMBLE (Data East 1994) Take the tag! Press the electronic plunger button as many times as possible to smash a chair over the other wrestler's head while the ball is still in play.

SPACE JAM (Sega 1996) Catch a total of 16 balls and two Loony Tunes characters with a basket for a perfect scoring round.

STAR TREK T.N.G. (Williams 1993) Navigate a shuttlecraft through a series of holodeck-created cave tunnels. Avoid running into mines and tunnel junctions, while at the same time picking up bonus point markers. There are 10 cave tunnels to complete per video mode round.

STAR TREK (Data East 1991) Fire at the Klingon, Romulan and Tholian spaceships as they cross the gunsights. Hit ten out of ten for a perfect score.

STAR WARS (Data East 1992) Shoot a platoon of stormtroopers using the plunger trigger while the ball is still in play.

STAR WARS TRILOGY (Sega 1997) Take a joyride through the streets of Mos Eisely space port on a landspeeder. Try to run over as many Stormtroopers as possible while avoiding other vehicles.

SUPER MARIO BROTHERS (Gottlieb 1992) Run and jump over obstacles to reach the castle. The usual Super Mario video game antics.

TERMINATOR 2: JUDGEMENT DAY (Williams 1991) Pinball's first dot matrix video mode! Shoot terminators before they shoot back by moving the gunsight left and right with the flipper buttons.

THE GETAWAY (Williams 1992) Overtake cars and trucks on the freeway. The faster the car goes the more the points. Don't forget to change gears with the plunger too!

THE SHADOW (Bally 1994) Move The Shadow left and right with the flipper buttons to try and avoid being hit by flying Phur-bu knives (ceremonial daggers used by Tibetan Buddhists).

THEATRE OF MAGIC (Bally 1995) Play video pinball! Knock down all the drop targets within a limited amount of time to collect the bonus prize, an extra ball.

TOMMY (Data East 1993) Guide a plane over houses and factories as it is dropping bombs. The more buildings destroyed the more the points.

Historical Summary

To complete this entire book, a compilation of all the chapter summaries is listed here in chronological order.

1871 A spring-loaded plunger first used on bagatelle games.

Early 1930s Battery-operated pinballs appear.

1933 First successful tilt mechanism (the pedestal tilt) invented by Harry Williams.

1934 Automatic scoring first appears in the form of clock counters.

1934 Kickout holes already appearing on pinballs.

1934-1976 Electromechanical sound produced using chimes, bells and buzzers.

1935 Transformers added to pinballs

1935 The small backglass appears and light-up scoring is introduced.

1935 Pendulum tilts invented by Harry Williams.

1935-1975 Electromechanical pinballs rule.

1936 Wire form rollover lanes already appearing on pinballs.

1937 Coil bumpers first appear on Bally's BUMPER.

1937 Automatic scoring becomes an essential part of pinball.

1937-1939 Coil bumpers used exclusively on most pinballs.

1938 The full size backglass appears along with backglass animation.

1939 Disc bumpers introduced.

1939-1948 Disc bumpers used on most pinballs, replacing coil bumpers.

1940 Genco's METRO introduces the bonus feature.

1947 Flippers introduced, two-inch size.

1947-1950 Back to front flippers used on pinballs.

1948 Thumper bumpers introduced on Williams' SARATOGA.

1948-1950 Flipper pinballs first use bullseye targets.

1948-1967/68 Thumper bumpers along with disc bumpers used on games.

1950 Turret shooter first used on several Gottlieb games.

1951 Slingshot kickers first used.

1952 Bingo-style ball traps become popular with pinball designers, but not for long.

1952 Gottlieb introduces the gobble hole.

1953 Drum score reels first appear on Williams pinballs.

1954 First multiple player game, SUPER JUMBO, is produced by Gottlieb using drum score reels.

1955 Flippers in modern position on most pinballs.

1956 First multiball feature used on Bally's BALLS-A-POPPIN.

1956 Roto-target introduced on Gottlieb's MAJESTIC.

1957 Pinballs begin using a match feature at end of game.

1958 Steel backbox doors begin to replace wooden doors.

1960 First add-a-ball game produced, Gottlieb's FLIPPER.

1960 Last American wood rail produced, Gottlieb's KEWPIE DOLL.

1960 Williams first uses the moving target on MAGIC CLOCK.

1961 Last American pinball built with light-up scoring.

1961 Captive ball targets already appearing on pinballs.

1962 The drop target is first used on Williams VAGABOND.

1963 Williams' first multiball pinball built.

1963 Last gobble hole pinball built.

1963 Spinners introduced to playfields.

1963-1966 Mechanical ball lift replaced by a ball return kicker.

1964 Gottlieb produces GIGI, a game that reinstated the bonus feature as a integral part of the game strategy.

1964 Earliest known appearance of a two player head-to head pinball game.

1964 Resettable tilts mechanisms first used.

1964 Bally introduces the mushroom bumper.

1965 Return lanes first used on Gottlieb's BANK-A-BALL.

1966 Bally introduces Zipper flippers (two-inch size).

1966 French company, Rally, produces the first pinball with digital scoring.

1966 First appearance of the captive ball spinner (roulette wheel).

1967 Replay pinballs have now the option of being converted to add-a-ball.

1967 Spinning posts and up-post features appearing on French pinballs.

1968 Three-inch flippers introduced.

1968 Thumper bumper used exclusively. Disc bumper no longer used.

1969 First appearance of the vari-target.

1969-1971 Most manufacturers converting from two to three inch flippers.

1970 First appearance of the spinning posts feature on American pinballs; Williams' ACES & KINGS.

1970 First pinballs built with the bonus feature collected at the end of each ball rather than at the end of the game.

1971 Multiple target banks first used by Gottlieb.

1972 FIREBALL, by Bally, uses the whirlwind spinner.

1973 Last pinball with Zipper flippers produced by Bally.

1975 The first solid state pinball is built.

1975-1979 Electromechanical pinballs are slowly phased out and solid state pinballs take over.

1976 First wide body pinball produced, Atari's THE ATARIANS.

1976 Chicago Coin, long time pinball manufacturer, produces its last game. Company is taken over and re-named Stern Electronics.

1976 Gottlieb bought by Colombia Pictures.

1976-1977 With solid state technology introduced, drum score reels are replaced by digital displays and 99% of all pinballs are produced with four-player capacity.

1976-1978 Solid state sound introduced.

1977 First non-commercial home version SS pinballs built.

1978 Cocktail table style pinballs become popular.

1979 Continuous background sound introduced.

1979 First talking pinball introduced by Williams.

1979 Last EM replay pinball, convertible to add-a-ball, built by Gottlieb.

1979 First appearance of in-line targets on Bally's PARAGON.

1980 Lane change introduced on Williams' FIREPOWER.

1980 First SS multiball pinball built by Williams.

1980 Williams releases BLACK KNIGHT, the first multi-level pinball.

1980-1982 Talking pinballs produced by most companies.

1981 Most pinballs have now a digital score capacity up to 9,999,990 points.

1982 Last add-a-ball pinballs built, Bally's SPEAK EASY & SPECTRUM.

1982 Flyaway targets first appear on Bally's SPEAK EASY.

1982-1985 Due to pinball recession and cost cutting, few talking pinballs produced.

1984 Colombia Pictures, owner of Gottlieb, decides to close pinball company. Company is then taken over by Premier Technology.

1985 Alphanumeric displays introduced.

1985 Separate plunger skill shots used on pinballs.

1986 Talking pinballs back in production.

1986 Automatic replay percentaging introduced.

1986 First photographic backglass appears on Gottlieb's RAVEN.

1986 Jackpot feature introduced during multiball play, replacing multiplied playfield scoring.

1987 First pinball with stereo sound introduced by Data East.

1988 Bally Manufacturing is taken over by Williams Electronics.

1989 Williams' EARTHSHAKER, first pinball with a vibrating cabinet.

1990 Data East introduces the solid state flipper.

1991 Dot matrix displays introduced along with a video mode feature.

1991 Electronic plungers become a standard feature on pinballs.

1991 Ball saver feature introduced.

1993 Buy-in option first available on Bally/Williams pinballs.

1996 Sega produces first curved backglass on SPACE JAM.

1996 Buy-in option no longer available on pinballs.

1996 Gottlieb, longtime pinball manufacturer, produces its last pinball.

Bibliography

Bueschel, Richard M. *Pinball 1; Illustrated Historical Guide to Pinball Machines Volume 1.* Wheat Ridge, Colorado: Hoflin Publishing Ltd., 1988.

Eiden, Heribert. Lukas, Jürgen. *Pinball Machines.* Atglen, Pennsylvania: Schiffer Publishing Ltd., 1992.

Flower, Gary. Kurtz, Bill. *Pinball: The Lure of the Silver Ball.* Secaucus, New Jersey: Chartwell Books Inc., 1988.

Kurtz, Bill. *Arcade Treasures.* Atglen, Pennsylvania: Schiffer Publishing Ltd., 1994.

Natkin, Bobbye Clare. Kirk, Steve. *All About Pinball.* New York, New York: Grosset & Dunlop., 1977.

Pettit, Daina. *Mr Pinball Flipper Pinball List.* Salt Lake City, Utah: Mr Pinball.,1998.

Zsolnay, Paul. *Pinball.* London, Great Britain: Tiger Books International., 1994.